America's ★ Best
BRAND-NAME RECIPES

Quick & Easy
Weeknight Favorites
Slow-Cooker Recipes, Casseroles, and More

America's ★ Best
BRAND-NAME RECIPES

Pictured on the front cover: Lasagna Supreme *(page 278)*.

Pictured on the back cover *(clockwise from bottom left):* Homestyle Chicken Pot Pie *(page 70),* Fiesta Black Bean Soup *(page 206)* and Main Dish Pie *(page 12).*

ISBN: 0-8487-2783-5

Library of Congress Control Number: 2003103919

Manufactured in China.

8 7 6 5 4 3 2 1

Microwave Cooking: Microwave ovens vary in wattage. Use the cooking times as guidelines and check for doneness before adding more time.

Preparation/Cooking Times: Preparation times are based on the approximate amount of time required to assemble the recipe before cooking, baking, chilling or serving. These times include preparation steps such as measuring, chopping and mixing. The fact that some preparations and cooking can be done simultaneously is taken into account. Preparation of optional ingredients and serving suggestions is not included.

278

186

90

248

The Basics

Slow Cooker Basics

Slow cookers were introduced in the 1970's and found a renewed popularity in the mid 1990's that continues into the new century. Considering the hectic pace of today's lifestyles, it's no wonder so many people have rediscovered this time-saving kitchen helper. Spend a few minutes preparing the ingredients, turn on the slow cooker and relax. Low heat and long cooking times take the stress out of meal preparation. Leave for work or a day of leisure and come home four, eight or even ten hours later to a hot, delicious meal.

There are two types of slow cookers. The most common models have heat coils circling the crockery inset, allowing

heat to surround the food and cook evenly. Two settings, LOW (about 200°F and HIGH (about 300°F regulate cooking temperatures. One hour on HIGH equals 2 to 2-1/2 hours on LOW. Less common models have heat coils on the bottom and have adjustable thermostats. If you own this type, consult your manufacturer's instructions for advice on converting the recipes in this publication.

The Benefits

- No need for constant attention or frequent stirring

- No worry about burning or overcooking

- No sink full of pots and pans to scrub at the end of a long day

- Great for parties and buffets

- Your kitchen stays cool because you don't turn on the oven

- Saves energy—cooking on the low setting uses less energy than most light bulbs

Tips and Techniques

Filling the Slow Cooker: Manufacturers recommend that slow cookers should be one-half to three-quarters full for best results.

Keep a Lid On It: A slow cooker can take as long as twenty minutes to regain heat lost when the cover is removed. If the recipe calls for stirring or checking the dish near the end of the cooking time, replace the cover as quickly as you can. Otherwise, resist the urge to remove the cover.

Cleaning Your Slow Cooker: To clean your slow cooker, follow the manufacturer's instructions. To make cleanup even easier, spray with nonstick cooking spray before adding food.

Tasting: Always taste the finished dish before serving to adjust seasonings to your preference. Consider adding a dash of the following: salt, freshly ground pepper, seasoned salt, seasoned herb blends, lemon juice, soy sauce, Worcestershire sauce, flavored vinegar or minced herbs.

Adapting Recipes: If you'd like to adapt your own favorite recipe to a slow cooker, you'll need to follow a few guidelines. First, try to find a similar slow cooker recipe in this publication or the manufacturer's guide. Note the cooking times, amount of liquid, and quantity and size of meat and vegetable pieces. Because the slow cooker captures moisture, you will want to reduce the amount of liquid, often by as much as half. Add dairy products toward the end of the cooking time so they do not curdle.

Follow this chart to estimate the cooking time you will need:

COOKING GUIDELINES		
Conventional Recipe	Cook on LOW	Cook on HIGH
30 to 45 minutes	6 to 10 hours	3 to 4 hours
50 minutes to 3 hours	8 to 15 hours	4 to 6 hours

Selecting the Right Meat: A good tip to keep in mind is that you can, and in fact should, use tougher, inexpensive cuts of meat. Top-quality cuts, such as loin chops or filet mignon, fall apart during long cooking periods and therefore are not good choices to use in the slow cooker. Keep those cuts for roasting, broiling or grilling, and save money when you use your slow cooker. You will be amazed to find even the

6

toughest cuts come out fork-tender and flavorful.

Reducing the Fat:
The slow cooker can help you make lower-fat meals because you won't be cooking in fat as you do when you sauté and stir-fry. And tougher, inexpensive cuts of meat have less fat than prime cuts. Many recipes call for trimming excess fat from meat.

If you do use fatty cuts of meat, such as ribs, consider browning them first on top of the range to cook off excess fat before adding them to the slow cooker.

Chicken skin tends to shrivel and curl in the slow cooker, so most recipes call for skinless chicken. If you use skin-on pieces, brown them before adding them to the slow cooker.

You can also remove most of the fat from accumulated juices and soups. The simplest way is to refrigerate the liquid for several hours or overnight. The fat will float to the top and congeal for easy removal. If you plan to serve the liquid right away, ladle it into a bowl or measuring cup. Let it stand about 5 minutes so the fat can rise to the surface. Skim with a large spoon. You can also lightly pull a sheet of clean paper towel over the surface, letting it absorb the fat.

Cutting Your Vegetables: Vegetables often take longer to cook than meats. Cut vegetables into small, thin pieces and place them near the bottom or sides of the slow cooker. Pay careful attention to the recipe instructions in order to cut vegetables to the proper size so they will cook in the amount of time given.

Food Safety Tips: If you do any advance preparation, such as trimming meat or cutting vegetables, make sure to cover and refrigerate the food until you are ready to start cooking. Store uncooked meats and vegetables separately. If you are preparing meat, poultry or fish, remember to wash your cutting board, utensils and hands with hot, soapy water before touching other food.

Once the food is cooked, don't keep it in the slow cooker too long. Foods need to be kept cooler than 40°F or hotter than 140°F to avoid growth of harmful bacteria. Remove food to a clean container, cover and refrigerate as soon as possible. For large amounts of leftovers, it is best to divide them into several containers so they will cool faster. Do not reheat leftovers in the slow

cooker. Use a microwave oven, the range top or the oven for reheating.

Foil to the Rescue: To easily lift a dish or a meatloaf out of the slow cooker, make foil handles according to the following directions.

Tear off three 18×3-inch strips of heavy-duty foil. Crisscross strips so they resemble the spokes of a wheel. Place the dish or food in the center of the strips.

Pull foil strips up and over and place them into the slow cooker. Leave them in while you cook so you can easily lift them out again when finished cooking.

By following these simple slow-cooker tips and techniques, you will soon be preparing some of the wonderful slow cooker recipes in this cookbook with the minimum of effort.

Casserole Basics

Casserole cookware comes in a variety of shapes, sizes and materials that fall into two general descriptions. They can be either deep, round containers with handles and tight-fitting lids or square and rectangular baking dishes. Casseroles are made of glass, ceramic or metal. When making a casserole, it's important to bake the casserole in the proper size dish so that the ingredients cook evenly in the time specified.

Size Unknown?

If the size of the casserole or baking dish isn't marked on the bottom of the dish, it can be measured to determine the size.

■ Round and oval casseroles are generally measured by volume, not inches, and are listed by quart capacity. Fill a measuring cup with water and pour it into the empty casserole. Repeat until the casserole is filled with water, keeping track of the amount of water added. The amount of water is equivalent to the size of the dish.

■ Square and rectangular baking dishes are usually measured in inches. If the dimensions are not marked on the bottom of a baking dish, use a ruler to measure on top from inside of one edge to the inside of the opposite edge. Repeat to determine the other dimension.

Prime-Time Beef

Beef and Vegetables in Rich Burgundy Sauce

Slow Cooker

1 package (8 ounces) sliced mushrooms
1 package (8 ounces) baby carrots
1 medium green bell pepper, cut into thin strips
1 boneless beef chuck roast (2½ pounds)
1 can (10½ ounces) condensed golden mushroom soup
¼ cup dry red wine or beef broth
1 tablespoon Worcestershire sauce
1 package (1 ounce) dry onion soup mix
¼ teaspoon black pepper
3 tablespoons cornstarch
2 tablespoons water
4 cups hot cooked noodles
Chopped fresh parsley (optional)

Slow Cooker Directions

1. Place mushrooms, carrots and bell pepper in slow cooker. Place roast on top of vegetables. Combine mushroom soup, wine, Worcestershire sauce, soup mix and black pepper in medium bowl; mix well. Pour soup mixture over roast. Cover; cook on LOW 8 to 10 hours.

2. Transfer roast to cutting board; cover with foil. Let stand 10 to 15 minutes before slicing.

3. Blend cornstarch and water until smooth. Turn slow cooker to HIGH. Stir cornstarch mixture into vegetable mixture; cook 10 minutes or until thickened. Serve beef and vegetables with sauce over cooked noodles. Garnish with parsley, if desired.

Makes 6 to 8 servings

Easy Taco-Macaroni Casserole

1 pound lean ground beef
1 package (1.25 ounces) LAWRY'S® Taco Spices & Seasonings
1 can (14½ ounces) tomatoes, undrained and cut up
1½ cups water
8 ounces dry macaroni or small spiral pasta
½ cup sliced celery
1 package (8½ ounces) corn muffin mix
1 egg
⅓ cup milk
½ cup (2 ounces) grated mild cheddar cheese

In medium skillet, brown ground beef until crumbly; drain. Add Taco Spices & Seasonings, tomatoes, water, macaroni and celery. Bring to a boil over medium-high heat; reduce heat to low and cover. Simmer 20 minutes, stirring occasionally. Spoon meat mixture into 2½-quart casserole dish; set aside. Heat oven to 400°F. In medium bowl, place corn muffin mix, egg and milk; stir with fork just to mix. Spoon half of the batter over meat mixture in dollops. Spoon remaining batter into 6 greased or paper-lined muffin cups. Bake casserole and muffins in 400°F. oven 15 to 20 minutes or until golden.

Makes 6 to 8 servings

Serving Suggestion: Sprinkle with grated cheese.

Beef and Vegetables in Rich Burgundy Sauce

Patchwork Casserole

2 pounds ground beef
2 cups chopped green bell
   pepper
1 cup chopped onion
2 pounds frozen Southern-style
   hash-brown potatoes,
   thawed
2 cans (8 ounces each) tomato
   sauce
1 cup water
1 can (6 ounces) tomato paste
1 teaspoon salt
½ teaspoon dried basil,
   crumbled
¼ teaspoon black pepper
1 pound pasteurized process
   American cheese, thinly
   sliced

1. Preheat oven to 350°F.

2. Brown beef in large skillet over medium heat about 10 minutes; drain off fat. Add bell pepper and onion; cook and stir until tender, about 4 minutes. Stir in potatoes, tomato sauce, water, tomato paste, salt, basil and black pepper.

3. Spoon half of mixture into 13×9×2-inch baking pan or 3-quart baking dish; top with half of cheese. Spoon remaining meat mixture evenly on top of cheese. Cover pan with aluminum foil. Bake 45 minutes.

4. Cut remaining cheese into decorative shapes; place on top of casserole. Let stand loosely covered until cheese melts, about 5 minutes.

Makes 8 to 10 servings

Helpful Hints

Frozen hash-brown potatoes are the fuss-free way to add potatoes to a dish. Southern-style hash-brown potatoes are diced rather than shredded.

Philly Steak Casserole

1 tablespoon vegetable oil
1 onion, sliced
1 green bell pepper, sliced
6 slices bread, divided
2 cups (8 ounces) shredded
   Swiss cheese, divided
3 packages (6 ounces each)
   HILLSHIRE FARM® Deli
   Select Smoked Beef
1 cup milk
3 eggs, beaten
1 teaspoon mustard
   Salt and black pepper to taste

Preheat oven to 325°F.

Heat oil in medium skillet over medium heat. Sauté onion and bell pepper until crisp-tender; set aside. Cut 3 slices bread into cubes; place in greased 12×8-inch baking dish. Top bread with 1 cup cheese. Spread onion mixture over cheese. Arrange Smoked Beef over onion mixture. Diagonally cut remaining 3 slices bread into halves. Arrange bread slices on top of beef, overlapping slightly. Combine milk, eggs, mustard, salt and black pepper in small bowl; pour over bread slices.

Bake, uncovered, 35 to 40 minutes. Top with remaining 1 cup cheese; bake, uncovered, 5 minutes or until cheese is melted. Let stand 10 minutes before serving.

Makes 6 to 8 servings

Taco Pie

1 pound ground beef
½ cup chopped onion
1 teaspoon dried cilantro leaves
½ teaspoon salt
½ teaspoon ground cumin
½ teaspoon pepper
1 can (4 ounces) chopped green
   chilies, drained
1 fresh jalapeño pepper,*
   minced
1 can (14½ ounces) FRANK'S®
   or SNOWFLOSS® Original
   Style Diced Tomatoes,
   drained slightly
1 can (15½ ounces) red kidney
   beans, rinsed and drained
1¼ cups milk
1 package (8½ ounces) corn
   bread mix
3 eggs
1 cup shredded Cheddar cheese
   Tortilla chips, any style
   Sour cream
   Shredded lettuce

Jalapeño peppers can sting and irritate the skin; wear rubber gloves when handling peppers and do not touch eyes. Wash hands after handling.

1. Preheat oven to 400°F. Brown ground beef and onion. Drain grease. Stir in seasonings.

2. Spread meat mixture in well-greased shallow 10-inch baking dish.

3. Spread chilies, jalapeño pepper, diced tomatoes and kidney beans over meat.

4. Beat milk, corn bread mix and eggs 1 minute with mixer. Pour over ingredients in baking dish.

5. Bake 30 minutes. Top with cheese and bake 10 minutes. Serve with tortilla chips, sour cream and lettuce.

Makes 4 servings

Prep Time: 15 minutes
Cook Time: 40 minutes

Patchwork Casserole

Baked Steak Flamenco

- ¼ **cup all-purpose flour**
- ½ **teaspoon seasoned salt**
- ⅛ **teaspoon ground black pepper**
- 1½ **pounds trimmed round steak, cut into strips**
- ½ **cup thinly sliced onion**
- 1 **cup thin green bell pepper rings**
- 1 **cup sliced fresh mushrooms**
- 1 **can (14.5 ounces) CONTADINA® Italian Style Stewed Tomatoes, undrained**
- ¼ **cup horseradish sauce**
- 1 **tablespoon Worcestershire sauce**

1. Combine flour, seasoned salt and pepper in large plastic food storage bag. Add steak; shake to evenly coat.

2. Place in greased 13×9-inch baking dish. Arrange onion slices, bell pepper rings and mushrooms on top of meat.

3. Drain tomatoes, reserving juice. Slice tomatoes lengthwise; arrange on top of vegetables.

4. Combine reserved juice, horseradish sauce and Worcestershire sauce in small bowl; pour evenly over all ingredients in baking dish. Bake, uncovered, in preheated 350°F oven for 45 minutes to 1 hour or until done as desired. Serve with hot cooked rice or potatoes, if desired.

Makes 6 servings

Main-Dish Pie

- 1 **package (8 rolls) refrigerated crescent rolls**
- 1 **pound lean ground beef**
- 1 **medium onion, chopped**
- 1 **can (12 ounces) beef or mushroom gravy**
- 1 **box (10 ounces) BIRDS EYE® frozen Green Peas, thawed**
- ½ **cup shredded Swiss cheese**
- 6 **slices tomato**

- Preheat oven to 350°F.

- Unroll dough and separate rolls. Spread to cover bottom of ungreased 9-inch pie pan. Press together to form lower crust. Bake 10 minutes.

- Meanwhile, in large skillet, brown beef and onion; drain excess fat.

- Stir in gravy and peas; cook until heated through.

- Pour mixture into partially baked crust. Sprinkle with cheese.

- Bake 10 to 15 minutes or until crust is brown and cheese is melted.

- Arrange tomato slices over pie; bake 2 minutes more.

Makes 6 servings

Prep Time: 10 minutes
Cook Time: 20 to 25 minutes

Chili Cornbread Casserole

- 1 **pound ground beef**
- 1 **medium onion, chopped**
- 1 **jar (1 pound) RAGÚ® Cheese Creations!® Double Cheddar Sauce**
- 1 **can (19 ounces) red kidney beans, rinsed and drained**
- 1 **can (8¾ ounces) whole kernel corn, drained**
- 2 to 3 **teaspoons chili powder**
- 1 **package (12 ounces) cornbread mix**

Preheat oven to 400°F. In 12-inch skillet, brown ground beef and onion over medium-high heat; drain. Stir in Ragú Cheese Creations! Sauce, beans, corn and chili powder.

Meanwhile, prepare cornbread mix according to package directions. Do not bake.

In ungreased 2-quart baking dish, spread ground beef mixture. Top with cornbread mixture. Bake uncovered 20 minutes or until toothpick inserted in center of cornbread comes out clean and top is golden.

Makes 6 servings

Prep Time: 10 minutes
Cook Time: 20 minutes

Corned Beef and Cabbage `Slow Cooker`

- 1 **head cabbage (1½ pounds), cut into 6 wedges**
- 4 **ounces baby carrots**
- 1 **corned beef (3 pounds) with seasoning packet***
- 1 **quart (4 cups) water**
- ⅓ **cup prepared mustard (optional)**
- ⅓ **cup honey (optional)**

*If seasoning packet is not perforated, poke several small holes with tip of paring knife.

Slow Cooker Directions

1. Place cabbage in slow cooker; top with carrots.

2. Place seasoning packet on top of vegetables. Place corned beef, fat side up, over seasoning packet and vegetables. Add water. Cover; cook on LOW 10 hours.

3. Discard seasoning packet. Just before serving, combine mustard and honey in small bowl. Use as dipping sauce, if desired.

Makes 6 servings

Main-Dish Pie

Western Wagon Wheels

1 pound lean ground beef or ground turkey
2 cups wagon wheel pasta, uncooked
1 can (14½ ounces) stewed tomatoes
1½ cups water
1 box (10 ounces) BIRDS EYE® frozen Sweet Corn
½ cup barbecue sauce
Salt and pepper to taste

• In large skillet, cook beef over medium heat 5 minutes or until well browned.

• Stir in pasta, tomatoes, water, corn and barbecue sauce; bring to boil.

• Reduce heat to low; cover and simmer 15 to 20 minutes or until pasta is tender, stirring occasionally. Season with salt and pepper.

Makes 4 servings

Serving Suggestion: Serve with corn bread or corn muffins.

Prep Time: 5 minutes
Cook Time: 25 minutes

Skillet Spaghetti and Sausage

¼ pound mild or hot Italian sausage links, sliced
½ pound ground beef
¼ teaspoon dried oregano, crushed
4 ounces spaghetti, broken in half
1 can (14½ ounces) DEL MONTE® Diced Tomatoes with Basil, Garlic & Oregano
1 can (8 ounces) DEL MONTE Tomato Sauce
1½ cups sliced fresh mushrooms
2 stalks celery, sliced

1. Brown sausage in large skillet over medium-high heat. Add beef and oregano; season to taste with salt and pepper, if desired.

2. Cook, stirring occasionally, until beef is browned; drain.

3. Add pasta, 1 cup water, undrained tomatoes, tomato sauce, mushrooms and celery. Bring to boil, stirring occasionally.

4. Reduce heat; cover and simmer 12 to 14 minutes or until spaghetti is tender. Garnish with grated Parmesan cheese and chopped parsley, if desired. Serve immediately.

Makes 4 to 6 servings

Prep Time: 5 minutes
Cook Time: 30 minutes

Texas Ranch Chili Beans

1 pound lean ground beef
1 can (28 ounces) whole peeled tomatoes, undrained
2 cans (15½ ounces each) chili beans
1 cup chopped onions
1 cup water
1 packet (1 ounce) HIDDEN VALLEY® The Original Ranch® Salad Dressing & Seasoning Mix
1 teaspoon chili powder
1 bay leaf

In Dutch oven, brown beef over medium-high heat; drain off fat. Add tomatoes, breaking up with spoon. Stir in beans, onions, water, salad dressing mix, chili powder and bay leaf. Bring to boil; reduce heat and simmer, uncovered, 1 hour, stirring occasionally. Remove bay leaf just before serving.

Makes 8 servings

French-American Rice

½ pound lean ground beef or ground turkey
1 box (10 ounces) BIRDS EYE® frozen White and Wild Rice
1½ teaspoons soy sauce
½ cup California walnuts

• In large skillet, cook beef over medium-high heat 5 minutes or until well browned.

• Stir in rice; cook 5 minutes more or until rice is tender, stirring occasionally.

• Stir in soy sauce and California walnuts; cook 1 minute or until heated.   *Makes 4 servings*

Prep Time: 5 minutes
Cook Time: 10 minutes

Quick Beef Stroganoff

1 pound ground beef
1 package LIPTON® Noodles & Sauce—Butter
2¼ cups water
1 jar (4½ ounces) sliced mushrooms, drained
2 tablespoons finely chopped pimiento
⅛ teaspoon garlic powder
½ cup sour cream

In 10-inch skillet, brown ground beef; drain. Stir in remaining ingredients except sour cream. Bring to a boil, then simmer, stirring frequently, 7 minutes or until noodles are tender. Stir in sour cream; heat through but do not boil.

Makes about 2 servings

Classic Beef & Noodles

- 2 pounds beef stew meat, trimmed and cut into cubes
- ¼ pound mushrooms, sliced into halves
- 2 tablespoons chopped onion
- 2 cloves garlic, minced
- 1 teaspoon salt
- 1 teaspoon dried oregano leaves
- ½ teaspoon black pepper
- ¼ teaspoon dried marjoram leaves
- 1 bay leaf
- 1½ cups beef broth
- ⅓ cup dry sherry
- 1 (8-ounce) container sour cream
- ½ cup all-purpose flour
- ¼ cup water
- 4 cups hot cooked noodles

Slow Cooker Directions

Heat oil in large skillet. Brown beef on all sides (Work in batches, if necessary.) Drain and discard fat.

Combine beef, mushrooms, onion, garlic, salt, oregano, pepper, marjoram and bay leaf in slow cooker. Pour in beef broth and sherry. Cover and cook on LOW 8 to 10 hours or on HIGH 4 to 5 hours. Remove and discard bay leaf.

If cooking on LOW, turn to HIGH. Stir together sour cream, flour and water in small bowl. Stir about 1 cup liquid from slow cooker into sour cream mixture. Stir mixture back into slow cooker. Cover and cook on HIGH 30 minutes or until thickened and bubbly. Serve over noodles. Garnish as desired. *Makes 8 servings*

Sloppy Joes

- 1 pound lean ground beef
- ½ cup chopped onion
- ⅓ cup chopped green pepper
- 1 bottle (12 ounces) HEINZ® Chili Sauce
- ¼ cup water
- 1 to 2 tablespoons brown sugar
- 1 tablespoon HEINZ® Worcestershire Sauce
- ¼ teaspoon salt
- ⅛ teaspoon pepper
- Sandwich buns

In large saucepan, cook beef, onion and green pepper until green pepper is tender; drain, if necessary. Stir in chili sauce, water, sugar, Worcestershire sauce, salt and pepper; simmer 10 minutes, stirring occasionally. Serve in sandwich buns.

Makes 6 to 8 (3-cup) servings

Classic Beef & Noodles

Beef Stroganoff Casserole

- 1 pound lean ground beef
- ¼ teaspoon salt
- ⅛ teaspoon black pepper
- 1 teaspoon vegetable oil
- 8 ounces sliced mushrooms
- 1 large onion, chopped
- 3 cloves garlic, minced
- ¼ cup dry white wine
- 1 can (10¾ ounces) condensed cream of mushroom soup
- ½ cup sour cream
- 1 tablespoon Dijon mustard
- 4 cups cooked egg noodles Chopped fresh parsley (optional)

1. Preheat oven to 350°F. Spray 13×9-inch baking dish with nonstick cooking spray.

2. Place beef in large skillet; season with salt and pepper. Brown beef over medium-high heat until no longer pink, stirring to separate beef. Drain fat from skillet; set aside.

3. Heat oil in same skillet over medium-high heat until hot. Add mushrooms, onion and garlic; cook and stir 2 minutes or until onion is tender. Add wine. Reduce heat to medium-low and simmer 3 minutes. Remove from heat; stir in soup, sour cream and mustard until well combined. Return beef to skillet.

4. Place noodles in prepared dish. Pour beef mixture over noodles; stir until noodles are well coated. Bake, uncovered, 30 minutes or until heated through. Sprinkle with parsley, if desired.   *Makes 6 servings*

Corny Sloppy Joes

- 1 pound lean ground beef or ground turkey
- 1 small onion, chopped
- 1 can (15½ ounces) sloppy joe sauce
- 1 box (10 ounces) BIRDS EYE® frozen Sweet Corn
- 6 hamburger buns

• In large skillet, cook beef and onion over high heat until beef is well browned.

• Stir in sloppy joe sauce and corn; reduce heat to low and simmer 5 minutes or until heated through.

• Serve mixture in hamburger buns.
      Makes 6 servings

Serving Suggestion: Sprinkle with shredded Cheddar cheese.

Prep Time: 5 minutes
Cook Time: 15 minutes

Easy Mostaccioli Casserole

- 1 pound ground beef
- ½ onion, chopped
- 1 can (14½ ounces) tomatoes, chopped and undrained
- 1 can (8 ounces) tomato sauce
- 1 cup chopped olives
- ¼ cup Parmesan cheese
- 2 teaspoons LAWRY'S® Garlic Pepper
- ¼ teaspoon LAWRY'S® Seasoned Salt
- ½ teaspoon oregano
- 8 ounces Mostaccioli noodles, cooked and drained
- 1 cup (8 ounces) grated mozzarella cheese

In large skillet, brown ground beef until crumbly; drain fat. Add onion, tomatoes, tomato sauce, olives, Parmesan cheese, Garlic Pepper, Seasoned Salt and oregano. Bring to a boil over medium-high heat; reduce heat to low and simmer, uncovered,

20 minutes. In 2-quart oven proof casserole dish place hot pasta, cover with meat mixture and top with cheese. Heat under broiler 3 minutes.
      Makes 8 servings

Serving Suggestion: Serve with tossed green salad and herbed French bread.

Italian Beef Burrito

- 1½ pounds ground beef
- 2 medium onions, finely chopped
- 2 medium red and/or green bell peppers, chopped
- 1 jar (1 pound 10 ounces) RAGÚ® Robusto!™ Pasta Sauce
- ½ teaspoon dried oregano leaves, crushed
- 8 (10-inch) flour tortillas, warmed
- 2 cups shredded mozzarella cheese (about 8 ounces)

1. In 12-inch skillet, brown ground beef over medium-high heat.

2. Stir in onions and red bell peppers and cook, stirring occasionally, 5 minutes or until tender; drain. Stir in Ragú Pasta Sauce and oregano; heat through.

3. To serve, top each tortilla with 1 cup ground beef mixture and ¼ cup cheese; roll up and serve.
      Makes 8 servings

Prep Time: 15 minutes
Cook Time: 15 minutes

Helpful Hints

To warm tortillas, loosely wrap them in plastic wrap. Microwave at HIGH about 1 minute or until tortillas are warm.

Beef Stroganoff Casserole

Oven-Baked Stew `Slow Cooker`

**2 pounds boneless beef chuck
   or round steak, cut into
   1-inch cubes**
¼ cup all-purpose flour
1⅓ cups sliced carrots
**1 can (14 to 16 ounces) whole
   peeled tomatoes, undrained
   and chopped**
**1 envelope LIPTON® RECIPE
   SECRETS® Onion Soup Mix***
½ cup dry red wine or water
**1 cup fresh or canned sliced
   mushrooms**
**1 package (8 ounces) medium
   or broad egg noodles,
   cooked and drained**

*Also terrific with LIPTON® RECIPE
SECRETS® Beefy Onion, Onion Mushroom or
Beefy Mushroom Soup Mix.*

1. Preheat oven to 425°F. In 2½-quart
shallow casserole, toss beef with
flour, then bake uncovered
20 minutes, stirring once.

2. Reduce heat to 350°F. Stir in
carrots, tomatoes, soup mix and wine.

3. Bake covered 1½ hours or until
beef is tender. Stir in mushrooms and
bake covered an additional
10 minutes. Serve over hot noodles.
                    Makes 8 servings

Slow Cooker Method: Toss beef with
flour and place in slow cooker. Add
carrots, tomatoes, soup mix and wine.
Cover. Cook on LOW 8 hours. Add
mushrooms; cover and cook
30 minutes or until beef is tender.
Serve over hot noodles.

Prep Time: 15 minutes
Cook Time: 2 hours

Twisty Beef Bake

1 pound ground beef
**2 cups rotini or elbow macaroni,
   cooked in unsalted water
   and drained**
**1⅓ cups *French's*® French Fried
   Onions, divided**
**1 cup (4 ounces) shredded
   Cheddar cheese, divided**
**1 can (10¾ ounces) condensed
   cream of mushroom soup,
   undiluted**
**1 can (14½ ounces) whole
   tomatoes, undrained and
   chopped**
**¼ cup chopped green bell
   pepper**
¼ teaspoon seasoned salt

Preheat oven to 375°F. In large skillet,
brown ground beef; drain. Stir in hot
macaroni, ⅔ cup French Fried
Onions, ½ cup cheese, soup,
tomatoes, bell pepper and seasoned
salt. Mix well. Pour into 2-quart
casserole. Bake, covered, for
30 minutes or until heated through.
Top with remaining ½ cup cheese and
⅔ cup onions; bake, uncovered,
3 minutes or until onions are golden
brown.   *Makes 4 to 6 servings*

Microwave Directions: Crumble
ground beef into 2-quart microwave-
safe casserole. Cook, covered, on
HIGH 4 to 6 minutes or until beef is
cooked. Stir beef halfway through
cooking time. Drain well. Add
remaining ingredients as above.
Cook, covered, 10 to 14 minutes or
until heated through. Stir beef mixture
halfway through cooking time. Top
with remaining cheese and onions;
cook, uncovered, 1 minute or until
cheese melts. Let stand 5 minutes.

Biscuit-Topped Hearty Steak Pie

**1½ pounds top round steak,
   cooked and cut into 1-inch
   cubes**
**1 package (9 ounces) frozen
   baby carrots**
**1 package (9 ounces) frozen
   peas and pearl onions**
**1 large baking potato, cooked
   and cut into ½-inch pieces**
**1 jar (18 ounces) home-style
   brown gravy**
½ teaspoon dried thyme leaves
½ teaspoon black pepper
**1 can (10 ounces) flaky
   buttermilk biscuits**

Preheat oven to 375°F. Spray 2-quart
casserole with nonstick cooking
spray.

Combine steak, frozen vegetables
and potato in prepared dish. Stir in
gravy, thyme and pepper.

Bake, uncovered, 40 minutes. Remove
from oven. *Increase oven temperature
to 400°F.* Top with biscuits and bake
8 to 10 minutes or until biscuits are
golden brown.   *Makes 6 servings*

Cook's Nook: This casserole can be
prepared with leftovers of almost any
kind. Other steaks, roast beef, stew
meat, pork, lamb or chicken can be
substituted for round steak; adjust
gravy flavor to complement meat. Red
potatoes can be used in place of
baking potato. Choose your favorite
vegetable combination, such as
broccoli, cauliflower and carrots or
broccoli, corn and red peppers, as a
substitute for the peas and carrots.

Helpful Hints

When cooking pasta for use in a casserole, cook it just until tender, but still
firm to the bite. The pasta will continue to cook and absorb more liquid
during the baking process.

Biscuit-Topped Hearty Steak Pie

Broccoli and Beef Pasta
`Slow Cooker`

2 cups broccoli florets *or*
    1 package (10 ounces)
    frozen broccoli, thawed
1 onion, thinly sliced
½ teaspoon dried basil leaves
½ teaspoon dried oregano leaves
½ teaspoon dried thyme leaves
1 can (14½ ounces) Italian-style
    diced tomatoes, undrained
¾ cup beef broth
1 pound lean ground beef
2 cloves garlic, minced
2 tablespoons tomato paste
2 cups cooked rotini pasta
3 ounces shredded Cheddar
    cheese or grated Parmesan
    cheese

Slow Cooker Directions

Layer broccoli, onion, basil, oregano, thyme, tomatoes with juice and beef broth in slow cooker. Cover and cook on LOW 2½ hours.

Combine beef and garlic in large nonstick skillet; cook over high heat 6 to 8 minutes or until meat is no longer pink, breaking meat apart with wooden spoon. Pour off drippings. Add beef mixture to slow cooker. Cover and cook 2 hours.

Stir in tomato paste. Add pasta and cheese. Cover and cook 30 minutes or until cheese melts and mixture is heated through. Sprinkle with additional shredded cheese, if desired.   *Makes 4 servings*

Serving Suggestion: Serve with garlic bread.

Chili Tamale Pie

1 pound ground beef
1 large onion, chopped
1 clove garlic, minced *or*
    ¼ teaspoon garlic powder
1 can (14½ ounces) stewed
    tomatoes, undrained
¼ cup *Frank's® RedHot®* Cayenne
    Pepper Sauce
2 tablespoons *plus* 1 teaspoon
    chili powder, divided
1 package (8½ ounces) corn
    muffin mix
1 green onion, thinly sliced

1. Preheat oven to 400°F. Cook beef, onion and garlic in large oven-safe* skillet 5 minutes or until meat is browned, stirring to separate meat. Drain fat. Stir in tomatoes, **Frank's RedHot** Sauce and 2 tablespoons chili powder. Heat to boiling. Reduce heat to medium-low. Cook 5 minutes, stirring occasionally.

2. Prepare corn muffin mix according to package directions. Stir in green onion and remaining 1 teaspoon chili powder. Spoon batter over meat mixture, spreading evenly to edges. Bake 15 minutes or until toothpick inserted in corn bread comes out clean. Garnish with avocados, cheese or olives, if desired. Serve with a crisp green salad.

Makes 6 servings

*If handle of skillet is not oven-safe, wrap handle with foil.

Prep Time: 10 minutes
Cook Time: 25 minutes

Reuben Casserole

1 cup FRANK'S® or
    SNOWFLOSS® Kraut,
    drained
½ cup chopped onion
2 tablespoons butter
1 apple, peeled and chopped
½ teaspoon caraway seeds
1 cup cubed corned beef
¼ cup Thousand Island dressing
1 cup cubed Swiss cheese
2 slices rye bread, toasted and
    cubed
2 tablespoons melted butter
1 small jar red pimiento
1 green bell pepper, sliced

1. Preheat oven to 400°F. Sauté the onion in 2 tablespoons butter until soft.

2. Add apple and sauté until soft.

3. Add caraway seeds, kraut and corned beef; sauté 1 minute to blend flavors. Place mixture in medium casserole dish.

4. Drizzle kraut mixture with Thousand Island dressing, top with Swiss cheese and with toasted bread cubes.

5. Pour remaining 2 tablespoons melted butter over top, dot with pimiento and decorate with bell pepper.

6. Bake at 400°F for 20 minutes.
Makes 4 servings

Prep Time: 15 minutes
Bake Time: 20 minutes

Helpful Hints

To reduce the amount of fat in slow cooker recipes, choose leaner cuts of meat and remove the skin from poultry before cooking. Excess fat may be skimmed off the surface of food just before serving.

Broccoli and Beef Pasta

Western Skillet Noodles

½ pound ground beef
2 teaspoons chili powder
2⅓ cups water
1 can (11 ounces) whole kernel corn with sweet peppers, drained
1 tablespoon margarine or butter
1 package LIPTON® Noodles & Sauce—Beef Flavor
½ cup shredded cheddar cheese (about 2 ounces), divided

Brown ground beef with chili powder in 12-inch nonstick skillet over medium-high heat; drain. Remove and set aside.

Add water, corn and margarine and bring to a boil. Stir in Noodles & Sauce—Beef Flavor and continue boiling over medium heat, stirring occasionally, 7 minutes or until noodles are tender.

Stir in beef mixture and ¼ cup cheese; heat through. Top with remaining ¼ cup cheese.

Makes about 2 servings

Steak San Marino [Slow Cooker]

¼ cup all-purpose flour
1 teaspoon salt
½ teaspoon black pepper
1 beef round steak, about 1 inch thick, cut into 4 pieces
1 can (8 ounces) tomato sauce
2 carrots, chopped
½ onion, chopped
1 rib celery, chopped
1 teaspoon dried Italian seasoning
½ teaspoon Worcestershire sauce
1 bay leaf
  Hot cooked rice

Slow Cooker Directions

Combine flour, salt and pepper in small bowl. Dredge each piece of steak in flour mixture. Place in slow cooker. Combine tomato sauce, carrots, onion, celery, Italian seasoning, Worcestershire sauce and bay leaf in small bowl; pour into slow cooker. Cover and cook on LOW 8 to 10 hours or on HIGH 4 to 5 hours.

Remove and discard bay leaf. Serve steaks and sauce over rice.

Makes 4 servings

Helpful Hints

Long cooking in a slow cooker may reduce the flavor of herbs and spices. Just before serving, taste the dish and add more seasoning, if necessary.

Texas-Style Deep-Dish Chili Pie

1 tablespoon vegetable oil
1 pound beef stew meat, cut into ½-inch cubes
2 cans (14½ ounces each) Mexican-style stewed tomatoes, undrained
1 medium green bell pepper, diced
1 package (1.0 ounce) LAWRY'S® Taco Spices & Seasonings
1 tablespoon yellow cornmeal
1 can (15¼ ounces) kidney beans, drained
1 package (15 ounces) flat refrigerated pie crusts
½ cup (2 ounces) shredded cheddar cheese, divided

In Dutch oven, heat oil. Add beef and cook over medium-high heat until browned; drain fat. Add stewed tomatoes, bell pepper, Taco Spices & Seasonings and cornmeal. Bring to a boil over medium-high heat; reduce heat to low and cook, uncovered, 20 minutes. Add kidney beans; mix well. In 10-inch pie plate, unfold 1 crust and fill with chili mixture and ¼ cup cheese. Top with remaining crust, fluting edges. Bake, uncovered, in 350°F oven 30 minutes. Sprinkle remaining cheese over crust; return to oven and bake 10 minutes longer.

Makes 6 servings

Serving Suggestion: Serve with a tossed green salad.

Steak San Marino

Picadillo `Slow Cooker`

- 1 pound ground beef
- 1 small onion, chopped
- 1 clove garlic, minced
- 1 can (14-12 ounces) diced tomatoes, undrained
- ¼ cup golden raisins
- 1 tablespoon chili powder
- 1 tablespoon cider vinegar
- ½ teaspoon ground cumin
- ½ teaspoon dried oregano leaves
- ½ teaspoon ground cinnamon
- ¼ teaspoon red pepper flakes
- 1 teaspoon salt
- ¼ cup slivered almonds (optional)

Slow Cooker Directions

1. Cook ground beef, onion and garlic in large nonstick skillet over medium heat until beef is no longer pink; drain. Place mixture into slow cooker.

2. Add tomatoes, raisins, chili powder, vinegar, cumin, oregano, cinnamon and pepper flakes to slow cooker. Cover; cook on LOW 6 to 7 hours. Stir in salt. Garnish with almonds, if desired.   *Makes 4 servings*

Steaks with Peppers

- 2 tablespoons BERTOLLI® Olive Oil
- 1½ pounds boneless beef chuck steaks, ½ inch thick (about 4 to 5)
- 2 medium red, green and/or yellow bell peppers, cut into thin strips
- 1 clove garlic, finely chopped (optional)
- 1 medium tomato, coarsely chopped
- 1 envelope LIPTON® RECIPE SECRETS® Onion or Onion-Mushroom Soup Mix
- 1 cup water

In 12-inch skillet, heat oil over medium-high heat and brown steaks. Remove steaks. Add peppers and garlic to skillet; cook over medium heat 5 minutes or until peppers are crisp-tender. Stir in tomato, then onion soup mix blended with water; bring to a boil over high heat. Reduce heat to low. Return steaks to skillet and simmer uncovered, stirring sauce occasionally, 25 minutes or until steaks and vegetables are tender.
          Makes about 4 servings

Menu Suggestion: Serve with steak fries or baked potatoes.

Creamy Beef and Vegetable Casserole

- 1 pound lean ground beef
- 1 small onion, chopped
- 1 bag (16 ounces) BIRDS EYE® frozen Farm Fresh Mixtures Broccoli, Corn & Red Peppers
- 1 can (10¾ ounces) cream of mushroom soup

- In medium skillet, brown beef and onion; drain excess fat.

- Meanwhile, in large saucepan, cook vegetables according to package directions; drain.

- Stir in beef mixture and soup. Cook over medium heat until heated through.   *Makes 4 servings*

Serving Suggestion: Serve over rice and sprinkle with ½ cup shredded Cheddar cheese.

Prep Time: 5 minutes
Cook Time: 10 to 15 minutes

Zesty Italian Stuffed Peppers

- 3 bell peppers (green, red or yellow)
- 1 pound ground beef
- 1 jar (14 ounces) spaghetti sauce
- 1⅓ cups *French's®* French Fried Onions, divided
- 2 tablespoons *Frank's® RedHot®* Cayenne Pepper Sauce
- ½ cup uncooked instant rice
- ¼ cup sliced ripe olives
- 1 cup (4 ounces) shredded mozzarella cheese

Preheat oven to 400°F. Cut bell peppers in half lengthwise through stems; discard seeds. Place pepper halves, cut side up, in shallow 2-quart baking dish; set aside.

Place beef in large microwavable bowl. Microwave on HIGH 5 minutes or until meat is browned, stirring once. Drain. Stir in spaghetti sauce, ⅔ cup French Fried Onions, *Frank's RedHot* Sauce, rice and olives. Spoon evenly into bell pepper halves.

Cover; bake 35 minutes or until bell peppers are tender. Uncover; sprinkle with cheese and remaining ⅔ cup onions. Bake 1 minute or until onions are golden.   *Makes 6 servings*

Prep Time: 10 minutes
Cook Time: 36 minutes

Helpful Hints

When cooking in a slow cooker, brown ground beef in a skillet to give it more flavor, then drain off the extra fat before adding it to the slow cooker.

Steaks with Peppers

Tacos in Pasta Shells

1 package (3 ounces) cream
   cheese with chives
18 jumbo pasta shells
1¼ pounds ground beef
1 teaspoon salt
1 teaspoon chili powder
2 tablespoons butter, melted
1 cup prepared taco sauce
1 cup (4 ounces) shredded
   Cheddar cheese
1 cup (4 ounces) shredded
   Monterey Jack cheese
1½ cups crushed tortilla chips
1 cup sour cream
3 green onions, chopped
   Leaf lettuce, small pitted ripe
   olives and cherry tomatoes
   for garnish

1. Cut cream cheese into ½-inch
cubes. Let stand at room temperature
until softened. Cook pasta according
to package directions. Place in
colander and rinse under warm
running water. Drain well. Return to
saucepan.

2. Preheat oven to 350°F. Butter
13×9-inch baking pan.

3. Cook beef in large skillet over
medium-high heat until brown, stirring
to separate meat; drain drippings.
Reduce heat to medium-low. Add
cream cheese, salt and chili powder;
simmer 5 minutes.

4. Toss shells with butter. Fill shells
with beef mixture. Arrange shells in
prepared pan. Pour taco sauce over
each shell. Cover with foil.

5. Bake 15 minutes. Uncover; top with
Cheddar cheese, Monterey Jack
cheese and chips. Bake 15 minutes
more or until bubbly. Top with sour
cream and onions. Garnish, if
desired.   *Makes 4 to 6 servings*

Texas-Style [Slow Cooker] Barbecued Brisket

1 beef brisket (3 to 4 pounds),
   cut into halves, if necessary,
   to fit slow cooker
3 tablespoons Worcestershire
   sauce
1 tablespoon chili powder
1 teaspoon celery salt
1 teaspoon black pepper
1 teaspoon liquid smoke
2 cloves garlic, minced
2 bay leaves
   Barbecue Sauce (recipe
   follows)

Slow Cooker Directions

Trim excess fat from meat and
discard. Place meat in resealable
plastic food storage bag. Combine
Worcestershire sauce, chili powder,
celery salt, pepper, liquid smoke,
garlic and bay leaves in small bowl.
Spread mixture on all sides of meat;
seal bag. Refrigerate 24 hours.

Place meat and marinade in slow
cooker. Cover and cook on LOW
7 hours. Meanwhile, prepare
Barbecue Sauce.

Remove meat from slow cooker and
pour juices into 2-cup measure; let
stand 5 minutes. Skim fat from juices.
Remove and discard bay leaves. Stir
1 cup defatted juices into Barbecue
Sauce. Discard remaining juices.
Return meat and Barbecue Sauce
mixture to slow cooker. Cover and
cook on LOW 1 hour or until meat is
fork-tender. Remove meat to cutting
board. Cut across grain into ¼-inch-
thick slices. Serve 2 to 3 tablespoons
Barbecue Sauce over each serving.
    Makes 10 to 12 servings

Barbecue Sauce

2 tablespoons vegetable oil
1 medium onion, chopped
2 cloves garlic, minced
1 cup ketchup
½ cup molasses
¼ cup cider vinegar
2 teaspoons chili powder
½ teaspoon dry mustard

Heat oil in medium saucepan over
medium heat. Add onion and garlic;
cook until onion is tender. Add
remaining ingredients. Simmer
5 minutes.

Zucchini Pasta Bake

1½ cups uncooked pasta tubes
½ pound ground beef
½ cup chopped onion
1 clove garlic, minced
   Salt and pepper
1 can (14½ ounces)
   DEL MONTE® Zucchini with
   Italian-Style Tomato Sauce
1 teaspoon dried basil, crushed
1 cup (4 ounces) shredded
   Monterey Jack cheese

1. Cook pasta according to package
directions; drain.

2. Cook beef with onion and garlic in
large skillet; drain. Season with salt
and pepper.

3. Stir in zucchini with tomato sauce
and basil. Place pasta in 8-inch
square baking dish. Top with meat
mixture.

4. Bake at 350°F for 15 minutes. Top
with cheese. Bake 3 minutes or until
cheese is melted.
    Makes 4 servings

Prep and Cook Time: 33 minutes

Tacos in Pasta Shells

Rice-Stuffed Peppers

1 package LIPTON® Rice &
    Sauce—Cheddar Broccoli
2 cups water
1 tablespoon margarine or
    butter
1 pound ground beef
4 large red or green bell
    peppers, halved lengthwise
    and seeded

Preheat oven to 350°F.

Prepare rice & sauce—cheddar broccoli with water and margarine according to package directions.

Meanwhile, in 10-inch skillet, brown ground beef over medium-high heat; drain. Stir into rice & sauce. Fill each pepper half with rice mixture. In 13×9-inch baking dish, arrange stuffed peppers. Bake covered 20 minutes. Remove cover and continue baking 10 minutes or until peppers are tender. Sprinkle, if desired, with shredded cheddar cheese.   *Makes about 4 servings*

Reuben Noodle Bake

8 ounces uncooked egg noodles
5 ounces thinly sliced deli-style
    corned beef
1 can (14½ ounces) sauerkraut
    with caraway seeds, drained
2 cups (8 ounces) shredded
    Swiss cheese
½ cup Thousand Island dressing
½ cup milk
1 tablespoon prepared mustard
2 slices pumpernickel bread
1 tablespoon butter, melted

1. Preheat oven to 350°F. Spray 13×9-inch baking dish with nonstick cooking spray.

2. Cook noodles according to package directions until al dente. Drain.

3. Meanwhile, cut corned beef into bite-size pieces. Combine noodles, corned beef, sauerkraut and cheese in large bowl. Spread in prepared dish.

4. Combine dressing, milk and mustard in small bowl. Spoon dressing mixture evenly over noodle mixture.

5. Tear bread into large pieces. Process in food processor or blender until crumbs form. Combine bread crumbs and margarine in small bowl; sprinkle evenly over casserole. Bake, uncovered, 25 to 30 minutes or until heated through.

Makes 6 servings

Old-Fashioned Beef Pot Pie

1 pound ground beef
1 can (11 ounces) condensed
    beef with vegetables and
    barley soup
½ cup water
1 package (10 ounces) frozen
    peas and carrots, thawed
    and drained
½ teaspoon seasoned salt
⅛ teaspoon garlic powder
⅛ teaspoon ground black pepper
1 cup (4 ounces) shredded
    Cheddar cheese, divided
1⅓ cups *French's*® French Fried
    Onions, divided
1 package (7½ ounces)
    refrigerated biscuits

Preheat oven to 350°F. In large skillet, brown ground beef in large chunks; drain. Stir in soup, water, vegetables and seasonings; bring to a boil. Reduce heat and simmer, uncovered, 5 minutes. Remove from heat; stir in ½ cup cheese and ⅔ cup French Fried Onions.

Pour mixture into 12×8-inch baking dish. Cut each biscuit in half; place, cut side down, around edge of casserole. Bake, uncovered, 15 to 20 minutes or until biscuits are done. Top with remaining ½ cup cheese and ⅔ *cup* onions; bake, uncovered, 5 minutes or until onions are golden brown.   *Makes 4 to 6 servings*

Reuben Noodle Bake

Easy Beef Lasagna

1 pound ground beef
1 jar (1 pound 10 ounces)
    RAGÚ® Old World Style®
    Pasta Sauce
1 container (15 ounces) ricotta
    cheese
2 cups shredded mozzarella
    cheese (about 8 ounces)
½ cup grated Parmesan cheese
2 eggs
12 lasagna noodles, cooked and
    drained

1. Preheat oven to 375°F. In 12-inch skillet, brown ground beef; drain. Stir in Ragú Pasta Sauce; heat through.

2. In large bowl, combine ricotta cheese, mozzarella cheese, ¼ cup Parmesan cheese and eggs.

3. In 13×9-inch baking dish, evenly spread 1 cup meat sauce. Arrange 4 lasagna noodles lengthwise over sauce, then 1 cup meat sauce and ½ of the ricotta cheese mixture; repeat, ending with sauce. Cover with aluminum foil and bake 30 minutes. Sprinkle with remaining ¼ cup Parmesan cheese. Bake uncovered 5 minutes. Let stand 10 minutes before serving.

Makes 10 servings

Prep Time: 30 minutes
Cook Time: 35 minutes

Helpful Hints

Ricotta is a fresh cheese. Check the sell-by date on the container to determine if it is fresh. Once the container is opened, the cheese must be used within 2 or 3 days.

Steak Fajitas Suprema

2 tablespoons vegetable oil,
    divided
1 medium-sized red bell pepper,
    thinly sliced
1 medium onion, very thinly
    sliced
1 pound beef sirloin steak,
    thinly sliced
1 package (1.27 ounces)
    LAWRY'S® Spices &
    Seasonings for Fajitas
¼ cup water
1 can (15 ounces) pinto beans,
    drained
6 medium flour or corn tortillas
1 cup (4 ounces) shredded
    cheddar cheese (optional)
    Salsa (optional)
    Dairy sour cream (optional)
    Sliced peeled avocado
    (optional)

In large skillet, heat 1 tablespoon oil. Add bell pepper and onion and cook over medium high heat until crisp-tender. Remove vegetables from skillet; set aside. In same skillet, heat remaining 1 tablespoon oil; add meat and cook 5 to 7 minutes or to desired doneness, drain fat. Add Spices & Seasonings for Fajitas, water and pinto beans; mix well. Bring to a boil over medium-high heat; reduce heat to low; simmer, uncovered, 3 to 5 minutes or until thoroughly heated, stirring occasionally. Return vegetables to skillet; heat 1 minute.

Makes 4 to 6 servings

Serving Suggestion: Serve in warm tortillas. If desired, add shredded cheddar cheese, salsa, sour cream and avocado to the inside for extra flavor.

Hint: Partially frozen meat is easier to slice thinly.

Chili Spaghetti Casserole

8 ounces uncooked spaghetti
1 pound lean ground beef
1 medium onion, chopped
¼ teaspoon salt
⅛ teaspoon black pepper
1 can (15 ounces) vegetarian
    chili with beans
1 can (14½ ounces) Italian-style
    stewed tomatoes, undrained
1½ cups (6 ounces) shredded
    sharp Cheddar cheese,
    divided
½ cup reduced-fat sour cream
1½ teaspoons chili powder
¼ teaspoon garlic powder

1. Preheat oven to 350°F. Spray 13×9-inch baking dish with nonstick cooking spray.

2. Cook pasta according to package directions until al dente. Drain and place in prepared dish.

3. Meanwhile, place beef and onion in large skillet; season with salt and pepper. Brown beef over medium-high heat until beef is no longer pink, stirring to separate meat. Drain fat. Stir in chili, tomatoes with juice, 1 cup cheese, sour cream, chili powder and garlic powder.

4. Add chili mixture to pasta; stir until pasta is well coated. Sprinkle with remaining ½ cup cheese.

5. Cover tightly with foil and bake 30 minutes or until hot and bubbly. Let stand 5 minutes before serving.

Makes 8 servings

Chili Spaghetti Casserole

Beefy Bean Skillet

    1 box (9 ounces) BIRDS EYE®
        frozen Cut Green Beans
    ½ pound lean ground beef
    ½ cup chopped onion
    1 cup instant rice
    1 can (10 ounces) au jus gravy*
    ¾ cup ketchup

Or, substitute 1 can (10 ounces) beef broth.

• In medium saucepan, cook green beans according to package directions; drain and set aside.

• Meanwhile, in large skillet, brown beef; drain excess fat. Add onion; cook and stir until onion is tender.

• Add rice, gravy and ketchup. Bring to boil over medium-high heat; cover and reduce heat to medium-low. Simmer 5 to 10 minutes or until rice is cooked, stirring occasionally.

• Stir in beans. Simmer until heated through. *Makes 4 servings*

Prep Time: 10 minutes
Cook Time: 20 minutes

Chili Beef Mac

    1 pound lean ground beef or
        ground turkey
    4 teaspoons Mexican
        seasoning*
    ⅔ cup milk
    1 (4.8-ounce) package
        PASTA RONI® Four Cheese
        Flavor with Corkscrew Pasta
    1 medium green, red or yellow
        bell pepper, diced
    ½ cup salsa
    ¼ cup chopped cilantro or sliced
        green onions

Substitute 2 teaspoons chili powder, 1 teaspoon ground cumin and 1 teaspoon garlic salt for the Mexican seasoning, if desired.

1. In large skillet over medium-high heat, cook ground beef and Mexican seasoning for 5 minutes, stirring occasionally.

2. Add 1¼ cups water, milk, pasta, bell pepper, salsa and Special Seasonings. Bring to a boil. Reduce heat to low. Cover; simmer 8 to 9 minutes or until pasta is tender. Stir in cilantro. Let stand 5 minutes before serving. *Makes 4 servings*

Prep Time: 5 minutes
Cook Time: 20 minutes

Stuffed Mexican Peppers

    1 package LIPTON® Rice &
        Sauce—Beef Flavor
    1¼ cups water, divided
    ½ pound ground beef
    1 cup frozen corn, partially
        thawed
    1 cup shredded cheddar cheese
        (about 4 ounces), divided
    1 medium tomato, chopped
    1 tablespoon chopped green
        chilies
    4 large green pepper cups

Preheat oven to 350°F.

In large bowl, combine rice & sauce—beef flavor with ¾ cup water; stir in ground beef, corn, ¾ cup cheese, tomato and chilies. Spoon into pepper cups; place upright in 8 or 9-inch baking pan filled with remaining ½ cup water. Cover tightly with aluminum foil and bake uncovered 45 minutes. Evenly top with remaining ¼ cup cheese and continue baking uncovered 10 minutes or until cheese melts.

Makes 4 servings

Spanish Skillet Supper

    ½ pound ground beef
    1 small onion, chopped
    2¼ cups water
    1 cup frozen whole kernel corn,
        partially thawed
    1 tablespoon margarine or
        butter
    1 package LIPTON® Rice &
        Sauce—Spanish
    ¼ cup shredded Cheddar cheese
        (about 1 ounce) (optional)

1. Brown ground beef and onion in 12-inch nonstick skillet over medium-high heat; drain. Remove and set aside.

2. Add water, corn, margarine and Rice & Sauce—Spanish and bring to a boil. Continue boiling over medium heat, stirring occasionally, 10 minutes or until rice is tender.

3. Stir in beef mixture; heat through. Sprinkle with cheese.
Makes about 2 servings

Prep Time: 5 minutes
Cook Time: 10 minutes

Beefy Bean Skillet

Beef Casserole Bourguignonne

        2 pounds boneless beef chuck,
            cut into 1-inch cubes
    ¼ cup all-purpose flour
    1⅓ cups sliced carrots
        1 can (14½ ounces) diced
            tomatoes, undrained
        1 cup thinly sliced onions
    ½ cup dry red wine
    ½ teaspoon salt
    ¼ teaspoon black pepper
        1 bay leaf
        1 cup sliced mushrooms
        1 package (8 ounces) medium
            or broad egg noodles

Preheat oven to 425°F. In 2½-quart shallow casserole, toss beef with flour. Bake uncovered 20 minutes, stirring halfway through cooking time. Add carrots, tomatoes, onions, wine, salt, pepper and bay leaf. Reduce heat to 350°F. Bake covered 1½ hours or until beef is tender. Add mushrooms and bake covered an additional 10 minutes. Remove bay leaf.

Meanwhile, cook noodles according to package directions. To serve, spoon bourguignonne over noodles.

Makes about 8 servings

Freezing/Reheating Directions:
Bourguignonne can be baked, then frozen. Simply wrap covered casserole in heavy-duty foil and freeze. To reheat, unwrap and bake covered at 400°F, stirring occasionally to separate beef and vegetables, 1 hour. Let stand covered 5 minutes.

Lasagna Roll-Ups

    1½ pounds ground beef
        1 (28-ounce) jar pasta sauce
    ½ teaspoon dried basil leaves
    ½ teaspoon dried oregano leaves
        1 (15-ounce) container ricotta
            cheese
        1 (10-ounce) package frozen
            chopped spinach, thawed
            and squeezed dry
        2 cups (8 ounces) shredded
            mozzarella cheese
    ½ cup grated Parmesan cheese,
            divided
        1 egg, beaten
    12 lasagna noodles, cooked,
            drained
        2 tablespoons chopped fresh
            parsley

Brown beef in large skillet over medium-high heat until no longer pink, stirring occasionally to break up beef; drain. Mix pasta sauce, basil and oregano in small bowl; stir 1 cup spaghetti sauce mixture into beef. Reverse remaining sauce mixture.

Preheat oven to 350°F. Mix ricotta cheese, spinach, mozzarella cheese, ⅓ cup Parmesan cheese and egg in medium bowl. On each lasagna noodle, spread about ¼ cup ricotta mixture. Top with about ⅓ cup beef mixture. Roll up each noodle from short end; lay each roll, seam side down, in lightly greased 13×9×2-inch baking dish. Pour reserved spaghetti sauce mixture over noodles. Sprinkle with remaining Parmesan cheese and parsley.

Bake, covered, 30 minutes. Uncover and bake 15 to 20 minutes more or until hot and bubbly. Serve with additional Parmesan cheese if desired.   *Makes 6 servings*

Countdown Casserole

        1 jar (8 ounces) pasteurized
            process cheese spread
    ¾ cup milk
        2 cups (12 ounces) cubed
            cooked roast beef
        1 bag (16 ounces) frozen
            vegetable combination
            (broccoli, corn, red pepper),
            thawed and drained
        4 cups frozen hash brown
            potatoes, thawed
    1⅓ cups *French's®* French Fried
            Onions, divided
    ½ teaspoon seasoned salt
    ¼ teaspoon freshly ground black
            pepper
    ½ cup (2 ounces) shredded
            Cheddar cheese

Preheat oven to 375°F. Spoon cheese spread into 12×8-inch baking dish; place in oven just until cheese melts, about 5 minutes. Using fork, stir milk into melted cheese until well blended. Stir in beef, vegetables, potatoes, ⅔ cup French Fried Onions and the seasonings. Bake, covered, at 375°F 30 minutes or until heated through. Top with Cheddar cheese; sprinkle remaining ⅔ cup onions down center. Bake, uncovered, 3 minutes or until onions are golden brown.

Makes 4 to 6 servings

Microwave Directions: In 12×8-inch microwave-safe dish, combine cheese spread and milk. Cook, covered, on HIGH 3 minutes; stir. Add ingredients as directed. Cook, covered, 14 minutes or until heated through, stirring beef mixture halfway through cooking time. Top with Cheddar cheese and remaining ⅔ cup onions as directed. Cook, uncovered, 1 minute or until cheese melts. Let stand 5 minutes.

Lasagna Roll-Ups

Irresistible Pork

Barbara's Pork Chop Dinner

1 tablespoon butter
1 tablespoon olive oil
6 bone-in pork loin chops
1 can (10¾ ounces) condensed cream of chicken soup, undiluted
1 can (4 ounces) mushrooms, drained and chopped
¼ cup Dijon mustard
¼ cup chicken broth
2 cloves garlic, minced
½ teaspoon salt
½ teaspoon dried basil leaves
¼ teaspoon black pepper
6 red potatoes, unpeeled, cut into thin slices
1 onion, sliced
Chopped fresh parsley

Slow Cooker Directions

Heat butter and oil in large skillet. Brown pork chops on both sides. Set aside.

Combine soup, mushrooms, mustard, chicken broth, garlic, salt, basil and pepper in slow cooker. Add potatoes and onion, stirring to coat. Place pork chops on top of potato mixture. Cover and cook on LOW 8 to 10 hours or on HIGH 4 to 5 hours. Sprinkle with parsley. *Makes 6 servings*

Orange Teriyaki Pork

Nonstick cooking spray
1 pound lean pork stew meat, cut into 1-inch cubes
1 package (16 ounces) frozen pepper blend for stir-fry
4 ounces sliced water chestnuts
½ cup orange juice
2 tablespoons quick-cooking tapioca
2 tablespoons packed light brown sugar
2 tablespoons teriyaki sauce
½ teaspoon ground ginger
½ teaspoon dry mustard
1⅓ cups hot cooked rice

Slow Cooker Directions

1. Spray large nonstick skillet with cooking spray; heat skillet over medium heat until hot. Add pork; brown on all sides. Remove from heat; set aside.

2. Place pepper blend and water chestnuts in slow cooker. Top with pork. Mix orange juice, tapioca, brown sugar, teriyaki sauce, ginger and mustard in bowl. Pour over pork mixture in slow cooker. Cover; cook on LOW 3 to 4 hours. Serve with rice.
Makes 4 servings

Cajun Sausage and Rice

8 ounces kielbasa sausage, cut in ¼-inch slices
1 can (14½ ounces) diced tomatoes, undrained
1 medium onion, diced
1 medium green bell pepper, diced
2 ribs celery, thinly sliced
1 tablespoon chicken bouillon granules
1 tablespoon steak sauce
3 bay leaves *or* 1 teaspoon dried thyme leaves
1 teaspoon sugar
¼ to ½ teaspoon hot pepper sauce
1 cup uncooked instant rice
½ cup water
½ cup chopped parsley

Slow Cooker Directions

1. Combine sausage, tomatoes with juice, onion, bell pepper, celery, bouillon, steak sauce, bay leaves, sugar and hot pepper sauce in slow cooker. Cover; cook on LOW 8 hours or on HIGH 4 hours.

2. Remove bay leaves; stir in rice and water. Cook on HIGH 25 minutes or until rice is tender. Stir in parsley.
Makes 5 servings

Barbara's Pork Chop Dinner

Baked Rigatoni with Sausage

½ pound Italian sausage
2 cups milk
2 tablespoons all-purpose flour
½ pound rigatoni pasta, cooked and drained
2½ cups (10 ounces) shredded mozzarella cheese
¼ cup grated Parmesan cheese
1 teaspoon LAWRY'S® Garlic Salt
¾ teaspoon LAWRY'S® Seasoned Pepper
2 to 3 tablespoons dry bread crumbs *or* ¾ cup croutons

In large skillet, crumble Italian sausage. Cook over medium-high heat until browned, 5 minutes; drain fat. Add milk and flour. Bring to a boil over medium-high heat, stirring constantly. Stir in pasta, cheeses, Garlic Salt and Seasoned Pepper. Place in 1½-quart baking dish. Bake in 350°F oven 25 minutes. Sprinkle with bread crumbs; place under broiler to brown about 2 to 4 minutes.

Makes 6 servings

Serving Suggestion: Serve with green beans and crusty bread.

Hint: ¼ pound cooked, diced ham can replace sausage.

Spicy Black Bean & Sausage Stew

1 tablespoon olive oil
½ cup chopped onion
¼ cup chopped green bell pepper
4 ounces kielbasa sausage, cut into ¼-inch pieces
2 cloves garlic, minced
1 cup drained canned black beans, rinsed
¾ cup undrained stewed tomatoes
1½ teaspoons dried oregano leaves
¾ teaspoon ground cumin
2 tablespoons minced fresh parsley
Hot pepper sauce
Hot cooked rice (optional)

1. Heat oil in medium skillet over medium heat. Add onion, bell pepper and sausage. Cook and stir 3 to 4 minutes or until vegetables are tender. Add garlic; cook and stir 1 minute.

2. Stir in beans, tomatoes with juice, oregano and cumin, breaking up tomatoes into small chunks. Bring to a boil; reduce heat to low. Cover and simmer 20 minutes, stirring occasionally. Stir in parsley and pepper sauce to taste. Serve with hot cooked rice, if desired.

Makes 2 servings

Potato and Pork Frittata

12 ounces (about 3 cups) frozen hash brown potatoes
1 teaspoon Cajun seasoning
4 egg whites
2 whole eggs
¼ cup low-fat (1%) milk
1 teaspoon dry mustard
¼ teaspoon black pepper
10 ounces (about 3 cups) frozen stir-fry vegetable blend
⅓ cup water
¾ cup chopped cooked lean pork
½ cup (2 ounces) shredded Cheddar cheese

1. Preheat oven to 400°F. Spray baking sheet with nonstick cooking spray. Spread potatoes on baking sheet; sprinkle with Cajun seasoning. Bake 15 minutes or until hot. Remove from oven. *Reduce oven temperature to 350°F.*

2. Beat egg whites, eggs, milk, mustard and pepper in small bowl. Place vegetables and water in medium ovenproof nonstick skillet. Cook over medium heat 5 minutes or until vegetables are crisp-tender; drain.

3. Add pork and potatoes to vegetables in skillet; stir lightly. Add egg mixture. Sprinkle with cheese. Cook over medium-low heat 5 minutes. Place skillet in oven and bake 5 minutes or until egg mixture is set and cheese is melted.

Makes 4 servings

Prep and Cook Time: 30 minutes

Helpful Hints

Kielbasa, also known as Polish sausage, is a smoked pork sausage that is usually precooked. Italian sausage is most commonly flavored with garlic and fennel seed. It is often sold in links and is also available in bulk.

Spicy Black Bean & Sausage Stew

Southwest Pork & Rice

1½ teaspoons chili powder, divided
¾ teaspoon ground cumin, divided
¾ teaspoon salt, divided
1½ pounds lean boneless pork, cut into 1-inch pieces
1 tablespoon vegetable oil
1 cup UNCLE BEN'S® ORIGINAL CONVERTED® Brand Rice
½ cup chopped onion
1 can (14½ ounces) diced tomatoes, undrained

1. In medium bowl, combine 1 teaspoon chili powder, ½ teaspoon cumin, ¼ teaspoon salt and pepper to taste; add pork and toss to coat.

2. In 12-inch skillet, heat oil over medium-high heat until hot. Add pork; cook, stirring occasionally, until browned, about 3 minutes. Remove pork from skillet; set aside.

3. Add rice and onion to skillet; cook and stir 2 minutes or until rice is opaque and onion is translucent. Stir in 1½ cups water, tomatoes, remaining ½ teaspoon chili powder, ½ teaspoon salt, ¼ teaspoon cumin and pepper to taste. Bring to a boil; stir in pork. Cover; reduce heat to low and simmer 25 to 30 minutes or until rice is tender and most of the liquid is absorbed.   *Makes 6 servings*

Serving Suggestions: For added flavor, sprinkle with minced fresh cilantro. Add 1 cup frozen corn and ½ cup chopped green bell pepper to rice mixture with tomatoes; proceed as directed.

Italian Sausage and Rice Frittata

7 large eggs
¾ cup milk
½ teaspoon salt
½ pound mild or hot Italian sausage, casing removed and sausage broken into small pieces
1½ cups uncooked UNCLE BEN'S® Instant Brown Rice
1 can (14½ ounces) Italian-style stewed tomatoes
¼ teaspoon Italian herb seasoning
1½ cups (6 ounces) shredded Italian cheese blend, divided

1. Whisk together eggs, milk and salt in medium bowl. Set aside.

2. Preheat oven to 325°F. Cook sausage about 7 minutes in 11-inch ovenproof nonstick skillet over high heat until no longer pink.

3. Reduce heat to medium-low. Stir in rice, stewed tomatoes with their juices, breaking up any large pieces, and Italian seasoning. Sprinkle evenly with 1 cup cheese.

4. Pour egg mixture into skillet; stir gently to distribute egg. Cover and cook 15 minutes or until eggs are just set.

5. Remove from heat. Sprinkle remaining ½ cup cheese over frittata. Bake about 10 minutes more or until puffed and cheese is melted.

6. Remove skillet from oven. Cover and let stand 5 minutes. Cut into 6 wedges before serving.
    Makes 6 servings

Cook's Tip: Choose a blend of shredded mozzarella and provolone for this frittata, or the blend of your choice.

Hot Dog Macaroni

1 package (8 ounces) hot dogs
1 cup uncooked corkscrew pasta
1 cup shredded Cheddar cheese
1 box (10 ounces) BIRDS EYE® frozen Green Peas
1 cup 1% milk

● Slice hot dogs into bite-size pieces; set aside.

● In large saucepan, cook pasta according to package directions; drain and return to saucepan.

● Stir in hot dogs, cheese, peas and milk. Cook over medium heat 10 minutes or until cheese is melted, stirring occasionally.
    Makes 4 servings

Prep Time: 10 minutes
Cook Time: 20 minutes

SPAM™ Skillet Dinner

3 medium zucchini
1 onion, thinly sliced
1 tablespoon vegetable oil
1 (12-ounce) can SPAM® Classic
3 medium potatoes, peeled, sliced
3 carrots, peeled, sliced
1 (16-ounce) can chopped tomatoes
¾ teaspoon garlic powder
½ teaspoon dried basil leaves
½ teaspoon dried oregano leaves

Cut zucchini into ½-inch slices. In large skillet, sauté zucchini and onion in oil 5 minutes. Cut SPAM® into 8 slices; halve each slice. Add potatoes, carrots and SPAM™ mixture to skillet; pour tomatoes over SPAM®. Sprinkle with garlic, basil and oregano. Cover; simmer 25 minutes or until potatoes are tender, stirring occasionally.   *Makes 8 servings*

Prep and Cook Time: 20 minutes

Hot Dog Macaroni

Shredded Pork Wraps

Slow Cooker

1 cup salsa, divided
2 tablespoons cornstarch
1 bone-in pork sirloin roast
    (2 pounds)
6 (8-inch) flour tortillas
3 cups broccoli slaw mix
⅓ cup shredded reduced-fat
    Cheddar cheese

Slow Cooker Directions

1. Combine ¼ cup salsa and cornstarch in small bowl; stir until smooth. Pour mixture into slow cooker. Top with pork roast. Pour remaining ¾ cup salsa over roast.

2. Cover; cook on LOW 6 to 8 hours or until internal temperature reaches 160°F when tested with meat thermometer inserted into thickest part of roast, not touching bone. Transfer roast to cutting board; cover with foil and let stand 10 to 15 minutes or until cool enough to handle. (Internal temperature will rise 5°F during stand time.) Trim and discard outer fat from pork. Using 2 forks, pull pork into coarse shreds.

3. Divide shredded meat evenly among tortillas. Spoon about 2 tablespoons salsa mixture on top of meat in each tortilla. Top evenly with broccoli slaw and cheese. Fold bottom edge of tortilla over filling; fold in sides. Roll up completely to enclose filling. Serve remaining salsa mixture as dipping sauce.

Makes 6 servings

Italian Pork Skillet

1 pound pork tenderloin
1 small eggplant
1 medium summer squash
2 tablespoons olive oil, divided
1½ teaspoons salt, divided
⅛ teaspoon black pepper
1 clove garlic, minced
1 medium onion, thinly sliced
1 small red bell pepper, cut into
    thin strips
1 teaspoon Italian seasoning
⅓ cup water
1 teaspoon cornstarch

Partially freeze tenderloin. Cut pork diagonally into ¼-inch thick slices; quarter slices. Cut squash lengthwise in half. Place on flat sides and cut crosswise into ¼-inch-thick slices. In skillet, brown half of pork in 1 tablespoon hot olive oil, stirring

Shredded Pork Wrap

constantly; remove from pan. Add remaining pork; cook, stirring constantly until pork is browned. Sprinkle ¾ teaspoon salt and pepper over pork. Place remaining 1 tablespoon olive oil, eggplant and minced garlic in skillet and cook over medium-high heat 3 minutes. Add squash, onion, bell pepper, Italian seasoning and remaining ¾ teaspoon salt; cook 7 minutes, stirring occasionally. Combine water and cornstarch; stir into vegetables. Return pork to skillet and cook 3 to 4 minutes or until thickened, stirring occasionally.   *Makes 4 servings*

Prep Time: 20 minutes

Favorite recipe from **National Pork Board**

Spanish Pork Chops

    4 pork chops (about 1 pound)
    1 (6.8-ounce) package
        RICE-A-RONI® Spanish Rice
    2 tablespoons margarine or
        butter
    1 (14½-ounce) can diced
        tomatoes, undrained

1. In large skillet over medium-high heat, brown pork chops 3 minutes on each side; set aside.

2. In same skillet, sauté rice-vermicelli with margarine until vermicelli is golden brown.

3. Slowly stir in 2¼ cups water, tomatoes and Special Seasonings; bring to a boil. Reduce heat to low. Cover; simmer 10 minutes.

4. Add pork chops; return to a simmer. Cover; simmer 8 to 10 minutes or until rice is tender and pork chops are no longer pink inside.
     Makes 4 servings

Prep Time: 5 minutes
Cook Time: 30 minutes

Hawaiian-Roni

    1 pound boneless pork loin
        chops, cut into 1-inch
        pieces
    ¼ cup teriyaki sauce
    1 (6.2-ounce) package
        RICE-A-RONI® Fried Rice
    ¼ cup chopped onion
    2 tablespoons margarine or
        butter
    1 (8-ounce) can pineapple
        chunks in juice, drained,
        reserving ¼ cup juice
    1 cup sliced carrots
    ¼ cup slivered almonds, toasted

1. In small bowl, combine pork and teriyaki sauce; set aside.

2. In large skillet over medium heat, sauté rice-vermicelli mix and onion with margarine until vermicelli is golden brown.

3. Slowly stir in 1 cup water, reserved ¼ cup pineapple juice, carrots, pork mixture and Special Seasonings; bring to a boil. Reduce heat to medium-low. Cover; simmer 15 to 20 minutes or rice is tender and pork is no longer pink inside.

4. Stir in pineapple chunks. Cover; let stand 5 minutes before serving. Sprinkle with almonds.
     Makes 4 servings

Tip: For variety, try sliced chicken or steak instead of pork.

Prep Time: 10 minutes
Cook Time: 30 minutes

Ham & Barbecued Bean Skillet

    1 tablespoon vegetable oil
    1 cup chopped onion
    1 teaspoon bottled minced
        garlic
    1 can (15 ounces) red or pink
        kidney beans, rinsed and
        drained
    1 can (15 ounces) cannellini or
        Great Northern beans,
        rinsed and drained
    1 cup chopped green bell
        pepper
    ½ cup packed light brown sugar
    ½ cup catsup
    2 tablespoons cider vinegar
    2 teaspoons dry mustard
    1 fully cooked smoked ham
        steak (about 12 ounces), cut
        ½ inch thick

1. Heat oil in large deep skillet over medium-high heat until hot. Add onion and garlic; cook 3 minutes, stirring occasionally.

2. Add kidney beans, cannellini beans, bell pepper, brown sugar, catsup, vinegar and mustard; mix well.

3. Trim fat from ham; cut into ½-inch pieces. Add ham to bean mixture; simmer over medium heat 5 minutes or until sauce thickens and mixture is heated through, stirring occasionally.
     Makes 4 servings

Serving Suggestion: Serve with a Caesar salad and crisp breadsticks.

Mexican Skillet Rice

¾ pound lean ground pork or lean ground beef
1 medium onion, chopped
1½ tablespoons chili powder
1 teaspoon ground cumin
½ teaspoon salt
3 cups cooked brown rice
1 can (16 ounces) pinto beans, drained
2 cans (4 ounces each) diced green chilies
1 medium tomato, seeded and chopped (optional)

Cook meat in large skillet over medium-high heat until brown, stirring to crumble; drain. Return meat to skillet. Add onion, chili powder, cumin and salt; cook until onion is soft but not brown. Stir in rice, beans and chilies; heat through. Top with tomato.

Makes 6 servings

Microwave Directions: Combine meat and onion in 2- to 3-quart microwave-safe baking dish, stirring well. Cover with waxed paper and cook on HIGH 4 to 5 minutes, stirring after 2 minutes, or until meat is no longer pink. Drain. Add chili powder, cumin, salt, rice, beans and chilies. Cook on HIGH 4 to 5 minutes, stirring after 2 minutes, or until thoroughly heated. Top with tomato.

Ham and Potato Casserole

`Slow Cooker`

1½ pounds red potatoes, peeled and sliced
8 ounces thinly sliced ham
2 poblano chili peppers, cut into thin strips
2 tablespoons olive oil
1 tablespoon dried oregano leaves
¼ teaspoon salt
1 cup (4 ounces) shredded Monterey Jack cheese with or without hot peppers
2 tablespoons finely chopped fresh cilantro

Slow Cooker Directions

1. Combine all ingredients, except cheese and cilantro, in slow cooker; mix well. Cover; cook on LOW 7 hours or on HIGH 4 hours.

2. Transfer potato mixture to serving dish; sprinkle with cheese and cilantro. Let stand 3 minutes or until cheese melts.

Makes 6 to 7 servings

Jambalaya

1 teaspoon vegetable oil
½ pound smoked deli ham, cubed
½ pound smoked sausage, cut into ¼-inch-thick slices
1 large onion, chopped
1 large green bell pepper, chopped (about 1½ cups)
3 ribs celery, chopped (about 1 cup)
3 cloves garlic, minced
1 can (28 ounces) diced tomatoes, undrained
1 can (10½ ounces) condensed chicken broth
1 cup uncooked rice
1 tablespoon Worcestershire sauce
1 teaspoon salt
1 teaspoon dried thyme leaves
½ teaspoon black pepper
¼ teaspoon ground red pepper
1 package (12 ounces) frozen ready-to-cook shrimp, thawed
Fresh chives (optional)

Preheat oven to 350°F. Spray 13×9-inch baking dish with nonstick cooking spray.

Heat oil in large skillet over medium-high heat until hot. Add ham and sausage. Cook and stir 5 minutes or until sausage is lightly browned on both sides. Remove from skillet and place in prepared dish. Place onion, bell pepper, celery and garlic in same skillet; cook and stir 3 minutes. Add to sausage mixture.

Combine tomatoes with juice, broth, rice, Worcestershire, salt, thyme, salt and black and red peppers in same skillet; bring to a boil over high heat. Reduce heat to low and simmer 3 minutes. Pour over sausage mixture and stir until combined.

Cover tightly with foil and bake 45 minutes or until rice is almost tender. Remove from oven; place shrimp on top of rice mixture. Bake, uncovered, 10 minutes or until shrimp are pink and opaque. Garnish with chives, if desired.

Makes 8 servings

Country Pork Skillet

4 boneless top loin pork chops, diced
1 (12-ounce) jar pork gravy
2 tablespoons ketchup
8 small red potatoes, diced
2 cups frozen mixed vegetables

In large skillet, brown pork cubes; stir in gravy, ketchup and potatoes; cover and simmer for 10 minutes. Stir in vegetables; cook for 10 to 15 minutes longer, until vegetables are tender.

Makes 4 servings

Favorite recipe from **National Pork Board**

Pork Chop & Wild Rice Bake

 1 package (6 ounces) seasoned long grain & wild rice mix
1½ cups *French's*® French Fried Onions, divided
 1 package (10 ounces) frozen cut green beans, thawed and drained
 ¼ cup orange juice
 1 teaspoon grated orange peel
 4 boneless pork chops (1 inch thick)

1. Preheat oven to 375°F. Combine rice mix and seasoning packet, 2 *cups water*, ⅔ *cup* French Fried Onions, green beans, orange juice and orange peel in 2-quart shallow baking dish. Arrange pork chops on top.

2. Bake, uncovered, 30 minutes or until pork chops are no longer pink near center. Sprinkle chops with remaining ⅔ *cup* onions. Bake 5 minutes or until onions are golden.

Makes 4 servings

Prep Time: 5 minutes
Cook Time: 35 minutes

Hash Brown Frittata

 1 (10-ounce) package BOB EVANS® Skinless Link Sausage
 6 eggs
 1 (12-ounce) package frozen hash brown potatoes, thawed
 1 cup (4 ounces) shredded Cheddar cheese
 ⅓ cup whipping cream
 ¼ cup chopped green and/or red bell pepper
 ¼ teaspoon salt
 Dash black pepper

Preheat oven to 350°F. Cut sausage into bite-size pieces. Cook in small skillet over medium heat until lightly browned, stirring occasionally. Drain off any drippings. Whisk eggs in medium bowl; stir in sausage and remaining ingredients. Pour into greased 2-quart casserole dish. Bake, uncovered, 30 minutes or until eggs are almost set. Let stand 5 minutes before cutting into squares; serve hot. Refrigerate leftovers.

Makes 6 servings

Helpful Hints

A frittata is an Italian omelet in which the eggs are combined with other ingredients, then cooked in a heavy skillet over medium heat. Frittatas are often finished in the oven or under a broiler.

Jambalaya

Cheesy Pork Chops 'n' Potatoes

1 jar (8 ounces) pasteurized processed cheese spread
1 tablespoon vegetable oil
6 thin pork chops, ¼ to ½ inch thick
Seasoned salt
½ cup milk
4 cups frozen cottage fries
1⅓ cups *French's*® French Fried Onions, divided
1 package (10 ounces) frozen broccoli spears,* thawed and drained

*One small head fresh broccoli (about ½ pound) may be substituted for frozen spears. Divide into spears and cook 3 to 4 minutes before using.

Preheat oven to 350°F. Spoon cheese spread into 12×8-inch baking dish; place in oven just until cheese melts, about 5 minutes. Meanwhile, in large skillet, heat oil. Brown pork chops on both sides; drain. Sprinkle chops with seasoned salt; set aside. Using fork, stir milk into melted cheese until well blended. Stir cottage fries and ⅔ cup French Fried Onions into cheese mixture. Divide broccoli spears into 6 small bunches. Arrange bunches of spears over potato mixture with flowerets around edges of dish. Arrange chops over broccoli *stalks*. Bake, covered, at 350°F for 35 to 40 minutes or until pork chops are no longer pink. Top chops with remaining ⅔ cup onions; bake, uncovered, 5 minutes or until onions are golden brown.   *Makes 4 to 6 servings*

Microwave Directions: Omit oil. Reduce milk to ¼ cup. In 12×8-inch microwave-safe dish, place cheese spread and milk. Cook, covered, on HIGH 3 minutes; stir to blend. Stir in cottage fries and ⅔ cup onions. Cook, covered, 5 minutes; stir. Top with broccoli spears as above. Arrange unbrowned pork chops over broccoli *stalks* with meatiest parts toward edges of dish. Cook, covered, on MEDIUM (50 to 60%)

24 to 30 minutes or until pork chops are no longer pink. Turn chops over, sprinkle with seasoned salt and rotate dish halfway through cooking time. Top with remaining ⅔ cup onions; cook, uncovered, on HIGH 1 minute. Let stand 5 minutes.

Creamy Pasta Primavera

1 bag (16 ounces) BIRDS EYE® frozen Pasta Secrets Primavera
½ cup 1% milk
2 packages (3 ounces each) cream cheese, cubed
1 cup cubed ham
¼ cup grated Parmesan cheese

• In large skillet, heat Pasta Secrets in milk over medium heat to a simmer; cover and simmer 7 to 9 minutes or until vegetables are tender.

• Add cream cheese; reduce heat to low and cook until cream cheese is melted, stirring often.

• Stir in ham and cheese; cover and cook 5 minutes more.

Makes 4 servings

Prep Time: 10 minutes
Cook Time: 20 minutes

Pork and Peach Bake

1 (6-ounce) package stuffing mix
½ cup SMUCKER'S® Peach Preserves, divided
4 pork chops (½ inch thick)
2 tablespoons oil
1 (8-ounce) can sliced peaches, drained
Parsley

Make stuffing mix according to package directions, decreasing water by ¼ cup; stir in ¼ cup preserves. Spoon stuffing into *ungreased* 1-quart casserole.

Brown pork chops in oil over medium heat. Arrange pork chops and peaches over stuffing. Spoon remaining ¼ cup preserves over chops.

Cover and bake at 350°F for 45 minutes to 1 hour or until pork chops are tender. Garnish with parsley.   *Makes 4 servings*

Sweet and Sour Spare Ribs

4 pounds pork spare ribs
2 cups dry sherry or chicken broth
½ cup pineapple, mango or guava juice
⅓ cup chicken broth
2 tablespoons packed light brown sugar
2 tablespoons cider vinegar
2 tablespoons soy sauce
1 clove garlic, minced
½ teaspoon salt
¼ teaspoon black pepper
⅛ teaspoon red pepper flakes
2 tablespoons cornstarch

Slow Cooker Directions
1. Preheat oven to 400°F. Place ribs in foil-lined shallow roasting pan. Bake 30 minutes, turning over after 15 minutes. Remove from oven. Slice meat into 2-rib portions. Place ribs in 5-quart slow cooker. Add remaining ingredients, except cornstarch, to slow cooker.

2. Cover; cook on LOW 6 hours. Transfer ribs to platter; keep warm. Let liquid in slow cooker stand 5 minutes to allow fat to rise. Skim off fat.

3. Combine cornstarch and ¼ cup liquid from slow cooker; stir until smooth. Stir mixture into liquid in slow cooker; mix well. Cook on HIGH 10 minutes or until slightly thickened.
Makes 4 servings

Sweet and Sour Spare Ribs

Apple, Bean and Ham Casserole

1 pound boneless ham
3 cans (15 ounces each) Great Northern beans, drained and rinsed
1 small onion, diced
1 medium Granny Smith apple, diced
3 tablespoons dark molasses
3 tablespoons packed brown sugar
1 tablespoon Dijon mustard
1 teaspoon ground allspice
¼ cup thinly sliced green onions *or* 1 tablespoon chopped fresh parsley

1. Preheat oven to 350°F. Cut ham into 1-inch cubes. Combine ham, beans, onion, apple, molasses, brown sugar, mustard and allspice in 3-quart casserole; mix well. Cover; bake 45 minutes or until most liquid is absorbed. Cool casserole completely. Cover and refrigerate up to 2 days.

2. To complete recipe, stir ⅓ cup water into casserole. Microwave at HIGH 10 minutes or until hot and bubbly. Or, heat in preheated 350°F oven 40 minutes or until hot and bubbly. Sprinkle with green onions before serving.

Makes 6 servings

Make-Ahead Time: up to 2 days in refrigerator
Final Cook Time: 15 minutes

Pork and Mushroom Ragoût

Slow Cooker

1 boneless pork loin roast (1¼-pounds)
1¼ cups canned crushed tomatoes, divided
2 tablespoons cornstarch
2 teaspoons dried savory leaves
3 sun-dried tomatoes, chopped
1 package (8 ounces) sliced mushrooms
1 large onion, sliced
1 teaspoon black pepper
3 cups hot cooked noodles

Slow Cooker Directions

1. Spray large nonstick skillet with nonstick cooking spray; heat skillet over medium heat until hot. Brown roast on all sides; set aside.

2. Place ½ cup crushed tomatoes, cornstarch, savory and sun-dried tomatoes into slow cooker; mix well. Layer mushrooms, onion and roast over tomato mixture.

3. Pour remaining tomatoes over roast; sprinkle with pepper. Cover; cook on LOW 4 to 6 hours or until internal temperature reaches 160°F when tested with meat thermometer inserted into the thickest part of roast.

4. Transfer roast to cutting board; cover with foil. Let stand 10 to 15 minutes. Internal temperature will continue to rise 5° to 10°F during stand time. Slice roast. Serve with sauce over hot cooked noodles.

Makes 6 servings

Pizza Pasta

1 medium green bell pepper, chopped
1 medium onion, chopped
1 cup sliced mushrooms
½ teaspoon LAWRY'S® Garlic Powder with Parsley OR Garlic Salt
1 tablespoon vegetable oil
¼ cup sliced ripe olives
1 package (1.5 ounces) LAWRY'S® Original-Style Spaghetti Sauce Spices & Seasonings
1¾ cups water
1 can (6 ounces) tomato paste
10 ounces mostaccioli, cooked and drained
3 ounces thinly sliced pepperoni
¾ cup shredded mozzarella cheese

In large skillet, heat oil. Add bell pepper, onion, mushrooms and Garlic Powder with Parsley and cook over medium-high heat. Stir in Spaghetti Sauce Spices & Seasonings, water and tomato paste; mix well. Bring sauce to a boil over medium-high heat; reduce heat to low and simmer, uncovered, 10 minutes. Add cooked mostaccioli and sliced pepperoni; mix well. Pour in 12×8×2-inch baking dish; top with cheese. Bake at 350°F 15 minutes until cheese is melted.

Makes 6 servings

Serving Suggestion: Serve with warm rolls or bread since this pizza doesn't have any crust.

Helpful Hints

Sun-dried tomatoes have an intense, sweet flavor that adds rich tomato flavor to soups and stews. They are available either packed in oil or dried. The oil-packed variety tends to be more expensive but it is ready to use. The dried variety needs to be softened in hot water for 30 minutes or boiling water for 5 minutes. Either variety is suitable for Pork and Mushroom Ragoût. For this recipe, the dried variety do not have to be pre-softened.

Apple, Bean and Ham Casserole

Pork Chops and Apple Stuffing Bake

> 6 (¾-inch-thick) boneless pork
>   loin chops (about
>   1½ pounds)
> ¼ teaspoon salt
> ⅛ teaspoon black pepper
> 1 tablespoon vegetable oil
> 1 small onion, chopped
> 2 ribs celery, chopped
> 2 Granny Smith apples, peeled
>   and coarsely chopped
>   (about 2 cups)
> 1 can (14½ ounces) reduced-
>   sodium chicken broth
> 1 can (10¾ ounces) condensed
>   cream of celery soup
> ¼ cup dry white wine
> 6 cups herb-seasoned stuffing
>   cubes

1. Preheat oven to 375°F. Spray 13×9-inch baking dish with nonstick cooking spray.

2. Season both sides of pork chops with salt and pepper. Heat oil in large deep skillet over medium-high heat until hot. Add chops and cook until browned on both sides, turning once. Remove chops from skillet; set aside.

3. Add onion and celery to same skillet. Cook and stir 3 minutes or until onion is tender. Add apples; cook and stir 1 minute. Add broth, soup and wine; mix well. Bring to a simmer; remove from heat. Stir in stuffing cubes until evenly moistened.

4. Spread stuffing mixture evenly in prepared dish. Place pork chops on top of stuffing; pour any accumulated juices over chops. Cover tightly with foil and bake 30 to 40 minutes or until pork chops are juicy and barely pink in center.   *Makes 6 servings*

Chicken in the Hay

> ⅓ cup WESSON® Best Blend Oil
> 2 cups frozen shredded hash
>   brown potatoes, thawed
> ¾ cup sliced green onions
> 1½ cups seasoned croutons
> 6 large eggs, beaten
> ¾ cup diced ham
> ⅔ cup shredded Cheddar cheese
> ⅛ to ¼ teaspoon coarsely
>   ground pepper (optional)
> Salt to taste
> Shredded Cheddar cheese for
>   garnish

In a large skillet, heat Wesson® Oil. Add hash browns and green onions; fry until potatoes are dark golden brown, stirring occasionally. If potatoes become dry, add more oil. Add *remaining* ingredients *except* salt and cheese for garnish; blend well. Cook egg mixture until eggs are set. Salt to taste and garnish with additional cheese.

Makes 6 servings

Cheesy Pork and Potatoes

Slow Cooker

> ½ pound ground pork, cooked
>   and crumbled
> ½ cup finely crushed saltine
>   crackers
> ⅓ cup barbecue sauce
> 1 egg
> 3 tablespoons margarine
> 1 tablespoon vegetable oil
> 4 potatoes, peeled and thinly
>   sliced
> 1 onion, thinly sliced
> 1 cup grated mozzarella cheese
> ⅔ cup evaporated milk
> 1 teaspoon salt
> ¼ teaspoon paprika
> ⅛ teaspoon black pepper
> Chopped fresh parsley

Slow Cooker Directions

Combine pork, crackers, barbecue sauce and egg in large bowl; shape mixture into 6 patties. Heat margarine and oil in medium skillet. Sauté potatoes and onion until lightly browned. Drain and place in slow cooker.

Combine cheese, milk, salt, paprika and pepper in small bowl. Pour into slow cooker. Layer pork patties on top. Cover and cook on LOW 3 to 5 hours. Garnish with parsley.

Makes 6 servings

Pork with Vegetable Rice

> 4 center-cut pork chops, about
>   ½ inch thick, or 4 boneless,
>   skinless chicken breast
>   halves
> 1 tablespoon vegetable oil
> 1 cup long grain rice
> 1 medium onion, chopped
> 2½ cups water
> 1 package KNORR® Recipe
>   Classics™ Vegetable Soup,
>   Dip and Recipe Mix

• Sprinkle pork chops with salt and pepper. In large skillet, heat oil over medium-high heat. Add chops and brown, turning occasionally, about 5 minutes. Remove.

• Add rice and onion; stirring constantly, cook 2 minutes. Stir in water and recipe mix; bring to a boil.

• Return pork chops to skillet. Reduce heat, cover and simmer 15 minutes or until rice is tender.

Makes 4 servings

Prep Time: 12 minutes
Cook Time: 15 minutes

Pork Chop and Apple Stuffing Bake

Hearty Potato and Sausage Bake

**1 pound new potatoes, cut in halves or quarters
1 large onion, sliced
½ pound baby carrots
2 tablespoons melted butter
1 teaspoon salt
1 teaspoon garlic powder
½ teaspoon dried thyme leaves
½ teaspoon black pepper
1 pound cooked sausage or turkey sausage**

1. Preheat oven to 400°F. Spray 13×9-inch baking pan with nonstick cooking spray.

2. Combine potatoes, onion, carrots, butter, salt, garlic powder, thyme, and pepper in large bowl. Toss to coat evenly.

3. Place potato mixture into prepared pan; bake, uncovered, 30 minutes. Add sausage to potato mixture; mix well. Continue to bake 15 to 20 minutes or until potatoes are tender and golden brown.

Makes 4 to 6 servings

SPAM™ Vegetable Hash

**½ cup chopped onion
2 tablespoons butter or margarine
2 cups frozen cubed hash brown potatoes, thawed
1 (12-ounce) can SPAM® Classic, cubed
1 (10-ounce) package frozen peas and carrots, thawed
½ teaspoon black pepper**

In large skillet over medium-high heat, sauté onion in butter until tender. Stir in potatoes. Cook, stirring occasionally, until potatoes are lightly browned. Stir in SPAM®, peas and carrots and pepper. Cook, stirring occasionally, until thoroughly heated.

Makes 4 to 6 servings

Quick Cassoulet

**2 slices bacon, cut into ½-inch pieces
¾ pound boneless pork chops, sliced crosswise ¼ inch thick
1 medium onion, chopped
1 clove garlic, minced
1 teaspoon dried thyme, crushed
1 can (14½ ounces) DEL MONTE® Stewed Tomatoes Original Recipe
½ cup dry white wine
1 can (15 ounces) white or pinto beans, drained**

1. Cook bacon in large skillet over medium-high heat until almost crisp.

2. Stir in meat, onion, garlic and thyme. Season with salt and pepper, if desired.

3. Cook 4 minutes. Add undrained tomatoes and wine; bring to boil. Cook, uncovered, over medium-high heat 10 minutes or until thickened, adding beans during last 5 minutes.

Makes 4 servings

Prep and Cook Time: 30 minutes

Pork Asado

**2 pounds lean, boneless pork shoulder, trimmed and cubed
1 clove garlic, minced
2 tablespoons salad oil
1 package (1.31 ounces) LAWRY'S® Spice & Seasonings for Taco Salad
1 cup water
1 can (28 ounces) whole tomatoes
2 stalks celery, cut into 1-inch pieces
2 medium onions, quartered
1 can (18 ounces) sweet potatoes or yams, drained
LAWRY'S® Seasoned Salt to taste
LAWRY'S® Seasoned Pepper to taste**

In Dutch oven, brown pork and garlic in oil; add Spice & Seasonings for Taco Salad, water, tomatoes, celery and onion. Bring to a boil over medium-high heat; reduce heat to low, cover and simmer 1 hour or until meat is tender. Add sweet potatoes and season with Seasoned Salt and Seasoned Pepper to taste during last 10 minutes of cooking.

Makes 6 to 8 servings

Serving Suggestion: Serve with warmed corn tortillas and a green salad.

Pork Chops and Yams

**4 pork chops (½ inch thick)
2 tablespoons oil
2 (16-ounce) cans yams or sweet potatoes, drained
¾ cup SMUCKER'S® Orange Marmalade or Apricot Preserves
½ large green bell pepper, cut into strips
2 tablespoons minced onion**

1. Brown pork chops in oil over medium heat.

2. Place yams in 1½-quart casserole. Stir in marmalade, bell pepper and onion. Layer pork chops over yam mixture. Cover and bake at 350°F for 30 minutes or until pork chops are tender.

Makes 4 servings

Hearty Potato and Sausage Bake

Oven Jambalaya

- 1 pound sweet Italian sausages
- 2 stalks celery, sliced
- 1 green bell pepper, diced
- 1 medium onion, diced
- 2 cloves garlic, minced
- 1 (28-ounce) can crushed tomatoes
- 2 cups chicken broth
- 1 cup long-grain rice
- 2 teaspoons TABASCO® brand Pepper Sauce
- 1 teaspoon salt
- 1 pound large raw shrimp, peeled and deveined

Preheat oven to 400°F. Cook sausages in 12-inch skillet over medium-high heat until well browned on all sides, turning frequently. Remove sausages to plate; reserve drippings in skillet. When cool enough to handle, cut sausages into ½-inch slices. Add celery, green bell pepper, onion and garlic to same skillet; cook 3 minutes over medium heat, stirring occasionally.

Combine tomatoes, chicken broth, rice, TABASCO® Sauce, salt, sausages and vegetable mixture in 3-quart casserole. Bake 40 minutes. Stir in shrimp; cook 5 minutes or until rice is tender and shrimp are cooked.

Makes 8 servings

Helpful Hints

To devein shrimp, cut a shallow slit along the back of the shrimp with a paring knife. Lift out the vein. (You may find this easier to do under cold running water.) The veins of large and jumbo shrimp are gritty; they must always be removed. The veins of medium and small shrimp are not gritty and need not be removed unless you wish a more elegant presentation.

Sausage & Noodle Casserole

- 1 pound BOB EVANS® Original Recipe Roll Sausage
- 1 cup chopped onion
- ¼ cup chopped green bell pepper
- 1 (10-ounce) package frozen peas
- 1 (10¾-ounce) can condensed cream of chicken soup
- 1 (8-ounce) package egg noodles, cooked according to package directions and drained
- Salt and black pepper to taste
- 1 (2.8-ounce) can French fried onions, crushed

Preheat oven to 350°F. Crumble sausage into large skillet. Add onion and green pepper. Cook over medium heat until meat is browned and vegetables are tender, stirring occasionally. Drain off any drippings. Cook peas according to package directions. Drain, reserving liquid in 2-cup glass measuring cup; set aside. Add enough water to pea liquid to obtain 1⅓ cups liquid. Combine liquid and soup in large bowl; stir in sausage mixture, noodles, reserved peas, salt and black pepper. Mix well. Spoon mixture into greased 2½-quart baking dish. Sprinkle with onions. Bake 30 minutes or until bubbly. Serve hot. Refrigerate leftovers.

Makes 6 servings

Easy Italian Skillet Supper

- 1 pound Italian sausage, casing removed and crumbled, or ground beef
- 1 medium onion, cut into wedges
- 1 medium green bell pepper, cut into strips
- 2 cloves garlic, minced
- 1 (6.8-ounce) package RICE-A-RONI® Spanish Rice
- 2 tablespoons margarine or butter
- 1 (14½-ounce) can diced tomatoes, undrained
- ½ cup sliced pimiento-stuffed olives
- 1 teaspoon dried oregano

1. In large skillet, sauté sausage, onion, bell pepper and garlic until sausage is well cooked. Remove with slotted spoon; set aside.

2. In same skillet over medium heat, sauté rice-vermicelli mix with margarine until vermicelli is golden brown.

3. Slowly stir in 2 cups water, tomatoes, olives, oregano and Special Seasonings; bring to a boil. Reduce heat to low. Cover; simmer 15 to 20 minutes or until rice is tender. Stir in sausage mixture; serve.

Makes 4 servings

Tip: Only canned whole tomatoes on hand? Simply snip them directly in the can using kitchen shears.

Prep Time: 10 minutes
Cook Time: 30 minutes

Oven Jambalaya

Sausage Tetrazzini

1 pound BOB EVANS® Italian
  Roll Sausage
1 medium onion, chopped
1 red or green bell pepper,
  chopped
½ pound spaghetti, cooked
  according to package
  directions and drained
1 (10½-ounce) can condensed
  cream of mushroom soup
1 (10-ounce) can condensed
  tomato soup
1 (16-ounce) can stewed
  tomatoes, undrained
½ pound fresh mushrooms,
  chopped
1 teaspoon minced garlic
½ teaspoon black pepper
  Salt to taste
1½ cups (6 ounces) shredded
  Cheddar cheese

Preheat oven to 350°F. Crumble
sausage into large skillet. Cook over
medium heat until lightly browned,
stirring occasionally. Remove
sausage; set aside. Add onion and
red pepper to drippings in skillet;
cook and stir until tender. Place in
large bowl. Stir in spaghetti, soups,
tomatoes with juice, mushrooms,
garlic, black pepper, salt and
reserved sausage; place in 3-quart
casserole dish. Sprinkle with cheese;
bake, uncovered, 30 to 35 minutes or
until heated through. Serve hot.
Refrigerate leftovers.

Makes 6 to 8 servings

Savory Lentil Casserole

1¼ cups uncooked dried brown or
  green lentils, rinsed and
  sorted
2 tablespoons olive oil
1 large onion, chopped
3 cloves garlic, minced
8 ounces fresh shiitake or
  button mushrooms, sliced
2 tablespoons all-purpose flour
1½ cups beef broth
1 tablespoon Worcestershire
  sauce
1 tablespoon balsamic vinegar
4 ounces Canadian bacon,
  minced
½ teaspoon salt
½ teaspoon black pepper
½ cup grated Parmesan cheese
2 to 3 plum tomatoes, seeded
  and chopped

1. Preheat oven to 400°F. Place lentils
in medium saucepan; cover with
1 inch water. Bring to a boil over high
heat. Reduce heat to low. Simmer,
covered, 20 to 25 minutes until lentils
are barely tender; drain.

2. Meanwhile, heat oil in large skillet
over medium heat. Add onion and
garlic; cook and stir 10 minutes. Add
mushrooms; cook and stir 10 minutes
or until liquid is evaporated and
mushrooms are tender. Sprinkle flour
over mushroom mixture; stir well.
Cook and stir 1 minute. Stir in beef
broth, Worcestershire, vinegar, bacon,
salt and pepper. Cook and stir until
mixture is thick and bubbly.

3. Grease 1½-quart casserole. Stir
lentils into mushroom mixture. Spread
evenly into prepared casserole.
Sprinkle with cheese. Bake
20 minutes.

4. Sprinkle tomatoes over casserole
just before serving. Garnish with
thyme and Italian parsley, if desired.

Makes 4 servings

Family-Style Frankfurters with Rice and Red Beans

1 tablespoon vegetable oil
1 medium onion, chopped
½ medium green bell pepper,
  chopped
2 cloves garlic, minced
1 can (14 ounces) red kidney
  beans, rinsed and drained
1 can (14 ounces) Great
  Northern beans, rinsed and
  drained
½ pound beef frankfurters, cut
  into ¼-inch-thick pieces
1 cup uncooked instant brown
  rice
1 cup vegetable broth
¼ cup packed brown sugar
¼ cup ketchup
3 tablespoons dark molasses
1 tablespoon Dijon mustard

Preheat oven to 350°F. Spray
13×9-inch baking dish with nonstick
cooking spray.

Heat oil in Dutch oven over medium-
high heat until hot. Add onion, pepper
and garlic; cook and stir 2 minutes or
until onion is tender.

Add beans, frankfurters, rice, broth,
sugar, ketchup, molasses and
mustard to vegetables; stir to
combine. Pour into prepared dish.

Cover tightly with foil and bake
30 minutes or until rice is tender.

Makes 6 servings

Savory Lentil Casserole

Fiesta Rice and Sausage
Slow Cooker

1 teaspoon vegetable oil
2 pounds spicy Italian sausage, casing removed
2 cloves garlic, minced
2 teaspoons ground cumin
4 onions, chopped
4 green bell peppers, chopped
3 jalapeño peppers,* seeded and minced
4 cups beef broth
2 packages (6¼ ounces each) long-grain and wild rice mix

Jalapeño peppers can sting and irritate the skin; wear rubber gloves when handling peppers and do not touch eyes. Wash hands after handling.

Slow Cooker Directions

Heat oil in large skillet; add sausage. Break up sausage with back of spoon while cooking; cook until browned, about 5 minutes. Add garlic and cumin; cook 30 seconds. Add onions, bell peppers and jalapeño peppers. Sauté mixture until onions are tender, about 10 minutes. Pour mixture into slow cooker. Stir in beef broth and rice.

Cover and cook on HIGH 1 to 2 hours or on LOW 4 to 6 hours.

Makes 10 to 12 servings

Vegetable-Stuffed Pork Chops
Slow Cooker

4 double pork loin chops, well trimmed
   Salt and black pepper
1 can (15¼ ounces) kernel corn, drained
1 green bell pepper, chopped
1 cup Italian-style seasoned dry bread crumbs
1 small onion, chopped
½ cup uncooked long-grain converted rice
1 can (8 ounces) tomato sauce

Slow Cooker Directions

Cut pocket in each pork chop, cutting from edge nearest bone. Lightly season pockets with salt and pepper to taste. Combine corn, bell pepper, bread crumbs, onion and rice in large bowl. Stuff pork chops with rice mixture. Secure along fat side with wooden toothpicks.

Place any remaining rice mixture into slow cooker. Add stuffed pork chops to slow cooker. Moisten top of each pork chop with tomato sauce. Pour any remaining tomato sauce over top. Cover and cook on LOW 8 to 10 hours or until done.

Remove pork chops to serving platter. Remove and discard toothpicks. Serve pork chops with rice mixture.

Makes 4 servings

Sausage Bake

1 cup uncooked egg noodles
1 bag (16 ounces) BIRDS EYE® frozen Cut Green Beans
1 pound smoked sausage links, fully cooked
1 can (15 ounces) cream of celery soup
½ teaspoon *each* sage, celery salt and garlic powder

• In large saucepan, cook noodles according to package directions. Add green beans during last 10 minutes; drain and return to pan.

• Meanwhile, cut sausage into ½-inch pieces.

• Add all ingredients to noodles and beans; toss together.

• Cook over medium heat 3 to 5 minutes or until heated through. Add salt and pepper to taste.

Makes 4 servings

Prep Time: 2 minutes
Cook Time: 15 minutes

Smokehouse Red Bean and Sausage Casserole

3 bacon slices, chopped
3 cups chopped onion
1 medium-sized green bell pepper, chopped
1 cup chopped fresh parsley
1 pound smoked sausage, cut into ¼-inch slices
2 cans (15¼ ounces each) kidney beans, undrained
1 can (8 ounces) tomato sauce
1 tablespoon Worcestershire sauce
1 tablespoon LAWRY'S® Seasoned Salt
¾ teaspoon hot pepper sauce
½ teaspoon LAWRY'S® Garlic Powder with Parsley
3 cups hot cooked white rice

In Dutch oven or large saucepan, cook bacon and onion over medium-high heat until bacon is just crisp and onion is transparent; drain fat. Add remaining ingredients except rice; mix well. Bring to a boil over medium-high heat; reduce heat to low and simmer, uncovered, 20 minutes, stirring occasionally.

Makes 8 servings

Serving Suggestion: Serve over rice; this is perfect with a green salad and crusty bread.

Hint: Use 1 bag (12 ounces) frozen chopped onion instead of fresh onion.

Fiesta Rice and Sausage

Smoked Sausage and Sauerkraut Casserole

6 fully-cooked smoked sausage
   links, such as German or
   Polish sausage (about
   1½ pounds)
⅓ cup water
¼ cup packed brown sugar
2 tablespoons country-style
   Dijon mustard, Dijon
   mustard or German-style
   mustard
1 teaspoon caraway seed
½ teaspoon dill weed
1 jar (32 ounces) sauerkraut,
   drained
1 small green bell pepper,
   stemmed, seeded and diced
½ cup (2 ounces) shredded
   Swiss cheese

1. Place sausage in large skillet with water. Cover; bring to a boil over medium heat. Reduce heat to low; simmer, covered, 10 minutes. Uncover and simmer until water evaporates and sausages brown lightly.

2. While sausage is cooking, combine sugar, mustard, caraway and dill in medium saucepan; stir until blended. Add sauerkraut and bell pepper; stir until well mixed. Cook, covered, over medium heat 10 minutes or until hot.

3. Spoon sauerkraut into microwavable 2- to 3-quart casserole; sprinkle with cheese. Place sausage into sauerkraut; cover. Microwave at HIGH 30 seconds or until cheese melts. *Makes 6 servings*

Prep and Cook Time: 20 minutes

Pork Chops with Jalapeño-Pecan Cornbread Stuffing

Slow Cooker

6 boneless loin pork chops,
   1 inch thick (1½ pounds)
   Nonstick cooking spray
¾ cup chopped onion
¾ cup chopped celery
½ cup coarsely chopped pecans
½ medium jalapeño pepper,*
   seeded and chopped
1 teaspoon rubbed sage
½ teaspoon dried rosemary
⅛ teaspoon black pepper
4 cups unseasoned cornbread
   stuffing mix
1¼ cups reduced-sodium chicken
   broth
1 egg, lightly beaten

Jalapeño peppers can sting and irritate the skin; wear rubber gloves when handling peppers and do not touch eyes. Wash hands after handling.

Slow Cooker Directions

Trim excess fat from pork and discard. Spray large skillet with nonstick cooking spray; heat over medium heat. Add pork; cook 10 minutes or until browned on all sides. Remove; set aside. Add onion, celery, pecans, jalapeño pepper, sage, rosemary and pepper to skillet. Cook 5 minutes or until tender; set aside.

Combine cornbread stuffing mix, vegetable mixture and broth in medium bowl. Stir in egg. Spoon stuffing mixture into slow cooker. Arrange pork on top. Cover and cook on LOW about 5 hours or until pork is tender and barely pink in center. Serve with vegetable salad, if desired. *Makes 6 servings*

Note: If you prefer a more moist dressing, increase the chicken broth to 1½ cups.

Vegetable Pork Skillet

1 tablespoon CRISCO® Oil*
4 (4 ounces *each*) lean,
   boneless, center-cut pork
   loin chops, ½ inch thick
2 medium onions, thinly sliced
   and separated into rings
1 can (14½ ounces) whole
   tomatoes, undrained
¾ cup water
2 teaspoons paprika
1 teaspoon salt
½ teaspoon celery seed
¼ teaspoon pepper
¼ teaspoon garlic powder
3 medium unpeeled potatoes,
   chopped
1 package (9 ounces) frozen cut
   green beans

Use your favorite Crisco Oil product.

1. Heat oil in large skillet on medium heat. Add meat. Cook until browned on both sides. Remove from skillet.

2. Add onions to skillet. Cook and stir until tender. Add tomatoes, water, paprika, salt, celery seed, pepper and garlic powder. Bring to a boil.

3. Return meat to skillet. Reduce heat to low. Cover. Simmer 15 minutes.

4. Add potatoes. Cover. Simmer 15 minutes.

5. Add beans. Cover. Simmer 5 to 7 minutes or until potatoes and beans are tender. *Makes 4 servings*

Pork Chop with Jalapeño-Pecan Cornbread Stuffing

Jamaican Pork Skillet

1 tablespoon vegetable oil
4 well-trimmed center cut pork
    chops, cut ½ inch thick
¾ teaspoon blackened or Cajun
    seasoning mix
¼ teaspoon ground allspice
1 cup chunky salsa, divided
1 can (15 ounces) black beans,
    drained and rinsed
1 can (about 8 ounces) whole
    kernel corn, drained *or*
    1 cup thawed frozen whole
    kernel corn
1 tablespoon fresh lime juice

1. Heat oil in large deep skillet over medium-high heat until hot. Sprinkle both sides of pork chops with blackened seasoning mix and allspice; cook 2 minutes per side or until browned.

2. Pour ½ cup salsa over pork chops; reduce heat to medium. Cover and simmer about 12 minutes or until pork is no longer pink.

3. While pork chops are simmering, combine beans, corn, remaining ½ cup salsa and lime juice in medium bowl; mix well. Serve bean mixture with pork chops.

Makes 4 servings

Note: For a special touch, add chopped fresh cilantro to the bean mixture.

Prep and Cook Time: 20 minutes

Helpful Hints

Cilantro is a fresh leafy green herb that looks a lot like Italian parsley. Its distinctive flavor complements spicy foods, especially Mexican, Caribbean, Thai and Vietnamese dishes.

Skillet Red Beans & Rice

1 tablespoon vegetable oil
1 medium onion, finely chopped
1 green bell pepper, finely
    chopped
1 rib celery, finely chopped
3 cloves garlic, minced
2½ cups water
1 can (about 15 ounces) kidney
    beans, rinsed and drained
1 cup uncooked converted white
    rice
¼ pound Canadian bacon, finely
    chopped
1 bay leaf
1 teaspoon dried thyme leaves
½ teaspoon black pepper

1. Heat oil in nonstick skillet over medium-high heat until hot. Add onion, bell pepper, celery and garlic; cook and stir 5 minutes or until vegetables are tender.

2. Add water, beans, rice, bacon, bay leaf, thyme and black pepper to skillet. Cover. Cook over medium heat 15 to 20 minutes or until liquid is absorbed and rice is tender. Remove bay leaf; discard. Garnish with sprigs of thyme, if desired.

Makes 6 servings

Cook's Tip: Avoid rinsing uncooked rice. Valuable B vitamins, such as thiamin and niacin, will be washed away in the water.

Spicy-Sweet Pineapple Pork

¾ cup LAWRY'S® Hawaiian
    Marinade with Tropical Fruit
    Juices
1 tablespoon minced fresh
    ginger
1 pound pork loin, cut into
    ½-inch strips or cubes
1 cup salsa
3 tablespoons brown sugar
2 tablespoons cornstarch
2 cans (8 ounces each)
    pineapple chunks,
    undrained, divided
2 tablespoons vegetable oil,
    divided
1 green bell pepper, cut into
    chunks
3 green onions, diagonally
    sliced into 1-inch pieces
½ cup whole cashews

In large resealable plastic food storage bag, combine Hawaiian Marinade with Tropical Fruit Juices and ginger. Add pork; seal bag. Marinate in refrigerator at least 1 hour. In small bowl, combine salsa, brown sugar, cornstarch and juice from 1 can pineapple; set aside. In large skillet or wok, heat 1 tablespoon oil. Stir-fry pepper and onions over high heat until onions are transparent; remove and set aside. Remove pork; discard used marinade. Add remaining 1 tablespoon oil and pork to skillet; stir-fry 5 minutes or until just browned. Return pepper and onions to skillet. Stir salsa mixture; add to skillet. Cook until thickened, stirring constantly. Drain remaining 1 can pineapple. Add pineapple chunks from both cans and cashews; simmer 5 minutes. *Makes 6 servings*

Serving Suggestion: Serve over steamed white rice and top with crunchy chow mein noodles.

Jamaican Pork Skillet

New Orleans Rice and Sausage

- ½ pound smoked sausage,* cut into slices
- 1 can (14½ ounces) stewed tomatoes, Cajun- or Italian-style
- ¾ cup water
- 1¾ cups uncooked instant rice
  Dash TABASCO® Pepper Sauce or to taste
- 1 bag (16 ounces) BIRDS EYE® frozen Farm Fresh Mixtures Broccoli, Corn and Red Peppers

For a spicy dish, use andouille sausage. Any type of kielbasa or turkey kielbasa can also be used.

Heat sausage in large skillet 2 to 3 minutes.

Add tomatoes, water, rice and TABASCO® Pepper Sauce; mix well.

Add vegetables; mix well. Cover and cook over medium heat 5 to 7 minutes or until rice is tender and vegetables are heated through.

Makes 6 servings

Prep Time: 5 minutes
Cook Time: 10 minutes

Chinese Pork & Vegetable Stir-Fry

- 2 tablespoons BERTOLLI® Olive Oil, divided
- 1 pound pork tenderloin or boneless beef sirloin, cut into ¼-inch slices
- 6 cups assorted fresh vegetables*
- 1 can (8 ounces) sliced water chestnuts, drained
- 1 envelope LIPTON® Recipe Secrets® Onion Soup Mix
- ¾ cup water
- ½ cup orange juice
- 1 tablespoon soy sauce
- ¼ teaspoon garlic powder

Use any of the following to equal 6 cups: broccoli florets, snow peas, thinly sliced red or green bell peppers or thinly sliced carrots.

In 12-inch skillet, heat 1 tablespoon oil over medium-high heat; brown pork. Remove and set aside.

In same skillet, heat remaining 1 tablespoon oil and cook assorted fresh vegetables, stirring occasionally, 5 minutes. Stir in water chestnuts and onion soup mix blended with water, orange juice, soy sauce and garlic powder. Bring to a boil over high heat. Reduce heat to low and simmer, uncovered, 3 minutes. Return pork to skillet and cook 1 minute or until heated through.

Makes about 4 servings

Tip: Pick up pre-sliced vegetables from your local salad bar.

Cajun Red Beans and Sausages

- 8 bacon slices, chopped
- 2 onions, chopped
- 1 green bell pepper, chopped
- 1 pound smoked sausage, sliced ¼ inch thick
- 3 cans (15 ounces each) red kidney beans, undrained
- 1 can (8 ounces) tomato sauce
- 1¼ teaspoon LAWRY'S® Red Pepper Seasoned Salt
- 1 teaspoon black pepper
- 1 teaspoon LAWRY'S® Garlic Powder with Parsley

In Dutch oven, cook bacon over medium-high heat 5 minutes, until almost crisp; drain fat. Add onions and green pepper and cook until tender, about 7 minutes. Stir in remaining ingredients. Bring to a boil over medium-high heat; reduce heat to medium, cover and simmer 10 minutes, stirring occasionally.

Makes 8 servings

Serving Suggestion: Serve over rice and accompany with crisp salad and corn muffins, if desired.

Hints: For parties, recipe can easily be doubled. Cook a day ahead then reheat on top of stove.

Prep Time: 30 minutes

Sweet and Sour Pork

- ¾ pound boneless pork
- 1 teaspoon vegetable oil
- 1 bag (16 ounces) BIRDS EYE® frozen Farm Fresh Mixtures Pepper Stir Fry vegetables
- 1 tablespoon water
- 1 jar (14 ounces) sweet and sour sauce
- 1 can (8 ounces) pineapple chunks, drained

- Cut pork into thin strips.
- In large skillet, heat oil over medium-high heat.
- Add pork; stir-fry until pork is browned.
- Add vegetables and water; cover and cook over medium heat 5 to 7 minutes or until vegetables are crisp-tender.
- Uncover; stir in sweet and sour sauce and pineapple. Cook until heated through.

Makes 4 servings

Serving Suggestion: Serve over hot cooked rice.

Birds Eye Idea: For a quick sweet and sour sauce for chicken nuggets or egg rolls, add sugar and vinegar to taste to jarred strained apricots or peaches.

Prep Time: 5 minutes
Cook Time: 15 to 18 minutes

New Orleans Rice and Sausage

Best-Loved Chicken

Forty-Clove Chicken

1 frying chicken (3 pounds), cut
    into serving pieces
    Salt and black pepper
1 to 2 tablespoons olive oil
¼ cup dry white wine
2 tablespoons dry vermouth
2 tablespoons chopped fresh
    parsley *or* 2 teaspoons
    dried parsley leaves
2 teaspoons dried basil leaves
1 teaspoon dried oregano leaves
    Pinch of red pepper flakes
40 cloves garlic (about 2 heads*),
    peeled
4 ribs celery, sliced
    Juice and peel of 1 lemon
    Fresh herbs (optional)

The whole garlic bulb is called a head.

Slow Cooker Directions

Remove skin from chicken, if desired.
Sprinkle chicken with salt and pepper.
Heat oil in large skillet over medium
heat. Add chicken; cook 10 minutes
or until browned on all sides. Remove
to platter.

Combine wine, vermouth, parsley,
basil, oregano and red pepper flakes
in large bowl. Add garlic and celery;
coat well. Transfer garlic and celery to
slow cooker with slotted spoon. Add
chicken to remaining herb mixture;
coat well. Place chicken on top of
celery in slow cooker. Sprinkle lemon
juice and peel in slow cooker; add
remaining herb mixture. Cover and
cook on LOW 6 hours or until chicken
is no longer pink in center. Garnish
with fresh herbs, if desired.

Makes 4 to 6 servings

Chicken Paprikash

1 pound boneless, skinless
    chicken breasts or thighs,
    cut into 1-inch chunks
2 teaspoons paprika
½ teaspoon salt
¼ teaspoon cayenne pepper
3 tablespoons margarine or
    butter, divided
3 cups (8 ounces) sliced white
    or crimini mushrooms
1 small onion, chopped
½ cup milk
1 (4.7-ounce) package
    PASTA RONI® Fettuccine
    Alfredo
¼ cup sour cream
¼ cup chopped parsley

1. Toss chicken with paprika, salt and
cayenne pepper. In large skillet over
medium-high heat, melt 1 tablespoon
margarine. Add chicken; sauté
3 minutes. Add mushrooms and
onion; sauté 7 minutes or until
chicken is no longer pink inside and
vegetables are tender. Remove from
skillet; set aside.

2. In same skillet, bring 1¼ cups
water, milk, remaining 2 tablespoons
margarine, pasta and Special
Seasonings to a boil. Reduce heat to
low. Gently boil uncovered, 5 to
6 minutes or until pasta is tender,
stirring occasionally.

3. Stir in chicken mixture and sour
cream. Let stand 3 to 5 minutes
before serving. Sprinkle with parsley.

Makes 4 servings

Prep Time: 15 minutes
Cook Time: 25 minutes

Forty-Clove Chicken

Roasted Chicken and Vegetables over Wild Rice

3½ pounds chicken pieces
¾ cup olive oil vinaigrette dressing, divided
1 tablespoon margarine or butter, melted
1 package (6 ounces) long-grain and wild rice mix
1 can (about 14 ounces) reduced-sodium chicken broth
1 small eggplant, cut into 1-inch pieces
2 medium red potatoes, cut into 1-inch pieces
1 medium yellow summer squash, cut into 1-inch pieces
1 medium zucchini, cut into 1-inch pieces
1 medium red onion, cut into wedges
1 package (4 ounces) crumbled feta cheese with basil
Chopped fresh cilantro (optional)
Fresh thyme sprigs (optional)

Remove skin from chicken; discard. Combine chicken and ½ cup dressing in large resealable plastic food storage bag. Seal bag and turn to coat. Refrigerate 30 minutes or overnight.

Preheat oven to 375°F. Coat bottom of 13×9-inch baking dish with margarine.

Add rice and seasoning packet to prepared dish; stir in broth. Combine eggplant, potatoes, squash, zucchini and onion in large bowl. Place on top of rice mixture.

Remove chicken from bag and place on top of vegetables; discard marinade. Pour remaining ¼ cup dressing over chicken.

Bake, uncovered, 45 minutes. Remove from oven and sprinkle with cheese. Bake 5 to 10 minutes or until chicken is no longer pink in centers, juices run clear and cheese is melted. Sprinkle with cilantro, if desired. Garnish with thyme, if desired.

Makes 4 to 6 servings

Honey-Dijon Chicken

4 boneless, skinless chicken breast halves (about 1 pound)
2 tablespoons all-purpose flour
3 tablespoons margarine or butter, divided
1 (6.9-ounce) package RICE-A-RONI® Chicken Flavor
1½ cups fresh or frozen sliced carrots
2 tablespoons honey
2 tablespoons Dijon mustard

1. Coat chicken with flour. In large skillet over medium heat, melt 2 tablespoons margarine. Add chicken; cook 5 minutes on each side or until browned. Remove from skillet; set aside.

2. In same skillet over medium heat, sauté rice-vermicelli mix with remaining 1 tablespoon margarine until vermicelli is golden brown.

3. Slowly stir in 2¼ cups water, carrots and Special Seasonings; bring to a boil. Place chicken over rice. Reduce heat to low. Cover; simmer 15 minutes.

4. In small bowl, combine honey and mustard. Drizzle over chicken. Simmer uncovered, 5 minutes or until rice is tender and chicken is no longer pink inside.   *Makes 4 servings*

Prep Time: 10 minutes
Cook Time: 35 minutes

Pennsylvania Dutch Chicken Bake

1 package (about 1¾ pounds) PERDUE® Fresh Skinless Chicken Thighs
Salt and pepper to taste
1 to 2 tablespoons canola oil
1 can (14 to 16 ounces) sauerkraut, undrained
1 can (14 to 15 ounces) whole onions, drained
1 tart red apple, unpeeled and sliced
6 to 8 dried whole apricots
½ cup raisins
¼ cup brown sugar, or to taste

Preheat oven to 350°F. Season thighs with salt and pepper. In large nonstick skillet over medium-high heat, heat oil. Cook thighs 6 to 8 minutes per side until browned. Meanwhile, in 12×9-inch shallow baking dish, mix sauerkraut, onions, apple, apricots, raisins and brown sugar until blended. Arrange thighs in sauerkraut mixture. Cover and bake 30 to 40 minutes or until chicken is cooked through and a meat thermometer inserted in thickest part of thigh registers 180°F.

Makes 6 servings

Note: If desired, substitute other fresh or dried fruit in this recipe, such as pears or pitted prunes.

Roasted Chicken and Vegetables over Wild Rice

Homestyle Chicken Pot Pie

2 tablespoons butter or margarine, divided
1 pound boneless skinless chicken breasts, cut into 1-inch pieces
½ teaspoon salt
½ teaspoon dried thyme leaves
¼ teaspoon black pepper
1 package (16 ounces) frozen mixed vegetables, such as potatoes, peas and carrots, thawed and drained
1 can (10¾ ounces) condensed cream of chicken or mushroom soup, undiluted
⅓ cup dry white wine or milk
1 refrigerated pie crust (½ of 15-ounce package), at room temperature

1. Preheat oven to 425°F. Melt 1 tablespoon butter in medium broilerproof skillet over medium-high heat. Add chicken; sprinkle with salt, thyme and pepper. Cook 1 minute, stirring frequently.

2. Reduce heat to medium-low. Stir in vegetables, soup and wine; simmer 5 minutes.

3. While soup mixture is simmering, unwrap pie crust. Using small cookie cutter, make 4 decorative cut-outs from pastry to allow steam to escape.

4. Remove chicken mixture from heat; top with pie crust. Melt remaining tablespoon butter. Brush pie crust with 2 teaspoons melted butter. Arrange cut-outs attractively over crust, if desired. Brush cut-outs with remaining 1 teaspoon melted butter. Bake 12 minutes. Turn oven to broil; broil 4 to 5 inches from heat source 2 minutes or until crust is golden brown and chicken mixture is bubbly.

Makes 4 to 5 servings

Tip: If you skin and debone chicken breasts, be sure to reserve both the bones and skin. Collect these scraps in a plastic bag in the freezer and soon you'll have enough to make a flavorful homemade chicken stock.

Prep Time: 5 minutes
Cook Time: 25 minutes

Broccoli, Chicken and Rice Casserole

1 box UNCLE BEN'S® COUNTRY INN® Broccoli Rice Au Gratin
4 TYSON® Individually Fresh Frozen® Boneless, Skinless Chicken Breasts
2 cups boiling water
¼ teaspoon garlic powder
2 cups frozen broccoli
1 cup shredded Cheddar cheese

COOK: Preheat oven to 425°F. In 13×9-inch baking pan, combine rice and contents of seasoning packet. Add boiling water; mix well. CLEAN: Wash hands. Add chicken, sprinkle with garlic powder; cover and bake 30 minutes. Add broccoli and cheese; bake, covered, 8 to 10 minutes or until internal juices of chicken run clear. (Or insert instant-read meat thermometer in thickest part of chicken. Temperature should read 170°F.)

SERVE: Serve hot out of the oven with yeast rolls, if desired.

CHILL: Refrigerate leftovers immediately. *Makes 4 servings*

Prep Time: none
Cook Time: 40 minutes

Chicken Dijon & Pasta

1 (3- to 4-pound) chicken, cut up and skinned, if desired
⅓ cup *French's®* Napa Valley Style Dijon Mustard
⅓ cup Italian salad dressing
1 can (10¾ ounces) condensed cream of chicken soup
4 cups hot cooked rotini pasta (8 ounces uncooked)
1⅓ cups *French's®* French Fried Onions, divided
1 cup diced tomatoes
1 cup diced zucchini
2 tablespoons minced parsley or basil leaves (optional)

1. Preheat oven to 400°F. Place chicken in shallow roasting pan. Mix mustard and dressing. Spoon half of mixture over chicken. Bake, uncovered, 40 minutes.

2. Combine soup, *½ cup water* and remaining mustard mixture. Toss pasta with sauce, *⅔ cup* French Fried Onions, vegetables and parsley. Spoon mixture around chicken.

3. Bake, uncovered, 15 minutes or until chicken is no longer pink in center. Sprinkle with remaining *⅔ cup* onions. Bake 1 minute or until onions are golden. *Makes 6 servings*

Prep Time: 15 minutes
Cook Time: about 1 hour

Helpful Hints

To remove skin from chicken pieces, using a paper towel, grasp the edge of the skin and pull it away from the chicken.

Homestyle Chicken Pot Pie

Pineapple Chicken and Sweet Potatoes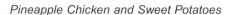

⅔ cup plus 3 tablespoons all-purpose flour, divided
1 teaspoon salt
1 teaspoon ground nutmeg
½ teaspoon ground cinnamon
⅛ teaspoon onion powder
⅛ teaspoon black pepper
6 chicken breasts
3 sweet potatoes, peeled and sliced
1 can (10¾ ounces) condensed cream of chicken soup, undiluted
½ cup pineapple juice
¼ pound mushrooms, sliced
2 teaspoons packed light brown sugar
½ teaspoon grated orange peel
Hot cooked rice

Slow Cooker Directions

Combine ⅔ cup flour, salt, nutmeg, cinnamon, onion powder and black pepper in large bowl. Thoroughly coat chicken with flour mixture. Place sweet potatoes on bottom of slow cooker. Top with chicken.

Combine soup, pineapple juice, mushrooms, remaining 3 tablespoons flour, brown sugar and orange peel in medium bowl; stir well. Pour soup mixture into slow cooker. Cover and cook on LOW 8 to 10 hours or on HIGH 3 to 4 hours. Serve chicken and sauce over rice.

Make 6 servings

Chicken Teriyaki

1 pound boneless skinless chicken tenders
1 can (6 ounces) pineapple juice
¼ cup soy sauce
1 tablespoon sugar
1 tablespoon minced fresh ginger
1 tablespoon minced garlic
1 tablespoon vegetable oil
1 tablespoon molasses
24 cherry tomatoes (optional)
2 cups hot cooked rice

Slow Cooker Directions

Combine all ingredients except rice in slow cooker. Cover; cook on LOW 2 hours or until chicken is tender. Serve chicken and sauce over rice.

Makes 4 servings

Pineapple Chicken and Sweet Potatoes

Cheesy Broccoli & Rice with Chicken

1½ pounds boneless skinless chicken, cut into strips
1 package (4.4 ounces) chicken flavor rice & sauce mix
1⅓ cups *French's*® French Fried Onions, divided
1 cup chopped broccoli
1 cup chopped red bell pepper
1 cup cubed pasteurized process cheese

1. Heat *1 tablespoon oil* in large skillet or wok until hot. Stir-fry chicken 5 minutes or until browned. Add rice mix and *2 cups water;* heat to boiling.

2. Stir in ⅔ cup French Fried Onions, vegetables and cheese. Simmer, uncovered, 10 minutes or until rice is tender, stirring.

3. Sprinkle remaining ⅔ *cup* onions over rice just before serving.

Makes 6 servings

Prep Time: 10 minutes
Cook Time: 15 minutes

Chicken Mexicana Casserole

10 boneless, skinless chicken breast halves (about 2½ pounds), cut into 1-inch cubes
2 packages (1.0 ounce each) LAWRY'S® Taco Spices & Seasonings
2 cans (14½ ounces each) whole tomatoes, undrained, cut up
3 cups (12 ounces) shredded sharp cheddar cheese, divided
1 can (7 ounces) diced green chiles, undrained
1 can (12 ounces) whole kernel corn, drained
1 package (8¼ ounces) corn muffin mix
2 eggs
¼ cup sour cream

In large bowl, toss chicken cubes with Taco Spices & Seasonings and tomatoes; mix well. Add 1 cup cheese. Spread mixture evenly into 13×9×2-inch baking dish. Spoon chiles over chicken mixture; sprinkle with remaining cheese. Set aside. In medium bowl, combine remaining ingredients; mix well. Drop by rounded spoonfuls on top of casserole, spacing evenly. Bake in 350°F oven 50 to 60 minutes or until top is lightly browned and sauce is bubbly. Remove from oven and let stand about 20 minutes before serving.

Makes 10 to 12 servings

Serving Suggestion: Serve with black beans and sliced tomatoes.

Cajun Chicken Bayou

2 cups water
1 can (10 ounces) diced tomatoes and green chilies, undrained
1 box UNCLE BEN'S CHEF'S RECIPE® Traditional Red Beans & Rice
3 TYSON® Individually Fresh Frozen® Boneless, Skinless Chicken Breasts

COOK: CLEAN: Wash hands. In large skillet, combine water, tomatoes, beans and rice, and contents of seasoning packet; mix well. Add chicken. Bring to a boil. Cover, reduce heat; simmer 30 to 35 minutes or until internal juices of chicken run clear. (Or insert instant-read meat thermometer in thickest part of chicken. Temperature should read 170°F.)

SERVE: Serve with sliced avocados and whole wheat rolls, if desired.

CHILL: Refrigerate leftovers immediately.   *Makes 3 servings*

Prep Time: none
Cook Time: 35 minutes

Skillet Chicken Parmesan

1 egg
1 tablespoon water or milk
4 boneless, skinless chicken breast halves (about 1¼ pounds)
½ cup Italian-seasoned dry bread crumbs
1 tablespoon BERTOLLI® Olive Oil
3½ cups water
1 package KNORR® Recipe Classics™ Tomato with Basil Soup, Dip and Recipe Mix
8 ounces pasta twists, uncooked
1 cup shredded mozzarella cheese (about 4 ounces)
1 tablespoon grated Parmesan cheese

• Beat egg lightly with 1 tablespoon water or milk. Dip chicken in egg mixture then coat with bread crumbs.

• In large skillet, heat oil over medium-high heat and brown chicken. Remove chicken and set aside.

• In same skillet, add water, recipe mix and *uncooked* pasta to skillet. Bring to a boil over medium-high heat stirring constantly. Return chicken to skillet, spooning some sauce over chicken. Reduce heat to low and simmer covered 10 minutes stirring occasionally or until pasta is tender and chicken is thoroughly cooked.

• Sprinkle with mozzarella and Parmesan cheeses. Cover and let stand until cheese is melted.

Makes 4 servings

Prep Time: 10 minutes
Cook Time: 16 minutes

Sweet & Sour Chicken and Rice

1 pound chicken tenders
1 can (8 ounces) pineapple chunks, drained and juice reserved
1 cup uncooked rice
2 carrots, thinly sliced
1 green bell pepper, cut into 1-inch pieces
1 large onion, chopped
3 cloves garlic, minced
1 can (14½ ounces) reduced-sodium chicken broth
⅓ cup soy sauce
3 tablespoons sugar
3 tablespoons apple cider vinegar
1 tablespoon sesame oil
1½ teaspoons ground ginger
¼ cup chopped peanuts (optional)
Chopped fresh cilantro (optional)

Preheat oven to 350°F. Spray 13×9-inch baking dish with nonstick cooking spray.

Combine chicken, pineapple, rice, carrots, bell pepper, onion and garlic in prepared dish.

Place broth, reserved pineapple juice, soy sauce, sugar, vinegar, sesame oil and ginger in small saucepan; bring to a boil over high heat. Remove from heat and pour over chicken mixture.

Cover tightly with foil and bake 40 to 50 minutes or until chicken is no longer pink in centers and rice is tender. Sprinkle with peanuts and cilantro, if desired.

Makes 6 servings

Chicken Fajita Casserole

8 TYSON® Fresh Chicken Breast Tenders or Individually Fresh Frozen® Boneless, Skinless Chicken Tenderloins
1 box UNCLE BEN'S CHEF'S RECIPE® Traditional Red Beans & Rice
1 can (4 ounces) sliced black olives, drained
1 can (4 ounces) diced green chilies, drained
2 cups boiling water
1 can (15 ounces) diced tomatoes
1 cup (4 ounces) shredded Monterey Jack cheese
1 cup crushed tortilla chips

PREP: Preheat oven to 350°F. CLEAN: Wash hands. Remove protective ice glaze from frozen chicken by holding under cool running water 1 to 2 minutes. Place red beans and rice (do not include seasoning packet) in 13×9-inch baking dish; top with olives and chilies. Place chicken in baking dish. CLEAN: Wash hands. In medium bowl, combine boiling water, tomatoes and contents of rice seasoning packet. Pour over chicken mixture.

COOK: Cover and bake 45 minutes. Remove cover; sprinkle with cheese and tortilla chips. Bake 5 minutes or until rice is cooked and internal juices of chicken run clear. (Or insert instant-read meat thermometer in thickest part of chicken. Temperature should read 170°F.)

SERVE: Serve with a tossed salad and lemon sherbet, if desired.

CHILL: Refrigerate leftovers immediately. *Makes 4 servings*

Prep Time: 10 minutes
Cook Time: 50 minutes

Chicken in French Onion Sauce

1 package (10 ounces) frozen baby carrots, thawed and drained *or* 4 medium carrots, cut into strips (about 2 cups)
2 cups sliced mushrooms
½ cup thinly sliced celery
1⅓ cups *French's®* French Fried Onions, divided
4 chicken breast halves, skinned and boned
½ cup white wine
¾ cup prepared chicken bouillon
½ teaspoon garlic salt
½ teaspoon pepper
Paprika

Preheat oven to 375°F. In 12×8-inch baking dish, combine vegetables and ⅔ cup French Fried Onions. Arrange chicken breasts on vegetables. In small bowl, combine wine, bouillon, garlic salt and pepper; pour over chicken and vegetables. Sprinkle chicken with paprika. Bake, covered, at 375°F for 35 minutes or until chicken is done. Baste chicken with wine sauce and top with remaining ⅔ cup onions; bake, uncovered, 3 minutes or until onions are golden brown. *Makes 4 servings*

Microwave Directions: In 12×8-inch microwave-safe dish, combine vegetables and ⅔ cup onions. Arrange chicken breasts, skinned side down, along sides of dish. Prepare wine mixture as above, except reduce bouillon to ⅓ cup; pour over chicken and vegetables. Cook, covered, on HIGH 6 minutes. Turn chicken breasts over and sprinkle with paprika. Stir vegetables and rotate dish. Cook, covered, 7 to 9 minutes or until chicken is done. Baste chicken with wine sauce and top with remaining ⅔ cup onions; cook, uncovered, 1 minute. Let stand 5 minutes.

Sweet & Sour Chicken and Rice

Lemon Garlic Chicken & Rice

4 boneless, skinless chicken breast halves (about 1 pound)
½ teaspoon paprika
⅛ teaspoon ground black pepper
2 tablespoons margarine or butter, divided
1 (6.9-ounce) package RICE-A-RONI® Chicken & Garlic Flavor
2 teaspoons lemon juice
1 medium red and/or green bell pepper, chopped

1. Sprinkle chicken with paprika and black pepper; set aside. In large skillet over medium heat, melt 1 tablespoon margarine. Add chicken; cook 2 minutes on each side. Remove from skillet; set aside.

2. In same skillet over medium heat, sauté rice-vermicelli mix with remaining 1 tablespoon margarine until vermicelli is golden brown.

3. Slowly stir in 2 cups water, lemon juice and Special Seasonings; bring to a boil. Place chicken over rice. Reduce heat to low. Cover; simmer 15 minutes.

4. Stir in bell pepper. Cover; cook 5 minutes or until rice is tender and chicken is no longer pink inside.

Makes 4 servings

Tip: No lemon juice in the house? Try orange juice.

Prep Time: 5 minutes
Cook Time: 30 minutes

Creamy Chicken and Pasta with Spinach

6 ounces uncooked egg noodles
1 tablespoon olive oil
¼ cup chopped onion
¼ cup chopped red bell pepper
1 package (10 ounces) frozen spinach, thawed and drained
2 boneless skinless chicken breasts (¾ pound), cooked and cut into 1-inch pieces
1 can (4 ounces) sliced mushrooms, drained
2 cups (8 ounces) shredded Swiss cheese
1 container (8 ounces) sour cream
¾ cup half-and-half
2 eggs, lightly beaten
½ teaspoon salt
Red onion and fresh spinach for garnish

1. Preheat oven to 350°F. Prepare noodles according to package directions; set aside.

2. Heat oil in large skillet over medium-high heat. Add onion and bell pepper; cook and stir 2 minutes or until onion is tender. Add spinach, chicken, mushrooms and cooked noodles; stir to combine.

3. Combine cheese, sour cream, half-and-half, eggs and salt in medium bowl; blend well.

4. Add cheese mixture to chicken mixture; stir to combine. Pour into 13×9-inch baking dish coated with nonstick cooking spray. Bake, covered, 30 to 35 minutes or until heated through. Garnish with red onion and fresh spinach, if desired.

Makes 8 servings

Serving Suggestion: Serve with orange slices sprinkled with coconut.

Simmered Tuscan Chicken

2 tablespoons BERTOLLI® Olive Oil
1 pound boneless, skinless chicken breasts, cut into 1-inch cubes
2 cloves garlic, finely chopped
4 medium potatoes, cut into ½-inch cubes (about 4 cups)
1 medium red bell pepper, cut into large pieces
1 jar (1 pound 10 ounces) RAGÚ® Old World Style® Pasta Sauce
1 pound fresh or frozen cut green beans
1 teaspoon dried basil leaves, crushed
Salt and ground black pepper to taste

In 12-inch skillet, heat oil over medium-high heat and cook chicken with garlic until chicken is thoroughly cooked. Remove chicken and set aside.

In same skillet, add potatoes and bell pepper. Cook over medium heat, stirring occasionally, 5 minutes. Stir in remaining ingredients. Bring to a boil over high heat. Reduce heat to low and simmer covered, stirring occasionally, 35 minutes or until potatoes are tender. Return chicken to skillet and heat through.

Makes 6 servings

Creamy Chicken and Pasta with Spinach

Chicken Caesar Tetrazzini

8 ounces uncooked spaghetti
2 cups shredded or cubed cooked chicken
1 cup chicken broth
1 cup HIDDEN VALLEY® Caesar Dressing
1 jar (4½ ounces) sliced mushrooms, drained
½ cup grated Parmesan cheese
2 tablespoons dry bread crumbs

Cook spaghetti according to package directions. Drain and combine with chicken, broth, dressing and mushrooms in a large mixing bowl. Place mixture in a 2-quart casserole. Mix together cheese and bread crumbs; sprinkle over spaghetti mixture. Bake at 350°F. for 25 minutes or until casserole is hot and bubbly.

Makes 4 servings

Classic Chicken Biscuit Pie

12 TYSON® Individually Fresh Frozen® Boneless, Skinless Chicken Tenderloins
2 boxes UNCLE BEN'S® COUNTRY INN® Chicken Flavored Rice
4 cups water
1 can (10¾ ounces) condensed cream of chicken soup
1 bag (16 ounces) frozen mixed vegetables
1 container (12 ounces) refrigerated buttermilk biscuits

PREP: Preheat oven to 400°F. CLEAN: Wash hands. Remove protective ice glaze from frozen chicken by holding under cool running water 1 to 2 minutes. Cut chicken into 1-inch pieces. CLEAN: Wash hands.

COOK: In large saucepan, combine chicken, water, rice, contents of seasoning packets, soup and mixed vegetables; mix well. Bring to a boil. Cover, reduce heat; simmer 10 minutes or until internal juices of chicken run clear. (Or insert instant-read meat thermometer in thickest part of chicken. Temperature should read 170°F.) Place in 13×9-inch baking pan; top with biscuits. Bake 10 to 12 minutes or until biscuits are deep golden brown.

SERVE: Serve immediately.

CHILL: Refrigerate leftovers immediately.   *Makes 8 servings*

Prep Time: 10 minutes
Cook Time: 30 minutes

Tortilla Stack Tampico

1¼ cups shredded, cooked chicken
1 package (1.0 ounces) LAWRY'S® Taco Spices & Seasonings
1 cup water
1 can (8 ounces) tomato sauce
8 medium corn tortillas
2 cups (8 ounces) shredded Monterey Jack or cheddar cheese
1 can (4 ounces) whole green chiles, rinsed and seeds removed
1 can (4¼ ounces) chopped black olives
½ cup salsa
Sliced green onions

In large skillet, combine chicken, Taco Spices & Seasonings, water and tomato sauce; mix well. Bring to a boil over medium-high heat; reduce heat to low and simmer, uncovered, 10 minutes. Lightly grease 12×8×2-inch baking dish. Dip tortillas in chicken mixture. Place 2 tortillas in bottom of baking dish. Top with ½ of chicken mixture. Sprinkle with ⅔ cup cheese and top with 2 more tortillas.

Layer whole chiles on top of tortillas. Sprinkle with ½ of olives, reserving 2 tablespoons for garnish. Sprinkle ⅔ cup cheese over olives. Top with 2 more tortillas and remaining chicken mixture. Top with remaining 2 tortillas. Pour salsa over tortillas. Garnish with remaining ⅔ cup cheese, reserved 2 tablespoons olives and green onions. Bake, uncovered, in 350°F oven 15 to 20 minutes or until heated through and cheese melts. Cut each stack into quarters to serve.

Makes 8 servings

Serving Suggestion: Serve with dollops of sour cream and wedges of fresh pineapple and watermelon, if desired.

Hint: If made in advance, cover tightly with foil or plastic wrap to prevent tortillas from drying out. One can (4 ounces) diced green chiles can be used in place of whole chiles.

Lemon Chicken Rice

1 tablespoon olive oil
1 pound boneless, skinless chicken breast, cut into strips
1 clove garlic, crushed
1 cup uncooked rice*
1 can (14½ ounces) chicken broth
1 tablespoon grated lemon peel
½ teaspoon ground black pepper

*Recipe based on regular-milled long grain white rice.

Heat oil in large skillet over medium-high heat until hot. Add chicken and garlic; cook and stir until browned. Stir in rice and broth. Cover and cook 15 minutes or until liquid is absorbed. Stir in lemon peel and pepper. Serve immediately.   *Makes 4 servings*

Favorite recipe from **USA Rice Federation**

Chicken Caesar Tetrazzini

Enchiladas

> 1 package (10 ounces) fully cooked carved chicken breast*
> 1 cup cooked rice
> 2 jars (12 ounces *each*) salsa, divided
> 1 can (15 to 19 ounces) black beans, rinsed and drained
> 1⅓ cups *French's®* French Fried Onions, divided
> 1 cup (4 ounces) shredded Cheddar cheese, divided
> 12 (8-inch) flour tortillas

You may substitute 2 cups shredded cooked chicken.

1. Preheat oven to 350°F. Combine chicken, rice, *1 cup* salsa, beans, ⅔ cup French Fried Onions and ½ cup cheese in large bowl. Spread about ½ cup mixture down center of each tortilla. Roll up tortillas enclosing filling. Place seam-side down in greased 15×10-inch baking pan.

2. Pour remaining salsa on top of tortillas. Cover dish. Bake 30 minutes or until heated through.

3. Top with remaining ½ cup cheese and ⅔ cup onions. Bake 5 minutes or until onions are golden.

Makes 6 servings

Prep Time: 10 minutes
Cook Time: 35 minutes

Herbed Chicken and Potatoes

> 2 medium all-purpose potatoes, thinly sliced (about 1 pound)
> 4 bone-in chicken breast halves (about 2 pounds)*
> 1 envelope LIPTON® RECIPE SECRETS® Savory Herb with Garlic Soup Mix
> ⅓ cup water
> 1 tablespoon BERTOLLI® Olive Oil

Substitution: Use 1 (2½- to 3-pound) chicken, cut into serving pieces.

1. Preheat oven to 425°F. In 13×9-inch baking or roasting pan, add potatoes; arrange chicken over potatoes.

2. Pour soup mix blended with water and oil over chicken and potatoes.

3. Bake uncovered 40 minutes or until chicken is thoroughly cooked and potatoes are tender.

Makes 4 servings

Oven Chicken & Rice

> 1 can (10¾ ounces) condensed cream of mushroom soup
> 1⅓ cups water
> 1 cup long-grain or converted rice
> 1 teaspoon dried dill weed, divided
> ¼ teaspoon black pepper
> 1 chicken (3 pounds), cut up and skinned
> ½ cup crushed multi-grain crackers
> 1 teaspoon paprika
> 2 tablespoons butter or margarine, melted
> Fresh dill sprigs for garnish

1. Preheat oven to 375°F. Combine soup, water, rice, ¾ teaspoon dill weed and pepper in 13×9-inch baking dish. Arrange chicken pieces on top of rice mixture. Cover tightly with foil. Bake 45 minutes.

2. Sprinkle chicken pieces with crackers, paprika and remaining ¼ teaspoon dill. Drizzle with butter. Bake 5 to 10 minutes or until chicken is tender. Season to taste with salt and pepper. Garnish with dill sprig, if desired. *Makes 4 to 5 servings*

Crunchy Topped Chicken Pot Pie

> 1 sheet frozen puff pastry (½ of a 17-ounce package), thawed according to package directions
> ½ cup (2 ounces) shredded Swiss cheese
> 1⅓ cups *French's®* French Fried Onions, divided
> 1 can (10¾ ounces) condensed cream of chicken soup
> 1 cup milk or half-and-half
> 2 cups (12 ounces) cooked chicken, cut into ½-inch cubes
> 1 bag (16 ounces) frozen vegetable combination, thawed

1. Preheat oven to 400°F. Unfold pastry and place on floured board. Invert 9-inch plate on top of pastry. With sharp knife, cut pastry into 9-inch circle. Remove plate. Cut pastry into 6 equal triangles. Place pastry triangles on ungreased baking sheet.

2. Bake pastry 15 minutes or until puffed and golden. Sprinkle pastry with cheese and ⅔ cup French Fried Onions. Bake 1 minute or until onions are golden. Set aside.

3. Combine soup and milk in large saucepan. Stir in chicken, vegetables and remaining ⅔ cup onions. Heat to boiling. Reduce heat to medium-low. Cook 5 minutes or until vegetables are tender and mixture is hot. To serve, spoon filling into bowls. Top each serving with pastry triangle.

Makes 6 servings

Prep Time: 10 minutes
Cook Time: about 15 minutes

Oven Chicken & Rice

Fiesta Chicken and Rice

1 tablespoon vegetable oil
¾ cup chopped onion
4 boneless, skinless chicken
    breast halves (about
    1 pound), cut into 2-inch
    strips
1 can (14½ ounces) chicken
    broth
1 cup sliced fresh mushrooms
¾ cup uncooked long-grain rice
½ cup dry white wine
1 teaspoon LAWRY'S® Garlic
    Powder with Parsley
½ teaspoon LAWRY'S® Seasoned
    Pepper
⅛ teaspoon ground saffron or
    turmeric
1 bag (16 ounces) frozen mixed
    vegetables, thawed and
    drained
1 jar (2 ounces) sliced pimiento,
    drained
    Grated Parmesan cheese

In large skillet heat oil. Add onion and cook over medium-high heat 5 minutes. Add chicken and cook over medium-high heat 5 minutes or just until chicken is browned on all sides. Stir in broth, mushrooms, rice, wine, Garlic Powder with Parsley, Seasoned Pepper and saffron. Bring to a boil over medium-high heat; reduce heat to low and simmer covered 20 minutes or until rice is tender and liquid is absorbed. Stir in mixed vegetables and pimiento; heat through, about 5 minutes.

Makes 4 servings

Serving Suggestion: For added color, sprinkle finished dish with grated Parmesan cheese and chopped fresh parsley, if desired.

Chicken Tetrazzini

8 ounces uncooked vermicelli,
    broken in half
1 can (10¾ ounces) condensed
    cream of mushroom soup,
    undiluted
¼ cup half-and-half
3 tablespoons dry sherry
½ teaspoon salt
⅛ to ¼ teaspoon red pepper
    flakes
2 cups chopped cooked chicken
    breasts (about ¾ pound)
1 cup frozen peas
½ cup grated Parmesan cheese
1 cup fresh coarse bread
    crumbs
2 tablespoons margarine or
    butter, melted
    Chopped fresh basil (optional)

1. Preheat oven to 375°F. Spray 8-inch square baking dish with nonstick cooking spray.

2. Cook pasta according to package directions until al dente. Drain and set aside.

3. Meanwhile, combine soup, half-and-half, sherry, salt and pepper flakes in large bowl. Stir in chicken, peas and cheese. Add pasta to chicken mixture; stir until pasta is well coated. Pour into prepared dish.

4. Combine bread crumbs and margarine in small bowl. Sprinkle evenly over casserole. Bake, uncovered, 25 to 30 minutes or until heated through and crumbs are golden brown. Sprinkle with basil, if desired. *Makes 4 servings*

Cook's Nook: Serve with Caesar salad. Have rotisserie chicken from your local supermarket for dinner one night and use 2 cups leftover chicken to make Tetrazzini the next.

Garlic Herb Chicken and Rice Skillet

4 boneless, skinless chicken
    breasts (about 1 pound)
1¾ cups water
1 box UNCLE BEN'S®
    COUNTRY INN® Chicken
    Flavored Rice
2 cups frozen broccoli, carrots
    and cauliflower
¼ cup garlic and herb flavored
    soft spreadable cheese

1. In large skillet, combine chicken, water and contents of seasoning packet. Bring to a boil. Reduce heat; cover and simmer 10 minutes.

2. Add rice, vegetables and cheese. Cook covered 10 to 15 minutes or until chicken is no longer pink in center. Remove from heat; let stand 5 minutes or until liquid is absorbed.

Makes 4 servings

Spicy Chicken & Rice Bake

4 boneless, skinless chicken
    breast halves (about
    1 pound)
1 jar (1 pound 10 ounces)
    RAGÚ® Robusto! Pasta
    Sauce
2 cups water
⅔ cup uncooked white rice
½ cup sliced pitted ripe olives
1 tablespoon capers, drained
    and chopped
1 teaspoon salt
½ teaspoon ground black pepper
¼ teaspoon dried oregano
    leaves, crushed
⅛ teaspoon crushed red pepper
    flakes

Preheat oven to 375°F. In 13×9-inch casserole, combine all ingredients. Bake uncovered 40 minutes or until rice is tender and chicken is thoroughly cooked.

Makes 4 servings

Chicken Tetrazzini

Chicken Divan

- 1 package (10 ounces) frozen broccoli spears, thawed and drained
- 1½ cups cooked unsalted regular rice (½ cup uncooked)
- 1⅓ cups *French's®* French Fried Onions, divided
- 1 can (10¾ ounces) condensed cream of chicken soup
- ½ cup sour cream
- ½ cup (2 ounces) shredded Cheddar cheese
- 1 teaspoon paprika
- ¼ teaspoon curry powder (optional)
- 1 cup (5 ounces) cubed cooked chicken

Preheat oven to 350°F. In 10-inch pie plate, arrange broccoli spears with flowerets around edge of dish. (May be necessary to halve stalks to obtain enough flowerets.) To hot rice in saucepan, add ⅔ cup French Fried Onions, the soup, sour cream, cheese, seasonings and chicken; stir well. Spoon chicken mixture evenly over broccoli stalks. Bake, covered, at 350°F for 30 minutes or until heated through. Top with remaining ⅔ cup onions; bake, uncovered, 5 minutes or until onions are golden brown.

Makes 4 servings

Jazzy Jambalaya

- 1 (6.8-ounce) package RICE-A-RONI® Spanish Rice
- 2 tablespoons margarine or butter
- 8 ounces boneless, skinless chicken breasts or cooked ham, cut into 1-inch pieces
- 1 (14½-ounce) can diced tomatoes, undrained
- 1 cup chopped onion
- 2 cloves garlic, minced
- ⅛ to ¼ teaspoon hot pepper sauce
- 8 ounces uncooked large shrimp, peeled and deveined
- 1 medium green bell pepper, chopped

1. In large skillet over medium heat, sauté rice-vermicelli mix with margarine until vermicelli is golden brown.

2. Slowly stir in 2 cups water, chicken, tomatoes, onion, garlic, hot pepper sauce and Special Seasonings; bring to a boil. Reduce heat to low. Cover; simmer 10 minutes.

3. Stir in shrimp and bell pepper. Cover; simmer 8 to 10 minutes or until rice is tender and shrimp turn pink.

Makes 5 servings

Prep Time: 15 minutes
Cook Time: 30 minutes

Zesty Garlic Chicken

- ¾ pound boneless skinless chicken breast, cut into 1-inch cubes
- 1 tablespoon vegetable oil
- 3 tablespoons lime or lemon juice
- 2 teaspoons Worcestershire sauce
- 2 teaspoons soy sauce
- 1 bag (16 ounces) BIRDS EYE® frozen Pasta Secrets Zesty Garlic

- In large skillet, cook and stir chicken in oil over medium heat until no longer pink in center.

- Stir in lime juice, Worcestershire and soy sauce.

- Add Pasta Secrets; stir well.

- Cover and cook 7 to 9 minutes or until vegetables are crisp-tender, stirring occasionally.

Makes 4 servings

Birds Eye Idea: Fill an empty squeeze bottle with vegetable oil and keep it near the stove for quick sautéing. This will allow you to use oil sparingly.

Prep Time: 5 minutes
Cook Time: 20 minutes

Chicken-Asparagus Casserole

- 2 teaspoons vegetable oil
- 1 cup seeded and chopped green and/or red bell peppers
- 1 medium onion, chopped
- 2 cloves garlic, minced
- 1 can (10¾ ounces) condensed cream of asparagus soup
- 1 container (8 ounces) ricotta cheese
- 2 cups (8 ounces) shredded Cheddar cheese, divided
- 2 eggs
- 1½ cups chopped cooked chicken
- 1 package (10 ounces) frozen chopped asparagus,* thawed and drained
- 8 ounces egg noodles, cooked
- Black pepper (optional)

Or, substitute ½ pound fresh asparagus cut into ½-inch pieces. Bring 6 cups water to a boil over high heat in large saucepan. Add fresh asparagus. Reduce heat to medium. Cover and cook 5 to 8 minutes or until crisp-tender. Drain.

1. Preheat oven to 350°F. Grease 13×9-inch casserole; set aside.

2. Heat oil in small skillet over medium heat. Add bell peppers, onion and garlic; cook and stir until vegetables are crisp-tender.

3. Mix soup, ricotta cheese, 1 cup Cheddar cheese and eggs in large bowl until well blended. Add onion mixture, chicken, asparagus and noodles; mix well. Season with pepper, if desired.

4. Spread mixture evenly in prepared casserole. Top with remaining 1 cup Cheddar cheese.

5. Bake 30 minutes or until center is set and cheese is bubbly. Let stand 5 minutes before serving. Garnish as desired.   *Makes 12 servings*

Chicken-Asparagus Casserole

Mile-High Enchilada Pie

Slow Cooker

8 (6-inch) corn tortillas
1 jar (12 ounces) prepared salsa
1 can (15½ ounces) kidney beans, rinsed and drained
1 cup shredded cooked chicken
1 cup shredded Monterey Jack cheese with jalapeño peppers

Slow Cooker Directions

Prepare foil handles for slow cooker (see below); place in slow cooker. Place 1 tortilla on bottom of slow cooker. Top with small amount of salsa, beans, chicken and cheese. Continue layering using remaining ingredients, ending with cheese. Cover and cook on Low 6 to 8 hours or on High 3 to 4 hours. Pull out by foil handles.

Makes 4 to 6 servings

Foil Handles: Tear off three 18×2-inch strips of heavy foil or use regular foil folded to double thickness. Crisscross foil strips in spoke design and place in slow cooker to make lifting of tortilla stack easier.

Hearty Chicken Bake

3 cups hot mashed potatoes
1 cup (4 ounces) shredded Cheddar cheese, divided
1⅓ cups *French's*® French Fried Onions, divided
1½ cups (7 ounces) cubed cooked chicken
1 package (10 ounces) frozen mixed vegetables, thawed and drained
1 can (10¾ ounces) condensed cream of chicken soup
¼ cup milk
½ teaspoon ground mustard
¼ teaspoon garlic powder
¼ teaspoon pepper

Preheat oven to 375°F. In medium bowl, combine mashed potatoes, ½ cup cheese and ⅔ cup French Fried Onions; mix thoroughly. Spoon potato mixture into greased 1½-quart casserole. Using back of spoon, spread potatoes across bottom and up sides of dish to form a shell. In large bowl, combine chicken, mixed vegetables, soup, milk and seasonings; pour into potato shell. Bake, uncovered, at 375°F for 30 minutes or until heated through. Top with remaining ½ cup cheese and ⅔ cup onions; bake, uncovered, 3 minutes or until onions are golden brown. Let stand 5 minutes before serving.   *Makes 4 to 6 servings*

Home-Style Chicken 'n Biscuits

1½ cups (7 ounces) cubed cooked chicken
1½ cups (6 ounces) shredded Cheddar cheese, divided
1 package (10 ounces) frozen mixed vegetables, thawed and drained
1 can (10¾ ounces) condensed cream of chicken soup
2 medium tomatoes, chopped (about 1 cup)
¾ cup milk
5 slices bacon, fried crisp and crumbled
1½ cups biscuit baking mix
⅔ cup milk
1⅓ cups *French's*® French Fried Onions, divided

Preheat oven to 400°F. In large bowl, combine chicken, *1 cup* cheese, mixed vegetables, soup, tomatoes, ¾ cup milk and bacon. Pour chicken mixture into greased 12×8-inch baking dish. Bake, covered, at 400°F for 15 minutes. Meanwhile, in medium bowl, combine baking mix, ⅔ cup milk and ⅔ cup French Fried Onions to form soft dough. Spoon biscuit dough in 6 mounds around edges of casserole. Bake, uncovered, 15 to 20 minutes or until biscuits are golden brown. Top biscuits with remaining ½ cup cheese and ⅔ cup onions; bake 1 to 3 minutes or until onions are golden brown.

Makes 6 servings

Microwave Directions: Prepare chicken mixture as directed, except reduce ¾ cup milk to ½ cup; pour into 12×8-inch microwave-safe dish. Cook, covered, on HIGH 10 minutes or until heated through. Stir chicken mixture halfway through cooking time. Prepare biscuit dough as directed. Stir casserole and spoon biscuit dough over hot chicken mixture as directed. Cook, uncovered, 7 to 8 minutes or until biscuits are done. Rotate dish halfway through cooking time. Top biscuits with remaining ½ cup cheese and ⅔ cup onions; cook, uncovered, 1 minute or until cheese melts. Let stand 5 minutes.

Lemony Roasted Chicken

Slow Cooker

1 fryer or roasting chicken (3 to 4 pounds)
½ cup chopped onion
2 tablespoons butter
Juice of one lemon
1 tablespoon fresh parsley
2 teaspoons grated lemon peel
¼ teaspoon salt
¼ teaspoon dried thyme leaves

Slow Cooker Directions

Rinse chicken and pat dry with paper towels. Remove and discard any excess fat. Place onion in chicken cavity and rub skin with butter. Place chicken in 5-quart slow cooker. Squeeze juice of lemon over chicken. Sprinkle with grated lemon peel, salt and thyme. Cover and cook on LOW 6 to 8 hours.   *Makes 6 servings*

Mile-High Enchilada Pie

Jambalaya

¼ cup **CRISCO® Oil,*** divided
1 large onion, peeled and diced
1 green or red bell pepper,
    seeds and ribs removed, cut
    into 1-inch squares
2 teaspoons jarred minced
    garlic *or* 1 large garlic clove,
    peeled and minced
1 boneless, skinless chicken
    breast, cut into 1-inch
    cubes
⅓ pound smoked sausage (such
    as kielbasa or turkey
    kielbasa), cut into ¼-inch
    slices
1 package (5 ounces) yellow rice
    or white rice
1 can (14½ ounces) chicken
    stock or broth
½ teaspoon salt
½ teaspoon Italian seasoning
½ teaspoon freshly ground black
    pepper
1 cup fresh or frozen green peas
½ pound peeled and deveined
    shrimp

*Use your favorite Crisco Oil product.

1. Heat oven to 375°F.

2. Heat 2 tablespoons oil in a large ovenproof skillet on medium-high heat. Add onion, bell pepper and garlic. Sauté 3 minutes, or until onion is translucent. Remove vegetables from pan.

3. Rinse chicken. Pat dry. Heat remaining 2 tablespoons oil in skillet on medium-high heat. Add chicken and sausage. Sauté 3 minutes, or until sausage is lightly browned. Add rice. Stir 1 minute. Return vegetables to pan. Add stock, salt, Italian seasoning and pepper. Bring to a boil. Cover pan.

4. Bake at 375°F for 15 minutes. Remove from oven. Stir in peas and shrimp. Recover. Return to oven for 15 minutes, or until shrimp are pink and cooked through and liquid is absorbed. Serve immediately.

Makes 4 servings

Note: The jambalaya can be prepared up to two days in advance and refrigerated, tightly covered. Reheat at 350°F for 15 minutes or until hot, stirring occasionally. For a spicier dish, use Cajun andouille sausage in place of kielbasa. If using shell-on shrimp, increase preparation time by 10 minutes.

Prep Time: 25 minutes
Total Time: 1 hour

Mexican Chicken Bake

1 pound boneless skinless
    chicken thighs, cut into
    strips
2 cans (8 ounces *each*) tomato
    sauce
1 can (11 ounces) Mexican-style
    corn kernels, drained
1⅓ cups *French's®* French Fried
    Onions, divided
2 tablespoons *Frank's® RedHot®*
    Cayenne Pepper Sauce
½ teaspoon dried oregano leaves
½ teaspoon ground cumin
¼ teaspoon garlic powder

1. Preheat oven to 350°F. Combine chicken, tomato sauce, corn, ⅔ cup French Fried Onions, **Frank's RedHot** Sauce and seasonings in lightly greased 2-quart baking dish. Stir until chicken is well coated.

2. Bake, uncovered, 30 minutes or until chicken is no longer pink and sauce is hot. Stir. Top with remaining ⅔ cup onions. Bake 5 minutes or until onions are golden. Serve with hot cooked rice, if desired.

Makes 4 servings

Prep Time: 10 minutes
Cook Time: 35 minutes

Lemon Pepper Pasta with Chicken and Dijon Teriyaki Sauce

1 package (12 ounces)
    PASTA LABELLA™ Lemon
    Pepper Penne Rigate
¼ cup olive oil
9 ounces boneless skinless
    chicken breasts, cut into
    1-inch cubes
½ cup sliced red onion
1½ cups broccoli florets
1 cup sliced mushrooms
1 tablespoon chopped garlic
1½ teaspoons ground ginger
¼ teaspoon salt
¼ teaspoon black pepper
1½ cups chicken broth
5 tablespoons Dijon mustard
¼ cup teriyaki sauce
¼ cup minced green onions

Cook pasta according to package directions. Meanwhile, heat olive oil in large skillet or saucepan over medium heat; sauté chicken for 5 minutes. Add onion, broccoli, mushrooms, garlic, ginger, salt and pepper. Continue to cook for 8 minutes. Add chicken broth; bring mixture to a simmer. Whisk in mustard and teriyaki sauce. Cook until sauce is of medium-thin consistency. Add hot pasta; mix well and heat thoroughly. Serve sprinkled with green onions.

Makes 4 servings

Chicken Seville

4 boneless, skinless chicken
    breast halves (1 to
    1½ pounds)
½ teaspoon paprika
2 tablespoons margarine or
    butter, divided
1 (4.9-ounce) package
    RICE-A-RONI® Chicken &
    Broccoli Flavor
1 cup orange juice
1 cup sliced carrots
6 large whole cloves garlic,
    peeled
¼ cup slivered almonds, toasted

1. Sprinkle chicken with paprika; set aside. In large skillet over medium-high heat, melt 1 tablespoon margarine. Sauté chicken 2 minutes on each side. Remove from skillet; set aside.

2. In same skillet over medium heat, sauté rice-vermicelli mix with remaining 1 tablespoon margarine until vermicelli is golden brown.

3. Slowly stir in 1 cup water, orange juice, carrots, garlic, and Special Seasonings; bring to a boil. Place chicken over rice. Reduce heat to low. Cover; simmer 18 to 20 minutes or until rice is tender and chicken is no longer pink inside. Let stand 3 minutes before serving. Sprinkle with almonds.   *Makes 4 servings*

Prep Time: 10 minutes
Cook Time: 30 minutes

Quick Chicken Pot Pie

1 pound boneless skinless chicken thighs, cut into 1-inch cubes
1 can (about 14 ounces) chicken broth
3 tablespoons all-purpose flour
2 tablespoons butter, softened
1 package (10 ounces) frozen mixed vegetables, thawed
1 can (about 4 ounces) button mushrooms, drained
¼ teaspoon dried basil leaves
¼ teaspoon dried oregano leaves
¼ teaspoon dried thyme leaves
1 cup biscuit baking mix
6 tablespoons milk

1. Preheat oven to 450°F. Place chicken and broth in large skillet; cover and bring to a boil over high heat. Reduce heat to medium; simmer, uncovered, 5 minutes or until chicken is tender.

2. While chicken is cooking, mix flour and butter; set aside. Combine mixed vegetables, mushrooms, basil, oregano and thyme in greased 2-quart casserole.

3. Add flour mixture to chicken and broth in skillet; stir with wire whisk until smooth. Cook and stir until thickened. Add to vegetable mixture; mix well.

4. Blend biscuit mix and milk in medium bowl until smooth. Drop 4 scoops batter onto chicken mixture.

5. Bake 18 to 20 minutes or until biscuits are browned and casserole is hot and bubbly.
   Makes 4 servings

Tip: This dish can be prepared through step 3, covered and refrigerated up to 24 hours, if desired. Proceed with step 4. Bake as directed for 20 to 25 minutes.

Quick Chicken Pot Pie

Green Chile Chicken Enchiladas

- **2 cups shredded cooked chicken**
- **1½ cups (6 ounces) shredded Mexican cheese blend or Cheddar cheese, divided**
- **½ cup HIDDEN VALLEY® The Original Ranch® Dressing**
- **¼ cup sour cream**
- **2 tablespoons canned diced green chiles, rinsed and drained**
- **4 (9 to 10-inch) flour tortillas, warmed**

Mix together chicken, ¾ cup cheese, dressing, sour cream and green chiles in a medium bowl. Divide evenly down center of each tortilla. Roll up tortillas and place, seam side down, in a 9-inch baking dish. Top with remaining ¾ cup cheese. Bake at 350°F. for 20 minutes or until cheese is melted and lightly browned.

Makes 4 servings

Note: Purchase rotisserie chicken at your favorite store to add great taste and save preparation time.

Chicken-Mac Casserole

- **1½ cups elbow macaroni, cooked in unsalted water and drained**
- **6 slices bacon, fried crisp and crumbled**
- **2 cups (10 ounces) cubed cooked chicken**
- **1⅓ cups *French's*® French Fried Onions, divided**
- **1 can (10¾ ounces) condensed cream of mushroom soup**
- **1 cup sour cream**
- **1 package (10 ounces) frozen chopped spinach, thawed and well drained**
- **⅛ teaspoon garlic powder**
- **1½ cups (6 ounces) shredded Cheddar cheese, divided**

Preheat oven to 375°F. Return cooked macaroni to saucepan; stir in bacon, chicken and ⅔ cup French Fried Onions. In medium bowl, combine soup, sour cream, spinach, garlic powder and 1 cup Cheddar cheese. Spoon half the macaroni mixture into greased 12×8-inch baking dish; cover with half the spinach mixture. Repeat layers. Bake, covered, at 375°F for 30 minutes or until heated through. Top with remaining cheese and ⅔ cup onions. Bake, uncovered, 3 minutes or until onions are golden brown.   *Makes 6 to 8 servings*

Broccoli Chicken au Gratin

- **1 (6.5-ounce) package RICE-A-RONI® Broccoli Au Gratin**
- **2½ tablespoons margarine or butter**
- **¾ pound boneless, skinless chicken breasts, cut into thin strips**
- **2 cups frozen chopped broccoli**
- **1 cup fresh sliced mushrooms**
- **¼ teaspoon coarse ground black pepper**

1. In large skillet over medium heat, sauté rice-pasta mix with margarine until pasta is light golden brown.

2. Slowly stir in 2¼ cups water, chicken and Special Seasonings; bring to a boil. Reduce heat to low. Cover; simmer 10 minutes.

3. Stir in broccoli, mushrooms and pepper. Cover; cook 5 to 10 minutes or until rice is tender and chicken is no longer pink inside. Let stand 3 to 5 minutes before serving.

Makes 4 servings

Prep Time: 5 minutes
Cook Time: 30 minutes

Mom's Best Chicken Tetrazzini

- **8 ounces uncooked vermicelli or thin noodles**
- **2 tablespoons butter**
- **8 ounces fresh mushrooms, sliced**
- **¼ cup chopped green onions**
- **1 can (about 14 ounces) chicken broth**
- **1 cup half-and-half, divided**
- **2 tablespoons dry sherry**
- **¼ cup all-purpose flour**
- **½ teaspoon salt**
- **¼ teaspoon ground nutmeg**
- **⅛ teaspoon white pepper**
- **1 jar (2 ounces) chopped pimiento, drained**
- **½ cup (4 ounces) grated Parmesan cheese, divided**
- **½ cup sour cream**
- **2 cups cubed cooked chicken**

1. Preheat oven to 350°F. Cook noodles according to package directions. Drain; set aside.

2. Melt butter in large nonstick skillet over medium-high heat. Add mushrooms and onions; cook and stir until onions are tender. Add chicken broth, ½ cup half-and-half and sherry to onion mixture. Pour remaining ½ cup half-and-half into small jar with tight-fitting lid; add flour, salt, nutmeg and pepper. Shake well. Slowly stir flour mixture into skillet. Bring to a boil; cook 1 minute. Reduce heat; stir in pimiento and ¼ cup Parmesan cheese. Stir in sour cream; blend well. Add chicken and noodles; mix well.

3. Coat 1½-quart casserole with nonstick cooking spray. Spread mixture evenly into prepared casserole. Sprinkle with remaining ¼ cup Parmesan cheese. Bake 30 to 35 minutes until hot. Let cool slightly before serving.

Makes 6 servings

Green Chile Chicken Enchilada

Mexican Chicken Casserole

- 8 ounces elbow noodles or small shell pasta
- 2 teaspoons olive oil
- 1 large carrot, grated
- 1 medium green bell pepper, finely chopped
- 1 tablespoon garlic
- ¾ pound chicken tenders, cut in ¾ inch pieces
- 2 teaspoons cumin
- 1½ teaspoons dried oregano leaves
- ½ teaspoon salt
- ¼ teaspoon ground red pepper
- 8 ounces (2 cups) shredded Monterey Jack cheese, divided
- 1 bottle (16 ounces) tomato salsa, divided

1. Cook pasta according to package directions. While pasta is cooking, heat oil in large nonstick skillet over medium heat. Add carrot, bell pepper and garlic; cook and stir 3 minutes until vegetables are tender. Add chicken, increase heat to medium-high; cook and stir 3 to 4 minutes or until chicken is no longer pink in center. Add cumin, oregano, salt and ground red pepper; cook and stir 1 minute. Remove from heat; set aside.

2. Grease 13×9-inch microwavable dish. Drain and rinse pasta under cold running water; place in large bowl. Add chicken mixture, 1 cup cheese and 1 cup salsa. Mix well; pour into prepared dish. Top with remaining 1 cup salsa and 1 cup cheese. Cover with plastic wrap; microwave at HIGH 4 to 6 minutes, turning dish halfway through cooking time. Serve immediately.

Makes 4 to 6 servings

Prep and Cook Time: 20 minutes

Snappy Pea and Chicken Pot Pie

- 2½ cups chicken broth
- 1 medium-size baking potato, peeled and cut into ½-inch chunks
- 1½ cups sliced carrots (½-inch slices)
- 1 cup frozen pearl onions
- ½ teaspoon dried rosemary
- ½ teaspoon TABASCO® brand Pepper Sauce
- ¼ teaspoon salt
- 1 medium red bell pepper, coarsely diced
- 4 ounces (about 1 cup) sugar-snap peas, trimmed and halved lengthwise
- 3 tablespoons butter or margarine
- ¼ cup flour
- 8 ounces cooked chicken-breast meat, cut in 3×1-inch strips
- 1 sheet frozen puff pastry
- 1 egg, beaten with 1 teaspoon water

In large heavy saucepan bring chicken broth to a boil over high heat. Add potato, carrots, pearl onions, rosemary, TABASCO® Sauce and salt. Reduce heat to medium; cover and simmer 8 to 10 minutes, until vegetables are tender. Add bell pepper and sugar-snap peas; boil 30 seconds, just until peas turn bright green. Drain vegetables, reserving chicken broth; set aside.

Melt butter in saucepan over low heat. Stir in flour and cook 3 to 4 minutes, stirring constantly. Pour in 2 cups of the reserved chicken broth and whisk until smooth. Bring to a boil over medium heat, stirring constantly. Reduce heat to low and simmer 5 minutes, stirring frequently, until thickened and bubbly.

Put chicken strips in bottoms of four lightly buttered ramekins or soufflé dishes. Top chicken with vegetables and sauce.

Heat oven to 475°F.

Thaw pastry and unfold on floured surface according to package directions. Cut pastry into four rectangles. Brush outside rims of ramekins with some of the beaten egg mixture. Place pastry rectangle over each ramekin and press firmly around edges to seal. Trim dough and flute edges. Brush tops with remaining beaten egg mixture.

Place ramekins on baking sheet and bake 10 to 12 minutes, until pastry is puffed and well browned. Serve at once.   *Makes 4 servings*

Cheesy Chicken, Coins & Strings

- 2 tablespoons margarine or butter
- 1 pound boneless, skinless chicken breasts, cut into 1-inch pieces
- 2 cups frozen crinkle-cut carrots
- ⅔ cup milk
- 1 (4.8-ounce) package PASTA RONI® Angel Hair Pasta with Herbs
- ½ cup pasteurized processed cheese, cut into ½-inch cubes

1. In large skillet over medium-high heat, melt margarine. Add chicken; sauté 5 to 7 minutes or until chicken is no longer pink inside. Remove from skillet; set aside.

2. In same skillet, bring 1⅓ cups water, carrots and milk to a boil. Stir in pasta and Special Seasonings; return to a boil. Reduce heat to medium. Gently boil uncovered, 4 to 5 minutes or until pasta is tender, stirring frequently.

3. Stir in chicken and cheese. Let stand 3 minutes or until cheese is melted.   *Makes 4 servings*

Prep Time: 10 minutes
Cook Time: 15 minutes

Mexican Chicken Casserole

3-Cheese Chicken & Noodles

3 cups chopped cooked chicken
1½ cups cottage cheese
1 can (10¾ ounces) condensed cream of chicken soup, undiluted
1 package (8 ounces) wide egg noodles, cooked and drained
1 cup grated Monterey Jack cheese
½ cup diced celery
½ cup diced onion
½ cup diced green bell pepper
½ cup diced red bell pepper
½ cup grated Parmesan cheese
½ cup chicken broth
1 can (4 ounces) sliced mushrooms, drained
2 tablespoons butter, melted
½ teaspoon dried thyme leaves

Slow Cooker Directions

Combine all ingredients in slow cooker. Stir to coat evenly. Cover and cook on LOW 6 to 10 hours or on HIGH 3 to 4 hours.

Makes 6 servings

Tortilla Chicken Bake

1 can (14½ ounces) DEL MONTE® Stewed Tomatoes Mexican Recipe
½ cup chopped onion
2 cloves garlic, crushed
½ teaspoon dried oregano, crushed
½ teaspoon chili powder
½ pound boneless chicken, skinned and cut into strips
4 cups tortilla chips
¾ cup shredded Monterey Jack cheese with jalapeño peppers or Cheddar cheese

1. Preheat oven to 375°F. Drain tomatoes, reserving liquid; chop tomatoes.

2. Combine reserved liquid, onion, garlic, oregano and chili powder in large skillet; boil 5 minutes, stirring occasionally.

3. Stir in tomatoes and chicken; cook over medium heat until chicken is no longer pink, about 5 minutes. Layer half of chips, chicken mixture and cheese in shallow 2-quart baking dish; repeat layers ending with cheese.

4. Cover and bake 15 minutes or until heated through. Serve with sour cream, if desired.

Makes 4 servings

Prep Time: 3 minutes
Cook Time: 25 minutes

3-Cheese Chicken & Noodles

Sour Cream Chicken Quiche

Crust
    Classic CRISCO® Single Crust
        (recipe follows)

Filling
    2 tablespoons CRISCO® Stick or
        2 tablespoons CRISCO®
        all-vegetable shortening
    2 tablespoons chopped green
        bell pepper
    2 tablespoons chopped onion
    1 cup cubed cooked chicken
    1 tablespoon all-purpose flour
    ¼ teaspoon salt
        Dash nutmeg
        Dash pepper
    ½ cup shredded sharp Cheddar
        cheese
    ¼ cup shredded Swiss cheese
    2 eggs, lightly beaten
    ¾ cup milk
    ¾ cup dairy sour cream

1. For crust, prepare as directed. Press into 9-inch pie pan. Do not bake. Heat oven to 400°F.

2. For filling, melt Crisco in small skillet. Add green pepper and onion. Cook on medium-high heat 3 minutes, stirring frequently. Add chicken and flour. Cook and stir 2 minutes. Spread in bottom of unbaked pie crust. Sprinkle with salt, nutmeg and pepper. Top with Cheddar cheese and Swiss cheese.

3. Combine eggs, milk and sour cream in medium bowl. Stir until smooth. Pour carefully over cheese.

4. Bake at 400°F for 20 minutes. Reduce oven temperature to 350°F. Bake 30 to 35 minutes or until knife inserted near center comes out clean. *Do not overbake.* Cool 10 minutes before cutting and serving. Refrigerate leftover pie.

Makes 1 (9-inch) pie

Classic Crisco® Single Crust

    1⅓ cups all-purpose flour
    ½ teaspoon salt
    ½ CRISCO® Stick or ½ cup
        CRISCO® all-vegetable
        shortening
    3 tablespoons cold water

1. Combine flour and salt in medium bowl.

2. Cut in shortening using pastry blender or 2 knives until all flour is blended to form pea-size chunks.

3. Sprinkle with water, 1 tablespoon at a time. Toss lightly with fork until dough forms a ball.

4. Press dough between hands to form 5- to 6-inch "pancake." Flour rolling surface and rolling pin lightly. Roll dough into circle. Trim circle 1 inch larger than upside-down pie plate. Carefully remove trimmed dough. Set aside to reroll and use for pastry cutout garnish, if desired.

5. Fold dough into quarters. Unfold and press into pie plate. Fold edge under. Flute.

6. For recipes using an unbaked pie crust, follow directions given for that recipe.

Makes 1 (9-inch) single crust

Chicken Casserole Olé

    12 boneless, skinless chicken
        tenders
    2 cups water
    1 can (15 ounces) mild chili
        beans, undrained
    1 cup salsa
    ½ cup chopped green bell
        pepper
    2 cups UNCLE BEN'S® Instant
        Rice
    2 cups (8 ounces) shredded
        Mexican cheese blend,
        divided
    2 cups bite-size tortilla chips

1. Spray large skillet with nonstick cooking spray. Add chicken; cook over medium-high heat 12 to 15 minutes or until lightly browned on both sides and chicken is no longer pink in center.

2. Add water, beans with liquid, salsa and bell pepper. Bring to a boil; add rice and 1 cup cheese. Cover; remove from heat and let stand 5 minutes or until liquid is absorbed. Top with tortilla chips and remaining 1 cup cheese; let stand, covered, 3 to 5 minutes or until cheese is melted.

Makes 6 servings

Helpful Hints

Chicken tenders are lean, tender strips that are found on the underside of the breast. They are skinless and boneless and have virtually no waste. They are available in the fresh poultry section of the supermarket.

Northwoods Mushroom Swiss Melt

4 TYSON® Individually Fresh Frozen® Boneless, Skinless Chicken Breasts
2 boxes UNCLE BEN'S® Long Grain & Wild Rice Original Recipe
3¾ cups water
½ cup chopped green bell pepper
½ cup chopped red bell pepper
1 cup sliced mushrooms
4 slices Swiss cheese

COOK: CLEAN: Wash hands. Remove protective ice glaze from frozen chicken by holding under cool running water 1 to 2 minutes. Spray large skillet with nonstick cooking spray. Add chicken; cook over medium-high heat 5 to 7 minutes or until light brown. Add water, rice and contents of seasoning packets. Bring to a boil. Cover; reduce heat. Simmer 20 minutes. Stir in bell peppers; sprinkle mushrooms over chicken. Cook, covered, 5 to 8 minutes or until internal juices of chicken run clear. (Or insert instant-read meat thermometer into thickest part of chicken. Temperature should read 170°F.) Place cheese over chicken; remove from heat. Let stand, covered, 5 minutes or until cheese is melted.

SERVE: Serve chicken while still hot with rolls and mixed vegetables, if desired.

CHILL: Refrigerate leftovers immediately.   *Makes 4 servings*

Prep Time: none
Cook Time: 40 minutes

Teriyaki Chicken Medley

2 cups cooked white rice (about ¾ cup uncooked)
2 cups (10 ounces) cooked chicken, cut into strips
1⅓ cups French's® French Fried Onions, divided
1 package (12 ounces) frozen bell pepper strips, thawed and drained*
1 jar (12 ounces) chicken gravy
3 tablespoons teriyaki sauce

Or, substitute 2 cups sliced bell peppers for frozen pepper strips.

Preheat oven to 400°F. Grease 2-quart oblong baking dish. Press rice into bottom of prepared dish.

Combine chicken, ⅔ cup French Fried Onions, bell pepper strips, gravy and teriyaki sauce in large bowl; mix well. Pour mixture over rice layer. Cover; bake 30 minutes or until heated through. Top with remaining ⅔ cup onions. Bake 1 minute or until onions are golden.

Makes 4 to 6 servings

Prep Time: 10 minutes
Cook Time: 31 minutes

Zesty Chicken Succotash

1 (3- to 4-pound) chicken, cut up and skinned, if desired
1 onion, chopped
1 rib celery, sliced
¼ cup Frank's® RedHot® Cayenne Pepper Sauce
1 package (10 ounces) frozen lima beans
1 package (10 ounces) frozen whole kernel corn
2 tomatoes, coarsely chopped

1. Heat *1 tablespoon oil* in large skillet until hot. Add chicken; cook 10 minutes or until browned on both sides. Drain off all but 1 tablespoon fat. Add onion and celery; cook and stir 3 minutes or until tender.

2. Stir in *¾ cup water*, **Frank's RedHot** Sauce and remaining ingredients. Heat to boiling. Reduce heat to medium-low. Cook, covered, 20 to 25 minutes or until chicken is no longer pink near bone. Sprinkle with chopped parsley, if desired.

Makes 6 servings

Prep Time: 10 minutes
Cook Time: 35 minutes

Chicken Jambalaya

2 tablespoons vegetable oil
¾ pound boneless chicken thighs or breasts, cut into cubes
1 cup ham cut into very thin strips (about 5 ounces)
1 can (14½ to 16 ounces) seasoned diced tomatoes in juice, undrained
1½ cups water
1 can (4 ounces) diced green chilies, undrained
1 package KNORR® Recipe Classics™ Vegetable Soup, Dip and Recipe Mix
1 cup uncooked rice

• In large skillet, heat oil over medium-high heat and brown chicken and ham.

• Stir in tomatoes, water, chilies and recipe mix. Bring to a boil over high heat. Stir in rice.

• Reduce heat to low and simmer covered, stirring occasionally, 20 minutes or until rice is tender.

Makes 4 servings

Prep Time: 15 minutes
Cook Time: 25 minutes

Northwoods Mushroom Swiss Melt

Chicken and Linguine in Creamy Tomato Sauce

1 tablespoon BERTOLLI® Olive Oil
1 pound boneless, skinless chicken breasts, cut into ½-inch strips
1 jar (1 pound 10 ounces) RAGÚ® Old World Style® Pasta Sauce
2 cups water
8 ounces linguine or spaghetti
½ cup whipping or heavy cream
1 tablespoon fresh basil leaves, chopped *or* ½ teaspoon dried basil leaves, crushed

1. In 12-inch skillet, heat oil over medium heat and brown chicken. Remove chicken and set aside.

2. In same skillet, stir in Ragú Pasta Sauce and water. Bring to a boil over high heat. Stir in uncooked linguine and return to a boil. Reduce heat to low and simmer covered, stirring occasionally, 15 minutes or until linguine is tender.

3. Stir in cream and basil. Return chicken to skillet and cook 5 minutes or until chicken is thoroughly cooked.

Makes 4 servings

Prep Time: 10 minutes
Cook Time: 30 minutes

Sautéed Chicken with Brown Rice

2 bags SUCCESS® Brown Rice
Vegetable cooking spray
¼ cup flour
½ teaspoon paprika
¼ teaspoon black pepper
2 cups chopped cooked chicken
1 medium onion, sliced
1 green bell pepper, chopped
1 jar (14 ounces) sliced mushrooms, drained
¼ cup apple juice
2 tablespoons packed brown sugar

Prepare rice according to package directions. Spray 13×9-inch baking dish with cooking spray.

Preheat oven to 425°F.

Combine flour, paprika and black pepper in shallow dish. Add chicken; coat with flour mixture. Place chicken in prepared baking dish; cover. Bake 30 minutes.

Remove chicken from baking dish; drain drippings from dish. Place rice in baking dish. Add onion, green pepper and mushrooms. Top with chicken. Combine apple juice and brown sugar; pour over chicken. Cover. Bake until chicken is no longer pink in center, 20 to 30 minutes.

Makes 8 servings

"Wildly" Delicious Casserole

1 package (14 ounces) ground chicken
1 package (14 ounces) frozen broccoli with red peppers
2 cups cooked wild rice
1 can (10¾ ounces) condensed cream of chicken soup
½ cup mayonnaise
½ cup plain yogurt
1 teaspoon lemon juice
½ teaspoon curry powder
¼ cup dry bread crumbs
3 to 4 slices process American cheese, cut in half diagonally

Preheat oven to 375°F. Grease 8-inch square casserole; set aside. In large skillet, cook chicken until no longer pink. Drain; set aside. Cook broccoli and peppers according to package directions; set aside. In large bowl, combine rice, soup, mayonnaise, yogurt, lemon juice and curry. Stir in chicken, broccoli and peppers. Pour into prepared casserole; sprinkle with bread crumbs. Bake 45 to 55 minutes. During last 5 minutes of baking, arrange cheese slices on top of casserole. Remove from oven; let stand 5 minutes.

Makes 6 to 8 servings

Favorite recipe from **Minnesota Cultivated Wild Rice Council**

Helpful Hints

It is easier to cut boneless chicken breasts into strips, if they are partially frozen. Allow the strips to thaw completely before cooking them.

Chicken and Linguine in Creamy Tomato Sauce

Indian-Spiced Chicken with Wild Rice

½ teaspoon salt
½ teaspoon ground cumin
½ teaspoon black pepper
¼ teaspoon ground cinnamon
¼ teaspoon ground turmeric
4 boneless skinless chicken breast halves (about 1 pound)
2 tablespoons olive oil
2 carrots, sliced
1 red bell pepper, chopped
1 rib celery, chopped
2 cloves garlic, minced
1 package (6 ounces) long grain and wild rice mix
2 cups reduced-sodium chicken broth
1 cup raisins
¼ cup sliced almonds

Combine salt, cumin, black pepper, cinnamon and turmeric in small bowl. Rub spice mixture on both sides of chicken. Place chicken on plate; cover and refrigerate 30 minutes.

Preheat oven to 350°F. Spray 13×9-inch baking dish with nonstick cooking spray.

Heat oil in large skillet over medium-high heat until hot. Add chicken; cook 2 minutes per side or until browned. Remove chicken; set aside.

Place carrots, bell pepper, celery and garlic in same skillet. Cook and stir 2 minutes. Add rice; cook 5 minutes, stirring frequently. Add seasoning packet from rice mix and broth; bring to a boil over high heat. Remove from heat; stir in raisins. Pour into prepared dish; place chicken on rice mixture. Sprinkle with almonds.

Cover tightly with foil and bake 35 minutes or until chicken is no longer pink in center and rice is tender.   *Makes 4 servings*

School Night Chicken Rice Taco Toss

1 (6.9-ounce) package RICE-A-RONI® Chicken Flavor
2 tablespoons margarine or butter
1 (16-ounce) jar salsa
1 pound boneless, skinless chicken breasts, chopped
1 cup frozen or canned corn, drained
4 cups shredded lettuce
½ cup (2 ounces) shredded Cheddar cheese
2 cups tortilla chips, coarsely broken
1 medium tomato, chopped

1. In large skillet over medium-high heat, sauté rice-vermicelli mix with margarine until vermicelli is golden brown.

2. Slowly stir in 2 cups water, salsa, chicken and Special Seasonings. Bring to a boil. Reduce heat to low. Cover; simmer 10 minutes.

3. Stir in corn. Cover; simmer 5 to 10 minutes or until rice is tender and chicken is no longer pink inside.

4. Arrange lettuce on large serving platter. Top with chicken-rice mixture. Sprinkle with cheese and tortilla chips. Garnish with tomato.
Makes 6 servings

Prep Time: 10 minutes
Cook Time: 30 minutes

Spicy Chicken 'n' Rice

2 tablespoons all-purpose flour
¾ teaspoon LAWRY'S® Seasoned Salt
6 chicken thighs, skin removed
2 tablespoons salad oil
2 cans (14½ ounces each) whole tomatoes, cut up
1 package (1.0 ounces) LAWRY'S® Taco Spices & Seasonings
1 cup thinly sliced celery
½ cup chopped onion
1 cup uncooked long-grain rice

In large plastic food storage bag, combine flour and Seasoned Salt. Dredge chicken in flour. In large skillet, heat oil. Add chicken over medium-high heat until brown. Continue cooking over low heat 15 minutes. Add remaining ingredients; mix well. Bring to a boil over medium-high heat; reduce heat to low, cover and simmer 20 minutes or until liquid is absorbed and rice is done.   *Makes 3 to 4 servings*

Serving Suggestion: Serve a fresh vegetable of your choice or a vegetable salad.

Indian-Spiced Chicken with Wild Rice

Artichoke-Olive Chicken Bake

1½ cups uncooked rotini
1 tablespoon olive oil
1 medium onion, chopped
½ green bell pepper, chopped
2 cups shredded cooked chicken
1 can (14½ ounces) diced tomatoes with Italian-style herbs, undrained
1 can (14 ounces) artichoke hearts, drained and quartered
1 can (6 ounces) sliced black olives, drained
1 teaspoon dried Italian seasoning
2 cups (8 ounces) shredded mozzarella cheese

Preheat oven to 350°F. Spray 2-quart casserole with nonstick cooking spray.

Cook pasta according to package directions until al dente. Drain and set aside.

Meanwhile, heat oil in large deep skillet over medium heat until hot. Add onion and pepper; cook and stir 1 minute. Add chicken, tomatoes with juice, pasta, artichokes, olives and Italian seasoning; mix until combined.

Place half of chicken mixture in prepared dish; sprinkle with half of cheese. Top with remaining chicken mixture and cheese.

Bake, covered, 35 minutes or until hot and bubbly.   *Makes 8 servings*

Sausage & Chicken-Stuffed Pita Sandwiches

¾ pound Italian sausage links, sliced
¾ pound boneless, skinless chicken breasts, cut into ¾-inch cubes
1 clove garlic, finely chopped
1½ cups RAGÚ® Old World Style® Pasta Sauce
1 cup shredded mozzarella cheese (about 4 ounces)
6 large pita breads, heated

Preheat oven to 350°F. In 12-inch nonstick skillet, cook sausage over medium-high heat, stirring occasionally, 5 minutes. Add chicken and garlic and cook, stirring occasionally, 5 minutes. Stir in Ragú® Old World Style Pasta Sauce and simmer uncovered 5 minutes or until sausage is done and chicken is thoroughly cooked. Remove from heat; stir in cheese. To serve, generously stuff pita bread with sausage mixture. Garnish, if desired, with grated Parmesan cheese.

Makes 6 servings

Chicken Divan

⅔ cup milk
2 tablespoons margarine or butter
1 package (4.8 ounces) PASTA RONI® Four Cheese Flavor with Corkscrew Pasta
2 cups chopped cooked chicken or turkey
2 cups broccoli flowerets
½ cup croutons, coarsely crushed

Microwave Directions

1. In round 3-quart microwaveable glass casserole, combine 1½ cups water, milk and margarine. Microwave, uncovered, on HIGH 4 to 5 minutes or until boiling.

2. Stir in pasta, Special Seasonings, chicken and broccoli.

3. Microwave, uncovered, on HIGH 12 to 13 minutes, stirring after 6 minutes.

4. Let stand 4 to 5 minutes or until desired consistency. Sauce will be thin, but will thicken upon standing. Stir before serving.

5. Sprinkle with croutons.

Makes 4 servings

Helpful Hints

The quickest way to peel garlic is to press each clove with the flat side of a chef's knife until the paper-like skin breaks; the skin will slip off easily.

Artichoke-Olive Chicken Bake

Chicken & Three-Cheese Rice Wraps

1 package (1 pound) TYSON®
   Fresh Ground Chicken
1 box UNCLE BEN'S®
   COUNTRY INN® Three
   Cheese Rice
1¾ cups water
3 tablespoons chopped green
   chilies
½ cup chopped tomato
12 (8- or 10-inch) flour tortillas

COOK: CLEAN: Wash hands. Heat large nonstick skillet over medium-high heat. Add chicken; cook, stirring frequently, 6 to 9 minutes or until chicken is no longer pink. CLEAN: Wash hands. Add rice, contents of seasoning packet, water and chilies; mix well. Bring to a boil. Reduce heat; cover. Simmer 10 to 15 minutes or until rice is tender and liquid is absorbed. Stir in tomato; let stand 5 minutes. Meanwhile, heat tortillas according to package directions. Spoon chicken mixture evenly down center of tortillas. Wrap or roll to enclose chicken mixture.

SERVE: Serve wraps with sour cream and salsa, if desired.

CHILL: Refrigerate leftovers immediately.   *Makes 6 servings*

Prep Time: none
Cook Time: 20 minutes

Creamy Chicken & Rice Bake

6 boneless, skinless chicken
   thighs (about 1½ pounds)
1 jar (1 pound) RAGÚ® Cheese
   Creations!® Classic Alfredo
   Sauce
1 can (14½ ounces) chicken
   broth
1½ cups uncooked converted rice
1 medium tomato, coarsely
   chopped
2 tablespoons grated Parmesan
   cheese

1. Preheat oven to 400°F. Season chicken, if desired, with salt and pepper.

2. In 13×9-inch baking dish, thoroughly combine Ragú Cheese Creations! Sauce, broth, uncooked rice and tomato. Arrange chicken on rice mixture.

3. Cover with aluminum foil and bake 35 minutes. Remove foil and sprinkle chicken with cheese. Bake an additional 10 minutes or until chicken juices run clearly.

Makes 6 servings

Tip: Substitute boneless, skinless chicken breasts for chicken thighs, if desired.

Prep Time: 5 minutes
Cook Time: 45 minutes

Fettuccine with Chicken Breasts

12 ounces uncooked fettuccine
   or egg noodles
1 cup HIDDEN VALLEY® The
   Original Ranch® Dressing
⅓ cup Dijon mustard
8 boneless, skinless chicken
   breast halves, pounded thin
½ cup butter
⅓ cup dry white wine

Cook fettuccine according to package directions; drain. Preheat oven to 425°F. Stir together dressing and mustard; set aside. Pour fettuccine into oiled baking dish. Sauté chicken in butter in a large skillet until no longer pink in center. Transfer cooked chicken to the bed of fettuccine. Add wine to the skillet; cook until reduced to desired consistency. Drizzle over chicken. Pour the reserved dressing mixture over the chicken. Bake at 425°F. about 10 minutes, or until dressing forms a golden brown crust.

Makes 8 servings

Helpful Hints

Pounding boneless chicken breasts to a uniform thickness, usually about ¼ inch, allows them to cook faster and more easily. Use the flat side of a meat mallet or a rolling pin to pound chicken. If you use a wooden rolling pin, wrap it tightly in plastic wrap to avoid contaminating it with salmonella bacteria, which is common in raw chicken; wash the rolling pin well in hot soapy water.

Chicken & Three-Cheese Rice Wraps

Tantalizing Turkey

Turkey and Macaroni

- 1 teaspoon vegetable oil
- 1½ pounds ground turkey
- 2 cans (10¾ ounces each) condensed tomato soup, undiluted
- 2 cups uncooked macaroni, cooked and drained
- 1 can (16 ounces) corn, drained
- ½ cup chopped onion
- 1 can (4 ounces) sliced mushrooms, drained
- 2 tablespoons ketchup
- 1 tablespoon mustard
  Salt and black pepper to taste

Slow Cooker Directions

Heat oil in medium skillet; cook turkey until browned. Transfer mixture to slow cooker. Add remaining ingredients to slow cooker. Stir to blend. Cover and cook on LOW 7 to 9 hours or on HIGH 3 to 4 hours.

Makes 4 to 6 servings

Red Beans With Sausage

- 1 pound lite turkey smoked sausage or smoked pork sausage, cut into ½-inch slices
- 2 tablespoons CRISCO® Oil*
- 2 celery stalks, chopped
- 1 large onion, peeled and diced
- 1 large green bell pepper, seeds and ribs removed, and chopped
- 2 teaspoons jarred minced garlic *or* 1 large garlic clove, peeled and minced
- 2 cans (16 ounces each) kidney beans, drained and rinsed
- 2 cups water
- 2 bay leaves
- 1 teaspoon Italian seasoning
- ½ to 1 teaspoon hot red pepper sauce
- ½ teaspoon salt

Use your favorite Crisco Oil product.

1. Heat 3-quart saucepan on medium-high heat. Add sausage. Cook 3 minutes, or until lightly brown. Remove sausage from pan with slotted spoon. Discard drippings from pan.

2. Reduce heat to medium. Add oil to pan, along with celery, onion, green pepper and garlic. Sauté 3 minutes, or until onions are translucent. Add beans, water, bay leaves, Italian seasoning, hot red pepper sauce and salt to pan. Return sausage to pan. Bring to boil.

3. Simmer mixture 30 to 45 minutes, or until thick. Stir occasionally. Discard bay leaves. Serve immediately over rice.

Makes 4 servings

Prep Time: 25 minutes
Total Time: 60 to 70 minutes

Helpful Hints

If you want to reduce the fat in a recipe using ground turkey, be sure to choose ground turkey breast meat. Products that contain dark meat and skin will be higher in fat.

Turkey and Macaroni

Turkey and Stuffing Bake

1 jar (4½ ounces) sliced mushrooms
¼ cup butter or margarine
½ cup diced celery
½ cup chopped onion
1¼ cups HIDDEN VALLEY® The Original Ranch® Dressing, divided
⅔ cup water
3 cups seasoned stuffing mix
⅓ cup sweetened dried cranberries
3 cups coarsely shredded cooked turkey (about 1 pound)

Drain mushrooms, reserving liquid; set aside. Melt butter over medium-high heat in a large skillet. Add celery and onion; sauté for 4 minutes or until soft. Remove from heat and stir in ½ cup dressing, water and reserved mushroom liquid. Stir in stuffing mix and cranberries until thoroughly moistened. Combine turkey, mushrooms and remaining ¾ cup dressing in a separate bowl; spread evenly in a greased 8-inch baking dish. Top with stuffing mixture. Bake at 350°F. for 40 minutes or until bubbly and brown.

Makes 4 to 6 servings

Helpful Hints

If you don't have leftover turkey for these recipes, purchase ½-inch-thick turkey slices from the deli counter of the supermarket.

Cheesy Turkey Veg•All® Bake

1 package (5½ ounces) au gratin potato mix
2⅔ cups boiling water
1 can (15 ounces) VEG•ALL® Original Mixed Vegetables, drained
1 cup cubed cooked turkey
2 tablespoons butter

Preheat oven to 350°F. Place au gratin potato mix and sauce packet into large mixing bowl. Add water, Veg•All, turkey and butter; mix well. Pour into ungreased 2-quart casserole. Bake for 20 minutes or until top is golden brown. Cool for 5 minutes before serving.   *Makes 6 servings*

Prep Time: 7 minutes
Cook Time: 20 minutes

Green Bean & Turkey Bake

1 can (10¾ ounces) condensed cream of mushroom soup
¾ cup milk
⅛ teaspoon pepper
2 packages (9 ounces *each*) frozen cut green beans, thawed
2 cups (12 ounces) cubed cooked turkey or chicken
1⅓ cups *French's®* French Fried Onions, divided
1½ cups (6 ounces) shredded Cheddar cheese, divided
3 cups hot mashed potatoes

1. Preheat oven to 375°F. In 3-quart casserole, combine soup, milk and pepper; mix well. Stir in beans, turkey, ⅔ cup French Fried Onions and *1 cup* cheese. Spoon mashed potatoes over top of turkey mixture.

2. Bake, uncovered, 45 minutes or until hot. Sprinkle with remaining *½ cup* cheese and ⅔ cup onions. Bake 3 minutes or until onions are golden.   *Makes 6 servings*

Microwave Directions: Prepare mixture as above except do not top with potatoes. Cover casserole with vented plastic wrap. Microwave on HIGH 15 minutes or until heated through, stirring halfway. Uncover. Top with mashed potatoes, remaining cheese and onions. Microwave on HIGH 2 to 4 minutes. Let stand 5 minutes.

Tip: Two (14½-ounce) cans cut green beans (drained) may be used instead of frozen beans. You may substitute instant mashed potatoes prepared according to package directions for 6 servings.

Prep Time: 10 minutes
Cook Time: 50 minutes

Turkey and Stuffing Bake

Tex-Mex Turkey

1 can (10¾ ounces) reduced-fat
    condensed tomato soup
½ cup nonfat sour cream
    Nonstick cooking spray
1 cup sliced green onions
½ cup diced green chilies
½ cup frozen corn
½ cup chopped red bell pepper
¼ cup sliced ripe olives
    (optional)
2 cloves garlic, minced
1 teaspoon chili powder
1 pound turkey tenderloins, cut
    into thin strips
½ teaspoon salt
    Hot cooked rice (optional)

Combine soup and sour cream in
small bowl; mix well. Set aside. Spray
large nonstick skillet with cooking
spray. Add onions, chilies, corn, bell
pepper, olives, if desired, garlic and
chili powder; cook and stir over
medium-high heat until onions and
pepper are tender.

Add turkey to skillet; brown evenly.
Add soup mixture and salt; bring to a
boil. Reduce heat to low; cover and
simmer 5 minutes. Serve with rice, if
desired.   *Makes 4 servings*

Mexican Rice and Turkey Bake

1 bag SUCCESS® Rice
    Vegetable cooking spray
3 cups chopped cooked turkey
1 can (10 ounces) tomatoes with
    chilies, undrained*
1 can (12 ounces) Mexican-style
    corn with sweet peppers,
    drained
1 cup fat-free sour cream
½ cup (2 ounces) shredded low-
    fat Cheddar cheese

*Or, use 1 can (14½ ounces) stewed
tomatoes. Add 1 can (4 ounces) drained
chopped mild green chilies. Prepare rice
according to package directions.*

Prepare rice according to package
directions.

Spray 1½-quart microwave-safe
casserole with cooking spray; set
aside. Combine rice, turkey, tomatoes
and corn in large bowl; mix well.
Spoon into prepared casserole.
Microwave on HIGH until hot and
bubbly, 8 to 10 minutes, stirring after
5 minutes. Top with sour cream and
cheese.   *Makes 6 servings*

Conventional Oven: Assemble
casserole as directed. Spoon into
ovenproof 1½-quart casserole
sprayed with vegetable cooking spray.
Bake at 350°F until thoroughly heated,
15 to 20 minutes.

Creamy Turkey & Broccoli

1 package (6 ounces) stuffing
    mix, plus ingredients to
    prepare mix*
1⅓ cups *French's*® French Fried
    Onions, divided
1 package (10 ounces) frozen
    broccoli spears, thawed and
    drained
1 package (about 1⅛ ounces)
    cheese sauce mix
1¼ cups milk
½ cup sour cream
2 cups (10 ounces) cubed
    cooked turkey or chicken

*Three cups leftover stuffing may be
substituted for stuffing mix. If stuffing is dry,
stir in water, 1 tablespoon at a time, until
moist but not wet.*

Preheat oven to 350°F. In medium
saucepan, prepare stuffing mix
according to package directions; stir
in ⅔ cup French Fried Onions. Spread
stuffing over bottom of greased
9-inch round baking dish. Arrange
broccoli spears over stuffing with
flowerets around edge of dish. In
medium saucepan, prepare cheese
sauce mix according to package
directions using 1¼ cups milk.
Remove from heat; stir in sour cream
and turkey. Pour turkey mixture over
broccoli stalks. Bake, covered, at
350°F for 30 minutes or until heated
through. Sprinkle remaining ⅔ cup
onions over turkey; bake, uncovered,
5 minutes or until onions are golden
brown.   *Makes 4 to 6 servings*

Microwave Directions: In 9-inch
round microwave-safe dish, prepare
stuffing mix according to package
microwave directions; stir in ⅔ cup
French Fried Onions. Arrange stuffing
and broccoli spears in dish as above;
set aside. In medium microwave-safe
bowl, prepare cheese sauce mix
according to package microwave
directions using 1¼ cups milk. Add
turkey and microwave, covered, on
HIGH 5 to 6 minutes, stirring turkey
halfway through cooking time. Stir in
sour cream. Pour turkey mixture over
broccoli stalks. Microwave, covered,
8 to 10 minutes or until heated
through. Rotate dish halfway through
cooking time. Top turkey with
remaining ⅔ cup onions; microwave,
uncovered, 1 minute. Let stand
5 minutes.

Tex-Mex Turkey

Sausage & Mushroom Pasta

1 can (10¾ ounces) reduced-fat condensed tomato soup
¼ cup fat-free (skim) milk
½ cup chopped onion
½ cup chopped green bell pepper
2 cloves garlic, minced
1 teaspoon dried Italian seasoning
1 cup sliced mushrooms
½ teaspoon salt (optional)
1 (7-ounce package) reduced-fat smoked turkey sausage, cut into ⅛-inch slices
4 cups cooked bow tie pasta

Combine soup and milk in small bowl; mix well and set aside. Spray large nonstick skillet with nonstick cooking spray; heat over medium-high heat until hot. Add onion, pepper, garlic and Italian seasoning; cook and stir until onion and peppers are tender. Add mushrooms and salt; cook and stir 2 to 3 minutes. Add sausage; mix well. Reduce heat; cover and simmer an additional 2 minutes. Add pasta; toss until coated with sauce.

Makes 6 servings

Cheesy Casserole

1½ cups skim milk
1 can (10¾ ounces) condensed cream of chicken soup
1 package (16 ounces) frozen mixed vegetables (thaw and drain)
2 cups finely diced cooked turkey, chicken or ham
1 cup uncooked instant rice
¾ cup (3 ounces) shredded cheddar cheese
¼ cup grated fresh Parmesan cheese
½ teaspoon LAWRY'S® Garlic Powder with Parsley
½ teaspoon LAWRY'S® Seasoned Pepper
1 tablespoon crushed potato chips or crumbled corn flakes

Lightly grease 9-inch square baking dish. Add milk and soup to dish; mix well with wire whisk. Stir in vegetables, turkey, rice, ½ cup cheddar cheese, 2 tablespoons Parmesan cheese, Garlic Powder with Parsley, and Seasoned Pepper; cover. Bake in 350°F. oven 30 minutes. Combine remaining ¼ cup cheddar cheese, 2 tablespoons Parmesan cheese and potato chips; sprinkle over top of casserole. Bake, uncovered, 15 minutes longer.

Makes 4 servings

Serving Suggestion: Serve with a crisp green salad or just by itself.

Turkey Orzo Italiano

¼ pound mushrooms, sliced
½ cup sliced green onions
2 tablespoons margarine
2 cups turkey broth or reduced-sodium chicken bouillon
1 cup uncooked orzo pasta
½ teaspoon Italian seasoning
½ teaspoon salt
⅛ teaspoon white pepper
2 cups cubed Cooked TURKEY

1. In large skillet, over medium-high heat, sauté mushrooms and onions in margarine for 1 minute. Add turkey broth and bring to a boil.

2. Stir in orzo, Italian seasoning, salt and pepper; bring to boil. Reduce heat and simmer, covered, 15 minutes or until orzo is tender and liquid has been absorbed. Stir in turkey and heat throughout.

Makes 4 servings

*Favorite recipe from **National Turkey Federation***

Helpful Hints

Orzo is a pasta that is shaped like rice kernels. Look for it in the pasta section of the supermarket.

Turkey Sausage Jambalaya

2 packages BUTTERBALL® Lean Fresh Turkey Hot Italian Sausage
2 tablespoons vegetable oil
2 cups chopped onion
⅔ cup chopped green bell pepper
⅔ cup chopped red bell pepper
⅔ cup chopped celery
4 to 6 cloves garlic, minced
4 cups chopped tomato
¼ to ½ teaspoon cayenne pepper
¼ teaspoon ground thyme
2 cans (14½ ounces each) chicken broth
2 cups uncooked long grain rice
⅓ cup chopped fresh parsley
Salt and black pepper

Heat oil in large skillet over medium heat until hot. Brown turkey sausage in skillet 8 minutes, turning occasionally. Add onion, bell peppers, celery and garlic. Cook and stir 3 to 5 minutes. Stir in tomato, cayenne pepper and thyme. Add chicken broth; bring to a boil. Stir in rice; cover. Reduce heat to low; simmer 20 minutes. Remove from heat. Stir in parsley. Add salt and pepper to taste. Cover; let stand 5 minutes before serving.

Makes 10 servings

Prep Time: 30 to 40 minutes

Sausage & Mushroom Pasta

Rice Lasagna

1 bag SUCCESS® Rice
  Vegetable cooking spray
2 tablespoons reduced-calorie
  margarine
1 pound ground turkey
1 cup chopped onion
1 cup sliced fresh mushrooms
1 clove garlic, minced
2 cans (8 ounces each) no-salt-
  added tomato sauce
1 can (6 ounces) no-salt-added
  tomato paste
1 teaspoon dried oregano
  leaves, crushed
1 carton (15 ounces) lowfat
  cottage cheese
½ cup (2 ounces) grated
  Parmesan cheese
2 cups (8 ounces) shredded
  mozzarella cheese
1 tablespoon dried parsley
  flakes

Prepare rice according to package
directions.

Preheat oven to 350°F.

Spray 13×9-inch baking dish with
cooking spray; set aside. Melt
margarine in large skillet over medium
heat. Add ground turkey, onion,
mushrooms and garlic; cook until
turkey is no longer pink and
vegetables are tender, stirring
occasionally to separate turkey. Drain.
Stir in tomato sauce, tomato paste
and oregano; simmer 15 minutes,
stirring occasionally. Layer half each
of rice, turkey mixture, cottage
cheese, Parmesan cheese and
mozzarella cheese in prepared
baking dish; repeat layers. Sprinkle
with parsley; cover. Bake 30 minutes.
Uncover; continue baking 15 minutes.

Makes 8 servings

Mexican Stuffed Peppers

  Nonstick cooking spray
6 ounces breakfast bulk turkey
  sausage
1 cup frozen corn
4 ounces uncooked orzo pasta
  or small shell pasta
1 cup canned black beans,
  rinsed and drained
  Salsa Cruda (recipe follows) or
  1¾ cups mild picante sauce,
  divided
½ cup water
¼ cup cornmeal
1 tablespoon chili powder
½ teaspoon ground cumin
4 medium green bell peppers,
  halved lengthwise with
  stems and seeds removed
½ cup (2 ounces) shredded
  reduced-fat sharp Cheddar
  cheese
½ cup nonfat sour cream
¼ cup chopped fresh cilantro
  leaves or finely chopped
  green onions

1. Preheat oven to 350°F. Spray large
nonstick skillet with cooking spray.
Heat over high heat until hot. Brown
turkey over medium-high heat 6 to
8 minutes or until no longer pink,
stirring to separate turkey; drain fat.
Add corn, pasta, beans, 1¼ cups
Salsa Cruda, water, cornmeal, chili
powder and cumin. Bring to a boil;
remove from heat.

2. Place pepper halves in 13×9-inch
baking pan. Fill each pepper half with
equal amounts of sausage mixture;
cover tightly with foil. Bake 1 hour and
15 minutes. Remove from oven; top
each pepper half with ⅛ remaining
Salsa Cruda. Sprinkle cheese over
peppers. Top each half with
1 tablespoon sour cream; sprinkle
with cilantro.   *Makes 4 servings*

Salsa Cruda

2 cups chopped tomato
¼ cup minced onion
¼ cup minced fresh cilantro
  (optional)
¼ cup lime juice
1 jalapeño pepper,* seeded,
  minced
2 cloves garlic, minced

*Jalapeño peppers can sting and irritate the
skin; wear rubber gloves when handling
peppers and do not touch eyes. Wash hands
after handling.*

1. Combine tomato, onion, cilantro,
lime juice, jalapeño pepper and garlic
in small bowl. Stir to combine.

Turkey Broccoli Bake

1 bag (16 ounces) frozen
  broccoli cuts, thawed,
  drained
2 cups cubed cooked turkey or
  chicken
2 cups soft bread cubes
8 ounces sliced American
  cheese, divided
1 jar (12 ounces) HEINZ®
  HomeStyle Turkey or
  Chicken Gravy
½ cup undiluted evaporated milk
  Dash pepper

In buttered 9-inch square baking
dish, layer broccoli, turkey, bread
cubes and cheese. Combine gravy,
milk and pepper; pour over cheese.
Bake in 375°F oven, 40 minutes. Let
stand 5 minutes.

Makes 6 servings

Rice Lasagna

Turkey and Rice Quiche

3 cups cooked rice, cooled to
    room temperature
1½ cups chopped cooked turkey
1 medium tomato, seeded and
    finely diced
¼ cup sliced green onions
¼ cup finely diced green bell
    pepper
1 tablespoon chopped fresh
    basil *or* 1 teaspoon dried
    basil leaves
½ teaspoon seasoned salt
⅛ to ¼ teaspoon ground red
    pepper
½ cup skim milk
3 eggs, beaten
    Vegetable cooking spray
½ cup (2 ounces) shredded
    Cheddar cheese
½ cup (2 ounces) shredded
    mozzarella cheese

Combine rice, turkey, tomato, onions, bell pepper, basil, salt, red pepper, milk and eggs in 13×9×2-inch pan coated with cooking spray. Top with cheeses. Bake at 375°F for 20 minutes or until knife inserted near center comes out clean. To serve, cut quiche into 8 squares; cut each square diagonally into 2 triangles.

Makes 8 servings
(2 triangles each)

Favorite recipe from **USA Rice Federation**

Helpful Hints

Store white rice in an airtight container in a cool, dry place. It will keep indefinitely. Brown rice is subject to rancidity because the bran is intact. It can be stored for only six months.

Skillet Turkey Tetrazzini

2 tablespoons margarine or
    butter
¾ pound boneless, skinless
    turkey breast or chicken
    breasts, cut into thin strips
1 cup sliced fresh mushrooms
½ cup chopped red or green bell
    pepper
⅔ cup milk
1 (5.1-ounce) package
    PASTA RONI® Angel Hair
    Pasta with Parmesan
    Cheese

1. In large skillet over medium-high heat, melt margarine. Add turkey, mushrooms and bell pepper. Sauté 5 minutes or until turkey is no longer pink inside. Remove from skillet; set aside.

2. In same skillet, bring 1⅓ cups water and milk to a boil.

3. Stir in pasta and Special Seasonings. Reduce heat to medium. Gently boil uncovered, 4 to 5 minutes or until pasta is tender. Stir in turkey mixture. Let stand 3 minutes before serving.   *Makes 4 servings*

Tip: To make slicing easier, place chicken or steak in the freezer for 10 minutes.

Prep Time: 10 minutes
Cook Time: 15 minutes

Southwestern Turkey in Chilies and Cream

Slow Cooker

1 can (15 ounces) corn, drained
1 can (4 ounces) diced green
    chilies, drained
1 boneless skinless turkey
    breast, cut into 1-inch
    pieces
2 tablespoons plus 2 teaspoons
    flour, divided
1 tablespoon butter
½ cup chicken broth
1 clove garlic, minced
1 teaspoon salt
½ teaspoon paprika
¼ teaspoon dried oregano leaves
¼ teaspoon black pepper
½ cup heavy cream
2 tablespoons chopped fresh
    cilantro
3 cups hot cooked rice or pasta

Slow Cooker Directions

1. Place corn and green chilies in slow cooker.

2. Coat turkey pieces with 2 tablespoons flour. Melt butter in large nonstick skillet over medium heat. Add turkey pieces; brown on all sides. Place turkey in slow cooker. Add broth, garlic, salt, paprika, oregano and pepper. Cover; cook on LOW 2 hours or until turkey is tender and no longer pink in center.

3. Combine cream and remaining 2 teaspoons flour in small bowl, stirring until smooth. Pour mixture into slow cooker. Cover; cook on HIGH 10 minutes or until slightly thickened. Stir in cilantro. Serve over rice.

Makes 6 (1½-cup) servings

Turkey and Rice Quiche

Turkey and Biscuits

    2 cans (10¾ ounces each)
        condensed cream of
        chicken soup
    ¼ cup dry white wine
    ¼ teaspoon poultry seasoning
    2 packages (8 ounces each)
        frozen cut asparagus,
        thawed
    3 cups cubed cooked turkey or
        chicken
        Paprika (optional)
    1 can (11 ounces) refrigerated
        flaky biscuits

1. Preheat oven to 350°F. Spray 13×9-inch baking dish with nonstick cooking spray.

2. Combine soup, wine and poultry seasoning in medium bowl.

3. Arrange asparagus in single layer in prepared dish. Place turkey evenly over asparagus. Spread soup mixture over turkey. Sprinkle lightly with paprika, if desired.

4. Cover tightly with foil and bake 20 minutes. Remove from oven. *Increase oven temperature to 425°F.* Top with biscuits and bake, uncovered, 8 to 10 minutes or until biscuits are golden brown.

Makes 6 servings

Helpful Hints

If poultry seasoning is not available, you may substitute ¼ teaspoon dried thyme leaves and ¼ teaspoon rubbed sage in this Turkey and Biscuits recipe.

Lasagna Verdi

Sauce
    ¼ cup (½ stick) butter or
        margarine
    3 tablespoons flour
    1 (14½-ounce) can chicken broth
    1 cup milk
    2 tablespoons TABASCO® brand
        Green Pepper Sauce

Filling
    2 tablespoons vegetable oil
    1 pound ground turkey
    1 medium onion, diced
    1 tablespoon TABASCO® brand
        Green Pepper Sauce
    1 teaspoon salt
    1 (15-ounce) container ricotta
        cheese
    1 egg
    2 tablespoons chopped fresh
        parsley
    12 no-boil lasagna noodles
    1 (8-ounce) package mozzarella
        cheese, shredded
    ¼ cup grated Parmesan cheese

For sauce, melt butter in 2-quart saucepan over medium heat; stir in flour until well blended and smooth. Gradually add chicken broth, milk and TABASCO® Green Pepper Sauce; cook over high heat until mixture boils and thickens, stirring frequently.

Preheat oven to 375°F. For filling, heat oil in 12-inch skillet over medium-high heat. Add turkey and onion; cook until meat is well browned, stirring frequently. Stir in TABASCO® Green Pepper Sauce and salt. Mix ricotta cheese, egg and parsley in small bowl.

Grease 12×8-inch baking dish. Spread 1 cup sauce on bottom of baking dish. Layer 3 lasagna noodles in baking dish. Spread ⅓ of turkey mixture, ⅓ of ricotta mixture, ¼ of mozzarella cheese and ¼ of remaining sauce over noodles. Repeat layers two more times. Top with remaining 3 lasagna noodles. Spread remaining sauce over noodles; sprinkle with remaining mozzarella cheese and Parmesan cheese.

Cover with foil and bake 30 minutes. Uncover and bake 10 minutes or until lasagna is hot and bubbly. Let stand 5 minutes before serving.

Makes 8 servings

Rice and Turkey Skillet Curry

    2 cups water
    1 cup UNCLE BEN'S®
        ORIGINAL CONVERTED®
        Brand Rice
    ¾ cup (6 ounces) pineapple juice
    ⅓ cup diced dried apricots
    ¼ cup dried cranberries
    1 teaspoon curry powder
    1½ cups (8 ounces) cooked turkey

1. In large skillet, bring 2 cups water, rice, pineapple juice, apricots, cranberries and curry powder to a boil. Cover; reduce heat and simmer 15 minutes or until rice is tender and liquid is absorbed.

2. Add turkey to rice. Cover and cook over low heat 5 minutes or until turkey is hot.

Makes 4 servings

Turkey and Biscuit

Chipotle Tamale Pie

¾ pound ground turkey breast or lean ground beef
1 cup chopped onion
¾ cup diced green bell pepper
¾ cup diced red bell pepper
4 cloves garlic, minced
2 teaspoons ground cumin
1 can (15 ounces) pinto or red beans, rinsed and drained
1 can (8 ounces) no-salt-added stewed tomatoes, undrained
2 canned chipotle chilies in adobo sauce, minced (about 1 tablespoon)
1 to 2 teaspoons adobo sauce from canned chilies (optional)
1 cup (4 ounces) reduced-fat shredded Cheddar cheese
½ cup chopped fresh cilantro
1 package (8½ ounces) corn bread mix
⅓ cup low-fat (1%) milk
1 large egg white

1. Preheat oven to 400°F.

2. Cook turkey, onion, bell peppers and garlic in large nonstick skillet over medium-high heat 8 minutes or until turkey is no longer pink, stirring occasionally. Drain fat; sprinkle mixture with cumin.

3. Add beans, tomatoes, chilies and adobo sauce; bring to a boil over high heat. Reduce heat to medium; simmer, uncovered, 5 minutes. Remove from heat; stir in cheese and cilantro.

4. Spray 8-inch square baking dish with nonstick cooking spray. Spoon turkey mixture evenly into prepared dish, pressing down to compact mixture. Combine corn bread mix, milk and egg white in medium bowl; mix just until dry ingredients are moistened. Spoon batter evenly over turkey mixture to cover completely.

5. Bake 20 to 22 minutes or until corn bread is golden brown. Let stand 5 minutes before serving.

Makes 6 servings

Turkey 'n' Stuffing Pie

1¼ cups water*
¼ cup butter or margarine*
3½ cups seasoned stuffing crumbs*
1⅓ cups *French's®* French Fried Onions
1½ cups (7 ounces) cubed cooked turkey
1 can (10¾ ounces) condensed cream of celery soup
1 package (10 ounces) frozen peas, thawed and drained
¾ cup milk

Three cups leftover stuffing may be substituted for water, butter and stuffing crumbs. If stuffing is dry, stir in water, 1 tablespoon at a time, until moist but not wet.

Preheat oven to 350°F. In medium saucepan, heat water and butter; stir until butter melts. Remove from heat. Stir in seasoned stuffing crumbs and ⅔ cup French Fried Onions. Spoon stuffing mixture into 9-inch round or fluted baking dish. Press stuffing evenly across bottom and up sides of dish to form a shell. In medium bowl, combine turkey, soup, peas and milk; pour into stuffing shell. Bake, covered, at 350°F for 30 minutes or until heated through. Top with remaining ⅔ cup onions; bake, uncovered, 5 minutes or until onions are golden brown.

Makes 4 to 6 servings

Microwave Directions: In 9-inch round or fluted microwave-safe dish, place water and butter. Cook, covered, on HIGH 3 minutes or until butter melts. Stir in stuffing crumbs and ⅔ cup onions. Press stuffing mixture into dish as above. Reduce milk to ½ cup. In large microwave-safe bowl, combine soup, milk, turkey and peas; cook, covered, 8 minutes. Stir turkey mixture halfway through cooking time. Pour turkey mixture into stuffing shell. Cook, uncovered, 4 to 6 minutes or until heated through. Rotate dish halfway through cooking time. Top with remaining ⅔ cup onions; cook, uncovered, 1 minute. Let stand 5 minutes.

Turkey Olé

½ cup diced onions
2 tablespoons butter or margarine
1 tablespoon all-purpose flour
1½ cups cubed cooked turkey
1½ cups prepared HIDDEN VALLEY® The Original Ranch® Dressing
3 ounces rotini (spiral macaroni), plain or spinach, cooked
½ (10-ounce) package frozen peas, thawed
⅓ cup canned diced green chiles, drained
1 teaspoon dried oregano, crushed
⅛ to ¼ teaspoon black pepper (optional)
3 tablespoons dry bread crumbs
1 tablespoon butter or margarine, melted
Tomato wedges

Preheat oven to 350°F. In skillet, sauté onions in 2 tablespoons butter until tender. Stir in flour and cook until smooth and bubbly; remove from heat. In 1½-quart casserole, combine turkey, salad dressing, rotini, peas, chiles, oregano and pepper; stir in onions. In small bowl, combine bread crumbs with melted butter; sprinkle over casserole. Bake until heated through and bread crumbs are browned, 15 to 20 minutes. Garnish with tomato wedges.

Makes 6 servings

Chipotle Tamale Pie

Turkey & Zucchini Enchiladas with Tomatillo-Green Chile Sauce

1¼ pound turkey leg
1 tablespoon olive oil
1 small onion, thinly sliced
1 tablespoon minced garlic
1 pound zucchini, quartered lengthwise and sliced thinly crosswise
1½ teaspoons cumin
½ teaspoon dried oregano leaves
¾ cup (3 ounces) shredded reduced-fat Monterey Jack cheese
12 (6-inch) corn tortillas
   Tomatillo-Green Chile Sauce (recipe follows)
½ cup crumbled feta cheese
6 sprigs fresh cilantro for garnish

1. Place turkey in large saucepan; cover with water. Bring to a boil over high heat. Reduce heat to medium-low. Cover and simmer 1½ to 2 hours or until meat pulls apart easily when tested with fork. Drain; discard skin and bone. Cut meat into small pieces. Place in medium bowl; set aside.

2. Preheat oven to 350°F.

3. Heat oil over medium-high heat in large skillet. Add onion; cook and stir 3 to 4 minutes or until tender. Reduce heat to medium. Add garlic; cook and stir 3 to 4 minutes or until onion is golden. Add zucchini, 2 tablespoons water, cumin and oregano. Cover; cook and stir over medium heat 10 minutes or until zucchini is tender. Add to turkey. Stir in Monterey Jack cheese.

4. Heat large nonstick skillet over medium-high heat. Place 1 inch water in medium bowl. Dip 1 tortilla in water; shake off excess. Place in hot skillet. Cook 10 to 15 seconds on each side or until tortilla is hot and pliable. Repeat with remaining tortillas.

5. Spray bottom of 13×9-inch baking pan with nonstick cooking spray. Spoon ¼ cup filling in center of each tortilla; fold sides over to enclose. Place seam side down in pan. Brush tops with ½ cup Tomatillo-Green Chile Sauce. Cover; bake 30 to 40 minutes or until heated through. Top enchiladas with remaining Tomatillo-Green Chile Sauce and feta cheese. Garnish with cilantro.

Makes 6 servings

Tomatillo-Green Chile Sauce

¾ pound fresh tomatillos *or* 2 cans (18 ounces each) whole tomatillos, drained
1 can (4 ounces) diced mild green chilies, drained
½ cup reduced-sodium chicken broth
½ teaspoon ground cumin
1 teaspoon dried oregano leaves, crushed
2 tablespoons chopped fresh cilantro (optional)

1. Place tomatillos in large saucepan; cover with water. Bring to a boil over high heat. Reduce heat to medium-high and simmer gently 20 to 30 minutes or until tomatillos are tender.

2. Place tomatillos, chilies, broth (omit broth if using canned tomatillos), cumin and oregano in food processor or blender; process until smooth. Return mixture to pan. Cover; heat over medium heat until bubbling. Stir in cilantro, if desired.

Makes about 3 cups

Cook's Tip: Herbs are a good way to add flavor to foods without adding calories, sodium or fat. This recipe combines oregano, cumin and fresh cilantro to pack it full of flavor.

Turkey Tamale Pie with Cornbread

2 tablespoons vegetable oil
1 small onion, chopped
1 small green bell pepper, chopped
1¼ pounds turkey cutlets, chopped
1 can (15¼ ounces) whole kernel corn, drained
1 can (15 ounces) kidney beans, drained
1 can (14½ ounces) stewed tomatoes
1 can (6 ounces) tomato paste
½ cup water
1 package (1.0 ounces) LAWRY'S® Taco Spices & Seasonings
1 can (4 ounces) chopped green chiles, drained
1 package (16 ounces) cornbread mix

In large skillet, heat oil. Add onion and bell pepper and cook 5 minutes. Add turkey and cook over medium-high heat 7 to 10 minutes or until no longer pink in center, stirring occasionally; reduce heat to low. Stir in corn, beans, stewed tomatoes, tomato paste, water, Taco Spices & Seasonings and green chiles. Cook over low heat 10 minutes, stirring occasionally. Pour mixture into lightly greased 13×9-inch baking pan. In medium bowl, prepare cornbread batter according to package directions. Spoon dollops of batter over turkey mixture. Spoon remaining batter into lightly greased muffin tins. Bake in 375°F oven 25 minutes for casserole (15 to 20 minutes for muffins) or until toothpick inserted into cornbread comes out clean.

Makes 8 to 10 servings

Serving Suggestion: Serve with a tossed green salad and your favorite cool beverage.

Hint: Cool muffins completely. Wrap tightly and freeze for later use, if desired.

One-Dish Meal

2 bags SUCCESS® Rice
  Vegetable cooking spray
1 cup cubed cooked turkey-
  ham*
1 cup (4 ounces) shredded low-
  fat Cheddar cheese
1 cup peas

*Or, use cooked turkey, ham or turkey franks.

Prepare rice according to package directions.

Spray 1-quart microwave-safe dish with cooking spray; set aside. Place rice in medium bowl. Add ham, cheese and peas; mix lightly. Spoon into prepared dish; smooth into even layer with spoon. Microwave on HIGH 1 minute; stir. Microwave 30 seconds or until thoroughly heated.

Makes 4 servings

Conventional Oven Directions:
Assemble casserole as directed. Spoon into ovenproof 1-quart baking dish sprayed with vegetable cooking spray. Bake at 350°F until thoroughly heated, about 15 to 20 minutes.

Spinach & Turkey Skillet

6 ounces turkey breast
  tenderloin
⅛ teaspoon salt
2 teaspoons olive oil
¼ cup chopped onion
2 cloves garlic, minced
⅓ cup uncooked rice
¾ teaspoon dried Italian
  seasoning
¼ teaspoon black pepper
1 cup chicken broth, divided
2 cups torn fresh spinach
⅔ cup diced plum tomatoes
3 tablespoons freshly grated
  Parmesan cheese

1. Cut turkey tenderloins into bite-size slices; sprinkle with salt. Heat oil in medium skillet over medium-high heat.

2. Add turkey slices; cook and stir until lightly browned. Remove from skillet. Reduce heat to low. Add onion and garlic; cook and stir until tender. Return turkey to skillet. Stir in rice, Italian seasoning and pepper.

3. Reserve 2 tablespoons chicken broth. Stir remaining broth into mixture in skillet. Bring to a boil. Reduce heat. Simmer, covered, 14 minutes. Stir in spinach and reserved broth. Cover and cook 2 to 3 minutes more or until liquid is absorbed and spinach is wilted. Stir in tomatoes. Heat through. Serve with Parmesan cheese.

Makes 2 servings

Spinach & Turkey Skillet

Tuscan Turkey Cutlets

1 pound turkey cutlets
¾ teaspoon salt, divided
¾ teaspoon black pepper, divided
3 teaspoons olive oil, divided
2 cups onions, coarsely chopped
1 cup carrots, coarsely chopped
3 to 4 cloves garlic, minced
½ teaspoon dried oregano
½ teaspoon dried thyme
1 (10-ounce) bag fresh spinach leaves, stems removed
1 (14½-ounce) can diced tomatoes, undrained
1 (19-ounce) can cannellini beans, drained and rinsed
¼ cup Parmesan cheese, divided

1. Place cutlets on cutting board and sprinkle with ¼ teaspoon salt and ¼ teaspoon pepper. Slice cutlets into ½-inch strips.

2. In 12-inch non-stick skillet over medium-high heat, sauté turkey strips in 1½ teaspoons oil, 4 to 5 minutes or until no longer pink (165°F). Remove from skillet; set aside.

3. Add remaining 1½ teaspoons oil to skillet. Sauté onion, carrots, garlic, oregano and thyme 5 minutes or until vegetables are tender. Gradually add spinach and stir an additional 2 minutes or until spinach is wilted, but not quite done. Add tomatoes and remaining ½ teaspoon salt and ½ teaspoon pepper; cook 2 minutes.

4. Stir in turkey strips and beans. Cook until heated through.

5. Serve topped with Parmesan cheese.   *Makes 4 servings*

Serving Suggestion: Serve over orzo, noodles or a whole grain such as quinoa.

*Favorite recipe from **National Turkey Federation***

Turkey-Spinach Manicotti

1 package (1.5 ounces) LAWRY'S® Original-Style Spaghetti Sauce Spices & Seasoning
1 can (28 ounces) whole tomatoes, cut up
1 can (8 ounces) tomato sauce
¼ cup chopped green onions
2 cups chopped fresh spinach
2 cups cooked, minced turkey or chicken
1 cup ricotta cheese
2 tablespoons milk
1 teaspoon LAWRY'S® Seasoned Pepper
½ teaspoon LAWRY'S® Garlic Powder with Parsley
8 manicotti shells, cooked and drained
⅓ cup grated Parmesan cheese

In medium saucepan, combine Spaghetti Sauce Spices & Seasoning, tomatoes, tomato sauce and onions. Bring to a boil over medium-high heat; reduce heat to low and cook, covered, 20 minutes, stirring occasionally. In medium bowl, combine spinach, turkey, ricotta cheese, milk, Seasoned Pepper and Garlic Powder with Parsley; mix well. Carefully spoon mixture into manicotti shells. Pour ½ of sauce in bottom of 12×8×2-inch baking dish. Place stuffed shells on top of sauce; pour remaining sauce over shells. Cover and bake in 375°F oven 30 minutes or until heated through. Sprinkle with Parmesan cheese.

Makes 4 to 8 servings

Serving Suggestion: Sprinkle with chopped parsley. Garnish with fresh basil leaves. Serve with garlic bread.

Hint: 1 package (10 ounces) frozen chopped spinach, thawed and drained, can be substituted for the fresh spinach.

Washington Apple Turkey Gyros

1 cup vertically sliced onion
1 cup thinly sliced red bell pepper
1 cup thinly sliced green bell pepper
2 tablespoons lemon juice
1 tablespoon vegetable oil
½ pound cooked turkey breast, cut into thin strips
1 medium Washington Golden Delicious or Winesap apple, cored and thinly sliced
8 pita rounds, lightly toasted
½ cup plain low fat yogurt

Cook and stir onion, bell peppers and lemon juice in oil in nonstick skillet until crisp-tender; stir in turkey and cook until heated through. Remove from heat; stir in apple. Fold pita in half and fill with apple mixture; drizzle with yogurt. Repeat with remaining ingredients. Serve warm.

Makes 8 servings

*Favorite recipe from **Washington Apple Commission***

Helpful Hints

Turkey breasts are sold whole or as halves. The breasts may be boneless, or with bone in. Prepare them by roasting or grilling. Or, purchase a thick slice of turkey from the supermarket deli and cut it into strips.

Tuscan Turkey Cutlets

Turkey-Tortilla Bake

9 (6-inch) corn tortillas
½ pound 93% fat-free ground turkey
½ cup chopped onion
¾ cup mild or medium taco sauce
1 can (4 ounces) chopped green chilies, drained
½ cup frozen corn, thawed
½ cup (2 ounces) shredded reduced-fat Cheddar cheese

1. Preheat oven to 400°F. Place tortillas on large baking sheet, overlapping tortillas as little as possible. Bake 4 minutes; turn tortillas. Continue baking 2 minutes or until crisp. Cool completely on wire rack.

2. Heat medium nonstick skillet over medium heat until hot. Add turkey and onion. Cook and stir 5 minutes or until turkey is browned and onion is tender. Add taco sauce, chilies and corn. Reduce heat and simmer 5 minutes.

3. Break 3 tortillas and arrange over bottom of 1½-quart casserole. Spoon half the turkey mixture over tortillas; sprinkle with half the cheese. Repeat layers. Bake 10 minutes or until cheese is melted and casserole is heated through. Break remaining tortillas and sprinkle over casserole. Garnish with sour cream, if desired.

Makes 4 servings

Prep and Cook Time: 30 minutes

Turkey Pot Pie

1 (1-pound) package frozen vegetables for stew, cooked according to package directions
1 cup frozen peas, cooked according to package directions
2 cups Cooked TURKEY from a TURKEY ROAST cut into ½-inch cubes (cook roast according to package directions)*
1 (12-ounce) jar non-fat turkey gravy
1 tablespoon dried parsley
1 teaspoon dried thyme
1 teaspoon dried rosemary
½ teaspoon salt
¼ teaspoon pepper
1 refrigerated pie crust (brought to room temperature)

Leftover cooked turkey may be substituted for the pre-packaged turkey roast.

1. Drain any cooking liquid from stew vegetables and peas.

2. Add turkey cubes, gravy, parsley, thyme, rosemary, salt and pepper to vegetables in oven-safe 2-quart cooking dish.

3. Unfold pie crust and place on top of dish, trimming edges to approximately 1 inch and securing edges to dish. Make several 1-inch slits on crust to allow steam to escape.

4. Bake in preheated 400°F oven for 25 to 30 minutes or until crust is brown and mixture is hot and bubbly.

Makes 5 servings

*Favorite recipe from **National Turkey Federation***

Turkey Wild Rice Chili

1 tablespoon oil
1 medium onion, chopped
1 clove garlic, minced
1¼ pounds turkey breast slices, cut into ½-inch pieces
2 cups cooked wild rice
1 can (15 ounces) great Northern beans, drained
1 can (11 ounces) white corn
2 cans (4 ounces each) diced green chilies
1 can (14½ ounces) low-sodium chicken broth
1 teaspoon ground cumin
Hot pepper sauce (optional)
4 ounces low-fat Monterey Jack Cheese, shredded
Parsley (optional)

Heat oil in large skillet over medium heat; add onion and garlic. Cook and stir until onion is tender. Add turkey, wild rice, beans, corn, chilies, broth and cumin. Cover and simmer over low heat 30 minutes or until turkey is tender. Stir in hot pepper sauce to taste. Serve with shredded cheese. Garnish with parsley, if desired.

Makes 8 servings

*Favorite recipe from **Minnesota Cultivated Wild Rice Council***

Helpful Hints

The next time you make a casserole, assemble and bake two. Allow one to cool completely, then wrap it in heavy-duty foil and freeze it. To reheat a frozen 2-quart casserole, unwrap it and microwave it, covered, at HIGH for 20 to 30 minutes, stirring once or twice during cooking.

Turkey-Tortilla Bake

Pizza Rice Casserole

1 bag SUCCESS® Rice
1 pound ground turkey or lean
  ground beef
½ cup chopped green bell
  pepper
½ cup chopped onion
1 jar (15½ ounces) pizza sauce
1 cup water
1 can (4 ounces) mushroom
  pieces, drained
¼ cup flour
½ cup chopped turkey ham
½ teaspoon garlic salt
1 cup (4 ounces) shredded
  Mozzarella cheese

Prepare rice according to package
directions.

Brown ground turkey with green
pepper and onion in large skillet or
saucepan, stirring occasionally to
separate turkey. Add rice, pizza
sauce, water, mushrooms, flour, ham
and garlic salt; heat thoroughly,
stirring occasionally. Sprinkle with
cheese.   *Makes 4 servings*

Turnip Shepherd's Pie

1 pound small turnips,* peeled
  and cut into ½-inch cubes
1 pound lean ground turkey
⅓ cup dry bread crumbs
¼ cup chopped onion
¼ cup ketchup
1 egg
½ teaspoon salt
½ teaspoon pepper
½ teaspoon beau monde
  seasoning
⅓ cup half-and-half
1 tablespoon butter or
  margarine
  Salt and black pepper
1 tablespoon chopped fresh
  parsley
¼ cup shredded sharp Cheddar
  cheese

*For Rutabaga Shepherd's Pie, use 1 pound
rutabagas in place of turnips.*

Preheat oven to 400°F. Place turnips
in large saucepan; cover with water.
Cover and bring to a boil; reduce heat
to medium-low. Simmer 20 minutes or
until fork-tender.

Mix turkey, crumbs, onion, ketchup,
egg, salt, pepper and seasoning. Pat
on bottom and side of 9-inch pie pan.
Bake 20 to 30 minutes until turkey is
no longer pink. Blot with paper towel
to remove any drippings.

Drain cooked turnips. Beat turnips
with electric mixer until smooth,
blending in half-and-half and butter.
Season with salt and pepper to taste.
Fill meat shell with turnip mixture;
sprinkle with parsley, then cheese.
Return to oven until cheese melts.
Garnish as desired.
          Makes 4 main-dish servings

Turkey with Mustard Sauce

1 tablespoon butter or
  margarine
1 pound turkey cutlets
1 cup BIRDS EYE® frozen Mixed
  Vegetables
1 box (9 ounces) BIRDS EYE®
  frozen Pearl Onions in
  Cream Sauce
1 teaspoon spicy brown
  mustard

• In large nonstick skillet, melt butter
over medium-high heat. Add turkey;
cook until browned on both sides.

• Add mixed vegetables, onions with
cream sauce and mustard; bring to
boil. Reduce heat to medium-low;
cover and simmer 6 to 8 minutes or
until vegetables are tender and turkey
is no longer pink in center.
          Makes 4 servings

Serving Suggestion: Serve with a
fresh garden salad.

Prep Time: 5 minutes
Cook Time: 15 minutes

Turkey-Spaghetti Pie

6 ounces spaghetti, cooked
  according to package
  directions and drained
1 egg white, lightly beaten
⅓ cup parmesan cheese
2½ tablespoons margarine,
  melted, divided
1 cup chopped onion
1 clove garlic, minced
1 package (10 ounces) frozen
  mixed vegetables, defrosted
  and drained
2 tablespoons flour
1 teaspoon poultry seasoning
⅛ teaspoon pepper
1½ cups skim milk
2 cups cubed Cooked TURKEY

1. Preheat oven to 350°F.

2. In medium-size bowl combine
spaghetti, egg white, cheese, and
1 tablespoon margarine. In well
greased 9-inch pie plate, press pasta
mixture over bottom and up sides of
pie plate. Grease 12×10-inch piece
aluminum foil. Press foil, greased-side
down, next to pasta shell. Bake 25 to
30 minutes or until pie shell is set and
slightly browned on edges.

3. In medium-size saucepan, over
medium-high heat, sauté onion and
garlic in remaining margarine 2 to
3 minutes or until onion is translucent.
Stir in vegetables and cook for
1 minute. Sprinkle flour, poultry
seasoning and pepper over mixture,
stirring to combine. Remove pan from
heat.

4. Slowly pour milk over vegetable
mixture, stirring constantly. Return
saucepan to medium heat; cook and
stir until mixture is thickened. Add
turkey, reduce heat to medium-low
and simmer 5 minutes or until heated
throughout. Pour mixture into cooked
pasta shell.

5. To serve, cut spaghetti pie into six
wedges.   *Makes 6 servings*

*Favorite recipe from **National Turkey
Federation***

Turnip Shepherd's Pie

Pasta and Spinach with Sun-Dried Tomatoes

⅓ pound BUTTERBALL® Oven Roasted Deli Turkey Breast, sliced thin and cut into strips
¼ cup sun-dried tomatoes, packed in oil, drained and chopped, oil reserved
1 clove garlic, minced
5 ounces fresh spinach, rinsed
2 ounces bow tie pasta, cooked and drained
¼ cup Italian salad dressing
3 tablespoons feta cheese, divided

Pour 1 teaspoon reserved sun-dried tomato oil in nonstick skillet. Add turkey, tomatoes and garlic. Cook and stir over medium heat 2 minutes. Add spinach, pasta, dressing and 2 tablespoons cheese; toss to coat. Cover; warm over low heat for about 1 minute. Sprinkle with remaining 1 tablespoon cheese.

Makes 2 servings

Prep Time: 20 minutes

Wild Rice Meatball Primavera

1 pound ground turkey
½ cup seasoned bread crumbs
1 egg, beaten
2 tablespoons oil
1 can (10¾ ounces) condensed cream of mushroom soup
2 cups water
1 package (16 ounces) frozen broccoli medley, thawed
1 box UNCLE BEN'S® Long Grain & Wild Rice Fast Cook Recipe

1. Combine turkey, bread crumbs and egg; mix well. Shape into 1¼- to 1½-inch meatballs (about 20 to 22 meatballs).

2. Heat oil in large skillet over medium-high heat until hot. Cook meatballs 6 to 7 minutes or until brown on all sides. Drain on paper towels.

3. Combine soup and water in skillet; bring to a boil. Add meatballs, vegetables and contents of seasoning packet, reserving rice. Cover; reduce heat and simmer 5 minutes, stirring occasionally.

4. Add reserved rice to skillet; mix well. Cover; cook 5 minutes more or until hot. Remove from heat; stir well. Cover and let stand 5 minutes before serving.   *Makes 6 servings*

Turkey Meatball & Olive Casserole

2 cups uncooked rotini pasta
½ pound ground turkey
¼ cup dry bread crumbs
1 egg, lightly beaten
2 teaspoons dried minced onion
2 teaspoons white wine Worcestershire sauce
½ teaspoon dried Italian seasoning
½ teaspoon salt
⅛ teaspoon black pepper
1 tablespoon vegetable oil
1 can (10¾ ounces) condensed cream of celery soup, undiluted
½ cup low-fat plain yogurt
¾ cup pimiento-stuffed green olives, sliced
3 tablespoons Italian-style bread crumbs
1 tablespoon margarine or butter, melted
Paprika (optional)

Preheat oven to 350°F. Spray 2-quart round casserole with nonstick cooking spray.

Cook pasta according to package directions until al dente. Drain and set aside.

Meanwhile, combine turkey, bread crumbs, egg, onion, Worcestershire sauce, Italian seasoning, salt and pepper in medium bowl. Shape mixture into ½-inch meatballs.

Heat oil in medium skillet over high heat until hot. Add meatballs in single layer; cook until lightly browned on all sides and still pink in centers, turning frequently. Do not overcook. Remove from skillet; drain on paper towels.

Mix soup and yogurt in large bowl. Add pasta, meatballs and olives; stir gently to combine. Transfer to prepared dish.

Combine bread crumbs and margarine in small bowl; sprinkle evenly over casserole. Sprinkle lightly with paprika, if desired.

Bake, covered, 30 minutes. Uncover and bake 12 minutes or until meatballs are no longer pink in centers and casserole is hot and bubbly.   *Makes 6 to 8 servings*

Wild Rice Meatball Primavera

Southwest Stir-Fry

- 1 bag SUCCESS® Rice
- 1 pound ground turkey
- 1 medium onion, chopped
- 1 package (1.7 ounces) taco seasoning mix
- 1 can (15¼ ounces) kidney beans, drained
- 1 can (8 ounces) Mexican-style corn, drained
- ½ cup fat-free sour cream

Prepare rice according to package directions.

Brown ground turkey with onion in large skillet, stirring occasionally to separate turkey; drain. Stir in taco seasoning. Add rice, beans and corn; heat thoroughly, stirring occasionally. Stir in sour cream.

Makes 4 servings

Chili Turkey Loaf `Slow Cooker`

- 2 pounds ground turkey
- 1 cup chopped onion
- ⅔ cup Italian-style seasoned dry bread crumbs
- ½ cup chopped green bell pepper
- ½ cup chili sauce
- 2 eggs, lightly beaten
- 2 tablespoons horseradish mustard
- 4 cloves garlic, minced
- 1 teaspoon salt
- ½ teaspoon dried Italian seasoning
- ¼ teaspoon black pepper
  Prepared salsa (optional)

Slow Cooker Directions

Make foil handles for loaf using technique described below. Mix all ingredients except salsa in large bowl. Shape into round loaf and place on foil strips. Transfer to bottom of slow cooker using foil handles. Cover and cook on LOW 4½ to 5 hours or until juices run clear and temperature is 170°F. Remove loaf from slow cooker using foil handles.

Place on serving plate. Let stand 5 minutes before serving. Cut into wedges and top with salsa, if desired. Serve with steamed carrots, if desired.   *Makes 8 servings*

Foil Handles: Tear off three 18×2-inch strips of heavy foil or use regular foil folded to double thickness. Crisscross foil strips in spoke design and place in slow cooker to allow for easy removal of turkey loaf.

Turkey Baked with Beans and Pasta

- 1 pound ½-inch slices deli-cut Honey Roasted Turkey Breast, cut into ½-inch cubes
- 1 (15½-ounce) can butter beans, drained
- 1 (15-ounce) can black beans, drained
- 1 (14½-ounce) can diced tomatoes, undrained
- 1 cup orzo, cooked according to package directions (for only 7 minutes)
- 1 cup chopped onion
- ¼ cup chopped black olives
- 1 teaspoon dried oregano leaves
  Nonstick vegetable cooking spray
- 4 ounces crumbled feta cheese with basil and tomato or plain

1. Preheat oven to 350°F. In large mixing bowl, combine turkey cubes, beans, tomatoes, cooked orzo, onion, olives and oregano.

2. Spray 2-quart casserole with cooking spray. Pour turkey mixture into prepared casserole. Sprinkle with cheese; cover with foil.

3. Bake 20 minutes; remove foil and continue baking until cheese is lightly browned. Serve hot.

Makes 4 servings

*Favorite recipe from **California Poultry Federation***

Vegetable Pasta Italiano

- ½ pound lean ground turkey
- 1 DOLE® Red Bell Pepper, seeded, sliced
- 1 tablespoon paprika
- 1 can (14½ ounces) crushed tomatoes
- 1 can (14½ ounces) reduced sodium chicken broth
- 2 cups uncooked bow tie pasta
- 2 cups DOLE® Broccoli, cut into florets
- 1 cup DOLE® Cauliflower, cut into florets
  Savory Topping (recipe follows)

- In 12-inch nonstick skillet, brown turkey 2 minutes.

- Stir in red pepper strips and paprika. Reduce heat to low, stirring 2 minutes longer.

- Stir in tomatoes, chicken broth and pasta. Bring to boil. Reduce heat to low, cover and simmer 15 minutes. Arrange broccoli and cauliflower on top. Cover, simmer 10 minutes or until pasta is soft.

- Sprinkle with Savory Topping. Let stand 3 minutes before serving.

Makes 6 servings

Savory Topping

- ¼ cup seasoned dry bread crumbs
- ¼ cup grated Parmesan cheese
- ¼ cup minced parsley

Combine all ingredients.

Chili Turkey Loaf

Fabulous Fish

Mediterranean Cod

**1 bag (16 ounces) BIRDS EYE®
  frozen Farm Fresh Mixtures
  Broccoli, Green Beans,
  Pearl Onions and Red
  Peppers**
**1 can (14½ ounces) stewed
  tomatoes**
½ teaspoon dried basil leaves
**1 pound cod fillets, cut into
  serving pieces**
½ cup orange juice, divided
2 tablespoons all-purpose flour
**¼ cup sliced black olives
  (optional)**

• Combine vegetables, tomatoes and basil in large skillet. Bring to boil over medium-high heat.

• Place cod on vegetables. Pour ¼ cup orange juice over fish. Cover and cook 5 to 7 minutes or until fish is tender and flakes with fork.

• Remove cod and keep warm. Blend flour with remaining ¼ cup orange juice; stir into skillet. Cook until liquid is thickened and vegetables are coated.

• Serve fish with vegetables; sprinkle with olives.

Makes about 4 servings

Serving Suggestion: Serve with rice or couscous.

Prep Time: 5 minutes
Cook Time: 15 minutes

Creamy Scalloped Potatoes and Tuna

2 cups milk
2 cups whipping cream
2 cloves garlic, minced
**2½ pounds (about 6 medium)
  white or russet potatoes**
¾ teaspoon salt
½ teaspoon white pepper
**1 tablespoon butter or
  margarine**
**1 (7-ounce) pouch of STARKIST®
  Premium Albacore or Chunk
  Light Tuna**
**1½ cups shredded mozzarella
  cheese**

In 3-quart saucepan over medium heat, heat milk, cream and garlic while preparing potatoes. Peel potatoes; slice about ⅛ to ¼ inch thick. Add potatoes, salt and white pepper to milk mixture; heat to simmering.

Grease 11×7-inch casserole with butter; spoon potato-milk mixture into dish. Bake in 350°F oven 25 minutes; remove from oven. Add tuna, stirring gently; top with cheese. Bake 35 more minutes or until potatoes are cooked through and top is golden brown. Let stand, covered, about 15 minutes to thicken.

Makes 6 to 8 servings

Prep Time: 70 minutes

Mediterranean Cod

No-Fuss Tuna Quiche

- 1 unbaked 9-inch deep-dish pastry shell
- 1½ cups low-fat milk
- 3 extra large eggs
- ⅓ cup chopped green onions
- 1 tablespoon chopped drained pimiento
- 1 teaspoon dried basil leaves, crushed
- ½ teaspoon salt
- 1 (3-ounce) pouch of STARKIST® Premium Albacore or Chunk Light Tuna
- ½ cup (2 ounces) shredded low-fat Cheddar cheese
- 8 spears (4 inches each) broccoli

Preheat oven to 450°F. Bake pastry shell for 5 minutes; remove to rack to cool. *Reduce oven temperature to 325°F.* For filling, in large bowl whisk together milk and eggs. Stir in onions, pimiento, basil and salt. Fold in tuna and cheese. Pour into prebaked pastry shell. Bake at 325°F for 30 minutes.

Meanwhile, in a saucepan steam broccoli spears over simmering water for 5 minutes. Drain; set aside. After 30 minutes baking time, arrange broccoli spears, spoke-fashion, over quiche. Bake 25 to 35 minutes more or until a knife inserted 2 inches from center comes out clean. Let stand for 5 minutes. Cut into 8 wedges, centering a broccoli spear in each wedge.   *Makes 8 servings*

Note: If desired, 1 cup chopped broccoli may be added to the filling before baking.

Herb-Baked Fish & Rice

- 1½ cups hot chicken bouillon
- ½ cup uncooked regular rice
- ¼ teaspoon Italian seasoning
- ¼ teaspoon garlic powder
- 1 package (10 ounces) frozen chopped broccoli, thawed and drained
- 1⅓ cups *French's®* French Fried Onions, divided
- 1 tablespoon grated Parmesan cheese
- 1 pound unbreaded fish fillets, thawed if frozen
  Paprika (optional)
- ½ cup (2 ounces) shredded Cheddar cheese

Preheat oven to 375°F. In 12×8-inch baking dish, combine hot bouillon, uncooked rice and seasonings. Bake, covered, at 375°F for 10 minutes. Top with broccoli, ⅔ cup French Fried Onions and the Parmesan cheese. Place fish fillets diagonally down center of dish; sprinkle fish lightly with paprika. Bake, covered, at 375°F for 20 to 25 minutes or until fish flakes easily with fork. Stir rice. Top fish with Cheddar cheese and remaining ⅔ cup French Fried Onions; bake, uncovered, 3 minutes or until onions are golden brown.

Makes 3 to 4 servings

Microwave Directions: In 12×8-inch microwave-safe dish, prepare rice mixture as above, except reduce bouillon to 1¼ cups. Cook, covered, on HIGH 5 minutes, stirring halfway through cooking time. Stir in broccoli, ⅔ cup onions and the Parmesan cheese. Arrange fish fillets in single layer on top of rice mixture; sprinkle fish lightly with paprika. Cook, covered, on MEDIUM (50-60%) 18 to 20 minutes or until fish flakes easily with fork and rice is done. Rotate dish halfway through cooking time. Top fish with Cheddar cheese and remaining ⅔ cup onions; cook, uncovered, on HIGH 1 minute or until cheese melts. Let stand 5 minutes.

By-the-Sea Casserole

- 1 bag (16 ounces) BIRDS EYE® frozen Mixed Vegetables
- 2 cans (6 ounces each) tuna in water, drained
- 1 cup uncooked instant rice
- 1 can (10¾ ounces) cream of celery soup
- 1 cup 1% milk
- 1 cup cheese-flavored fish-shaped crackers

- In medium bowl, combine vegetables and tuna.

- Stir in rice, soup and milk.

- Place tuna mixture in 1½-quart microwave-safe casserole dish; cover and microwave on HIGH 6 minutes. Stir; microwave, covered, 6 to 8 minutes more or until rice is tender.

- Stir casserole and sprinkle with crackers.   *Makes 6 servings*

Prep Time: 10 minutes
Cook Time: 15 minutes

By-the-Sea Casserole

Tuna Pot Pie

1 tablespoon butter
1 small onion, chopped
1 can (10¾ ounces) condensed cream of potato soup
¼ cup milk
½ teaspoon dried thyme leaves
¼ teaspoon salt
⅛ teaspoon black pepper
1 package (16 ounces) frozen vegetable medley, such as broccoli, green beans, carrots and red peppers, thawed
2 cans (6 ounces each) albacore tuna in water, drained
2 tablespoons chopped fresh parsley
1 can (8 ounces) refrigerated crescent roll dough

1. Preheat oven to 350°F. Spray 11×7-inch baking dish with nonstick cooking spray.

2. Melt butter in large skillet over medium heat. Add onion; cook and stir 2 minutes or until onion is tender. Add soup, milk, thyme, salt and pepper; cook and stir 3 to 4 minutes or until thick and bubbly. Stir in vegetables, tuna and parsley. Pour mixture into prepared dish.

3. Unroll crescent roll dough and divide into triangles. Place triangles over tuna filling without overlapping dough. Bake, uncovered, 20 minutes or until triangles are golden brown. Let stand 5 minutes before serving.

Makes 6 servings

Cook's Nook: Experiment with different vegetable combinations and create an exciting recipe every time. Just substitute a new medley for the one listed and enjoy the results.

Bacon-Tuna Parmesano

½ cup milk
2 tablespoons margarine or butter
1 package (4.8 ounces) PASTA RONI® Parmesano
1 package (10 ounces) frozen peas
1 can (6 ounces) white tuna in water, drained, flaked
4 slices crisply cooked bacon, crumbled
½ cup sliced green onions

Microwave Directions

1. In round 3-quart microwaveable glass casserole, combine 1⅔ cups water, milk and margarine. Microwave, uncovered, on HIGH 4 to 5 minutes or until boiling.

2. Stir in pasta, Special Seasonings, frozen peas, tuna, bacon and onions.

3. Microwave, uncovered, on HIGH 9 to 10 minutes or until peas are tender, stirring after 3 minutes.

4. Cover; let stand 3 to 4 minutes. Sauce will thicken upon standing. Stir before serving.

Makes 4 servings

Tuna Mac and Cheese

1 package (7¼ ounces) macaroni and cheese dinner
1 (7-ounce) pouch of STARKIST® Premium Albacore or Chunk Light Tuna
1 cup frozen peas
½ cup shredded Cheddar cheese
½ cup milk
1 teaspoon Italian herb seasoning
¼ teaspoon garlic powder (optional)
1 tablespoon grated Parmesan cheese

Prepare macaroni and cheese dinner according to package directions. Add remaining ingredients except Parmesan cheese. Pour into 1½-quart microwavable serving dish. Cover with vented plastic wrap; microwave on HIGH 2 minutes. Stir; continue heating on HIGH 2½ to 3½ more minutes or until cheese is melted and mixture is heated through. Sprinkle with Parmesan cheese.

Makes 5 to 6 servings

Prep Time: 20 minutes

Potato Tuna au Gratin

1 package (5 or 6 ounces) Cheddar cheese au gratin potatoes
1 (7-ounce) pouch of STARKIST® Premium Albacore or Chunk Light Tuna
¼ cup chopped onion
1 package (16 ounces) frozen broccoli cuts, cooked and drained
¾ cup shredded Cheddar cheese
¼ cup breadcrumbs

Prepare potatoes according to package directions. While potatoes are standing, stir in tuna and onion. Arrange cooked broccoli in bottom of lightly greased 11×7-inch baking dish. Pour tuna-potato mixture over broccoli; top with cheese. Broil 3 to 4 minutes or until cheese is bubbly. Sprinkle breadcrumbs over top.

Makes 6 servings

Prep Time: 35 minutes

Tuna Pot Pie

Lemony Dill Salmon and Shell Casserole

Nonstick cooking spray
1½ cups sliced mushrooms
⅓ cup sliced green onions
1 clove garlic, minced
2 cups fat-free (skim) milk
3 tablespoons all-purpose flour
1 tablespoon grated lemon peel
¾ teaspoon dried dill weed
¼ teaspoon salt
⅛ teaspoon black pepper
1½ cups frozen green peas
6 ounces uncooked medium shell pasta, cooked, rinsed and drained
1 can (7½ ounces) salmon, drained and flaked

1. Preheat oven to 350°F.

2. Spray medium nonstick saucepan with cooking spray; heat over medium heat until hot. Add mushrooms, onions and garlic; cook and stir 5 minutes or until vegetables are tender.

3. Whisk milk into flour in medium bowl until smooth. Stir in lemon peel, dill weed, salt and pepper. Stir into saucepan; heat over medium-high heat 5 to 8 minutes or until thickened, stirring constantly. Remove saucepan from heat. Stir in peas, pasta and salmon. Pour pasta mixture into 2-quart casserole.

4. Bake, covered, 35 to 40 minutes. Serve immediately. Garnish as desired.   *Makes 6 servings*

StarKist® Swiss Potato Pie

4 cups frozen shredded hash brown potatoes, thawed
2 cups shredded Swiss cheese
1 cup milk
4 large eggs, beaten
½ to 1 cup chopped green onions, including tops
½ cup chopped green bell pepper (optional)
½ cup sour cream
1 (3-ounce) pouch of STARKIST® Premium Albacore Tuna
½ teaspoon garlic powder

In large bowl, combine all ingredients. Pour into lightly greased deep 10-inch pie plate. Bake in 350°F oven 1 hour and 20 minutes or until golden and crusty. Let stand a few minutes before slicing into serving portions.   *Makes 6 servings*

Prep & Cook Time: 90 minutes

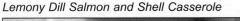

Lemony Dill Salmon and Shell Casserole

Mediterranean-Style Tuna Noodle Casserole

1 tablespoon Lucini Premium Select extra virgin olive oil
4 cloves garlic, minced
2 large onions, chopped (1½ cups)
12 ounces mushrooms, chopped (4 cups)
2 large tomatoes, chopped
1 red bell pepper, diced (1 cup)
1 green bell pepper, diced (1 cup)
1 to 2 teaspoons ground red pepper
1 cup chopped fresh cilantro leaves or ¼ cup dried oregano leaves
2 tablespoons dried marjoram or oregano leaves
1 pound JARLSBERG LITE™ cheese, shredded (4 cups)
1 (16-ounce) can black-eyed peas, rinsed and drained
2 (7-ounce) cans tuna, drained and flaked
6 ounces cooked pasta (tricolor rotelle, bows or macaroni)

Preheat oven to 350°F. Heat oil in large skillet; sauté garlic until golden. Add onions; sauté until transparent, about 2 minutes on medium-high heat.

Add mushrooms, tomatoes and bell peppers, stirring 3 to 5 minutes or until mushrooms begin to brown. Add ground red pepper, cilantro and marjoram.

Toss with cheese, peas, tuna and pasta. Pour into greased baking dish. Bake, covered, 45 minutes or until cooked through.

Makes 6 to 8 servings

Serving Suggestion: Serve with crusty bread and homemade coleslaw.

Crunchy Tuna Squares

1 (7-ounce) pouch of STARKIST® Premium Albacore Tuna
1 cup chopped celery
1 cup chopped roasted cashews
½ cup drained sliced water chestnuts
½ cup chopped green onions, including tops
⅓ cup chopped drained roasted red peppers
1½ cups shredded Cheddar cheese, divided
½ cup mayonnaise or light mayonnaise
½ cup sour cream or light sour cream
2 tablespoons lemon juice
¾ teaspoon seasoned salt
1 cup cheese crackers, crushed into coarse crumbs

In medium bowl, place tuna, celery, cashews, water chestnuts, onions, peppers and 1 cup cheese; mix lightly with fork. In small bowl, whisk together mayonnaise, sour cream, lemon juice and seasoned salt. Add to tuna mixture; mix gently.

Spoon into greased 11×7-inch baking pan. Sprinkle with crushed cracker crumbs; top with remaining ½ cup cheese. Bake in 450°F oven 12 to 15 minutes or until mixture bubbles and begins to brown. Let stand several minutes before cutting into 6 squares.

Makes 6 servings

Prep Time: 20 minutes

Tag-Along Tuna Bake

3 to 4 tablespoons butter or margarine, softened
12 slices bread
1 can (12½ ounces) water-packed tuna, drained and flaked
1 cup chopped celery
1⅓ cups *French's®* French Fried Onions, divided
2 cups milk
1 cup mayonnaise
4 eggs, slightly beaten
1 can (10¾ ounces) condensed cream of mushroom soup
3 slices (¾ ounce each) processed American cheese, cut diagonally into halves

Butter 1 side of each bread slice; arrange 6 slices, buttered-side down in 13×9-inch baking dish. Layer tuna, celery and ⅔ cup French Fried Onions evenly over bread. Top with remaining bread slices, buttered side down. In medium bowl, combine milk, mayonnaise, eggs and soup; mix well. Pour evenly over layers in baking dish; cover and refrigerate overnight. Bake, covered, at 350°F for 30 minutes. Uncover and bake 15 minutes or until center is set. Arrange cheese slices down center of casserole, overlapping slightly, points all in 1 direction. Top with remaining ⅔ cup onions; bake, uncovered, 5 minutes or until onions are golden brown.

Makes 8 servings

Flounder Fillets over Zesty Lemon Rice

¼ cup butter
3 tablespoons fresh lemon juice
2 teaspoons chicken bouillon granules
½ teaspoon black pepper
1 package (10 ounces) frozen chopped broccoli, thawed
1 cup cooked rice
1 cup (4 ounces) shredded sharp Cheddar cheese
1 pound flounder fillets
½ teaspoon paprika

1. Preheat oven to 375°F. Spray 2-quart square casserole with nonstick cooking spray.

2. Melt butter in small saucepan over medium heat. Add lemon juice, bouillon and pepper; cook and stir 2 minutes or until bouillon dissolves.

3. Combine broccoli, rice, cheese and ¼ cup lemon sauce in medium bowl; spread on bottom of prepared dish. Place fillets over rice mixture. Pour remaining lemon sauce over fillets.

4. Bake, uncovered, 20 minutes or until fish flakes easily when tested with fork. Sprinkle evenly with paprika.

Makes 6 servings

Helpful Hints

When buying fish fillets and steaks, look for those with moist flesh and shiny skin. They should have a mild, slightly oceanlike odor rather than a fishy or sour smell. Store fresh fish in the coldest part of the refrigerator.

Old-Fashioned Tuna Noodle Casserole

¼ cup plain dry bread crumbs
3 tablespoons margarine or butter, melted and divided
1 tablespoon finely chopped parsley
½ cup chopped onion
½ cup chopped celery
1 cup water
1 cup milk
1 package LIPTON® Noodles & Sauce—Butter
2 cans (6 ounces each) tuna, drained and flaked

In small bowl, thoroughly combine bread crumbs, 1 tablespoon margarine and parsley; set aside.

In medium saucepan, melt remaining 2 tablespoons margarine over medium heat and cook onion and celery, stirring occasionally, 2 minutes or until onion is tender. Add water and milk; bring to the boiling point. Stir in Noodles & Sauce—Butter. Continue boiling over medium heat, stirring occasionally, 8 minutes or until noodles are tender. Stir in tuna. Turn into greased 1-quart casserole, then top with bread crumb mixture. Broil until bread crumbs are golden.

Makes about 4 servings

Biscuit-Topped Tuna Bake

2 tablespoons vegetable oil
½ cup chopped onion
½ cup chopped celery
1 (7-ounce) pouch of STARKIST® Premium Albacore or Chunk Light Tuna
1 can (10¾ ounces) condensed cream of potato soup
1 package (10 ounces) frozen peas and carrots, thawed
¾ cup milk
¼ teaspoon ground black pepper
¼ teaspoon garlic powder
1 can (7½ ounces) refrigerator flaky biscuits

In large skillet, heat oil over medium-high heat; sauté onion and celery until onion is soft. Add remaining ingredients except biscuits; heat thoroughly. Transfer mixture to 1½-quart casserole. Arrange biscuits around top edge of dish; bake in 400°F oven 10 to 15 minutes or until biscuits are golden brown.

Makes 4 to 6 servings

Prep and Cook Time: 25 minutes

Mushroom and Tuna Bake

1 can (10¾ ounces) cream of celery soup
1 cup milk
1 jar (4 ounces) sliced mushrooms, drained
½ cup grated Parmesan cheese, divided
1 teaspoon dried Italian herb blend
½ teaspoon seasoned salt
⅛ to ¼ teaspoon garlic powder
1 (7-ounce) pouch of STARKIST® Premium Albacore or Chunk Light Tuna
3 cups cooked egg noodles
1 cup crispy rice cereal

In medium saucepan, combine soup and milk; blend well. Add mushrooms, ¼ cup Parmesan cheese, Italian herb blend, seasoned salt, garlic powder and tuna; cook over low heat until heated through. Remove from heat; stir in egg noodles. Transfer mixture to lightly greased 11×7-inch baking dish. Top with remaining ¼ cup Parmesan cheese and cereal. Bake in 350°F oven 30 minutes.

Makes 6 servings

Prep Time: 40 minutes

Flounder Fillets over Zesty Lemon Rice

Idaho Potato & Tuna Stove-Top Casserole

2½ pounds Idaho Potatoes, scrubbed and cut into bite-sized cubes (about 7 cups)
1 (10-ounce) package frozen peas and carrots
1 (12-ounce) can tuna packed in water, drained
1 (10¾-ounce) can condensed Cheddar cheese soup
¼ teaspoon garlic powder
¼ teaspoon black pepper

1. Bring 1½ quarts of water to a boil in medium saucepan. Add potatoes. Return to a boil and cook 5 minutes.

2. Add frozen vegetables. Return to a boil and cook 2 minutes (or to desired tenderness). Drain.

3. Stir tuna, soup and seasonings into same saucepan. Add hot potato mixture. Stir and serve. (Note: If necessary, reheat on very low heat. Add water if needed.)

Makes 6 servings

Serving Suggestion: Serve with green salad and vinaigrette dressing.

Favorite recipe from **Idaho Potato Commission**

Tuna and Pasta Frittata

1 tablespoon olive oil
2 cups cooked spaghetti
4 large eggs
¼ cup prepared pesto sauce
2 tablespoons milk
1 (3-ounce) pouch of STARKIST® Premium Albacore or Chunk Light Tuna
½ cup shredded mozzarella cheese

Preheat broiler. In medium ovenproof skillet, heat oil over medium-high heat; sauté spaghetti. In bowl, combine eggs, pesto sauce and milk; blend well. Add tuna; pour mixture over hot spaghetti. Cook over medium-low heat, stirring occasionally until eggs are almost completely set. Sprinkle cheese over cooked eggs; place under broiler until cheese is bubbly and golden. Serve hot or at room temperature.

Makes 2 to 4 servings

Prep Time: 8 minutes

Tuna Vegetable Medley

8 ounces cooked egg noodles
1 package (10 ounces) frozen chopped broccoli, thawed and well drained
1 package (10 ounces) frozen carrots, thawed and well drained
1 cup corn
1 can (10¾ ounces) cream of mushroom soup
1 (7-ounce) pouch of STARKIST® Premium Albacore or Chunk Light Tuna
⅔ cup milk
1 cup shredded Swiss, Cheddar or Monterey Jack Cheese
Salt and pepper to taste
¼ cup grated Parmesan cheese

In large bowl, combine all ingredients except Parmesan cheese; mix well. Pour mixture into 2-quart baking dish; top with Parmesan cheese. Bake in 400°F oven 20 to 30 minutes or until thoroughly heated and golden on top.

Makes 6 servings

Prep Time: 40 minutes

Tempting Tuna Parmesano

2 large cloves garlic
1 package (9 ounces) refrigerated fresh angel hair pasta
¼ cup butter or margarine
1 cup whipping cream
1 cup frozen peas
¼ teaspoon salt
1 can (6 ounces) white tuna in water, drained
¼ cup grated Parmesan cheese, plus additional cheese for serving
Black pepper

1. Fill large deep skillet ¾ full with water. Cover and bring to a boil over high heat. Meanwhile, peel and mince garlic.

2. Add pasta to skillet; boil 1 to 2 minutes or until pasta is al dente. Do not overcook. Drain; set aside.

3. Add butter and garlic to skillet; cook over medium-high heat until butter is melted and sizzling. Stir in cream, peas and salt; bring to a boil.

4. Break tuna into chunks and stir into skillet with ¼ cup cheese. Return pasta to skillet. Cook until heated through; toss gently. Serve with additional cheese and pepper to taste.   *Makes 2 to 3 servings*

Serving Suggestion: Serve with a tossed romaine and tomato salad with Italian dressing.

Prep and Cook Time: 16 minutes

Tempting Tuna Parmesano

Mom's Tuna Casserole

Slow Cooker

- 2 cans (12 ounces each) tuna, drained and flaked
- 3 cups diced celery
- 3 cups crushed potato chips, divided
- 6 hard-cooked eggs, chopped
- 1 can (10¾ ounces) condensed cream of mushroom soup, undiluted
- 1 can (10¾ ounces) condensed cream of celery soup, undiluted
- 1 cup mayonnaise
- 1 teaspoon dried tarragon leaves
- 1 teaspoon black pepper

Slow Cooker Directions

Combine all ingredients, except ½ cup potato chips, in slow cooker; stir well. Top mixture with remaining ½ cup potato chips. Cover and cook on LOW 5 to 8 hours.

Makes 8 servings

Fish Burritos

- PAM® No-Stick Cooking Spray
- 1 cup diced onion
- 1 pound orange roughy fillets or any white fish fillets
- 3 limes
- 1 (16-ounce) can ROSARITA® No Fat Traditional Refried Beans
- 8 burrito-size fat-free flour tortillas
- 2 cups cooked white rice
- 1½ cups shredded cabbage
- ¾ cup reduced-fat shredded sharp Cheddar cheese
- ¾ cup diced tomatoes
- ROSARITA® Traditional Mild Salsa

1. Spray large no-stick skillet with PAM Cooking Spray. Sauté onion until tender.

2. Add fish and juice from 1 lime. Cook until fish becomes flakey; shred with fork. Remove from heat. Set aside.

3. Evenly divide Rosarita Beans among *each* tortilla; spread beans down center of tortillas. Top beans with even amounts of fish, rice, cabbage, cheese and tomatoes.

4. Roll burrito-style, folding in edges. Serve with Rosarita Salsa and lime wedges.

Makes 8 burritos

Spicy Tuna and Linguine with Garlic and Pine Nuts

- 2 tablespoons olive oil
- 4 cloves garlic, minced
- 2 cups sliced mushrooms
- ½ cup chopped onion
- ½ teaspoon crushed red pepper
- 2½ cups chopped plum tomatoes
- 1 can (14½ ounces) chicken broth plus water to equal 2 cups
- ½ teaspoon salt
- ¼ teaspoon coarsely ground black pepper
- 1 package (9 ounces) uncooked fresh linguine
- 1 (7-ounce) pouch of STARKIST® Premium Albacore Tuna
- ⅓ cup chopped fresh cilantro
- ⅓ cup toasted pine nuts or almonds

In 12-inch skillet, heat olive oil over medium-high heat; sauté garlic, mushrooms, onion and red pepper until golden brown. Add tomatoes, chicken broth mixture, salt and black pepper; bring to a boil.

Separate uncooked linguine into strands; place in skillet and spoon sauce over. Reduce heat to simmer; cook, covered, 4 more minutes or until cooked through. Toss gently; add tuna and cilantro and toss again. Sprinkle with pine nuts.

Makes 4 to 6 servings

Spicy Snapper & Black Beans

- 1½ pounds fresh red snapper fillets, cut into 4 portions (6 ounces each)
- Juice of 1 lime
- ½ teaspoon coarsely ground black pepper
- Nonstick cooking spray
- 1 cup GUILTLESS GOURMET® Spicy Black Bean Dip
- ½ cup water
- ½ cup (about 35) crushed GUILTLESS GOURMET® Baked Tortilla Chips (yellow or white corn)
- 1 cup GUILTLESS GOURMET® Roasted Red Pepper Salsa

Wash fish thoroughly; pat dry with paper towels. Place fish in 13×9-inch glass baking dish. Pour juice over top; sprinkle with pepper. Cover and refrigerate 1 hour.

Preheat oven to 350°F. Coat 11×7-inch glass baking dish with cooking spray. Combine bean dip and water in small bowl; spread 1 cup bean mixture in bottom of prepared baking dish. Place fish over bean mixture, discarding juice. Spread remaining bean mixture over top of fish; sprinkle with crushed chips.

Bake about 20 minutes or until chips are lightly browned and fish turns opaque and flakes easily when tested with fork. To serve, divide fish among 4 serving plates; spoon ¼ cup salsa over top of each serving.

Makes 4 servings

Note: This recipe can be made with 4 boneless skinless chicken breast halves in place of red snapper fillets. Prepare as directed and bake about 40 minutes or until chicken is no longer pink in center. Serve as directed.

Mom's Tuna Casserole

Broccoli-Fish Rollups

1 can (10¾ ounces) cream of
    broccoli soup
½ cup fat-free (skim) milk
2 cups seasoned stuffing
    crumbs
¾ pound flounder (4 medium
    pieces)
1 box (10 ounces) broccoli
    spears, thawed
    Paprika

1. Preheat oven to 375°F. Grease
9×9-inch baking pan. Combine soup
and milk in medium bowl. Set aside
½ cup soup mixture.

2. Combine stuffing crumbs and
remaining soup mixture. Pat into
prepared pan.

3. Place fish on clean work surface.
Arrange 1 broccoli spear across
narrow end of fish. Starting at narrow
end, gently roll up fish. Place over
stuffing mixture, seam side down.
Repeat with remaining fish and
broccoli.

4. Arrange any remaining broccoli
spears over stuffing mixture. Spoon
reserved ½ cup soup mixture over
broccoli-fish rollups. Sprinkle with
paprika.

5. Bake 20 minutes or until fish flakes
easily when tested with fork.
Makes 4 servings

Variation: Asparagus spears and
cream of asparagus soup may be
substituted for broccoli spears and
cream of broccoli soup.

Prep and Cook Time: 30 minutes

Pasta with Tuna

1 pound uncooked pasta, such
    as spaghetti or penne
¼ cup CRISCO® Oil,* divided
1 medium red onion, peeled and
    diced
2 teaspoons jarred minced
    garlic *or* 1 large garlic clove,
    peeled and minced
1½ teaspoons Italian seasoning
½ to 1 teaspoon dried red pepper
    flakes, depending on taste
½ teaspoon salt
2 cans (8 ounces each) tomato
    sauce
2 cans (6 ounces each) white
    tuna packed in water,
    drained and broken into
    chunks
3 tablespoons chopped fresh
    parsley
¼ cup sliced black or green
    olives (optional)
    Freshly grated Parmesan
    cheese (optional)

Use your favorite Crisco Oil product.

1. Bring large pot of salted water to a
boil. Add pasta and 2 tablespoons oil.
Cook pasta according to package
directions until al dente. Drain pasta.
Keep warm.

2. While pasta is boiling, heat
remaining 2 tablespoons oil in large
skillet on medium-high heat. Add
onion and garlic. Sauté 3 minutes, or
until onion is translucent. Add Italian
seasoning, pepper flakes and salt.
Cook 1 minute. Add tomato sauce.
Bring to a boil. Reduce heat to low.
Simmer 5 minutes.

3. Add tuna, parsley and olives, if
used, to sauce. Simmer 2 minutes.
Toss sauce with cooked pasta and
Parmesan cheese, if used. Serve
immediately.   *Makes 4 servings*

Note: The sauce can be prepared
one day in advance and refrigerated,
tightly covered. Reheat in pan used to
cook pasta while pasta drains.

Prep Time: 15 minutes
Total Time: 30 minutes

Homestyle Tuna Pot Pie

    Salt and pepper to taste
1 package (15 ounces)
    refrigerated pie crusts
1 (7-ounce) pouch of STARKIST®
    Premium Albacore or Chunk
    Light Tuna
1 package (10 ounces) frozen
    peas and carrots, thawed
    and drained
1 can (10¾ ounces) condensed
    cream of potato or cream of
    mushroom soup
½ cup chopped onion
⅓ cup milk
½ teaspoon poultry seasoning or
    dried thyme leaves

Line 9-inch pie pan with one crust;
set aside. Reserve second crust. In
medium bowl, combine remaining
ingredients; mix well. Pour tuna
mixture into pie shell; top with second
crust. Crimp edges to seal. Cut slits
in top crust to vent. Bake in 375°F
oven 45 to 50 minutes or until golden
brown.   *Makes 6 servings*

Prep & Cook Time: 55 to 60 minutes

Broccoli-Fish Rollups

Rice Pilaf with Fish Fillets

1 cup **UNCLE BEN'S® ORIGINAL CONVERTED® Brand Rice**
1 can (14½ ounces) fat-free reduced-sodium chicken broth
2 cups sugar snap peas or snow peas
1 cup sliced green onions
12 ounces Dover sole fillets
¼ cup reduced-fat Caesar salad dressing
2 tomatoes, cut into wedges
¼ cup chopped parsley

1. In large skillet, combine rice, chicken broth and ½ cup water. Bring to a boil. Cover; reduce heat and simmer 12 minutes.

2. Add peas and green onions to rice pilaf. Season to taste with salt and pepper. Place fish fillets on pilaf. Spoon salad dressing onto fillets. Cover and cook over low heat 8 minutes or until fish flakes when tested with a fork and rice is tender.

3. Garnish with tomatoes and parsley.
Makes 4 servings

Variation: Orange roughy fillets or swordfish steaks can be substituted for sole fillets.

Tuna Noodle Casserole

1 can (10¾ ounces) condensed cream of mushroom soup
1 cup milk
3 cups hot cooked rotini pasta (2 cups uncooked)
1 can (12 ounces) tuna packed in water, drained and flaked
1⅓ cups *French's®* French Fried Onions, divided
1 package (10 ounces) frozen peas and carrots
½ cup (2 ounces) shredded Cheddar or grated Parmesan cheese

Microwave Directions

Combine soup and milk in 2-quart microwavable shallow casserole. Stir in pasta, tuna, ⅔ *cup* French Fried Onions, vegetables and cheese. Cover; microwave on HIGH 10 minutes* or until heated through, stirring halfway through cooking time. Top with remaining ⅔ *cup* onions. Microwave 1 minute or until onions are golden.   *Makes 6 servings*

*Or, bake, covered, in 350°F oven 25 to 30 minutes.

Tip: Garnish with chopped pimiento and parsley sprigs, if desired.

Prep Time: 10 minutes
Cook Time: 11 minutes

Tuna and Broccoli Bake

1 package (16 ounces) frozen broccoli cuts, thawed and well drained
2 slices bread, cut in ½-inch cubes
1 (7-ounce) pouch of STARKIST® Premium Albacore or Chunk Light Tuna
2 cups cottage cheese
1 cup shredded Cheddar cheese
3 eggs
¼ teaspoon ground black pepper

Place broccoli on bottom of 2-quart baking dish. Top with bread cubes and tuna. In medium bowl, combine cottage cheese, Cheddar cheese, eggs and pepper. Spread evenly over tuna mixture. Bake in 400°F oven 30 minutes or until golden brown and puffed.   *Makes 4 servings*

Prep Time: 35 minutes

Helpful Hints

Choose solid white tuna or chunk tuna for Tuna Noodle Casserole. Solid white tuna is firm; break up any large pieces with a fork. Chunk tuna is not as firm and pieces are generally smaller than those of solid white tuna.

Tuna and Broccoli Bake

Tuna & Shrimp Fajitas

1 large red onion, cut in half and thinly sliced
1 red bell pepper, cut into bite-sized strips
1 large green bell pepper, cut into bite-sized strips
2 tablespoons vegetable oil
1 jar (12 ounces) salsa
1 (3-ounce) pouch of STARKIST® Premium Albacore or Chunk Light Tuna
½ pound frozen cooked bay shrimp, thawed
8 (8-inch) flour tortillas, warmed if desired
Diced avocado, shredded low-fat Cheddar or Monterey Jack cheese, sliced pitted ripe olives and bottled salsa for toppings

In large skillet or wok stir-fry onion and bell peppers in oil for 3 minutes over high heat. Add ¼ cup of the salsa, the tuna and shrimp; stir-fry for 2 minutes more, or until heated through.

To assemble fajitas, spoon some of the tuna mixture in center of each tortilla, then add desired toppings and serve immediately.

Makes 4 servings

Prep Time: 10 minutes

Veggie Tuna Pasta

1 package (16 ounces) medium pasta shells
1 bag (16 ounces) BIRDS EYE® frozen Farm Fresh Mixtures Broccoli, Corn & Red Peppers
1 can (10 ounces) chunky light tuna, packed in water
1 can (10¾ ounces) reduced-fat cream of mushroom soup

• In large saucepan, cook pasta according to package directions. Add vegetables during last 10 minutes; drain and return to saucepan.

• Stir in tuna and soup. Add salt and pepper to taste. Cook over medium heat until heated through.

Makes 4 servings

Variation: Stir in 1 can (4 to 6 ounces) chopped ripe olives with tuna.

Serving Suggestion: For a creamier dish, add a few tablespoons water; blend well.

Birds Eye Idea: Be prepared for unexpected company by stocking your freezer with your favorite Birds Eye® Easy Recipe entrées and chicken breasts.

Prep Time: 2 minutes
Cook Time: 12 to 15 minutes

Linguine with Tuna Antipasto

1 package (9 ounces) uncooked refrigerated flavored linguine, such as tomato and herb
1 can (6 ounces) tuna in water, drained and broken into pieces
1 jar (6½ ounces) marinated artichoke hearts, coarsely chopped and liquid reserved
½ cup roasted red peppers, drained and coarsely chopped
⅓ cup olive oil
¼ cup coarsely chopped black olives
½ teaspoon minced garlic
¼ teaspoon salt
¼ teaspoon red pepper flakes
⅛ teaspoon black pepper
½ cup grated Parmesan cheese

1. Cook linguine according to package directions.

2. While linguine is cooking, combine remaining ingredients except cheese in large microwavable bowl. Mix well; cover with vented plastic wrap. Microwave at HIGH 2 to 3 minutes or until heated through.

3. Drain linguine; add to bowl. Toss well; arrange on 4 plates. Sprinkle with cheese; garnish as desired.

Makes 4 servings

Prep and Cook Time: 18 minutes

Linguine with Tuna Antipasto

Sensational Shellfish

Spicy Shrimp Puttanesca

- **8 ounces uncooked linguine, capellini or spaghetti**
- **1 tablespoon olive oil**
- **12 ounces medium shrimp, peeled and deveined**
- **4 cloves garlic, minced**
- **¾ teaspoon red pepper flakes**
- **1 cup finely chopped onion**
- **1 can (14½ ounces) no-salt-added stewed tomatoes, undrained**
- **2 tablespoons tomato paste**
- **2 tablespoons chopped pitted calamata or black olives**
- **1 tablespoon drained capers**
- **¼ cup chopped fresh basil or parsley**

1. Cook linguine according to package directions, omitting salt. Drain; set aside.

2. Meanwhile, heat oil in large nonstick skillet over medium high heat. Add shrimp, garlic and red pepper flakes; cook and stir 3 to 4 minutes or until shrimp are opaque. Transfer shrimp mixture to bowl with slotted spoon; set aside.

3. Add onion to same skillet; cook over medium heat 5 minutes, stirring occasionally. Add tomatoes with juice, tomato paste, olives and capers; simmer, uncovered, 5 minutes.

4. Return shrimp mixture to skillet; simmer 1 minute. Stir in basil; simmer 1 minute. Place linguine in large serving bowl; top with shrimp mixture.

Makes 4 servings

Chicken and Shrimp Jambalaya

- **1 package (7 ounces) wild pecan aromatic rice *or* 1 cup basmati rice**
- **2½ to 3 cups fat-free reduced-sodium chicken broth, divided**
- **¾ teaspoon salt**
- **⅛ teaspoon black pepper**
- **⅛ teaspoon ground red pepper**
- **½ pound boneless skinless chicken breast, cut into ½-inch pieces**
- **1 tablespoon vegetable oil**
- **2 cups chopped red, yellow and green bell peppers**
- **1 large onion, chopped**
- **2 cloves garlic, minced**
- **1 large ripe tomato, chopped**
- **6 ounces peeled and deveined medium shrimp**
- **2 tablespoons chopped fresh parsley**

1. Cook rice according to package directions, substituting 2 cups chicken broth for the water and omitting salt.

2. Meanwhile, combine salt, black pepper and red pepper in small bowl; sprinkle half over chicken. Heat oil in large nonstick skillet over medium heat. Add chicken; cook without stirring 2 minutes or until golden. Turn chicken; cook 2 minutes more. Remove chicken; set aside.

3. Add bell peppers and onion to same skillet; cook and stir 2 to 3 minutes or until onion is translucent. Add garlic; cook 1 minute longer. Stir in chicken, tomato, shrimp, remaining pepper mixture and ½ cup chicken broth; bring to a boil. Reduce heat; simmer 5 minutes or until shrimp are opaque.

4. Stir in parsley and rice. Add additional chicken broth if needed to moisten rice. Cook 3 minutes longer or until liquid is absorbed and jambalaya is hot.

Makes 4 servings

Spicy Shrimp Puttanesca

Shrimp Primavera Pot Pie

1 can (10¾ ounces) condensed cream of shrimp soup, undiluted
1 package (12 ounces) frozen peeled uncooked medium shrimp
2 packages (1 pound each) frozen mixed vegetables, such as green beans, potatoes, onions and red peppers, thawed and drained
1 teaspoon dried dill weed
¼ teaspoon salt
¼ teaspoon black pepper
1 can (11 ounces) refrigerated breadstick dough

1. Preheat oven to 400°F. Heat soup in medium ovenproof skillet over medium-high heat 1 minute. Add shrimp; cook and stir 3 minutes or until shrimp begin to thaw. Stir in vegetables, dill, salt and pepper; mix well. Reduce heat to medium-low; cook and stir 3 minutes.

2. Unwrap breadstick dough; separate into 8 strips. Twist strips, cutting to fit skillet. Arrange attractively over shrimp mixture in crisscross pattern. Press ends of dough lightly to edges of skillet to secure. Bake 18 minutes or until crust is golden brown and shrimp mixture is bubbly.   *Makes 4 to 6 servings*

Prep and Cook Time: 30 minutes

Creamy Alfredo Seafood Lasagna

1 jar (1 pound) RAGÚ® Cheese Creations!® Classic Alfredo Sauce
1 container (15 ounces) ricotta cheese
1 pound imitation crabmeat, separated into bite-sized pieces
1 green onion, chopped (optional)
¼ teaspoon ground white pepper
⅛ teaspoon ground nutmeg (optional)
9 lasagna noodles, cooked and drained
2 cups shredded mozzarella cheese (about 8 ounces)
2 tablespoons grated Parmesan cheese

1. Preheat oven to 350°F. In medium bowl, combine ½ cup Ragú Cheese Creations! Sauce, ricotta cheese, crabmeat, green onion, pepper and nutmeg; set aside.

2. In 13×9-inch baking dish, spread ½ cup Ragú Cheese Creations! Sauce. Arrange 3 lasagna noodles lengthwise over sauce. Spread ½ of the ricotta mixture over noodles; evenly top with ¾ cup mozzarella cheese. Repeat layers, ending with noodles. Top with remaining ½ cup sauce, then sprinkle with remaining ½ cup mozzarella cheese and Parmesan cheese.

3. Cover with aluminum foil and bake 40 minutes. Remove foil and continue baking 10 minutes or until cheese is melted and lightly golden. Let stand 10 minutes before serving. Garnish, if desired, with additional chopped green onions.   *Makes 8 servings*

Prep Time: 20 minutes
Cook Time: 50 minutes

Roasted Red Pepper Pasta with Shrimp

1 jar (7 ounces) roasted red peppers packed in oil, undrained
2 tablespoons finely chopped fresh basil leaves,* divided
2 teaspoons finely chopped garlic, divided
2 tablespoons BERTOLLI® Olive Oil
1 pound uncooked medium shrimp, cleaned
2 tablespoons dry white wine
1½ cups water
½ cup milk
1 package LIPTON® Noodles & Sauce—Alfredo
Ground black pepper to taste

Substitution: Use 1 teaspoon dried basil leaves, crushed.

In food processor or blender, process red peppers, 1 tablespoon basil and 1 teaspoon garlic until smooth; set aside.

In 12-inch skillet, heat oil over medium-high heat and cook remaining 1 teaspoon garlic with shrimp, stirring constantly, until shrimp turn pink; remove and set aside.

In same skillet, add wine and cook 1 minute. Add water and milk; bring to the boiling point. Stir in noodles & sauce—Alfredo, then simmer, stirring occasionally, 8 minutes or until noodles are tender. Stir in red pepper purée and black pepper; heat through. To serve, arrange shrimp over noodles, then sprinkle with remaining 1 tablespoon basil. Garnish, if desired, with fresh basil.
      Makes about 4 servings

Shrimp Primavera Pot Pie

Creamy Alfredo Seafood Newburg

2 tablespoons margarine or butter
¼ cup finely chopped onion
1 pound uncooked medium shrimp, peeled, deveined and coarsely chopped
1 jar (1 pound) RAGÚ® Cheese Creations!® Classic Alfredo Sauce
¼ teaspoon ground white pepper
4 croissants or crescent rolls

1. In 12-inch nonstick skillet, melt margarine over medium-high heat and cook onion, stirring occasionally, 2 minutes or until tender.

2. Stir in shrimp and cook, stirring constantly, 2 minutes or until shrimp are almost pink. Stir in Ragú Cheese Creations! Sauce and pepper. Bring to a boil over high heat.

3. Reduce heat to low and simmer uncovered, stirring occasionally, 5 minutes or until shrimp turn pink. To serve, spoon shrimp mixture onto bottom of croissants and sprinkle, if desired, with chopped fresh parsley. Top with remaining croissant halves.

Makes 4 servings

Variation: For a light dish, substitute Ragú Cheese Creations! Light Parmesan Alfredo Sauce

Tip: Substitute 1 pound imitation crabmeat for shrimp.

Prep Time: 5 minutes
Cook Time: 15 minutes

French Quarter Shrimp Creole

½ cup chopped onion
½ cup chopped celery
½ cup chopped green bell pepper
1 clove garlic, minced
1 can (14½ ounces) stewed tomatoes, undrained
¼ cup *Frank's® RedHot®* Cayenne Pepper Sauce
1 pound medium shrimp, peeled and deveined
Hot cooked rice

1. Melt *2 tablespoons butter* in medium skillet; blend in *2 tablespoons flour*. Add onion, celery, bell pepper and garlic; cook

Creamy Alfredo Seafood Newburg

and stir over medium-high heat 5 minutes or until vegetables are tender and flour mixture is lightly golden.

2. Stir in tomatoes and **Frank's RedHot** Sauce. Heat to boiling. Reduce heat to medium-low. Cook, uncovered, 5 minutes or until slightly thickened. Stir occasionally. Add shrimp. Cook 5 minutes or just until shrimp are pink. Serve over rice. Garnish with chopped parsley, if desired.   *Makes 4 servings*

Prep Time: 10 minutes
Cook Time: 15 minutes

Shrimp Omelets

    3 to 5 tablespoons vegetable oil,
        divided
    8 fresh medium mushrooms,
        finely chopped
    4 teaspoons cornstarch
    1 cup water
    2 teaspoons soy sauce
    2 teaspoons instant chicken
        bouillon granules
    1 teaspoon sugar
    8 eggs
    ½ teaspoon salt
    ⅛ teaspoon black pepper
    8 ounces bean sprouts
    8 ounces shrimp, shelled,
        deveined and finely
        chopped
    4 green onions with tops, finely
        chopped
    1 stalk celery, finely chopped
        Cooked whole shrimp and
        slivered green onions for
        garnish

1. Heat 1 tablespoon oil in small skillet. Add mushrooms; cook 1 minute. Remove from skillet; set aside.

2. Combine cornstarch, water, soy sauce, bouillon granules and sugar in small saucepan. Cook and stir over medium heat until mixture boils and thickens, about 5 minutes. Keep warm.

3. Combine eggs, salt and pepper in large bowl. Beat until frothy. Add sprouts, shrimp, chopped onions, celery and mushrooms; mix well.

4. For each omelet, heat ½ tablespoon oil in 7-inch omelet pan or skillet. Pour ½ cup egg mixture into pan. Cook until lightly browned, 2 to 3 minutes on each side, gently pushing cooked portion to center and tilting skillet to allow uncooked portion to flow underneath.

5. Stack omelets on serving plate. Pour warm soy sauce mixture over omelets. Garnish, if desired.
            Makes 4 servings

Crab and Brown Rice Casserole

    1 pound Florida blue crab meat,
        fresh, or frozen, thawed
    3 eggs, lightly beaten
    1 cup mayonnaise
    1 cup cooked brown rice
    ¾ cup evaporated milk
    ¾ cup (3 ounces) shredded
        Cheddar cheese
    ¼ teaspoon hot pepper sauce

Preheat oven to 350°F. Grease 1½-quart casserole; set aside. Remove any pieces of cartilage from crab meat. Set aside.

Combine eggs, mayonnaise, brown rice, milk, cheese and hot pepper sauce in large bowl. Stir in crab meat. Bake 30 to 35 minutes or until knife inserted 1 inch from center comes out clean.   *Makes 6 servings*

Favorite recipe from **Florida Department of Agriculture and Consumer Services, Bureau of Seafood and Aquaculture**

Shrimp Dijon with Asparagus

    1 package (9 ounces) fresh
        linguine pasta
    1 cup chicken broth
    ⅓ cup dry white wine
    3 tablespoons *French's®* Napa
        Valley Style Dijon Mustard
    ½ pound fresh asparagus, cut
        into 1-inch pieces
    3 cloves garlic, minced
    1 pound large shrimp, peeled
        and deveined

1. Cook pasta according to package directions; drain. Transfer to heated platter. Whisk together broth, wine, mustard and *2 teaspoons flour;* set aside.

2. Melt *1 tablespoon butter* in large nonstick skillet over medium-high heat. Cook asparagus and garlic 2 minutes or until asparagus is crisp-tender. Stir in shrimp. Cook and stir 2 minutes or until shrimp just turn pink.

3. Add broth mixture to skillet. Heat to boiling. Reduce heat to low. Cook 2 minutes or until sauce thickens slightly. Spoon shrimp and asparagus mixture over pasta; toss to coat pasta with sauce. Serve with freshly cracked black pepper, if desired.
            Makes 4 servings

Prep Time: 5 minutes
Cook Time: 10 minutes

Shrimp La Louisiana

1 tablespoon margarine
1½ cups uncooked long-grain white rice*
1 medium onion, chopped
1 green bell pepper, chopped
2¾ cups beef broth
¼ teaspoon salt
¼ teaspoon ground black pepper
¼ teaspoon hot pepper sauce
1 pound medium shrimp, peeled and deveined
1 can (4 ounces) sliced mushrooms, drained
3 tablespoons snipped parsley
¼ cup sliced green onions for garnish (optional)

Recipe based on regular-milled long grain white rice.

Melt margarine in 3-quart saucepan. Add rice, onion and green pepper. Cook 2 to 3 minutes. Add broth, salt, black pepper and pepper sauce; bring to a boil. Cover and simmer 15 minutes. Add shrimp, mushrooms and parsley. Cook 5 minutes longer or until shrimp turn pink. Garnish with green onions.   *Makes 8 servings*

Favorite recipe from **USA Rice Federation**

Egg Noodle-Crab Casserole

12 ounces wide egg noodles, uncooked
1 can (10¾ ounces) Cheddar cheese soup
1 cup milk
1 tablespoon minced dried onions
¼ teaspoon paprika
¼ teaspoon dried marjoram
1 pound crabmeat
1 cup SONOMA® Dried Tomato Halves, snipped into strips, parboiled and drained

Cook noodles according to package directions until al dente. Set aside and keep warm.

In medium mixing bowl, combine soup and milk. Add onions, paprika and marjoram; stir. Place noodles in 2½- to 3-quart casserole. Break up crabmeat into bite-size pieces; sprinkle crabmeat and tomatoes over noodles. Pour soup mixture over crab mixture; blend well.

Cover and bake in 350°F oven for 30 minutes or until hot and bubbly.
Makes 6 servings

Shrimp & Ham Jambalaya

1 onion, cut into wedges
1 large green bell pepper, chopped
2 cloves garlic, minced
¼ teaspoon ground red pepper
2 tablespoons FLEISCHMANN'S® Original Margarine
3 cups cooked rice
2 cups large shrimp, cleaned and cooked (about 1 pound)
2 cups cubed cooked ham (about 1¼ pounds)
1 (16-ounce) can peeled tomatoes, chopped (undrained)
1 teaspoon natural hickory seasoning

1. Cook and stir onion, bell pepper, garlic and red pepper in margarine in large skillet over medium heat until vegetables are tender.

2. Stir in remaining ingredients. Cook for 10 to 15 minutes or until heated through, stirring occasionally. Serve immediately.   *Makes 8 servings*

Prep Time: 30 minutes
Cook Time: 20 minutes
Total Time: 50 minutes

Sonora Shrimp

2 tablespoons butter
1 medium green bell pepper, chopped
½ cup chopped onion
½ cup chopped celery
1 can (14½ ounces) whole peeled tomatoes, undrained and cut up
½ cup dry white wine
½ teaspoon LAWRY'S® Seasoned Salt
½ teaspoon LAWRY'S® Seasoned Pepper
¼ teaspoon LAWRY'S® Garlic Powder with Parsley
¼ teaspoon dried thyme, crushed
1 pound medium shrimp, peeled and deveined
1 can (2¼ ounces) sliced black olives, drained

In large skillet, heat butter. Add bell pepper, onion and celery and cook over medium-high heat until onion is tender. Add remaining ingredients except shrimp and olives; mix well. Bring to a boil over medium-high heat; reduce heat to low and cook, uncovered, 15 minutes, stirring occasionally. Add shrimp and olives; cook additional 10 minutes or until shrimp turn pink.
Makes 4 to 6 servings

Serving Suggestion: Serve over hot fluffy rice.

Helpful Hints

Shrimp may be peeled and deveined either before or after they are cooked. If cooked, peel and devein them while they are still warm. The shell is easily removed with your fingers.

Shrimp & Ham Jambalaya

Basil Shrimp Fettuccine

3 tablespoons butter
3 tablespoons olive oil
2 tomatoes, peeled, seeded and chopped
1 garlic clove, minced
⅓ cup evaporated skim milk
½ cup HOLLAND HOUSE® White Cooking Wine
½ cup fresh basil, chopped
½ cup shrimp, peeled and deveined
4 tablespoons Parmesan cheese, grated and divided
4 tablespoons fresh parsley, chopped and divided
1 pound fettuccine, cooked and drained

Melt butter and oil in medium saucepan over medium heat. Add tomatoes and garlic; simmer until tomatoes are softened. Add milk and cooking wine; simmer 10 minutes. Stir in basil and shrimp; simmer 3 minutes or until shrimp turn pink and are opaque. Add 2 tablespoons cheese and 2 tablespoons parsley. Serve over cooked fettuccine. Sprinkle with remaining 2 tablespoons each cheese and parsley.

Makes 4 to 6 servings

Hoisin-Flavored Mushrooms and Shrimp

2 tablespoons vegetable oil
1 pound fresh white mushrooms, sliced (about 5 cups)
1 tablespoon minced fresh ginger
1 teaspoon minced garlic
1⅓ cups uncooked orzo pasta
2 cans (about 14 ounces each) chicken broth
¼ cup hoisin sauce
Pinch ground red pepper
12 ounces cooked cleaned deveined shrimp
½ cup green onions, cut into 1-inch pieces

In large saucepan, heat oil until hot; add mushrooms, ginger and garlic. Cook until mushrooms release their liquid, about 5 minutes. Stir in pasta, chicken broth, hoisin sauce and pepper; bring to a boil. Simmer, covered, stirring occasionally until pasta is firm-tender and some liquid remains, about 10 minutes. Stir in shrimp and onions; cook until shrimp are heated through, 1 to 2 minutes.

Makes 4 servings

*Favorite recipe from **Mushroom Council***

Jambalaya Stir-Fry on Cajun Rice

1 cup uncooked converted rice
1 can (16 ounces) diced tomatoes, undrained
½ cup finely chopped celery
2 teaspoons chicken bouillon granules
1 bay leaf
8 ounces andouille sausage, cut into ¼-inch rounds*
1½ cups chopped onions
1 cup chopped green bell pepper
½ pound raw large shrimp, peeled and deveined
½ pound boneless chicken breasts, cut into 1-inch pieces
¾ teaspoon dried thyme leaves
¼ cup chopped fresh parsley
1 teaspoon salt
½ teaspoon ground red pepper
½ teaspoon paprika
Hot pepper sauce

If unavailable, use kielbasa sausage.

1. Bring 1¾ cups water to a boil in medium saucepan. Add rice, tomatoes and their liquid, celery, bouillon granules and bay leaf. Return to a boil; reduce heat, cover tightly and simmer 20 minutes or until all liquid is absorbed.

2. Meanwhile, heat large skillet over medium-high heat 1 minute. Add sausage, onions and bell pepper; cook and stir 10 minutes.

3. Increase heat to high; add shrimp, chicken and thyme. Cook and stir 5 minutes. Add parsley, salt, ground red pepper and paprika. Stir to blend thoroughly.

4. Place rice on platter. Spoon shrimp mixture over rice and serve with pepper sauce.　　*Makes 4 servings*

Noodles with Baby Shrimp

1 package (3¾ ounces) bean thread noodles
1 tablespoon vegetable oil
3 green onions with tops
1 package (16 ounces) frozen mixed vegetables (such as cauliflower, broccoli and carrots)
1 cup vegetable broth
8 ounces frozen baby shrimp
1 tablespoon soy sauce
2 teaspoons sesame oil
¼ teaspoon black pepper

Place noodles in large bowl. Cover with hot tap water; let stand 10 to 15 minutes or just until softened. Drain noodles and cut into 5- or 6-inch pieces; set aside.

Cut onions into 1-inch pieces.

Heat wok over high heat about 1 minute or until hot. Drizzle vegetable oil into wok and heat 30 seconds. Add onions; stir-fry 1 minute. Add mixed vegetables; stir-fry 2 minutes. Add broth; bring to a boil. Reduce heat to low; cover and cook about 5 minutes or until vegetables are crisp-tender.

Add shrimp to wok and cook just until thawed. Stir in noodles, soy sauce, sesame oil and black pepper; stir-fry until heated through. Transfer to serving dish.

Makes 4 to 6 servings

Jambalaya Stir-Fry on Cajun Rice

Elegant Crabmeat Frittata

3 tablespoons butter or
    margarine, divided
¼ pound fresh mushrooms,
    sliced
2 green onions, cut into thin
    slices
8 eggs, separated
¼ cup milk
¼ teaspoon salt
½ teaspoon hot pepper sauce
½ pound lump crabmeat or
    imitation crabmeat, flaked
    and picked over to remove
    any shells
½ cup (2 ounces) shredded
    Swiss cheese

1. Melt 2 tablespoons butter in large ovenproof skillet over medium-high heat. Add mushrooms and onions; cook and stir 3 to 5 minutes or until vegetables are tender. Remove from skillet; set aside.

2. Beat egg yolks with electric mixer at high speed until slightly thickened and lemon color. Stir in milk, salt and hot pepper sauce.

3. Beat egg whites in clean large bowl with electric mixer at high speed until foamy. Gradually add to egg yolk mixture, whisking just until blended.

4. Melt remaining 1 tablespoon butter in skillet. Pour egg mixture into skillet. Cook until egg is almost set. Remove from heat.

5. Preheat broiler. Broil frittata 4 to 6 inches from heat until top is set. Top with crabmeat, mushroom mixture and cheese. Return frittata to broiler; broil until cheese is melted. Garnish, if desired. Serve immediately.

Makes 4 servings

Seafood Lasagna

4 ounces lasagna noodles
1 jar (28-ounces) spaghetti,
    pasta sauce or favorite
    homemade recipe
1 package (6 ounces) frozen
    cooked salad shrimp,
    thawed and drained
4 ounces Surimi Seafood,
    thawed and thinly sliced
½ cup low-fat ricotta cheese
¼ cup freshly grated Parmesan
    cheese
1 tablespoon minced fresh
    parsley
⅛ teaspoon black pepper
⅔ cup shredded low-fat
    mozzarella cheese

Heat oven to 375°F. Prepare lasagna according to package directions. Empty spaghetti sauce into saucepan and simmer for 10 minutes until thickened and reduced to about 3 cups; stir in shrimp and Surimi Seafood. Combine ricotta cheese, Parmesan cheese, parsley and pepper in small bowl.

To assemble lasagna, place half of noodles in 8×8-inch casserole. Top with half of seafood sauce and drop half of ricotta mixture by small teaspoonfuls on top. Sprinkle with half of mozzarella cheese. Repeat layers. Bake for 35 minutes or until bubbly. Let stand 10 minutes before cutting.

Makes 6 servings

*Favorite recipe from **National Fisheries Institute***

Cajun-Style Corn with Crayfish

6 ears corn on the cob
1 tablespoon vegetable oil
1 medium onion, chopped
½ cup chopped green bell
    pepper
½ cup chopped red bell pepper
1 cup water
1 teaspoon salt
⅛ teaspoon black pepper
⅛ teaspoon ground red pepper
¾ pound crayfish tail meat

1. Cut corn from cobs in two or three layers so that kernels are not left whole. Scrape cobs to remove remaining juice and pulp.

2. Heat oil in large skillet over medium heat. Add onion and bell peppers; cook 5 minutes, stirring occasionally. Add corn, water, salt, black pepper and ground red pepper; bring to a boil. Reduce heat to low; simmer 10 to 15 minutes.

3. Add crayfish; return mixture to a simmer. Cook 3 to 5 minutes or just until crayfish turn opaque. Garnish, if desired.   *Makes 6 servings*

Crabmeat with Herbs and Pasta

1 small onion, minced
1 carrot, shredded
1 clove garlic, minced
⅓ cup olive oil
3 tablespoons butter or
    margarine
6 ounces canned crabmeat,
    drained and flaked
¼ cup chopped fresh basil *or*
    1 teaspoon dried basil
    leaves, crushed
2 tablespoons chopped fresh
    parsley
1 tablespoon lemon juice
½ cup chopped pine nuts
    (optional)
½ teaspoon salt
½ package (8 ounces) uncooked
    vermicelli, hot cooked and
    drained

In large skillet over medium-high heat, cook and stir onion, carrot and garlic in hot oil and butter until vegetables are tender, but not brown. Reduce heat to medium. Stir in crabmeat, basil, parsley and lemon juice. Cook 4 minutes, stirring constantly. Stir in pine nuts and salt. Pour sauce over vermicelli in large bowl; toss gently to coat. Garnish as desired.

Makes 4 servings

*Favorite recipe from **New Jersey Department of Agriculture***

Elegant Crabmeat Frittata

Linguine with Savory Clam Sauce

2 tablespoons BERTOLLI® Olive Oil, margarine or butter
3 cloves garlic, minced
1 can (10½ ounces) whole baby clams or 2 cans (6½ ounces each) minced clams in juice, undrained
1 package KNORR® Recipe Classics™ Vegetable Soup, Dip and Recipe Mix
½ cup water
½ cup milk
¼ teaspoon dried oregano
8 ounces linguine, cooked and drained

• In large skillet, heat oil over medium-high heat and cook garlic 30 seconds. Add clams with juice, recipe mix, water, milk and oregano. Bring to a boil over high heat. Reduce heat to low and simmer, stirring occasionally, 3 minutes.

• Toss with hot linguine.

Makes 4 servings

Prep Time: 20 minutes
Cook Time: 5 minutes

Chesapeake Crab Strata

4 tablespoons butter or margarine
4 cups unseasoned croutons
2 cups shredded Cheddar cheese
2 cups milk
8 eggs, beaten
½ teaspoon dry mustard
½ teaspoon seafood seasoning
Salt and black pepper to taste
1 pound crabmeat, picked over to remove any shells

1. Preheat oven to 325°F. Place butter in 11×7-inch baking dish. Heat in oven until melted, tilting to coat dish. Remove dish from oven; spread croutons over melted butter. Top with cheese; set aside.

2. Combine milk, eggs, dry mustard, seafood seasoning, salt and black pepper; mix well. Pour egg mixture over cheese in dish; sprinkle with crabmeat. Bake 50 minutes or until mixture is set. Remove from oven and let stand about 10 minutes. Garnish, if desired. *Makes 6 to 8 servings*

Easy Crab Asparagus Pie

4 ounces crabmeat, shredded
12 ounces fresh asparagus, cut into 1-inch pieces and cooked
½ cup chopped onion, cooked
1 cup (4 ounces) shredded Monterey Jack cheese
¼ cup (1 ounce) grated Parmesan cheese
Black pepper
¾ cup all-purpose flour
¾ teaspoon baking powder
½ teaspoon salt
2 tablespoons cold butter or margarine
1½ cups milk
4 eggs, lightly beaten

1. Preheat oven to 350°F. Lightly grease 10-inch quiche dish or pie plate.

2. Layer crabmeat, asparagus and onion in prepared pie plate; top with cheeses. Season with pepper.

3. Combine flour, baking powder and salt in large bowl. With pastry blender or 2 knives, cut in butter until mixture forms coarse crumbs. Stir in milk and eggs; pour over cheese mixture.

4. Bake 30 minutes or until filling is puffed and knife inserted near center comes out clean. Serve hot.

Makes 6 servings

Hot Crab and Cheese on Muffins

4 English muffins, split
1 tablespoon butter or margarine
3 green onions, chopped
⅓ cup chopped red bell pepper
½ pound fresh crabmeat, drained and flaked*
1 to 2 teaspoons hot pepper sauce
1 cup (4 ounces) shredded Cheddar cheese
1 cup (4 ounces) shredded Monterey Jack cheese

Two cans (6 ounces each) fancy crabmeat, drained, can be substituted for fresh crabmeat.

1. Preheat broiler. Place muffin halves on lightly greased baking sheet. Broil 4 inches from heat 2 minutes or until muffins are lightly toasted. Place on large microwavable plate.

2. Melt butter in medium skillet over medium heat. Add green onions and bell pepper; cook and stir 3 to 4 minutes or until tender. Remove from heat; stir in crabmeat, hot pepper sauce and cheeses. Spoon about ⅓ cup crab mixture onto muffin halves.

3. Microwave at HIGH 2 to 3 minutes, rotating platter once, or until crab mixture is heated through.

Makes 8 servings

Prep and Cook Time: 12 minutes

Chesapeake Crab Strata

Linguine with Red Clam Sauce

Nonstick cooking spray
1 onion, finely chopped
2 cloves garlic, minced
2 tablespoons finely chopped fresh parsley
2 teaspoons dried oregano leaves
1 can (14 ounces) Italian plum tomatoes, undrained and coarsely chopped
1 can (8 ounces) tomato sauce
2 cans (7½ ounces each) baby clams, undrained
1 tablespoon lemon juice
Salt and black pepper
8 ounces linguine, cooked and kept warm

1. Spray large saucepan with cooking spray. Heat over medium heat until hot. Add onion and garlic; cook and stir about 3 minutes or until tender. Stir in parsley and oregano; cook 1 to 2 minutes.

2. Add tomatoes with juice and tomato sauce to saucepan; bring to a boil. Reduce heat and simmer, uncovered, about 10 minutes or until mixture is of medium sauce consistency. Stir in clams and lemon juice; cook about 3 minutes or until heated through. Season to taste with salt and pepper.

3. Spoon sauce over linguine in large bowl and toss.

Makes 4 main-dish servings

Seafood Lasagna

1 package (16 ounces) lasagna noodles
2 tablespoons margarine or butter
1 large onion, finely chopped
1 package (8 ounces) cream cheese, cut into ½-inch pieces, at room temperature
1½ cups cream-style cottage cheese
2 teaspoons dried basil leaves
½ teaspoon salt
⅛ teaspoon black pepper
1 egg, lightly beaten
2 cans (10¾ ounces each) cream of mushroom soup
⅓ cup milk
1 clove garlic, minced
½ pound bay scallops, rinsed and patted dry
½ pound flounder fillets, rinsed, patted dry and cut into ½-inch cubes
½ pound medium raw shrimp, peeled and deveined
½ cup dry white wine
1 cup (4 ounces) shredded mozzarella cheese
2 tablespoons grated Parmesan cheese

1. Cook lasagna noodles according to package directions; drain.

2. Melt margarine in large skillet over medium heat. Cook onion in hot margarine until tender, stirring frequently. Stir in cream cheese, cottage cheese, basil, salt and pepper; mix well. Stir in egg; set aside.

3. Combine soup, milk and garlic in large bowl until well blended. Stir in scallops, fillets, shrimp and wine.

4. Preheat oven to 350°F. Grease 13×9-inch baking pan.

5. Place a layer of noodles in prepared pan, overlapping the noodles. Spread half the cheese mixture over noodles. Place a layer of noodles over cheese mixture and top with half the seafood mixture. Repeat layers. Sprinkle with mozzarella and Parmesan cheeses.

6. Bake 45 minutes or until bubbly. Let stand 10 minutes before cutting.

Makes 8 to 10 servings

Helpful Hints

Bay scallops are tiny scallops harvested mainly along the east coast of the United States; they are generally fairly expensive. Sea scallops are much larger than bay scallops and if cut into halves or quarters they make an inexpensive alternative to bay scallops.

Linguine with Red Clam Sauce

Paella

1 pound littleneck clams
8 to 10 ounces sea scallops
6 ounces raw medium shrimp
4 teaspoons olive oil, divided
3¼ cups reduced-sodium chicken broth, divided
1 medium onion, finely chopped
3 cloves garlic, chopped
2 cups long-grain rice
1 teaspoon dried thyme leaves
½ teaspoon saffron threads, crushed
1 pint cherry tomatoes, halved
1 cup frozen petit peas, thawed
1 tablespoon chopped fresh parsley

1. Discard any clams that remain open when tapped with fingers. To clean clams, scrub with stiff brush under cold running water. Soak clams in mixture of ⅓ cup salt to 1 gallon of water 20 minutes. Drain water; repeat 2 more times. Slice sea scallops in half crosswise into rounds. Peel shrimp leaving tails on, if desired; devein.

2. Heat 1 teaspoon oil over medium-high heat in large saucepan. Add shrimp; cook, stirring occasionally, 3 minutes or until shrimp turn pink. Transfer to bowl; cover. Add scallops to saucepan and cook 2 minutes or until scallops are opaque. Transfer to bowl with shrimp. Add clams and ¼ cup broth to pan. Cover; boil 2 to 8 minutes or until clams open. Transfer clams and broth to bowl with shrimp and scallops; discard any unopened clams.

3. Heat remaining 3 teaspoons oil in same saucepan. Add onion and garlic; cook and stir 4 minutes or until tender. Add rice; cook and stir 2 minutes. Add remaining 3 cups broth, thyme and saffron; reduce heat to medium-low. Cover; simmer 15 minutes or until rice is tender. Stir in tomatoes, peas and parsley. Stir in seafood and accumulated juices. Cover; remove from heat. Let stand 3 to 5 minutes or until seafood is hot.
Makes 6 servings

Scallop Stir-Fry

6 ounces uncooked ramen noodles
1 tablespoon olive oil
1 pound asparagus, cut into 1-inch pieces
1 red bell pepper, cut into thin rings
3 green onions, chopped
1 large clove garlic, minced
1 pound sea scallops, halved crosswise
2 tablespoons soy sauce
1 teaspoon hot pepper sauce
1 teaspoon sesame oil
Juice of ½ lime

1. Cook noodles in lightly salted boiling water according to package directions.

2. Meanwhile, heat olive oil in wok or large skillet over high heat. Add asparagus, red pepper, onions and garlic. Stir-fry 2 minutes.

3. Add scallops; stir-fry until scallops turn opaque.

4. Stir in soy sauce, hot pepper sauce, sesame oil and lime juice. Add noodles; heat thoroughly, stirring occasionally.   *Makes 4 servings*

Note: Substitute vermicelli for ramen noodles.

Shrimp Creole

2 tablespoons BERTOLLI® Olive Oil
1 medium onion, chopped
1 medium green bell pepper, chopped
1 jar (1 pound 10 ounces) RAGÚ® Chunky Gardenstyle Pasta Sauce
½ cup bottled clam juice
2 to 3 teaspoons hot pepper sauce
1½ pounds medium shrimp, peeled and deveined

1. In 12-inch skillet, heat oil over medium-high heat and cook onion and green pepper, stirring frequently, 6 minutes or until tender.

2. Stir in Ragú Pasta Sauce, clam juice and hot pepper sauce. Bring to a boil over high heat. Reduce heat to medium and continue cooking, stirring occasionally, 5 minutes. Stir in shrimp and cook, stirring occasionally, 3 minutes or until shrimp turn pink.

3. Serve, if desired, over hot cooked rice.   *Makes 4 servings*

Tip: For a more classic dish, stir in 1 package (9 ounces) chopped frozen okra with Ragú Chunky Gardenstyle Pasta Sauce. Okra is a vegetable native to the Southeastern United States and is used in cooking for thickening and flavor.

Prep Time: 10 minutes
Cook Time: 20 minutes

Paella

Make It Meatless

Hearty Lentil Stew

Slow Cooker

1 cup dried lentils, rinsed and drained
1 package (16 ounces) frozen green beans
2 cups cauliflower florets
1 cup chopped onion
1 cup baby carrots, cut in half crosswise
3 cups fat-free chicken broth
2 teaspoons ground cumin
¾ teaspoon ground ginger
1 can (15 ounces) chunky tomato sauce with garlic and herbs
½ cup dry-roasted peanuts

Slow Cooker Directions

1. Place lentils in slow cooker. Top with green beans, cauliflower, onion and carrots. Combine broth, cumin and ginger in large bowl; mix well. Pour mixture over vegetables. Cover; cook on LOW 9 to 11 hours.

2. Stir in tomato sauce. Cover; cook on LOW 10 minutes. Ladle stew into bowls. Sprinkle peanuts evenly over each serving.   *Makes 6 servings*

Broccoli & Cheese Strata

Slow Cooker

2 cups chopped broccoli florets
4 slices firm white bread, ½-inch thick
4 teaspoons butter
1½ cups (6 ounces) shredded Cheddar cheese
1½ cups low-fat (1%) milk
3 eggs
½ teaspoon salt
½ teaspoon hot pepper sauce
⅛ teaspoon black pepper

Slow Cooker Directions

1. Cook broccoli in boiling water 10 minutes or until tender. Drain. Spread one side of each bread slice with 1 teaspoon butter. Arrange 2 slices bread, buttered sides up, in greased 1-quart casserole that will fit in slow cooker. Layer cheese, broccoli and remaining 2 bread slices, buttered sides down.

2. Beat remaining ingredients in bowl. Gradually pour over bread.

3. Place small wire rack in 5-quart slow cooker. Pour in 1 cup water. Place casserole on rack. Cover; cook on HIGH 3 hours.

Makes 4 servings

Baked Ziti with Walnuts

1 cup uncooked ziti pasta
1 box (10 ounces) BIRDS EYE® frozen Peas & Pearl Onions
1 cup tomato sauce
½ cup chopped walnuts
1 tablespoon olive oil
2 tablespoons grated Parmesan cheese

- Preheat oven to 350°F.

- Cook ziti according to package directions; drain and set aside.

- In large bowl, combine vegetables, tomato sauce, walnuts and oil. Add ziti; toss well.

- Place mixture in 13×9-inch baking pan. Sprinkle with cheese.

- Bake 20 minutes or until heated through.   *Makes 4 servings*

Prep Time: 10 minutes
Cook Time: 20 minutes

Hearty Lentil Stew

Broccoli-Stuffed Shells

1 tablespoon butter or
    margarine
¼ cup chopped onion
1 cup ricotta cheese
1 egg
2 cups chopped cooked broccoli
    or 1 package (10 ounces)
    frozen chopped broccoli,
    thawed and well drained
1 cup (4 ounces) shredded
    Monterey Jack cheese
20 jumbo pasta shells
1 can (28 ounces) crushed
    tomatoes with added purée
1 package (1 ounce)
    HIDDEN VALLEY® The
    Original Ranch® Salad
    Dressing & Seasoning Mix
¼ cup grated Parmesan cheese

Preheat oven to 350°F. In small skillet, melt butter over medium heat. Add onion; cook until onion is tender but not browned. Remove from heat; cool. In large bowl, stir ricotta cheese and egg until well blended. Add broccoli and Monterey Jack cheese; mix well. In large pot of boiling water, cook pasta shells 8 to 10 minutes or just until tender; drain. Rinse under cold running water; drain again. Stuff each shell with about 2 tablespoons broccoli-cheese mixture.

In medium bowl, combine tomatoes, sautéed onion and salad dressing & seasoning mix; mix well. Pour one third of the tomato mixture into 13×9-inch baking dish. Arrange filled shells in dish. Spoon remaining tomato mixture over top. Sprinkle with Parmesan cheese. Bake, covered, until hot and bubbly, about 30 minutes.   *Makes 4 servings*

Moroccan Supper

1 (7.2-ounce) package
    RICE-A-RONI® Rice Pilaf
½ cup chopped onion
2 cloves garlic, minced
2 tablespoons margarine or
    olive oil
1 teaspoon ground cumin
¼ teaspoon ground cinnamon
1 (15-ounce) can garbanzo
    beans (chick-peas), rinsed
    and drained
1½ cups broccoli flowerets
¼ cup dried apricots, slivered or
    raisins
⅓ cup slivered or sliced
    almonds, toasted
¼ cup chopped cilantro
    (optional)

1. In large skillet over medium heat, sauté rice-pasta mix, onion and garlic with margarine until pasta is light golden brown.

2. Slowly stir in 2 cups water, cumin, cinnamon and Special Seasonings; bring to a boil. Cover; reduce heat to low. Simmer 10 minutes.

3. Stir in beans, broccoli and apricots. Cover; simmer 10 to 12 minutes or until rice is tender. Serve topped with almonds and cilantro, if desired.
     Makes 4 servings

Tip: For a Southwestern flair, use black beans, 1½ cups corn and ¼ teaspoon chili powder instead of garbanzo beans, apricots and cinnamon.

Prep Time: 10 minutes
Cook Time: 30 minutes

Classic Stuffed Shells

1 jar (1 pound 10 ounces)
    RAGÚ® Old World Style®
    Pasta Sauce, divided
2 pounds part-skim ricotta
    cheese
2 cups part-skim shredded
    mozzarella cheese (about
    8 ounces)
¼ cup grated Parmesan cheese
3 eggs
1 tablespoon finely chopped
    fresh parsley
⅛ teaspoon ground black pepper
1 box (12 ounces) jumbo shells
    pasta, cooked and drained

Preheat oven to 350°F. In 13×9-inch baking pan, evenly spread 1 cup Ragú® Old World Style Pasta Sauce; set aside.

In large bowl, combine cheeses, eggs, parsley and black pepper. Fill shells with cheese mixture, then arrange in baking pan. Evenly top with remaining sauce. Bake 45 minutes or until sauce is bubbling.
     Makes 8 servings

Recipe Tip: For a change of shape, substitute cooked and drained cannelloni or manicotti tubes for the jumbo shells. Use a teaspoon or pastry bag to fill the tubes from end to end, being careful not to overfill them.

Classic Stuffed Shells

Eggplant and Feta Skillet

- ¼ cup olive oil
- 1 medium eggplant, cut into 1-inch pieces
- 1 medium zucchini, cut into ½-inch slices
- 1 package (16 ounces) frozen bell peppers and onions blend, thawed and drained
- 2 teaspoons bottled minced garlic
- 2 cans (14½ ounces each) Italian-style diced tomatoes, drained
- 1 can (2¼ ounces) sliced black olives, drained
- 1½ cups prepared croutons
- ¾ cup feta cheese with basil and tomato, crumbled

1. Heat oil in large skillet over high heat until hot.

2. Add eggplant, zucchini, peppers and onions and garlic; cook and stir 6 minutes. Add tomatoes; simmer 3 minutes. Stir in olives.

3. Sprinkle croutons and feta cheese over top.   *Makes 6 servings*

Prep and Cook Time: 20 minutes

Baked Bow-Tie Pasta in Mushroom Cream Sauce

- 1 teaspoon BERTOLLI® Olive Oil
- 1 package (10 ounces) sliced mushrooms
- 1 large onion, thinly sliced
- ⅛ teaspoon ground black pepper
- 1 jar (1 pound) RAGÚ® Cheese Creations!® Light Parmesan Alfredo Sauce
- 8 ounces bow tie pasta, cooked and drained
- 1 tablespoon grated Parmesan cheese
- 1 tablespoon plain dry bread crumbs (optional)

1. Preheat oven to 400°F. In 10-inch nonstick skillet, heat oil over medium heat and cook mushrooms, onion and pepper, stirring frequently, 10 minutes or until vegetables are golden. Stir in Ragú Cheese Creations! Sauce.

2. In 2-quart shallow baking dish, combine sauce mixture with hot pasta. Sprinkle with cheese combined with bread crumbs. Cover with aluminum foil and bake 20 minutes. Remove foil and bake an additional 5 minutes.   *Makes 6 servings*

Prep Time: 10 minutes
Cook Time: 35 minutes

Vegetables with Spicy Honey Peanut Sauce

- ½ cup honey
- ¼ cup peanut butter
- 2 tablespoons soy sauce
- 1 tablespoon chopped fresh cilantro
- ⅛ teaspoon crushed red pepper flakes
- 4 cups broccoli florets
- 4 cups sliced carrots
- 4 cups snow peas
- 6 cups cooked white rice

Combine honey, peanut butter, soy sauce, cilantro and red pepper in small bowl; mix well and set aside. Steam vegetables until crisp-tender; drain well. Toss steamed vegetables with peanut sauce in large bowl. Serve immediately over rice.

Makes 6 servings

*Favorite recipe from **National Honey Board***

Bow Ties with Vegetables Alfredo

- 1 package (8 ounces) bow tie pasta, uncooked
- 1 bag (16 ounces) BIRDS EYE® frozen Farm Fresh Mixtures Broccoli, Cauliflower & Carrots
- 1 package (1.6 ounces) alfredo pasta sauce mix
- ½ teaspoon pepper

- In large saucepan, cook pasta according to package directions. Add vegetables during last 5 minutes of pasta cooking. Drain; return to saucepan.

- Meanwhile, in medium saucepan, prepare sauce according to package directions.

- Stir sauce into vegetables and pasta; cook over medium heat until heated through.

- Season with pepper.
          Makes 4 servings

Variation: Stir 2 tablespoons prepared pesto sauce into Alfredo sauce.

Serving Suggestion: Sprinkle with grated Parmesan cheese.

Birds Eye Idea: For pasta perfection, cook pasta in an abundant amount of boiling water. Stir frequently while cooking to avoid sticking.

Prep Time: 5 minutes
Cook Time: 20 minutes

Eggplant and Feta Skillet

Cheesy Baked Barley

2 cups water
½ cup medium pearled barley
½ teaspoon salt, divided
   Nonstick cooking spray
½ cup diced onion
½ cup diced zucchini
½ cup diced red bell pepper
1½ teaspoons all-purpose flour
   Seasoned pepper
¾ cup milk
1 cup (4 ounces) shredded
   Italian blend cheese, divided
1 tablespoon Dijon mustard

1. Bring water to a boil in 1-quart saucepan. Add barley and ¼ teaspoon salt. Cover; reduce heat and simmer 45 minutes or until barley is tender and most water is evaporated. Let stand covered, 5 minutes.

2. Preheat oven to 375°F. Spray medium skillet with cooking spray. Cook onion, zucchini and bell pepper over medium-low heat about 10 minutes or until soft. Stir in flour, remaining ¼ teaspoon salt and seasoned pepper to taste; cook 1 to 2 minutes. Add milk, stirring constantly; cook and stir until slightly thickened. Remove from heat and add barley, ¾ cup cheese and mustard; stir until cheese is melted.

3. Spread in even layer in casserole. Sprinkle with remaining ¼ cup cheese. Bake 20 minutes or until hot. Preheat broiler. Broil casserole 1 to 2 minutes or until cheese is lightly browned.   *Makes 2 servings*

Chili Relleno Casserole

1½ cups (6 ounces) SARGENTO®
   Light 4 Cheese Mexican
   Shredded Cheese or
   SARGENTO® Light Shredded
   Cheese for Tacos, divided
1 can (12 ounces) evaporated
   skim milk
¾ cup (6 ounces) fat-free liquid
   egg substitute *or* 3 eggs,
   beaten
6 (7-inch) corn tortillas, torn into
   2-inch pieces
2 cans (4 ounces each) chopped
   green chilies
½ cup mild chunky salsa
¼ teaspoon salt (optional)
2 tablespoons chopped fresh
   cilantro
   Light or fat-free sour cream
   (optional)

1. Coat 10-inch deep dish pie plate or 8-inch square baking dish with nonstick cooking spray. In medium bowl, combine 1 cup cheese, milk, egg substitute, tortillas, chilies, salsa and salt, if desired. Mix well; pour into prepared dish.

2. Bake at 375°F 30 to 32 minutes or until set. Remove from oven; sprinkle with remaining ½ cup cheese and cilantro. Return to oven; bake 1 minute or until cheese is melted. Serve with sour cream, if desired.
          Makes 4 servings

Pasta Primavera with Lemon Pepper Sauce

1 package (8 ounces) linguine
1 bag (16 ounces) BIRDS EYE®
   frozen Farm Fresh Mixtures
   Broccoli, Cauliflower &
   Carrots
1 packet (1.8 ounces) white
   sauce mix
¼ cup grated Parmesan cheese
2 teaspoons grated lemon peel
¼ teaspoon pepper

• In large saucepan, cook pasta according to package directions. Add vegetables during last 8 minutes; drain and set aside.

• In same saucepan, prepare sauce according to package directions; stir in cheese, lemon peel and pepper. Stir in vegetables and pasta; cook over medium heat until heated through.   *Makes 4 servings*

Variation: Add 2 cans (6 ounces each) drained and flaked tuna when you add pasta and vegetables to sauce.

Prep Time: 5 minutes
Cook Time: 20 minutes

Penne Pasta with Portobello Mushroom Tomato Sauce

1 tablespoon margarine or
   butter
2 medium portobello
   mushrooms, stems removed
   and coarsely chopped
1 tablespoon balsamic vinegar
1 jar (1 pound 10 ounces)
   RAGÚ® Light Pasta Sauce
¼ teaspoon ground black pepper
1 box (16 ounces) penne or ziti
   pasta, cooked and drained

In 12-inch skillet, melt margarine over medium heat and cook mushrooms, stirring occasionally, 7 minutes or until tender. Stir in vinegar and cook, stirring constantly, 1 minute. Stir in pasta sauce and pepper; simmer uncovered, stirring occasionally, 15 minutes. Serve over hot pasta and garnish, if desired, with fresh grated Parmesan cheese.
          Makes 8 servings

Cheesy Baked Barley

Eggplant Crêpes with Roasted Tomato Sauce

Roasted Tomato Sauce (recipe follows) or 1 cup prepared marinara sauce
2 eggplants (about 8 to 9 inches long), cut into 18 (¼-inch-thick) slices
Nonstick olive oil cooking spray
1 package (10 ounces) frozen chopped spinach, thawed and pressed dry
1 cup ricotta cheese
½ cup grated Parmesan cheese
1¼ cups (5 ounces) shredded Gruyère* cheese
Fresh oregano leaves for garnish

*Gruyère cheese is a Swiss cheese that has been aged for 10 to 12 months. Any Swiss cheese may be substituted.

1. Prepare Roasted Tomato Sauce. *Reduce oven temperature to 425°F.*

2. Arrange eggplant on nonstick baking sheets in single layer. Spray both sides of eggplant slices with cooking spray. Bake eggplant 10 minutes; turn and bake 5 to 10 minutes or until tender. Cool. *Reduce oven temperature to 350°F.*

3. Combine spinach, ricotta and Parmesan cheese; mix well. Spray 12×8-inch baking pan with cooking spray. Spread spinach mixture evenly on eggplant slices; roll up slices, beginning at short ends. Place rolls, seam side down, in baking dish.

4. Cover dish with foil. Bake 25 minutes. Uncover; sprinkle rolls with Gruyère cheese. Bake, uncovered, 5 minutes or until cheese is melted.

5. Serve with Roasted Tomato Sauce. Garnish, if desired.

Makes 4 to 6 servings

Roasted Tomato Sauce

20 ripe plum tomatoes (about 2⅔ pounds), cut in half and seeded
3 tablespoons olive oil, divided
½ teaspoon salt
⅓ cup minced fresh basil
½ teaspoon black pepper

Preheat oven to 450°F. Toss tomatoes with 1 tablespoon oil and salt. Place, cut sides down, on nonstick baking sheet. Bake 20 to 25 minutes or until skins are blistered. Cool. Process tomatoes, remaining 2 tablespoons oil, basil and pepper in food processor until smooth.

Makes about 1 cup

Pasta with Spicy Tomato Sauce

8 whole cloves garlic, peeled
1 can (28 ounces) crushed tomatoes in purée, undrained
½ cup chopped black olives
¼ cup *Frank's® RedHot®* Cayenne Pepper Sauce
¼ cup minced basil or parsley
1 tablespoon capers (optional)
4 cups hot cooked tube-shaped pasta

1. Heat *2 tablespoons oil* in large skillet; cook and stir garlic until lightly golden. Add remaining ingredients *except* pasta. Heat to boiling. Simmer, stirring, 10 minutes.

2. In serving bowl, toss pasta with half of sauce. Serve remaining sauce on the side. Garnish with shredded cheese, if desired.

Makes 4 servings
(3 cups sauce)

Prep Time: 10 minutes
Cook Time: 15 minutes

Layered Mexican Tortilla Cheese Casserole

1 can (14½ ounces) salsa-style or Mexican-style stewed tomatoes, undrained
½ cup chopped fresh cilantro, divided
2 tablespoons fresh lime juice
Nonstick vegetable cooking spray
6 (6-inch) corn tortillas, torn into 1½-inch pieces
1 can (15 ounces) black beans, rinsed and drained
1 can (8 ounces) whole kernel corn, drained *or* 1 cup frozen whole kernel corn, thawed
2 cups (8 ounces) SARGENTO® Mexican Blend Shredded Cheese

1. In small bowl, combine tomatoes, ¼ cup cilantro and lime juice; set aside.

2. Coat 8-inch square baking dish with cooking spray. Arrange ¼ of tortillas in bottom of dish; spoon ¼ of tomato mixture over tortillas. Top with ¼ of beans, ¼ of corn and ¼ of cheese. Repeat layering 3 more times with remaining tortillas, tomato mixture, beans, corn and cheese.

3. Bake uncovered at 375°F 25 minutes or until cheese is melted and sauce is bubbly. Sprinkle with remaining ¼ cup cilantro. Let stand 10 minutes before serving.

Makes 4 servings

Eggplant Crêpes with Roasted Tomato Sauce

Gourmet Bean & Spinach Burritos

  Avocado Relish (recipe
    follows)
  1 pound spinach leaves, divided
  2 teaspoons olive oil
  1 cup finely chopped onion
  2 cloves garlic, minced
  2 cans (15 ounces each) black
    beans, drained
  1 can (10 ounces) whole
    tomatoes with green chilies,
    undrained
  2 teaspoons ground cumin
  ½ teaspoon ground oregano
  8 flour tortillas (8-inch diameter)
  2 cups (8 ounces) shredded
    Monterey Jack cheese
  Sour cream (optional)

1. Prepare Avocado Relish.

2. Wash and dry spinach. Remove and discard stems from spinach leaves. Set aside 24 to 30 large leaves. Stack remaining leaves and cut crosswise into ¼-inch-wide pieces. Set aside.

3. Heat olive oil in large nonstick skillet over medium heat until hot. Add onion and garlic; cook and stir 5 minutes or until tender. Add beans, tomatoes, cumin and oregano. Simmer, uncovered, until mixture is dry. Remove from heat; mash bean mixture with potato masher.

4. Preheat oven to 350°F. Arrange 3 to 4 whole spinach leaves on each tortilla. Spoon bean mixture onto bottom half of tortillas; sprinkle cheese evenly over bean mixture.

5. Roll up to enclose filling. Repeat with remaining tortillas, spinach and bean mixture.

6. Arrange, seam side down, in 12×8-inch baking dish. Cover with foil. Bake 20 minutes or until heated through.

7. To serve, arrange about ½ cup spinach pieces on each serving plate; top with 2 burritos. Serve with Avocado Relish. Garnish, if desired.
Makes 4 servings

Avocado Relish

  1 large, firm, ripe avocado, finely
    diced
  2 tablespoons fresh lime juice
  ¾ cup finely chopped seeded
    tomato
  ½ cup minced green onions
  ⅓ cup minced fresh cilantro
  ½ to 1 teaspoon hot pepper
    sauce

Combine avocado and lime juice in bowl; toss. Add tomato, onions, cilantro and hot sauce; toss gently. Cover and refrigerate 1 hour. Serve at room temperature.
Makes about 2¼ cups

Creamy Vegetable Casserole

  1 large butternut squash, (about
    2½ pounds), peeled and cut
    into ¼-inch-thick slices
  1 teaspoon chopped fresh
    thyme leaves *or* ¼ teaspoon
    dried thyme leaves, crushed
  1 package (10 ounces) frozen
    chopped spinach, thawed
    and squeezed dry
  1 jar (1 pound) RAGÚ® Cheese
    Creations!® Classic Alfredo
    Sauce
  ½ cup chicken broth or water
  ⅔ cup grated Parmesan cheese
  3 tablespoons fresh bread
    crumbs

1. Preheat oven to 400°F. In greased 2½-quart casserole, arrange ½ of the squash. Season, if desired, with salt and ground black pepper. Sprinkle with ½ teaspoon thyme, then top with spinach and remaining squash.

2. In medium bowl, combine Ragú Cheese Creations! Sauce and broth; evenly pour over vegetables. Cover with aluminum foil and bake 40 minutes or until squash is tender.

3. Remove foil and sprinkle with cheese combined with bread crumbs. Bake an additional 15 minutes or until golden.   *Makes 6 servings*

Tip: Make this dish one day ahead, then reheat before serving.

Prep Time: 15 minutes
Cook Time: 55 minutes

Mushroom-Laced Fettuccine

  3 tablespoons margarine or
    butter
  ½ pound assorted fresh
    mushrooms*
  1 envelope LIPTON®
    RECIPE SECRETS® Savory
    Herb with Garlic Soup Mix**
  1½ cups milk
  8 ounces fettuccine or linguine,
    cooked and drained

Use any of the following, sliced: portobello, crimini, shiitake, white, morels, porcini or enoki mushrooms.

**Also terrific with LIPTON® Recipe Secrets® Golden Onion Soup Mix.*

In 10-inch skillet, melt margarine over medium heat and cook mushrooms, stirring occasionally, 4 minutes or until tender. Add savory herb with garlic soup mix blended with milk. Bring to a boil over high heat. Reduce heat to low and simmer 3 minutes, stirring frequently. Toss with hot fettuccine. Serve immediately.
Makes about 2 servings

Gourmet Bean & Spinach Burritos

Lasagna à la Zucchini

8 (2-inch-wide) uncooked lasagna noodles
3 medium zucchini, cut into thin slices
1 can (16 ounces) Italian-style sliced stewed tomatoes, drained
¼ pound fresh mushrooms, cut into thin slices
1 small onion, chopped
2 cloves garlic, minced
1 teaspoon dried Italian seasoning
¼ teaspoon salt
⅛ teaspoon black pepper
1 can (6 ounces) tomato paste
1 container (16 ounces) small curd cottage cheese
6 eggs, lightly beaten
¼ cup freshly grated Parmesan cheese
2 cups (8 ounces) shredded mozzarella cheese

1. Preheat oven to 350°F.

2. Cook lasagna noodles according to package directions until tender but still firm. Drain; set aside.

3. Combine zucchini, tomatoes, mushrooms, onion, garlic, Italian seasoning, salt and pepper in large skillet. Cook over medium-high heat 5 to 7 minutes or until zucchini is tender. Stir in tomato paste; remove from heat.

4. Combine cottage cheese, eggs and Parmesan cheese in medium bowl; stir until well blended.

5. Place 4 noodles on bottom of greased 13×9-inch baking dish. Pour ½ of egg mixture evenly over noodles. Cover egg mixture with ½ of tomato mixture; sprinkle with 1½ cups mozzarella. Repeat layers with remaining ingredients, ending with ½ cup mozzarella.

6. Bake covered 30 minutes. Uncover; bake 10 minutes or until heated through. Let stand 10 minutes before serving.   *Makes 8 to 10 servings*

Mushroom Frittata

1 teaspoon butter or margarine
1 medium zucchini, shredded
1 medium tomato, chopped
1 can (4 ounces) sliced mushrooms, drained
6 eggs, beaten
2 cups (8 ounces) shredded Swiss cheese
¼ cup milk
2 teaspoons Dijon mustard
½ teaspoon LAWRY'S® Seasoned Salt
½ teaspoon LAWRY'S® Seasoned Pepper

Lasagna à la Zucchini

In large, ovenproof skillet, heat butter. Cook zucchini, tomato and mushrooms over medium high heat 1 minute. In large bowl, combine remaining ingredients; mix well. Pour egg mixture into skillet; cook 10 minutes over low heat. To brown top, place skillet under broiler 2 to 3 minutes.   *Makes 4 servings*

Serving Suggestion: Serve directly from skillet or remove frittata to serving dish. Serve with additional Swiss cheese and fresh fruit.

Hint: Try serving frittata with prepared LAWRY'S® Spaghetti Sauce Seasoning Blend with Imported Mushrooms.

Eggplant Pasta Bake

4 ounces dry bow-tie pasta
1 pound eggplant, diced
1 clove garlic, minced
¼ cup olive oil
1½ cups shredded Monterey Jack cheese, divided
1 cup sliced green onions
½ cup grated Parmesan cheese
1 can (14½ ounces) DEL MONTE® Diced Tomatoes with Basil, Garlic & Oregano, undrained

1. Preheat oven to 350°F. Cook pasta according to package directions; drain.

2. Cook eggplant and garlic in oil in large skillet over medium-high heat until tender.

3. Toss eggplant with cooked pasta, 1 cup Jack cheese, green onions and Parmesan cheese.

4. Place in greased 9-inch square baking dish. Top with undrained tomatoes and remaining ½ cup Jack cheese. Bake 15 minutes or until heated through.

Makes 6 servings

Prep and Cook Time: 30 minutes

Pasta Roll-Ups

1 package (1.5 ounces) LAWRY'S® Original-Style Spaghetti Sauce Spices & Seasonings
1 can (6 ounces) tomato paste
2¼ cups water
2 tablespoons butter or vegetable oil
2 cups cottage cheese or ricotta cheese
1 cup (4 ounces) shredded mozzarella cheese
¼ cup grated Parmesan cheese
2 eggs, lightly beaten
½ to 1 teaspoon LAWRY'S® Garlic Salt
½ teaspoon dried basil, crushed (optional)
8 ounces lasagna noodles, cooked and drained

In medium saucepan, prepare Spaghetti Sauce Spices & Seasonings according to package directions using tomato paste, water and butter. In large bowl, combine remaining ingredients except noodles; mix well. Spread ¼ cup cheese mixture on entire length of each lasagna noodle; roll up. Place noodles, seam side down, in microwave-safe baking dish. Cover with vented plastic wrap and microwave on HIGH 6 to 7 minutes or until cheese begins to melt. Pour sauce over rolls and microwave on HIGH 1 minute longer, if necessary, to heat sauce.   *Makes 6 servings*

Serving Suggestion: Sprinkle with additional grated Parmesan cheese. Garnish with fresh basil leaves.

Rotini with Fresh Tomato, Basil and Ricotta Sauce

1 container (15 ounces) ricotta cheese
¼ cup grated Parmesan cheese Black pepper
2 large tomatoes, cored and cut into thin wedges
2 tablespoons extra-virgin olive oil
½ teaspoon salt
1 package (16 ounces) BARILLA® Rotini
2 tablespoons slivered basil leaves

1. Whisk ricotta, Parmesan and pepper to taste in large serving bowl. Combine tomatoes, olive oil and salt in separate bowl.

2. Cook rotini according to package directions. Remove ¼ cup pasta-cooking water and stir into ricotta mixture. Drain rotini.

3. Add rotini to ricotta cheese mixture with tomatoes and basil; mix well. Serve immediately.
Makes 6 to 8 servings

Helpful Hints

To sliver basil easily, stack the leaves together and roll them up like a cigar. With a sharp knife, cut the leaves crosswise into thin strips.

Penne Puttanesca

3 tablespoons BERTOLLI® Olive Oil
2 cloves garlic, finely chopped
1 jar (1 pound 10 ounces) RAGÚ® Old World Style® Pasta Sauce
¼ cup chopped pitted oil-cured olives
1 tablespoon capers, rinsed
½ teaspoon dried oregano leaves, crushed
¼ teaspoon crushed red pepper flakes
1 box (16 ounces) penne pasta, cooked, drained

In 12-inch skillet, heat oil over low heat and cook garlic 30 seconds. Stir in remaining ingredients except pasta. Simmer uncovered, stirring occasionally, 15 minutes. Serve sauce over hot pasta. Garnish, if desired, with chopped fresh parsley.

Makes 8 servings

Celebration Pasta

2 cups fresh tortellini
1 bag (16 ounces) BIRDS EYE® frozen Farm Fresh Mixtures Broccoli, Corn & Red Peppers
1 tablespoon olive oil
1 teaspoon salt
1 teaspoon lemon juice
½ cup fresh or canned diced tomatoes

• In large saucepan, cook tortellini according to package directions; drain and return to saucepan.

• Cook vegetables according to package directions; drain and add to tortellini.

• In small bowl, combine oil, salt and lemon juice. Stir in tomatoes.

• Stir tomato mixture into pasta and vegetables; cook over medium heat 5 minutes or until heated through.

Makes 4 servings

Prep Time: 10 minutes
Cook Time: 10 minutes

Greek-Style Stuffed Shells

1 jar (1 pound 10 ounces) RAGÚ® Chunky Gardenstyle Pasta Sauce
1 container (15 ounces) ricotta cheese
8 ounces feta cheese, crumbled
1 large egg, lightly beaten
1 teaspoon dried oregano leaves, crushed
6 ounces jumbo shells pasta, cooked and drained (about 21)

1. Preheat oven to 350°F. In 13×9-inch baking dish, evenly spread 1 cup Ragú® Chunky Gardenstyle Pasta Sauce; set aside.

2. In large bowl, combine cheeses, egg and oregano. Fill shells with cheese mixture, then arrange in baking dish. Evenly top with remaining sauce.

3. Bake 30 minutes or until sauce is bubbling. Garnish, if desired, with sliced pitted ripe olives.

Makes 6 servings

Tip: Try using a small ice cream scoop to neatly fill shells.

Prep Time: 20 minutes
Cook Time: 30 minutes

Latin-Style Pasta & Beans

8 ounces uncooked mostaccioli, penne or bow tie pasta
1 tablespoon olive oil
1 medium onion, chopped
1 yellow or red bell pepper, diced
4 cloves garlic, minced
1 can (15 ounces) red or black beans, rinsed and drained
¾ cup canned vegetable broth
¾ cup medium-hot salsa or picante sauce
2 teaspoons ground cumin
⅓ cup coarsely chopped fresh cilantro
Lime wedges

1. Cook pasta according to package directions, omitting salt. Drain; set aside.

2. Meanwhile, heat oil in large skillet over medium heat. Add onion; cook 5 minutes, stirring occasionally. Add bell pepper and garlic; cook 3 minutes, stirring occasionally. Add beans, vegetable broth, salsa and cumin; simmer, uncovered, 5 minutes.

3. Add pasta to skillet; cook 1 minute, tossing frequently. Stir in cilantro; spoon onto 4 plates. Serve with lime wedges. *Makes 4 servings*

Helpful Hints

Lime juice adds a refreshing tang to both sweet and savory dishes. A sprinkle of lime juice heightens the flavor of fruits, such as melons, mangoes and papayas.

Latin-Style Pasta & Beans

Spaghetti with Tomatoes and Olives

2 tablespoons extra-virgin olive oil
3 cloves garlic, finely chopped
1½ pounds fresh ripe tomatoes, seeded and chopped (about 3 cups)
1 tablespoon tomato paste
1 teaspoon dried oregano
⅛ teaspoon ground red pepper
½ cup pitted brine-cured black olives, coarsely chopped
2 tablespoons capers
Salt and pepper
1 package (16 ounces) BARILLA® Thin Spaghetti
Grated Parmesan cheese

1. Heat olive oil and garlic in large skillet over low heat until garlic begins to sizzle. Add tomatoes, tomato paste, oregano and red pepper; simmer, uncovered, until sauce is thickened, about 15 minutes. Add olives, capers and salt and pepper to taste.

2. Meanwhile, cook spaghetti according to package directions; drain.

3. Toss spaghetti with sauce. Sprinkle with cheese before serving.

Makes 6 to 8 servings

Meatless Ravioli Bake

4 cups finely chopped eggplant
½ cup chopped onion
¼ cup chopped carrots
¼ cup chopped celery
3 tablespoons olive oil
2 cans (8 ounces each) HUNT'S® No Salt Added Tomato Sauce
1 can (14.5 ounces) HUNT'S® Crushed Tomatoes
½ teaspoon sugar
⅛ teaspoon pepper
1 package (18 ounces) frozen large ravioli, prepared according to package directions

1. Preheat oven to 375°F.

2. In saucepan, sauté eggplant, onion, carrots and celery in hot oil; cook until tender.

3. Stir in Hunt's Tomato Sauce, Hunt's Tomatoes, sugar and pepper. Simmer, uncovered, 10 minutes; stirring occasionally.

4. Spoon *1½ cups* of tomato mixture into 13×9×2-inch baking dish; top with *half* the ravioli and *half of the remaining* sauce. Repeat layers.

5. Bake, uncovered, 30 minutes or until bubbly.

Makes 6 (7-ounce) servings

Pasta with Onions and Goat Cheese

2 teaspoons olive oil
4 cups thinly sliced sweet onions
¾ cup (3 ounces) goat cheese
¼ cup skim milk
6 ounces uncooked baby bow tie or other small pasta
1 clove garlic, minced
2 tablespoons dry white wine or fat-free reduced-sodium chicken broth
1½ teaspoons chopped fresh sage *or* ½ teaspoon dried sage leaves
½ teaspoon salt
¼ teaspoon black pepper
2 tablespoons chopped toasted walnuts

Heat oil in large nonstick skillet over medium heat. Add onions; cook slowly until golden and caramelized, about 20 to 25 minutes, stirring occasionally.

Combine goat cheese and milk in small bowl; stir until well blended. Set aside.

Cook pasta according to package directions, omitting salt. Drain and set aside.

Add garlic to onions in skillet; cook until softened, about 3 minutes. Add wine, sage, salt and pepper; cook until moisture is evaporated. Remove from heat; add pasta and goat cheese mixture, stirring to melt cheese. Sprinkle with walnuts.

Makes 8 (½-cup) servings

Quick Skillet Quiche

4 eggs
⅓ cup 1% milk
2 teaspoons Cajun seasoning
1 cup reduced-fat Cheddar cheese, divided
1 cup UNCLE BEN'S® Instant Rice
1 cup chopped fresh asparagus
¾ cup chopped green onions
½ cup chopped red bell pepper

1. Preheat oven to 350°F. In medium bowl, whisk eggs, milk, Cajun seasoning and ½ cup cheese. Set aside.

2. Cook rice according to package directions.

3. Meanwhile, spray medium skillet with nonstick cooking spray. Heat over medium heat until hot. Add asparagus, green onions and bell pepper. Cook and stir 5 minutes. Add rice and mix well.

4. Shape rice mixture to form crust on bottom and halfway up side of skillet. Pour egg mixture over crust. Sprinkle with remaining ½ cup cheese. Cover; cook over medium-low heat 10 minutes or until eggs are nearly set. Transfer skillet to oven and bake 5 minutes or until eggs are completely set.

Makes 6 servings

Pasta with Onions and Goat Cheese

Polenta Lasagna

1½ cups whole grain yellow
      cornmeal
4 teaspoons finely chopped
      fresh marjoram
1 teaspoon olive oil
1 pound fresh mushrooms,
      sliced
1 cup chopped leeks
1 clove garlic, minced
½ cup (2 ounces) shredded part-
      skim mozzarella cheese
2 tablespoons chopped fresh
      basil
1 tablespoon chopped fresh
      oregano
⅛ teaspoon black pepper
2 red bell peppers, chopped
¼ cup freshly grated Parmesan
      cheese, divided

1. Bring 4 cups water to a boil in medium saucepan over high heat. Slowly add cornmeal to water, stirring constantly with wire whisk. Reduce heat to low; stir in marjoram. Simmer 15 to 20 minutes or until polenta thickens and pulls away from side of saucepan. Spread on 13×9-inch ungreased baking sheet. Cover and chill about 1 hour or until firm.

2. Heat oil in medium nonstick skillet. Cook and stir mushrooms, leeks and garlic over medium heat 5 minutes or until vegetables are crisp-tender. Stir in mozzarella, basil, oregano and black pepper.

3. Place bell peppers and ¼ cup water in food processor or blender; process until smooth. Preheat oven to 350°F. Spray 11×7-inch baking dish with nonstick cooking spray.

4. Cut cold polenta into 12 (3½-inch) squares; arrange 6 squares in bottom of prepared pan. Spread with half of bell pepper mixture, half of vegetable mixture and 2 tablespoons Parmesan.

Place remaining 6 squares polenta over Parmesan; top with remaining bell pepper and vegetable mixtures and Parmesan. Bake 20 minutes or until cheese is melted and polenta is golden brown.

Makes 6 servings

Saucy Mediterranean Frittata

Tomato Sauce (recipe follows)
1 tablespoon olive oil
1 small onion, chopped
1 medium tomato, seeded and
      diced
1 tablespoon finely chopped
      fresh basil *or* 1 teaspoon
      dried basil leaves
¼ teaspoon dried oregano leaves
⅓ cup cooked orzo
⅓ cup chopped pitted black
      olives
8 eggs
½ teaspoon salt
⅛ teaspoon black pepper
2 tablespoons butter
½ cup (2 ounces) shredded
      mozzarella cheese

1. Prepare Tomato Sauce.

2. Heat oil in ovenproof 10-inch skillet over medium-high heat. Cook and stir onion until tender. Add tomato, basil and oregano; cook and stir 3 minutes. Stir in orzo and olives; remove from skillet and set aside.

3. Beat eggs, salt and pepper in medium bowl with electric mixer at low speed. Stir in tomato mixture; set aside.

4. Melt butter in same skillet over medium heat. Add egg mixture; top with cheese. Reduce heat to low. Cook 8 to 10 minutes or until bottom and most of middle is set.

5. Place skillet on rack 4 inches from broiler. Broil 1 to 2 minutes or until top is browned. Cut into wedges; serve with Tomato Sauce. Garnish as desired.   *Makes 4 to 6 servings*

Tomato Sauce

1 can (8 ounces) tomato sauce
1 teaspoon minced dried onion
¼ teaspoon dried basil leaves
¼ teaspoon dried oregano leaves
⅛ teaspoon minced dried garlic
⅛ teaspoon black pepper

Combine all ingredients in small saucepan. Bring to a boil over high heat. Reduce heat to low. Simmer, uncovered, over medium-low heat 5 minutes, stirring often. Set aside; keep warm.   *Makes about 1 cup*

Pesto Linguine Tossed with Olive Oil and Broccoli

1 (12 ounce) package
      PASTA LABELLA™ Pesto
      Linguine
¼ cup extra-virgin olive oil
½ cup julienned yellow onion
½ cup diced red bell pepper
1½ cups broccoli florets
      Salt and pepper, to taste
1 cup pasta cooking liquid*
¼ cup grated Parmesan cheese

Cook pasta according to package directions until al dente. *Before draining pasta, reserve 1 cup cooking liquid for recipe. Meanwhile, heat olive oil in large skillet. Sauté onion and bell pepper 1 minute. Add broccoli; sauté 4 minutes. Season with salt and pepper; add pasta liquid. Simmer vegetables 2 minutes. Add hot linguine to vegetable mixture; mix well. Sprinkle with Parmesan cheese and serve.

Makes 4 servings

Polenta Lasagna

Quick Veg•All® Enchiladas

1 can (15 ounces) VEG•ALL®
   Original Mixed Vegetables,
   drained
1 can (15 ounces) refried beans
8 (6-inch) corn tortillas
1 can (10 ounces) enchilada
   sauce
1 cup shredded Cheddar cheese
1 cup sour cream
½ cup chopped green onions
½ cup chopped ripe olives

Preheat oven to 350°F. Combine Veg•All and beans in medium bowl. Divide mixture and place in center of each tortilla; roll up. Place rolled tortillas in baking dish. Cover tortillas with enchilada sauce and cheese. Bake for 30 minutes. Top with sour cream, green onions, and ripe olives.

Makes 4 servings

Note: If tortillas unfold as you are assembling them, turn seam side down.

Prep Time: 7 minutes
Cook Time: 30 minutes

Eggplant Cheese Casserole

1 package (1.5 ounce) LAWRY'S®
   Original-Style Spaghetti
   Sauce Spices & Seasoning
1 can (8 ounce) tomato sauce
1½ cups water
1 teaspoon LAWRY'S® Seasoned
   Salt
½ cup finely chopped onion
1 large eggplant, peeled and cut
   into ¼-inch slices
¾ to 1 cup salad oil
½ pound mozzarella cheese,
   thinly sliced
¼ cup grated Parmesan cheese

In medium saucepan, combine Original-Style Spaghetti Sauce Spices & Seasonings, tomato sauce, water, Seasoned Salt and onion; mix well. Bring to a boil over medium-high heat; reduce heat to low and simmer, uncovered, 20 minutes. In large skillet, heat oil. Add eggplant and cook over medium-high heat until browned, adding oil as needed. Drain eggplant thoroughly on paper towels. Pour ⅓ of sauce into 8-inch square dish. Cover sauce with layers of eggplant and mozzarella slices. Repeat layers, ending with sauce and top with Parmesan cheese. Bake, uncovered, in 350°F. oven 20 minutes.

Makes 6 servings

Serving Suggestion: Let stand 10 minutes before cutting into squares. Serve with a vegetable salad and fruit dessert, or as an accompaniment to roast lamb or grilled lamb chops.

Florentine-Stuffed Shells

24 uncooked jumbo pasta shells
   for filling
1 package (10 ounces) frozen
   chopped spinach, thawed
1 egg, slightly beaten
2 cups (15 ounces) SARGENTO®
   Ricotta Cheese*
1½ cups (6 ounces) SARGENTO®
   Chef Style or Fancy
   Mozzarella Shredded
   Cheese
⅓ cup finely chopped onion
2 cloves garlic, minced
¼ teaspoon salt
⅛ teaspoon ground nutmeg
2 cups meatless spaghetti
   sauce
½ cup (2 ounces) SARGENTO®
   Fancy Parmesan Shredded
   Cheese

SARGENTO® Whole Milk Ricotta, Part-Skim Ricotta or Light Ricotta can be used.

Cook pasta shells according to package directions; drain. Meanwhile, squeeze spinach to remove as much moisture as possible. Combine egg, spinach, Ricotta cheese, Mozzarella cheese, onion, garlic, salt and nutmeg; stir to blend well. Stuff shells with Ricotta mixture, using about 2 tablespoons mixture for each shell. Place in lightly greased 13×9-inch baking dish. Pour spaghetti sauce over shells. Sprinkle with grated cheese; cover. Bake at 350°F, 30 to 40 minutes or until thoroughly heated.

Makes 8 servings

Quick Veg•All® Enchiladas

Ratatouille Pot Pie

¼ cup olive oil
1 medium eggplant (about
    1 pound), peeled and cut
    into ½-inch pieces
1 large onion, chopped
1 green or yellow bell pepper,
    chopped
1½ teaspoons minced garlic
1 can (14½ ounces) pasta-ready
    diced tomatoes with garlic
    and herbs or Italian stewed
    tomatoes, undrained
1 teaspoon dried basil leaves
½ teaspoon red pepper flakes
¼ teaspoon salt
1 tablespoon balsamic vinegar
2 cups (8 ounces) shredded
    mozzarella cheese, divided
1 package (10 ounces)
    refrigerated pizza dough

1. Preheat oven to 425°F. Heat oil in large skillet over medium heat until hot. Add eggplant, onion, bell pepper and garlic. Cook 10 minutes or until eggplant begins to brown, stirring occasionally. Stir in tomatoes with juice, basil, pepper flakes and salt. Cook, uncovered, over medium-low heat 5 minutes.

2. Remove from heat; stir in vinegar. Let stand 10 minutes; stir in 1 cup cheese. Transfer mixture to ungreased 11×7-inch casserole dish. Sprinkle with remaining 1 cup cheese.

3. Unroll pizza dough; arrange over top of casserole. Make decorative cut-outs using small cookie cutter, if desired. Spray dough with nonstick cooking spray. Bake 15 minutes or until crust is golden brown and vegetable mixture is bubbly. Let stand 5 minutes before serving.

Makes 6 servings

Spinach Stuffed Manicotti

1 package (10 ounces) frozen
    spinach
8 uncooked manicotti shells
1½ teaspoons olive oil
1 teaspoon dried rosemary
1 teaspoon dried sage leaves
1 teaspoon dried oregano leaves
1 teaspoon dried thyme leaves
1 teaspoon chopped garlic
1½ cups chopped fresh tomatoes
½ cup ricotta cheese
½ cup fresh whole wheat bread
    crumbs
2 egg whites, lightly beaten
    Yellow pepper rings and sage
    sprig for garnish

1. Cook spinach according to package directions. Place in colander to drain. Let stand until cool enough to handle. Squeeze spinach with hands to remove excess moisture. Set aside.

2. Cook pasta according to package directions, drain. Rinse under cold running water until cool enough to handle; drain.

3. Preheat oven to 350°F. Heat oil in small saucepan over medium heat. Cook and stir rosemary, sage, oregano, thyme and garlic in hot oil about 1 minute. *Do not let herbs turn brown.* Add tomatoes; reduce heat to low. Simmer, uncovered, 10 minutes, stirring occasionally.

4. Combine spinach, cheese and crumbs in bowl. Fold in egg whites. Fill shells with spinach mixture using spoon.

5. Place one third of tomato mixture on bottom of 13×9-inch baking pan. Arrange manicotti in pan. Pour tomato mixture over top. Cover with foil.

6. Bake 30 minutes or until bubbly. Garnish, if desired.

Makes 4 servings

Spicy Ravioli and Cheese

1 medium red bell pepper, thinly
    sliced
1 medium green bell pepper,
    thinly sliced
1 medium yellow bell pepper,
    thinly sliced
1 tablespoon olive or vegetable
    oil
½ teaspoon LAWRY'S® Seasoned
    Salt
¼ teaspoon LAWRY'S® Garlic
    Powder with Parsley
¼ teaspoon sugar
1 package (8 or 9 ounces) fresh
    or frozen ravioli
1½ cups chunky salsa
4 ounces mozzarella cheese,
    thinly sliced
2 green onions, sliced

Place bell peppers in broilerproof baking dish; sprinkle with oil, Seasoned Salt, Garlic Powder with Parsley and sugar. Broil 15 minutes or until tender and browned, turning once. Prepare ravioli according to package directions. Pour ¾ cup salsa in bottom of 8-inch square baking dish. Alternate layers of bell peppers, ravioli, cheese and green onions. Pour remaining ¾ cup salsa over layers. Cover with foil; bake in 350°F oven 15 to 20 minutes or until heated through and cheese melts.

Makes 4 to 6 servings

Serving Suggestion: Excellent with thin, crisp bread sticks and a small green salad.

Ratatouille Pot Pie

Skillet Pesto Tortellini

1¼ cups water
1¼ cups milk
1 envelope (1¼ ounces) creamy pesto sauce mix
1 package (16 ounces) frozen vegetable medley
1 package (12 ounces) frozen tortellini
Dash ground red pepper
½ cup (2 ounces) shredded mozzarella cheese

1. Blend water, milk and sauce mix in large deep skillet. Bring to a boil over high heat. Stir in vegetables, tortellini and ground red pepper; return to a boil.

2. Cook vegetables and tortellini, uncovered, over medium-high heat 8 to 10 minutes or until tortellini is tender and sauce has thickened, stirring occasionally.

3. Sprinkle with cheese just before serving.   *Makes 4 servings*

Prep and Cook Time: 22 minutes

Wisconsin Cheesy Pasta Primavera

1 cup diagonally sliced carrots
6 tablespoons butter, divided
1 cup sliced yellow summer squash
2 cups quartered mushroom
1 cup halved Chinese pea pods
¼ cup sliced green onions
1 tablespoon chopped fresh basil leaves *or* 1 teaspoon dried basil leaves
8 ounces hot cooked fettuccine
1 cup low-fat or cream-style cottage cheese
½ cup grated Wisconsin Parmesan cheese
Salt and pepper

In large skillet sauté carrots in 4 tablespoons butter for 5 minutes. Add squash; cook 2 minutes. Add pea pods and green onions; cook until vegetables are tender, about 5 minutes. Stir in basil. Combine fettuccine and remaining 2 tablespoons butter; toss until butter is melted. Toss in cottage cheese and Parmesan cheese. Place fettuccine mixture on serving platter; top with vegetable mixture. Season with salt and pepper to taste.

Makes 4 servings

*Favorite recipe from **Wisconsin Milk Marketing Board***

Vegetarian Stir-Fry

1 bag (16 ounces) BIRDS EYE® frozen Mixed Vegetables
2 tablespoons water
1 can (14 ounces) kidney beans, drained
1 jar (14 ounces) spaghetti sauce
½ teaspoon garlic powder
½ cup grated Parmesan cheese

• In large skillet, place vegetables in water. Cover; cook 7 to 10 minutes over medium heat.

• Uncover; stir in beans, spaghetti sauce and garlic powder; cook until heated through.

• Sprinkle with cheese.

Makes 4 servings

Serving Suggestion: Serve over hot cooked rice or pasta.

Prep Time: 2 minutes
Cook Time: 12 to 15 minutes

Puttenesca Sauce

1 pound dry pasta (fettuccine, spaghetti or penne)
2 tablespoons olive oil
2 cloves garlic, minced
1 can (14.5 ounces) CONTADINA® Recipe Ready Diced Tomatoes, undrained
1 can (6 ounces) sliced pitted ripe olives, drained
1 can (6 ounces) CONTADINA Tomato Paste
⅓ cup chopped fresh parsley *or* 4 teaspoons dried parsley flakes, crushed
⅓ cup water
2 tablespoons dry red wine or chicken broth
1 tablespoon capers
1 tablespoon Worcestershire sauce
1 teaspoon dried oregano leaves, crushed
⅛ teaspoon crushed red pepper flakes

1. Cook pasta according to package directions; drain and keep warm.

2. Meanwhile, heat oil in medium skillet. Add garlic; sauté for 30 seconds.

3. Stir in undrained tomatoes, olives, tomato paste, parsley, water, wine, capers, Worcestershire sauce, oregano and red pepper flakes.

4. Bring to a boil. Reduce heat to low; simmer, uncovered, for 10 minutes. Serve over pasta.

Makes 8 servings

Prep Time: 5 minutes
Cook Time: 12 minutes

Skillet Pesto Tortellini

Spicy African Chick-Pea and Sweet Potato Stew

Spice Paste (recipe follows)
1½ pounds sweet potatoes, peeled and cubed
2 cups canned vegetable broth or water
1 can (16 ounces) plum tomatoes, undrained and chopped
1 can (16 ounces) chick-peas, drained and rinsed
1½ cups sliced fresh okra *or* 1 package (10 ounces) frozen cut okra, thawed
Yellow Couscous (recipe follows)
Hot pepper sauce
Fresh cilantro for garnish

1. Prepare Spice Paste.

2. Combine sweet potatoes, broth, tomatoes with juice, chick-peas, okra and Spice Paste in large saucepan. Bring to a boil over high heat. Reduce heat to low. Cover and simmer 15 minutes. Uncover; simmer 10 minutes or until vegetables are tender.

3. Meanwhile, prepare Yellow Couscous.

4. Serve stew with couscous and red pepper sauce. Garnish, if desired.
Makes 4 servings

Spice Paste

6 cloves garlic, peeled
1 teaspoon coarse salt
2 teaspoons sweet paprika
1½ teaspoons cumin seeds
1 teaspoon cracked black pepper
½ teaspoon ground ginger
½ teaspoon ground allspice
1 tablespoon olive oil

Process garlic and salt in blender or small food processor until garlic is finely chopped. Add remaining spices. Process 15 seconds. While blender is running, pour oil through cover opening; process until mixture forms paste.   *Makes 3 cups*

Yellow Couscous

1 tablespoon olive oil
5 green onions, sliced
1⅔ cups water
⅛ teaspoon saffron threads *or* ½ teaspoon ground turmeric
¼ teaspoon salt
1 cup precooked couscous*

*Check ingredient label for "precooked semolina."

Heat oil in medium saucepan over medium heat until hot. Add onions; cook and stir 4 minutes. Add water, saffron and salt. Bring to a boil. Stir in couscous. Remove from heat. Cover; let stand 5 minutes.
Makes 3 cups

Vegetable Cheese Frittata

½ cup fresh green beans, cut into 1-inch pieces
1 small onion, chopped
3 tablespoons butter or margarine
¼ red bell pepper, chopped
¼ cup sliced fresh mushrooms
¼ cup dry bread crumbs
½ cup prepared HIDDEN VALLEY® The Original Ranch® Dressing
6 eggs, beaten
⅓ cup shredded Cheddar cheese
¼ cup grated Parmesan cheese

Preheat oven to 350°F. In medium saucepan, steam green beans over boiling water until crisp-tender, about 4 minutes. In medium skillet, sauté onion in butter until onion is softened; stir in beans, red pepper and mushrooms. Fold vegetables, bread crumbs and salad dressing into eggs. Pour into buttered quiche dish. Sprinkle with cheeses. Bake until set, about 25 minutes.
Makes 6 servings

Note: Substitute chopped tomatoes, diced green chili peppers, sliced black olives, chopped zucchini or any vegetable combination for green beans, onion and mushrooms.

Penne Primavera

2 tablespoons WESSON® Vegetable Oil
1 cup sliced mushrooms
½ cup chopped onion
¼ cup chopped zucchini
¼ cup each: chopped red bell peppers, yellow bell peppers, and green bell peppers
1 teaspoon minced fresh garlic
1 can (26 ounces) HUNT'S® Traditional Spaghetti Sauce
1 can (2¾ ounces) sliced black olives, drained
Hot cooked penne pasta
TREASURE CAVE® Shredded Parmesan Cheese

1. In large skillet, heat Wesson Oil. Sauté mushrooms, onion, zucchini, peppers and garlic until tender.

2. Add Hunt's Spaghetti Sauce and olives; simmer, covered, 15 minutes.

3. Serve over hot pasta. Sprinkle with cheese.
Makes 8 (5-ounce) servings

Helpful Hints

Penne is narrow tubes of pasta that have been cut on the diagonal. Mostaccioli may be substituted.

Spicy African Chick-Pea and Sweet Potato Stew

Springtime Pasta

1 package (12 ounces)
    fettuccine or other long
    pasta, uncooked
1 bag (16 ounces) BIRDS EYE®
    frozen Farm Fresh Mixtures
    Cauliflower, Carrots and
    Snow Pea Pods
⅓ cup creamy Caesar, Italian or
    ranch salad dressing
1 teaspoon dried basil
1 teaspoon garlic powder
⅓ cup grated Parmesan cheese

• Cook pasta according to package directions; drain.

• Cook vegetables according to package directions.

• Combine pasta, vegetables, dressing and spices in large skillet; mix well.

• Cook over medium heat just until heated through.

• Add cheese; toss to coat pasta.

Makes 4 to 6 servings

Prep Time: 5 minutes
Cook Time: 15 minutes

Herbed Veggie Cheese and Rice

1 bag (16 ounces) BIRDS EYE®
    frozen Farm Fresh Mixtures
    Broccoli, Green Beans,
    Pearl Onions & Red Peppers
2 cups cooked white rice
2 tablespoons grated Parmesan
    cheese
1 teaspoon dried basil
1 teaspoon dill weed
½ cup reduced-fat shredded
    Cheddar cheese
½ cup reduced-fat shredded
    Monterey Jack cheese

• In large saucepan, cook vegetables according to package directions; drain and return to saucepan.

• Add rice, using fork to keep rice fluffy.

• Add Parmesan cheese, basil, dill and salt and pepper to taste.

• Add Cheddar and Monterey Jack cheeses; toss together. Cook over medium heat until heated through.

Makes 4 servings

Prep Time: 6 minutes
Cook Time: 12 to 15 minutes

Tomato-Caper Sauce

1 pound dry pasta
2 tablespoons olive or vegetable
    oil
2 cloves garlic, minced
1 can (29 ounces) CONTADINA®
    Tomato Sauce
½ cup capers
¼ cup chopped fresh cilantro
1 tablespoon chopped fresh
    basil *or* 1 teaspoon dried
    basil leaves, crushed
1 tablespoon chopped fresh
    thyme *or* 1 teaspoon dried
    thyme leaves, crushed

1. Cook pasta according to package directions; drain and keep warm.

2. Meanwhile, heat oil in medium saucepan. Add garlic; sauté for 30 seconds. Stir in tomato sauce and capers.

3. Bring to a boil. Reduce heat to low; simmer, uncovered, for 20 minutes, stirring occasionally.

4. Stir in cilantro, basil and thyme; simmer for 5 minutes. Serve over pasta.   *Makes 8 servings*

Prep Time: 6 minutes
Cook Time: 26 minutes

Spinach and Mushroom Enchiladas

2 packages (10 ounces each)
    frozen chopped spinach,
    thawed
1½ cups sliced mushrooms
1 can (15 ounces) pinto beans,
    drained and rinsed
3 teaspoons chili powder,
    divided
¼ teaspoon red pepper flakes
1 can (8 ounces) tomato sauce
2 tablespoons water
½ teaspoon hot pepper sauce
8 (8-inch) corn tortillas
1 cup shredded Monterey Jack
    cheese
    Shredded lettuce (optional)
    Chopped tomatoes (optional)
    Reduced-fat sour cream
    (optional)

1. Combine spinach, mushrooms, beans, 2 teaspoons chili powder and red pepper flakes in large skillet over medium heat. Cook and stir 5 minutes; remove from heat.

2. Combine tomato sauce, water, remaining 1 teaspoon chili powder and pepper sauce in medium skillet. Dip tortillas into tomato sauce mixture; stack tortillas on waxed paper.

3. Divide spinach filling into 8 portions. Spoon onto center of tortillas; roll up and place in 11×8-inch microwavable dish. (Secure rolls with wooden picks, if desired.) Spread remaining tomato sauce mixture over enchiladas.

4. Cover with vented plastic wrap. Microwave, uncovered, at MEDIUM (50%) 10 minutes or until heated through. Sprinkle with cheese. Microwave at MEDIUM 3 minutes or until cheese is melted. Serve with lettuce, tomatoes and sour cream.

Makes 4 servings

Spinach and Mushroom Enchiladas

Vegetable Lasagna

Tomato-Basil Sauce (recipe
    follows)
2 tablespoons olive oil
4 medium carrots, thinly sliced
    (1½ cups)
3 medium zucchini (1 pound),
    thinly sliced
6 ounces spinach leaves,
    washed, stemmed and torn
    in bite-sized pieces
¼ teaspoon salt
¼ teaspoon black pepper
1 egg
3 cups ricotta cheese
½ cup plus 2 tablespoons grated
    Parmesan cheese, divided
12 uncooked lasagna noodles
1½ cups (6 ounces) shredded
    mozzarella cheese
1½ cups (6 ounces) shredded
    Monterey Jack cheese
½ cup water
    Belgian endive leaves, Bibb
    lettuce leaves and fresh
    basil sprigs for garnish

1. Prepare Tomato-Basil Sauce.

2. Heat oil in 12-inch skillet over
medium heat until hot. Add carrots;
cook and stir 4 minutes. Add
zucchini; cook and stir 8 minutes or
until crisp-tender. Add spinach; cook
and stir 1 minute or until spinach is
wilted. Stir in salt and pepper.

3. Preheat oven to 350°F. Beat egg in
medium bowl. Stir in ricotta cheese
and ½ cup Parmesan cheese.

4. Spread 2 cups Tomato-Basil Sauce
in bottom of 13×9×3-inch baking
pan; top with 4 uncooked lasagna
noodles. Spoon ⅓ of ricotta cheese
mixture over noodles; carefully spread
with spatula.

5. Spoon ⅓ of vegetable mixture over
cheese. Top with 2 cups Tomato-Basil
Sauce. Sprinkle with ½ cup each
mozzarella and Monterey Jack
cheeses. Repeat layers 2 times
beginning with noodles and ending
with mozzarella and Monterey Jack
cheeses. Sprinkle with remaining
2 tablespoons Parmesan cheese.

6. Carefully pour water around sides
of pan. Cover pan tightly with foil.

7. Bake lasagna 1 hour 20 to 1 hour
40 minutes or until bubbly. Uncover.
Let stand 10 to 15 minutes. Cut into
squares. Garnish, if desired.
Makes 8 servings

Tomato-Basil Sauce

4 cans (28 ounces each) plum
    tomatoes
2 teaspoons olive oil
2 medium onions, chopped
5 cloves garlic, minced
1 tablespoon sugar
2 tablespoons dried basil leaves
½ teaspoon salt
¼ teaspoon black pepper

1. Drain tomatoes, reserving 1 cup
juice. Seed and chop tomatoes.

2. Heat oil in large skillet over medium
heat until hot. Add onions and garlic;
cook and stir 5 minutes or until tender.
Stir in tomatoes, reserved juice, sugar,
basil, salt and pepper.

3. Bring to a boil over high heat.
Reduce heat to low. Simmer,
uncovered, 25 to 30 minutes or until
most of juices have evaporated.
Makes 8 cups

Spring Vegetable Linguine

8 ounces BARILLA® Linguine
8 ounces asparagus, stems
    trimmed, cut into 3-inch
    pieces
8 ounces sugar snap peas,
    trimmed
1 jar (26 ounces) BARILLA®
    Tomato and Basil Pasta
    Sauce
    Grated Parmesan cheese

1. Begin cooking linguine according
to package directions; add
asparagus and sugar snap peas
during last 5 minutes of cooking.

2. Meanwhile, heat pasta sauce in
medium saucepan over medium heat,
stirring frequently.

3. Pour sauce over hot drained
linguine and vegetables. Serve with
cheese.   *Makes 6 to 8 servings*

Speedy Mac & Cheese

1 can (10¾ ounces) condensed
    Cheddar cheese soup
1 cup milk
4 cups hot cooked medium shell
    macaroni (3 cups uncooked)
1⅓ cups *French's®* French Fried
    Onions, divided
1 cup (4 ounces) shredded
    Cheddar cheese

Combine soup and milk in 2-quart
microwavable casserole. Stir in
macaroni, ⅔ *cup* French Fried Onions
and cheese. Cover; microwave on
HIGH 10 minutes* or until heated
through, stirring halfway through
cooking time. Top with remaining
⅔ *cup* onions. Microwave 1 minute or
until onions are golden.
Makes 6 servings

*Or, bake, covered, in 350°F oven 25 to
30 minutes.

Prep Time: 10 minutes
Cook Time: 11 minutes

Vegetable Lasagna

Comforting Soups

Farmhouse Ham and Vegetable Chowder

Slow Cooker

2 cans (10½ ounces each) condensed cream of celery soup
2 cups diced cooked ham
1 package (10 ounces) frozen corn
1 large baking potato, cut in ½-inch pieces
1 medium red bell pepper, diced
½ teaspoon dried thyme leaves
2 cups small broccoli florets
½ cup milk

Slow Cooker Directions

1. Combine all ingredients except broccoli and milk in slow cooker; stir to blend. Cover; cook on LOW 6 to 8 hours or on HIGH 3 to 4 hours.

2. If cooking on LOW, turn to HIGH; stir in broccoli and milk. Cover; cook 15 minutes or until broccoli is crisp tender. *Makes 6 servings*

Campfire Sausage and Potato Soup

Slow Cooker

8 ounces kielbasa sausage, cut lengthwise into halves, then crosswise into ½-inch pieces
1 can (15½ ounces) dark kidney beans, rinsed and drained
1 can (14½ ounces) diced tomatoes, undrained
1 can (10½ ounces) condensed beef broth
1 large baking potato, cut into ½-inch cubes
1 medium onion, diced
1 medium green bell pepper, diced
1 teaspoon dried oregano leaves
½ teaspoon sugar
1 to 2 teaspoons ground cumin

Slow Cooker Directions

Combine all ingredients except cumin in slow cooker. Cover; cook on LOW 8 hours or on HIGH 4 hours. Stir in cumin; serve.

Makes 6 to 7 servings

Ham and Navy Bean Soup

Slow Cooker

8 ounces dried navy beans, rinsed and drained
6 cups water
1 ham bone
1 medium yellow onion, chopped
2 celery stalks, finely chopped
2 bay leaves
1½ teaspoons dried tarragon leaves
1½ teaspoons salt
¼ teaspoon black pepper

Slow Cooker Directions

1. Place beans in large bowl; cover completely with water. Soak 6 to 8 hours or overnight. Drain beans; discard water.

2. Combine beans, 6 cups water, ham bone, onion, celery, bay leaves, tarragon and salt in slow cooker. Cover; cook on LOW 8 hours or on HIGH 4 hours. Discard ham bone and bay leaves; stir in pepper.

Makes 8 servings

205

205205

Farmhouse Ham and Vegetable Chowder

Ground Beef, Spinach and Barley Soup

- 12 ounces 95% lean ground beef
- 4 cups water
- 1 can (14½ ounces) no-salt-added stewed tomatoes, undrained
- 1½ cups thinly sliced carrots
- 1 cup chopped onion
- ½ cup quick-cooking barley
- 1½ teaspoons beef bouillon granules
- 1½ teaspoons dried thyme leaves
- 1 teaspoon dried oregano leaves
- ½ teaspoon garlic powder
- ¼ teaspoon black pepper
- ⅛ teaspoon salt
- 3 cups torn stemmed washed spinach leaves

Cook beef in large saucepan over medium heat until no longer pink, stirring to separate. Rinse beef under warm water; drain. Return beef to saucepan; add water, stewed tomatoes with juice, carrots, onion, barley, bouillon granules, thyme, oregano, garlic powder, pepper and salt.

Bring to a boil over high heat. Reduce heat to medium-low. Cover and simmer 12 to 15 minutes or until barley and vegetables are tender, stirring occasionally. Stir in spinach; cook until spinach starts to wilt.

Makes 4 servings

Ranch Clam Chowder

- 3 cans (6½ ounces each) chopped clams
- 6 slices bacon, chopped*
- ¼ cup finely chopped onion
- ¼ cup all-purpose flour
- 2½ cups milk
- 1 packet (1 ounce) HIDDEN VALLEY® The Original Ranch® Salad Dressing & Seasoning Mix
- 2 cups frozen cubed O'Brien potatoes
- 2 cups frozen corn kernels
- ⅛ teaspoon dried thyme (optional)

Bacon pieces may be used.

Drain clams, reserving juice (about 1⅓ cups); set aside. Cook bacon until crisp in a large pot or Dutch oven; remove with slotted spoon, reserving ¼ cup drippings.** Set aside bacon pieces. Heat bacon drippings over medium heat in same pot. Add onion; sauté 3 minutes. Sprinkle with flour; cook and stir 1 minute longer. Gradually whisk in reserved clam juice and milk, stirring until smooth. Whisk in salad dressing & seasoning mix until blended. Stir in potatoes, corn and thyme, if desired. Bring mixture just to a boil; reduce heat and simmer 10 minutes, stirring occasionally. Stir in clams; heat through. Sprinkle bacon on each serving. *Makes 4 to 6 servings*

**You can substitute ¼ cup butter.

Fiesta Black Bean Soup

- 6 cups chicken broth
- ¾ pound potatoes, peeled and diced
- 1 can (16 ounces) black beans, drained
- ½ pound ham, diced
- ½ onion, diced
- 1 can (4 ounces) chopped jalapeño peppers*
- 2 cloves garlic, minced
- 2 teaspoons dried oregano leaves
- 1½ teaspoons dried thyme leaves
- 1 teaspoon ground cumin
  Sour cream, chopped bell peppers and chopped tomatoes for garnish

Jalapeño peppers can sting and irritate the skin; wear rubber gloves when handling peppers and do not touch eyes. Wash hands after handling.

Slow Cooker Directions

Combine all ingredients, except garnishes, in slow cooker. Cover and cook on LOW 8 to 10 hours or on HIGH 4 to 5 hours. Garnish, if desired. *Makes 6 to 8 servings*

Helpful Hints

Barley is available in several forms: hulled, grits, scotch barley and pearled. The most common form, pearled barley, has been polished to remove the bran and most of the germ. Pearled barley is also available in a quick-cooking form.

Fiesta Black Bean Soup

Navy Bean Bacon Chowder

Slow Cooker

1½ cups dried navy beans, rinsed
2 cups cold water
6 slices thick-cut bacon
1 medium carrot, cut lengthwise into halves, then cut into 1-inch pieces
1 rib celery, chopped
1 medium onion, chopped
1 small turnip, cut into 1-inch pieces
1 teaspoon dried Italian seasoning
⅛ teaspoon black pepper
1 large can (46 ounces) reduced-sodium chicken broth
1 cup milk

Slow Cooker Directions

Soak beans overnight in cold water.

Cook bacon in medium skillet over medium heat. Drain and crumble. Combine carrot, celery, onion, turnip, Italian seasoning, pepper, beans and bacon in slow cooker; mix slightly. Pour broth over top. Cover and cook on LOW 7½ to 9 hours or until beans are crisp-tender.

Ladle 2 cups of soup mixture into food processor or blender. Process until smooth; return to slow cooker. Add milk; cover and heat on HIGH 10 minutes or until heated through.

Makes 6 servings

Creamy Reuben Soup

1 cup FRANK'S® or SNOWFLOSS® Kraut, well drained
½ cup chopped onion
¼ cup chopped celery
3 tablespoons butter or margarine
¼ cup unsifted flour
3 cups water
4 teaspoons beef-flavored bouillon granules *or* 4 beef bouillon cubes
½ pound corned beef, shredded
3 cups half-and-half
3 cups (12 ounces) shredded Swiss cheese, divided
6 to 8 slices rye or pumpernickel bread, toasted and cut into quarters

1. In large saucepan cook onion and celery in butter until tender.

2. Stir in flour until smooth.

3. Gradually stir in water and bouillon and bring to boil. Reduce heat and simmer uncovered 5 minutes.

4. Add corned beef, kraut, half-and-half and 1 cup cheese.

5. Cook over low heat for 30 minutes until slightly thickened, stirring frequently.

6. Ladle into 8 oven-proof bowls. Top each with toasted bread and ¼ cup cheese. Broil until cheese melts. Serve immediately.

Makes 8 servings

Prep Time: 20 minutes
Cook Time: 45 minutes

Sausage Vegetable Rotini Soup

6 ounces bulk sausage
1 cup chopped yellow onion
1 cup chopped green bell pepper
3 cups water
1 can (14½ ounces) diced tomatoes, undrained
¼ cup ketchup
2 teaspoons reduced-sodium beef granules
2 teaspoons chili powder
4 ounces uncooked tri-colored rotini
1 cup frozen corn kernels, thawed

Heat Dutch oven over medium-high heat until hot. Coat with nonstick cooking spray. Add sausage and cook 3 minutes or until no longer pink, breaking up sausage into small pieces. Add onion and pepper; cook 3 to 4 minutes or until onion is translucent.

Add water, tomatoes with juice, ketchup, beef granules and chili powder; bring to a boil over high heat. Stir in pasta and return to a boil. Reduce heat to medium-low and simmer, uncovered, 12 minutes. Stir in corn and cook 2 minutes.

Makes 4 servings (6½ cups)

Helpful Hints

Cooking times for rotini may vary from brand to brand. For Sausage Vegetable Rotini Soup, choose a brand with a shorter cooking time.

Navy Bean Bacon Chowder

Beef and Pasta Soup

1 tablespoon vegetable oil
½ pound round steak, cut into
    ½-inch cubes
1 medium onion, chopped
3 cloves garlic, minced
4 cups beef broth
1 can (10¾ ounces) tomato
    purée
2 teaspoons dried Italian
    seasoning
2 bay leaves
1 package (9 ounces) frozen
    Italian green beans
½ cup uncooked orzo or
    rosamarina (rice-shaped
    pastas)
    Salt
    Lemon slices and fresh
    oregano for garnish
    Freshly grated Parmesan
    cheese (optional)
    French bread (optional)

1. Heat oil in 5-quart Dutch oven over medium-high heat; add beef, onion and garlic. Cook and stir until meat is crusty brown and onion is slightly tender.

2. Stir in broth, tomato purée, Italian seasoning and bay leaves. Bring to a boil over high heat. Reduce heat to medium-low; simmer, uncovered, 45 minutes.

3. Add beans and uncooked pasta. Bring to a boil over high heat. Simmer, uncovered, 8 minutes or until beans and pasta are tender, stirring frequently. Season with salt to taste.

4. Remove bay leaves. Ladle into bowls. Garnish, if desired. Serve with freshly grated Parmesan cheese and French bread, if desired.

Makes 5 servings

Potato-Bacon Soup

2 cans (about 14 ounces each)
    chicken broth
3 russet potatoes (1¾ to
    2 pounds), peeled and cut
    into ½-inch cubes
1 medium onion, finely chopped
1 teaspoon dried thyme leaves
4 to 6 strips bacon (4 to
    6 ounces), chopped
½ cup (2 ounces) shredded
    Cheddar cheese

1. Combine broth, potatoes, onion and thyme in Dutch oven; bring to a boil over high heat. Reduce heat to medium-high and boil 10 minutes or until potatoes are tender.

2. While potatoes are cooking, place bacon in microwavable container. Cover with paper towels and cook on HIGH 6 to 7 minutes or until bacon is crisp, stirring after 3 minutes. Break up bacon.

3. Immediately transfer bacon to broth mixture; simmer 3 to 5 minutes. Season to taste with salt and pepper. Ladle into bowls and sprinkle with cheese.   *Makes 4 servings*

Tip: Instead of using a knife to chop the bacon, try snipping it with a pair of scissors while it is partially frozen—you'll find this method quicker and easier.

Prep and Cook Time: 27 minutes

Mexican Vegetable Beef Soup

1 pound ground beef
½ cup chopped onion
1 package (1.0 ounce)
    LAWRY'S® Taco Spices &
    Seasonings
1 can (28 ounces) whole
    tomatoes, cut up
1 package (16 ounces) frozen
    mixed vegetables, thawed
1 can (15¼ ounces) kidney
    beans, undrained
1 can (14½ ounces) beef broth
    Corn chips
    Shredded cheddar cheese

In Dutch oven, brown ground beef and onion, stirring until beef is crumbly and onion is tender; drain fat. Add Taco Spices & Seasonings, tomatoes, vegetables, beans and broth. Bring to a boil over medium-high heat; reduce heat to low and cook, uncovered, 5 minutes, stirring occasionally.   *Makes 6 servings*

Serving Suggestion: Top each serving with corn chips and shredded cheddar cheese.

Hint: For extra flavor, add chopped cilantro to beef mixture.

Beef and Pasta Soup

Kansas City Steak Soup

Nonstick cooking spray
½ pound ground sirloin or
    ground round beef
1 cup chopped onion
3 cups frozen mixed vegetables
2 cups water
1 can (14½ ounces) stewed
    tomatoes, undrained
1 cup sliced celery
1 beef bouillon cube
½ to 1 teaspoon black pepper
1 can (10½ ounces) beef broth
½ cup all-purpose flour

1. Spray Dutch oven with cooking spray. Heat over medium-high heat until hot. Add beef and onion. Cook and stir 5 minutes or until beef is browned.

2. Add vegetables, water, tomatoes with juice, celery, bouillon cube and pepper. Bring to a boil. Whisk together beef broth and flour until smooth; add to beef mixture, stirring constantly. Return mixture to a boil. Reduce heat to low. Cover and simmer 15 minutes, stirring frequently.

Makes 6 servings

Note: If time permits, allow the soup to simmer an additional 30 minutes— the flavors just get better and better

Beef Soup with Noodles

2 tablespoons soy sauce
1 teaspoon minced fresh ginger
¼ teaspoon red pepper flakes
1 boneless beef top sirloin
    steak, cut 1 inch thick
    (about ¾ pound)
1 tablespoon peanut or
    vegetable oil
2 cups sliced fresh mushrooms
2 cans (about 14 ounces each)
    beef broth
3 ounces (1 cup) fresh snow
    peas, cut diagonally into
    1-inch pieces
1½ cups hot cooked fine egg
    noodles (2 ounces
    uncooked)
1 green onion, cut diagonally
    into thin slices
1 teaspoon dark sesame oil
    (optional)
    Red bell pepper strips for
    garnish

1. Combine soy sauce, ginger and red pepper flakes in small bowl. Spread mixture evenly over both sides of steak. Marinate at room temperature 15 minutes.

2. Heat deep skillet over medium-high heat. Add peanut oil; heat until hot. Drain steak; reserve soy sauce mixture (there will only be a small amount of mixture). Add steak to skillet; cook 4 to 5 minutes per side.* Let stand on cutting board 10 minutes.

3. Add mushrooms to skillet; stir-fry 2 minutes. Add broth, snow peas and reserved soy sauce mixture; bring to a boil, scraping up browned meat bits. Reduce heat to medium-low. Stir in noodles.

4. Cut steak across the grain into ⅛-inch slices; cut each slice into 1-inch pieces. Stir into soup; heat through. Stir in onion and sesame oil. Ladle into soup bowls. Garnish with red pepper strips.

Makes 4 servings
(about 6 cups)

*Cooking time is for medium-rare doneness. Adjust time for desired doneness.

Chili Corn Soup

2 tablespoons vegetable oil
2 medium potatoes, diced
1 medium onion, diced
1 tablespoon chili powder
1 (16-ounce) can red kidney
    beans, drained and rinsed
1 (15¼-ounce) can corn, drained
1 (13¾-ounce) can vegetable
    broth
1½ teaspoons TABASCO® brand
    Pepper Sauce
1 teaspoon salt

Heat oil in 4-quart saucepan over medium heat. Add potatoes and onion; cook about 5 minutes, stirring occasionally. Add chili powder; cook 1 minute, stirring frequently.

Stir in beans, corn, vegetable broth, TABASCO® Sauce and salt. Heat to boiling over high heat. Reduce heat to low; cover and simmer 15 to 20 minutes or until potatoes are tender, stirring occasionally.

Makes 6 servings

Kansas City Steak Soup

Savory Pea Soup with Sausage `Slow Cooker`

8 ounces smoked sausage, cut lengthwise into halves, then cut into ½-inch pieces
1 package (16 ounces) dried split peas, sorted and rinsed
3 medium carrots, sliced
2 ribs celery, sliced
1 medium onion, chopped
¾ teaspoon dried marjoram leaves
1 bay leaf
2 cans (14½ ounces each) reduced-sodium chicken broth

Slow Cooker Directions

Heat small skillet over medium heat. Add sausage; cook 5 to 8 minutes or until browned. Drain well. Combine sausage and remaining ingredients in slow cooker. Cover and cook on LOW 4 to 5 hours or until peas are tender. Turn off heat. Remove and discard bay leaf. Cover and let stand 15 minutes to thicken.

Makes 6 servings

Turkey Vegetable Soup

2½ pounds TURKEY WINGS
5 cups water
2 onions, quartered
1 carrot, cut into chunks
1 bay leaf
5 peppercorns
2 cubes low-sodium chicken bouillon
4 medium tomatoes, peeled and cut into quarters
1 cup green beans
1 medium zucchini, cut into ½- to ¾-inch slices
1 carrot, cut into ½-inch slices
1 stalk celery, cut into ½-inch slices
1 leek, thinly sliced
½ cup lima beans
3 tablespoons pearl barley
3 tablespoons fresh parsley, chopped *or* 1 tablespoon dry parsley
1½ teaspoons fresh oregano *or* ½ teaspoon dry oregano
1 clove garlic mashed with ¼ teaspoon salt
¾ teaspoon seasoned pepper
½ cup peas
1 ear corn, cut into ½-inch slices
1 cup broccoli flowerettes

1. In 5-quart saucepan, combine first seven ingredients. Bring to a boil over high heat. Skim off any foam. Reduce heat, cover and simmer for 1 to 1¼ hours or until turkey is tender.

2. Remove turkey from cooking liquid and allow to cool. Cut meat from bones, discard skin and bones. Cube meat.

3. Strain broth. Discard vegetables, seasonings and spices. Skim off any remaining fat. Return broth to saucepan.

4. Add tomatoes, green beans, zucchini, carrot, celery, leek, lima beans, barley and seasonings. Over high heat, bring mixture to a boil. Cover and reduce heat to a simmer. Cook 20 minutes.

5. Add turkey, peas, corn and broccoli; cook 5 minutes. Adjust seasoning to taste.

Makes 4 servings

Favorite recipe from **National Turkey Federation**

Mexican Fiesta Soup

3 cans (14½ ounces each) chicken broth
2 cups cooked chicken, cubed
1 cup peeled potatoes, cubed
1 cup chopped carrots
1 cup chopped onions
1 cup chopped celery
1 can (17 ounces) whole kernel corn, undrained
1 can (12 ounces) vegetable or tomato juice
1 cup tomato salsa
½ cup HOLLAND HOUSE® Vermouth Cooking Wine
1 can (4 ounces) chopped green chilies, undrained
¼ cup chopped fresh cilantro (optional)
Shredded Monterey Jack cheese (optional)
Tortilla chips (optional)

In large saucepan, combine chicken broth, chicken, potatoes, carrots, onions, celery, corn, vegetable juice, salsa, cooking wine, green chilies and cilantro, if desired, and place over medium-high heat. Bring to a boil; reduce heat. Simmer 20 to 30 minutes or until vegetables are tender. Serve with cheese and tortilla chips as garnishes, if desired.

Makes 8 (1½-cup) servings

Savory Pea Soup with Sausage

Chicken and Vegetable Chowder

Slow Cooker

1 pound boneless skinless chicken breasts, cut into 1-inch pieces
10 ounces frozen broccoli cuts
1 cup sliced carrots
1 jar (4½ ounces) sliced mushrooms, drained
½ cup chopped onion
½ cup whole kernel corn
2 cloves garlic, minced
½ teaspoon dried thyme leaves
1 can (14½ ounces) reduced-sodium chicken broth
1 can (10¾ ounces) condensed cream of potato soup
⅓ cup half-and-half

Slow Cooker Directions

Combine all ingredients except half-and-half in slow cooker. Cover and cook on LOW 5 hours or until vegetables are tender and chicken is no longer pink in center. Stir in half-and-half. Turn to HIGH. Cover and cook 15 minutes or until heated through.   *Makes 6 servings*

Variation: If desired, ½ cup (2 ounces) shredded Swiss or Cheddar cheese can be added during last 5 minutes of cooking, stirring over LOW heat until melted.

Tortellini Vegetable Soup

1 package (14 ounces) turkey or pork breakfast sausage, crumbled
2 quarts water
6 HERB-OX® Beef Bouillon cubes*
½ teaspoon garlic powder
1 package (9 ounces) fresh tortellini cheese pasta
1 package (16 ounces) frozen vegetable combination (broccoli, cauliflower, red pepper), thawed

1 bouillon cube = 1 teaspoon instant bouillon = 1 packet instant broth and seasoning.

In Dutch oven over medium-high heat, cook sausage until browned; drain. Add water, bouillon and garlic powder; bring to a boil. Add pasta; boil 5 minutes. Stir in vegetables. Simmer, uncovered, 10 minutes until vegetables and pasta are tender.

Makes 8 servings

Chicken & Orzo Soup

Nonstick olive oil cooking spray
3 ounces boneless skinless chicken breast, cut into bite-size pieces
1 can (about 14 ounces) fat-free, reduced-sodium chicken broth
1 cup water
⅔ cup shredded carrot
⅓ cup sliced green onion
¼ cup uncooked orzo pasta
1 teaspoon grated fresh ginger
⅛ teaspoon ground turmeric
2 teaspoons lemon juice
Black pepper
Sliced green onions (optional)

1. Spray medium saucepan with cooking spray. Heat over medium-high heat. Add chicken. Cook and stir 2 to 3 minutes or until no longer pink. Remove from saucepan and set aside.

2. In same saucepan combine broth, water, carrot, onion, orzo, ginger and turmeric. Bring to a boil. Reduce heat and simmer, covered, 8 to 10 minutes or until orzo is tender. Stir in chicken and lemon juice; cook until hot. Season to taste with pepper.

3. Ladle into serving bowls. Sprinkle with green onions, if desired.

Makes 2 servings

Corn and Chicken Chowder

3 tablespoons butter or margarine, divided
1 pound boneless skinless chicken breasts, cut into chunks
2 medium leeks, sliced (2 cups)
2 medium potatoes, cut into bite-size chunks
1 large green pepper, diced
2 tablespoons paprika
2 tablespoons flour
3 cups chicken broth
2½ cups fresh corn kernels
1½ teaspoons TABASCO® brand Pepper Sauce
1 teaspoon salt
1 cup half-and-half

In 4-quart saucepan over medium-high heat, melt 1 tablespoon butter. Cook chicken chunks until well browned on all sides, stirring frequently. With slotted spoon, remove chicken; set aside.

Add 2 tablespoons butter to drippings remaining in saucepan. Over medium heat, cook leeks, potatoes and green pepper until tender, stirring occasionally. Stir in paprika and flour until well blended; cook for 1 minute. Add chicken broth, corn kernels, TABASCO® Sauce, salt and chicken chunks. Over high heat, heat to boiling. Reduce heat to low; cover and simmer 20 minutes. Stir in half-and-half; heat through.

Makes 8 cups

Chicken and Vegetable Chowder

Mulligatawny Soup

2 tablespoons butter or
     margarine
1½ cups chopped onions
1 (10-ounce) package frozen
     mixed vegetables, thawed
2 tablespoons flour
2 teaspoons curry powder
1 teaspoon salt
½ teaspoon TABASCO® brand
     Pepper Sauce
¼ teaspoon ground cloves
1 quart water
1 (10½-ounce) can condensed
     chicken with rice soup
1 cup diced cooked chicken
1 cup chopped pared apple

Melt butter in large soup pot over
medium heat. Add onions and mixed
vegetables; cook and stir about
5 minutes or just until onion is tender.
Stir in flour, curry powder, salt,
TABASCO® Sauce and cloves. Add
water, soup, chicken and apple. Heat
to boiling; reduce heat to low and
simmer, covered, 20 minutes. Ladle
into serving bowls. Serve with
additional TABASCO® Sauce, if
desired.   *Makes 6 servings*

Country Chicken Chowder

Slow Cooker

2 tablespoons margarine or
     butter
1½ pounds chicken tenders, cut
     into ½-inch pieces
2 small onions, chopped
2 ribs celery, sliced
2 small carrots, sliced
2 cups frozen corn
2 cans (10¾ ounces each)
     cream of potato soup
1½ cups chicken broth
1 teaspoon dried dill weed
½ cup half-and-half

Slow Cooker Directions

Melt margarine in large skillet. Add
chicken; cook until browned. Add
cooked chicken, onions, celery,
carrots, corn, soup, chicken broth and
dill to slow cooker. Cover and cook on
LOW 3 to 4 hours or until chicken is
no longer pink and vegetables are
tender.

Turn off heat; stir in half-and-half.
Cover and let stand 5 to 10 minutes or
just until heated through.
          Makes 8 servings

Note: For a special touch, garnish
soup with croutons and fresh dill.

Tortilla Rice Soup

Vegetable cooking spray
⅓ cup sliced green onions
4 cups chicken broth
2 cups cooked rice
1 can (10½ ounces) diced
     tomatoes with green chiles,
     undrained
1 cup cooked chicken breast
     cubes
1 can (4 ounces) chopped green
     chiles, undrained
1 tablespoon lime juice
     Salt to taste
     Tortilla chips
½ cup chopped tomato
½ avocado, cut into small cubes
4 lime slices for garnish
     Fresh cilantro for garnish

Heat Dutch oven or large saucepan
coated with cooking spray over
medium-high heat until hot. Add
onions; cook and stir until tender. Add
broth, rice, tomatoes with juice,
chicken and chiles. Reduce heat to
low; cover and simmer 20 minutes.
Stir in lime juice and salt. Just before
serving, pour into soup bowls; top
with tortilla chips, chopped tomato
and avocado. Garnish with lime slices
and cilantro.   *Makes 4 servings*

Favorite recipe from **USA Rice Federation**

Chicken Rotini Soup

½ pound boneless skinless
     chicken breasts, cut into
     ½-inch pieces
1 cup water
2 tablespoons butter or
     margarine
½ medium onion, chopped
4 ounces fresh mushrooms,
     sliced
4 cups chicken broth
1 teaspoon Worcestershire
     sauce
¼ teaspoon dried tarragon
     leaves
¾ cup uncooked rotini
1 small zucchini
     Fresh basil for garnish

Combine chicken and water in
medium saucepan. Bring to a boil
over high heat. Reduce heat to
medium-low; simmer 2 minutes. Drain
water and rinse chicken. Melt butter in
5-quart Dutch oven or large
saucepan over medium heat. Add
mushrooms and onion. Cook and stir
until onion is tender. Stir in chicken,
chicken broth, Worcestershire and
tarragon. Bring to a boil over high
heat. Stir in uncooked pasta. Reduce
heat to medium-low; simmer,
uncovered, 5 minutes. Cut zucchini
into ⅛-inch slices; halve any large
slices. Add to soup; simmer,
uncovered, about 5 minutes, or until
pasta is tender. Ladle into bowls.
Garnish, if desired.
          Makes 4 servings

Chicken Rotini Soup

Oriental Chicken and Rice Soup

12 TYSON® Fresh Chicken Breast Tenders or Individually Fresh Frozen® Boneless, Skinless Chicken Tenderloins
1½ cups UNCLE BEN'S® Instant Rice
6 cups defatted reduced-sodium chicken broth
2 slices gingerroot (about ¼ inch thick)
½ cup chopped carrots
1 cup sliced pea pods
¼ cup chopped green onions

PREP: CLEAN: Wash hands. Remove protective ice glaze from frozen chicken by holding under cool running water 1 to 2 minutes. Cut into 1-inch pieces. CLEAN: Wash hands.

COOK: Heat chicken broth and gingerroot in large saucepan; add chicken. Simmer 5 minutes (8 minutes if using frozen chicken). Add carrots; simmer about 5 minutes or until internal juices of chicken run clear. (Or insert instant-read meat thermometer in thickest part of chicken. Temperature should read 170°F.) Stir in pea pods and rice. Remove from heat; cover. Let stand 5 minutes. Remove gingerroot.

SERVE: Sprinkle with green onions. Serve with herb bread and tea, if desired.

CHILL: Refrigerate leftovers immediately.   *Makes 4 servings*

Prep Time: 10 minutes
Cook Time: 25 minutes

Creamy Turkey Soup   `Slow Cooker`

2 cans (10½ ounces each) condensed cream of chicken soup
2 cups chopped cooked turkey breast meat
1 package (8 ounces) sliced mushrooms
1 medium yellow onion, chopped
1 teaspoon rubbed sage *or* ½ teaspoon dried poultry seasoning
1 cup frozen peas, thawed
½ cup milk
1 jar (about 4 ounces) diced pimiento

Slow Cooker Directions

1. Combine soup, turkey, mushrooms, onion and sage in slow cooker. Cover; cook on LOW 8 hours or on HIGH 4 hours.

2. If cooking on LOW, turn to HIGH; stir in peas, milk and pimientos. Cook an additional 10 minutes or until heated through.

Makes 5 to 6 servings

Minute Minestrone Soup

½ pound turkey sausage, cut into small pieces
2 cloves garlic, crushed
3 cans (14½ ounces *each*) low-sodium chicken broth
2 cups frozen Italian blend vegetables
1 can (15 ounces) white kidney beans, rinsed and drained
1 can (14½ ounces) Italian stewed tomatoes, undrained
1 cup cooked ditalini or small shell pasta (½ cup uncooked)
3 tablespoons *French's®* Worcestershire Sauce

1. In medium saucepan, stir-fry sausage and garlic 5 minutes or until sausage is cooked; drain. Add broth, vegetables, beans and tomatoes. Heat to boiling. Simmer, uncovered, 5 minutes or until vegetables are crisp-tender.

2. Stir in pasta and Worcestershire. Cook until heated through. Serve with grated cheese and crusty bread, if desired.   *Makes 6 servings*

Prep Time: 10 minutes
Cook Time: about 10 minutes

Manhattan Clam Chowder

2 pieces bacon, diced
1 large red bell pepper, diced
1 large green bell pepper, diced
1 rib celery, chopped
1 carrot, peeled and chopped
1 small onion, chopped
1 clove garlic, finely chopped
2 cups bottled clam juice
1 cup CLAMATO® Tomato Cocktail
2 medium potatoes, peeled and diced
1 large tomato, chopped
1 teaspoon oregano
½ teaspoon black pepper
2 cups fresh or canned clams, chopped (about 24 shucked clams)

In heavy 4-quart saucepan, sauté bacon, peppers, celery, carrot, onion and garlic over medium heat until tender, about 10 minutes. (Do not brown bacon.) Add clam juice, Clamato, potatoes, tomato, oregano and pepper. Simmer 35 minutes or until potatoes are tender. Add clams; cook 5 minutes more.

Makes 8 servings

Creamy Turkey Soup

Black Bean Bisque with Crab

- 3 cups low sodium chicken broth, defatted
- 1 jar (16 ounces) GUILTLESS GOURMET® Black Bean Dip (Spicy or Mild)
- 1 can (6 ounces) crabmeat, drained
- 2 tablespoons brandy (optional)
- 6 tablespoons low fat sour cream
- Chopped fresh chives (optional)

Microwave Directions

Combine broth and bean dip in 2-quart glass measure or microwave-safe casserole. Cover with vented plastic wrap or lid; microwave on HIGH (100% power) 6 minutes or until soup starts to bubble.

Stir in crabmeat and brandy, if desired; microwave on MEDIUM (50% power) 2 minutes or to desired serving temperature. To serve, ladle bisque into 8 individual ramekins or soup bowls, dividing evenly. Swirl 1 tablespoon sour cream into each serving. Garnish with chives, if desired.   *Makes 8 servings*

Stove Top Directions: Combine broth and bean dip in 2-quart saucepan; bring to a boil over medium heat. Stir in crabmeat and brandy, if desired; cook 2 minutes or to desired serving temperature. Serve as directed.

Potato-Crab Chowder

Slow Cooker

- 1 package (10 ounces) frozen corn
- 1 cup frozen hash brown potatoes
- ¾ cup finely chopped carrots
- 1 teaspoon dried thyme leaves
- ¾ teaspoon garlic-pepper seasoning
- 3 cups fat-free chicken broth
- ½ cup water
- 1 cup evaporated milk
- 3 tablespoons cornstarch
- 1 can (6 ounces) crabmeat, drained
- ½ cup sliced green onions

Slow Cooker Directions

1. Place corn, potatoes and carrots in slow cooker. Sprinkle with thyme and garlic-pepper seasoning. Add broth and water. Cover; cook on LOW 3½ to 4½ hours.

2. Stir together evaporated milk and cornstarch in medium bowl. Stir into slow cooker. Cover; cook on HIGH 1 hour. Just before serving, stir in crabmeat and green onions. Garnish as desired.   *Makes 5 servings*

Oyster Soup

- ¼ cup (½ stick) butter or margarine
- ½ cup thinly sliced green onions
- 2 tablespoons flour
- 2 cups half-and-half
- 2 cups fresh, shucked oysters and their liquid
- ½ teaspoon TABASCO® brand Pepper Sauce
- 2 tablespoons chopped fresh parsley

Melt butter in 3-quart saucepan over medium heat. Add green onions and cook 5 minutes. Add flour; cook 1 minute, stirring constantly. Gradually stir in half-and-half until smooth.

Heat to boiling, stirring constantly. Add oyster liquid and TABASCO® Sauce; return to boil. Cook until soup thickens, stirring constantly. Add oysters and parsley; simmer over low heat 5 to 10 minutes, stirring frequently. (Do not boil.)
    Makes 4 servings

Potato-Crab Chowder

Beer and Cheese Soup

Slow Cooker

2 to 3 slices pumpernickel or rye bread
¼ cup finely chopped onion
2 cloves garlic, minced
¾ teaspoon dried thyme leaves
1 can (about 14 ounces each) chicken broth
1 cup beer
6 ounces American cheese, shredded or diced
4 to 6 ounces sharp Cheddar cheese, shredded
1 cup milk
½ teaspoon paprika

Slow Cooker Directions

Preheat oven to 425°F. Slice bread into ½-inch cubes; place on baking sheet. Bake 10 to 12 minutes, stirring once, or until crisp; set aside.

Combine onion, garlic, thyme, chicken broth and beer in slow cooker. Cover and cook on LOW 4 hours. Turn to HIGH. Stir cheeses, milk and paprika into slow cooker. Cook 45 to 60 minutes or until soup is hot and cheeses are melted. Stir soup well to blend cheeses. Ladle soup into bowls; top with croutons.

Makes 4 (1-cup) servings

Cream of Asparagus Soup

1 tablespoon margarine or butter
1 small onion, chopped
2 cans (14½ ounces each) chicken broth
1 jar (1 pound) RAGÚ® Cheese Creations!® Classic Alfredo Sauce
2 packages (10 ounces each) frozen asparagus spears, thawed

1. In 3½-quart saucepan, melt margarine over medium heat and cook onion, stirring occasionally, 5 minutes or until tender. Stir in broth, Ragú Cheese Creations! Sauce and asparagus. Bring to a boil over medium heat, stirring frequently. Reduce heat to low and simmer 5 minutes or until asparagus is tender.

2. In blender or food processor, purée hot soup mixture until smooth. Return soup to saucepan and heat through. Season, if desired, with salt and ground black pepper.

Makes 8 servings

Variation: For a Cream of Broccoli Soup, substitute frozen broccoli spears for asparagus.

Tip: Serve soup with cheese toast croutons. Simply place Swiss cheese on sliced French bread rounds and broil until cheese is melted.

Prep Time: 5 minutes
Cook Time: 20 minutes

French Mushroom Soup

1 pound fresh mushrooms, sliced
1 large onion, thinly sliced
2 tablespoons butter
2 tablespoons all-purpose flour
4 cups beef broth
¾ cup HARVEYS® Bristol Cream®
½ cup shredded Gruyère cheese
6 slices French bread

In 4-quart saucepan, cook mushrooms and onion in butter until onion is soft. Stir in flour. Cook, stirring, 1 to 2 minutes. Add broth. Simmer, covered, 10 minutes. Stir in Harveys® Bristol Cream®. Sprinkle cheese on bread, broil until melted. Place toast on each serving of soup.

Makes 6 servings

Pasta e Fagioli

2 tablespoons olive oil
1 cup chopped onion
3 cloves garlic, minced
2 cans (14½ ounces each) Italian-style stewed tomatoes, undrained
3 cups ⅓-less-salt chicken broth
1 can (about 15 ounces) cannellini beans (white kidney beans), undrained*
¼ cup chopped fresh Italian parsley
1 teaspoon dried basil leaves
¼ teaspoon black pepper
4 ounces uncooked small shell pasta

One can (about 15 ounces) Great Northern beans, undrained, may be substituted for cannellini beans.

1. Heat oil in 4-quart Dutch oven over medium heat until hot; add onion and garlic. Cook and stir 5 minutes or until onion is tender.

2. Stir tomatoes with juice, chicken broth, beans with liquid, parsley, basil and pepper into Dutch oven; bring to a boil over high heat, stirring occasionally. Reduce heat to low. Simmer, covered, 10 minutes.

3. Add pasta to Dutch oven. Simmer, covered, 10 to 12 minutes or until pasta is just tender. Serve immediately. Garnish as desired.

Makes 8 servings

Pasta e Fagioli

Oniony Mushroom Soup

2 cans (10¾ ounces each) condensed golden mushroom soup
1 can (13¾ ounces) reduced-sodium beef broth
1⅓ cups *French's®* French Fried Onions, divided
½ cup water
⅓ cup dry sherry wine
4 slices French bread, cut ½ inch thick
1 tablespoon olive oil
1 clove garlic, finely minced
1 cup (4 ounces) shredded Swiss cheese

Combine mushroom soup, beef broth, *1 cup* French Fried Onions, water and sherry in large saucepan. Bring to a boil over medium-high heat, stirring often. Reduce heat to low. Simmer 15 minutes, stirring occasionally.

Preheat broiler. Place bread on baking sheet. Combine oil and garlic in small bowl. Brush oil over both sides of bread slices. Broil bread until toasted and crisp, turning once.

Ladle soup into 4 broiler-safe bowls. Place 1 slice of bread in each bowl. Sprinkle evenly with cheese and remaining *⅓ cup* onions. Place bowls on baking sheet. Place under broiler about 1 minute or until cheese is melted and onions are golden.

Makes 4 servings

Tip: Make all your soups special by topping with French Fried Onions. They'll give your soups a wonderful oniony flavor.

Prep Time: 20 minutes
Cook Time: 18 minutes

Double Thick [Slow Cooker] Baked Potato-Cheese Soup

2 pounds baking potatoes, peeled and cut into ½-inch cubes
2 cans (10½ ounces each) condensed cream of mushroom soup
1½ cups finely chopped green onions, divided
¼ teaspoon garlic powder
⅛ teaspoon ground red pepper
1½ cups (6 ounces) shredded sharp Cheddar cheese
1 cup (8 ounces) sour cream
1 cup milk
Black pepper

Slow Cooker Directions

1. Combine potatoes, soup, 1 cup green onions, garlic powder and red pepper in slow cooker. Cover; cook on HIGH 4 hours or on LOW 8 hours.

2. Add cheese, sour cream and milk; stir until cheese has completely melted. Cover; cook on HIGH an additional 10 minutes. Season to taste with black pepper. Garnish with remaining green onions.

Makes 7 servings

Lentil Soup

2 tablespoons BERTOLLI® Olive Oil
1 medium onion, chopped
1 medium carrot, chopped
3 quarts chicken broth
1 jar (1 pound 10 ounces) RAGÚ® Light Pasta sauce
1½ cups uncooked lentils, rinsed and drained
2 cups coarsely shredded fresh spinach or escarole

1. In 6-quart saucepot, heat oil over medium-high heat and cook onion and carrot, stirring occasionally, 4 minutes or until vegetables are golden.

2. Stir in broth, Ragú Pasta Sauce and lentils. Bring to a boil over high heat. Reduce heat to low and simmer, stirring occasionally, 30 minutes or until lentils are tender. Stir in spinach and cook an additional 10 minutes or until spinach is tender.

Makes 3½ quarts soup

Prep Time: 15 minutes
Cook Time: 50 minutes

Easy Italian [Slow Cooker] Vegetable Soup

1 can (14½ ounces) diced tomatoes, undrained
1 can (10½ ounces) condensed beef broth
1 package (8 ounces) sliced mushrooms
1 medium yellow onion, chopped
1 medium zucchini, thinly sliced
1 medium green bell pepper, chopped
⅓ cup dry red wine or beef broth
1½ tablespoons dried basil leaves
2½ teaspoons sugar
1 tablespoon olive oil
½ teaspoon salt
1 cup (4 ounces) shredded Mozzarella cheese (optional)

Slow Cooker Directions

1. Combine tomatoes, broth, mushrooms, onion, zucchini, bell pepper, wine, basil and sugar in slow cooker. Cover; cook on LOW 8 hours or on HIGH 4 hours.

2. Stir oil and salt into soup. Serve; garnish with cheese, if desired.

Makes 5 to 6 servings

Oniony Mushroom Soup

Spectacular Stews

Panama Pork Stew

2 small sweet potatoes, peeled
   and cut into 2-inch pieces
   (about 12 ounces total)
1 package (10 ounces) frozen
   corn
1 package (9 ounces) frozen cut
   green beans
1 cup chopped onion
1¼ pounds lean pork stew meat,
   cut into 1-inch cubes
1 can (14½ ounces) diced
   tomatoes, undrained
¾ cup water
1 to 2 tablespoons chili powder
½ teaspoon salt
½ teaspoon ground coriander

Slow Cooker Directions

Place potatoes, corn, green beans
and onion in slow cooker. Top with
pork. Combine tomatoes with juice,
water, chili powder, salt and coriander
in large bowl. Pour over pork in slow
cooker. Cover; cook on LOW 7 to
9 hours.   *Makes 6 servings*

Beef Stew in Red Wine

1½ pounds boneless beef round,
   cut into 1-inch cubes
1½ cups dry red wine
2 teaspoons olive oil
   Peel of half an orange
2 large cloves garlic, thinly
   sliced
1 bay leaf
½ teaspoon dried thyme leaves
⅛ teaspoon black pepper
8 ounces fresh mushrooms,
   quartered
8 sun-dried tomatoes, quartered
1 can (about 14 ounces) fat-free
   beef broth
6 small potatoes, unpeeled, cut
   into wedges
1 cup baby carrots
1 cup fresh pearl onions, outer
   skins removed
1 tablespoon cornstarch mixed
   with 2 tablespoons water

1. Combine beef, wine, oil, orange
peel, garlic, bay leaf, thyme and
pepper in large glass bowl.
Refrigerate, covered, at least 2 hours
or overnight.

2. Place beef mixture, mushrooms
and tomatoes in large nonstick skillet
or Dutch oven. Add enough beef
broth to just cover ingredients. Bring
to a boil over high heat. Cover;
reduce heat to low. Simmer 1 hour.
Add potatoes, carrots and onions;
cover and cook 20 to 25 minutes or
until vegetables are tender and meat
is no longer pink. Remove meat and
vegetables from skillet with slotted
spoon; cover and set aside. Discard
orange peel and bay leaf.

3. Stir cornstarch mixture into skillet
with sauce. Increase heat to medium;
cook and stir until sauce is slightly
thickened. Return meat and
vegetables to sauce; heat thoroughly.

Makes 6 servings

Panama Pork Stew

Favorite Beef Stew
[Slow Cooker]

- 3 carrots, cut lengthwise into halves, then cut into 1-inch pieces
- 3 ribs celery, cut into 1-inch pieces
- 2 large potatoes, peeled and cut into ½-inch pieces
- 1½ cups chopped onions
- 3 cloves garlic, chopped
- 1 bay leaf
- 4½ teaspoons Worcestershire sauce
- ¾ teaspoon dried thyme leaves
- ¾ teaspoon dried basil leaves
- ½ teaspoon black pepper
- 2 pounds lean beef stew meat, cut into 1-inch pieces
- 1 can (14½ ounces) diced tomatoes, undrained
- 1 can (about 14 ounces) beef broth
- ½ cup cold water
- ¼ cup all-purpose flour

Slow Cooker Directions

Layer ingredients in slow cooker in the following order: carrots, celery, potatoes, onions, garlic, bay leaf, Worcestershire sauce, thyme, basil, pepper, beef, tomatoes with juice and broth. Cover and cook on LOW 8 to 9 hours.

Remove beef and vegetables to large serving bowl; cover and keep warm. Remove and discard bay leaf. Turn slow cooker to HIGH; cover. Stir water into flour in small bowl until smooth. Add ½ cup cooking liquid; mix well. Stir flour mixture into slow cooker. Cover and cook 15 minutes or until thickened. Pour sauce over meat and vegetables. Serve immediately.

Makes 6 to 8 servings

Brunswick Stew

- **Nonstick cooking spray**
- 12 ounces smoked ham or cooked chicken breast, cut into ¾- to 1-inch cubes
- 1 cup sliced onion
- 4½ teaspoons all-purpose flour
- 1 can (14½ ounces) stewed tomatoes, undrained
- 2 cups frozen mixed vegetables for soup (such as okra, lima beans, potatoes, celery, corn, carrots, green beans and onions)
- 1 cup chicken broth

1. Spray large saucepan with cooking spray; heat over medium heat until hot. Add ham and onion; cook 5 minutes or until ham is browned. Stir in flour; cook over medium to medium-low heat 1 minute, stirring constantly.

2. Stir in remaining tomatoes, mixed vegetables and broth; bring to a boil. Reduce heat to low; simmer, covered, 5 to 8 minutes or until vegetables are tender. Simmer, uncovered, 5 to 8 minutes or until slightly thickened. Season to taste with salt and pepper.

Makes 4 (1-cup) servings

Serving Suggestion: Brunswick Stew is excellent served over rice or squares of cornbread.

Cook's Notes: In 1828, Brunswick County, Virginia, was the birthplace of Brunswick stew, originally made of squirrel meat and onion.

Prep and Cook Time: 30 minutes

French-Style Pork Stew
[Slow Cooker]

- 1 tablespoon vegetable oil
- 1 pork tenderloin (16 ounces), cut into ¾- to 1-inch cubes
- 1 medium onion, coarsely chopped
- 1 rib celery, sliced
- ½ teaspoon dried basil leaves
- ¼ teaspoon dried rosemary, crushed
- ¼ teaspoon dried oregano leaves
- 1 cup chicken broth
- 2 tablespoons all-purpose flour
- ½ package (16 ounces) frozen mixed vegetables (carrots, potatoes and peas)
- 1 jar (4½ ounces) sliced mushrooms, drained
- 1 package (about 6 ounces) long grain and wild rice
- 2 teaspoons lemon juice
- ⅛ teaspoon ground nutmeg

Slow Cooker Directions

Heat oil in large skillet over high heat. Add pork, onion, celery, basil, rosemary and oregano. Cook until pork is browned. Place pork mixture in slow cooker. Stir chicken broth into flour until smooth; pour into slow cooker.

Stir in frozen vegetables and mushrooms. Cover and cook on LOW 4 hours or until pork is barely pink in center. Prepare rice according to package directions, discarding spice packet, if desired.

Stir lemon juice, nutmeg and salt and pepper to taste into slow cooker. Cover and cook 15 minutes. Serve stew over rice.

Makes 4 (1-cup) servings

Favorite Beef Stew

New Orleans Pork Gumbo

- 1 pound pork loin roast
  Nonstick cooking spray
- 1 tablespoon margarine
- 2 tablespoons all-purpose flour
- 1 cup water
- 1 can (16 ounces) stewed tomatoes, undrained
- 1 package (10 ounces) frozen cut okra
- 1 package (10 ounces) frozen succotash
- 1 beef bouillon cube
- 1 teaspoon hot pepper sauce
- 1 teaspoon black pepper
- 1 bay leaf

1. Cut pork into ½-inch cubes. Spray large Dutch oven with cooking spray. Heat over medium heat until hot. Add pork; cook and stir 4 minutes or until pork is browned. Remove pork from Dutch oven.

2. Melt margarine in same Dutch oven. Stir in flour. Cook and stir until flour mixture is browned. Gradually whisk in water until smooth. Add pork and remaining ingredients. Bring to a boil. Reduce heat to low and simmer 15 minutes. Remove bay leaf.

Makes 4 servings

Prep and Cook Time: 30 minutes

Dijon Lamb Stew

- ½ pound boneless lamb, cut into small pieces*
- ½ medium onion, chopped
- ½ teaspoon dried rosemary
- 1 tablespoon olive oil
- 1 can (14½ ounces) DEL MONTE® Stewed Tomatoes Italian Recipe
- 1 carrot, julienne cut
- 1 tablespoon Dijon mustard
- 1 can (15 ounces) white beans or pinto beans, drained

*Top sirloin steak may be substituted for lamb.

1. Brown meat with onion and rosemary in oil in large skillet over medium-high heat, stirring occasionally. Season with salt and pepper, if desired.

2. Add undrained tomatoes, carrot and mustard. Cover and cook over medium heat, 10 minutes; add beans.

3. Cook, uncovered, over medium heat 5 minutes, stirring occasionally. Garnish with sliced ripe olives and chopped parsley, if desired.

Makes 4 servings

Prep Time: 10 minutes
Cook Time: 20 minutes

Golden Harvest Pork Stew

- 1 pound boneless pork cutlets, cut into 1-inch pieces
- 2 tablespoons all-purpose flour, divided
- 1 tablespoon vegetable oil
- 2 medium Yukon gold potatoes, unpeeled and cut into 1-inch cubes
- 1 large sweet potato, peeled and cut into 1-inch cubes
- 1 cup chopped carrots
- 1 ear corn, broken into 4 pieces *or* ½ cup corn
- ½ cup chicken broth
- 1 jalapeño pepper,* seeded and finely chopped
- 1 clove garlic, minced
- 1 teaspoon salt
- ¼ teaspoon black pepper
- ¼ teaspoon dried thyme leaves

*Jalapeño peppers can sting and irritate the skin; wear rubber gloves when handling peppers and do not touch eyes.

Slow Cooker Directions

1. Toss pork pieces with 1 tablespoon flour; set aside. Heat oil in large nonstick skillet over medium-high heat until hot. Brown pork 2 to 3 minutes per side; transfer to 5-quart slow cooker.

2. Add remaining ingredients to slow cooker. Cover; cook on LOW 5 to 6 hours.

3. Combine remaining 1 tablespoon flour and ¼ cup broth from stew in small bowl; stir until smooth. Stir flour mixture into stew. Cook on HIGH 10 minutes or until thickened. Adjust seasonings, if desired.

Makes 4 (2½-cup) servings

Easy Oven Beef Stew

- 2 pounds boneless beef stew meat, cut into 1½-inch cubes
- 1 can (16 ounces) tomatoes, undrained, cut up
- 1 can (10½ ounces) condensed beef broth
- 1 cup HOLLAND HOUSE® Red Cooking Wine
- 1 tablespoon dried Italian seasoning*
- 6 potatoes, peeled, quartered
- 6 carrots cut into 2-inch pieces
- 3 ribs celery cut into 1-inch pieces
- 2 medium onions, peeled, quartered
- ⅓ cup instant tapioca
- ¼ teaspoon black pepper
  Chopped fresh parsley

*You can substitute 1½ teaspoons each of dried basil and oregano for Italian seasonings.

Heat oven to 325°F. Combine all ingredients except parsley in ovenproof Dutch oven; cover. Bake 2½ to 3 hours or until meat and vegetables are tender. Garnish with parsley.

Makes 8 servings

New Orleans Pork Gumbo

Southwestern-Style Beef Stew

¼ cup all-purpose flour
1 teaspoon seasoned salt
¼ teaspoon ground black pepper
2 pounds beef stew meat, cut into bite-size pieces
2 tablespoons vegetable oil
1 large onion, cut into wedges
2 large cloves garlic, finely chopped
1 can (14½ ounces) stewed tomatoes, undrained
1 jar (16 ounces) ORTEGA® SALSA (any flavor)
1 cup beef broth
1 tablespoon ground oregano
1 teaspoon ground cumin
½ teaspoon salt
3 large carrots, peeled, cut into 1-inch slices
1 can (15 ounces) garbanzo beans, drained
1 cup frozen corn kernels

COMBINE flour, salt and pepper in medium bowl or large resealable plastic food-storage bag. Add meat; toss well to coat.

HEAT oil in large skillet over medium-high heat. Add meat, onion and garlic; cook for 5 to 6 minutes or until meat is browned on outside and onion is tender. Stir in tomatoes, salsa, broth, oregano, cumin and salt. Bring to a boil; cover. Reduce heat to low; cook, stirring occasionally, for 45 minutes or until meat is tender.

STIR in carrots, beans and corn. Increase heat to medium-low. Cook, stirring occasionally, for 30 to 40 minutes or until carrots are tender.

Makes 8 servings

Hungarian Beef Stew

¼ cup vegetable oil
1 medium onion, chopped
1 cup sliced mushrooms
2 teaspoons paprika
1 boneless beef sirloin steak, ½ inch thick, trimmed and cut into ½-inch pieces (about 2 pounds)
½ cup beef broth
½ teaspoon caraway seeds
Salt and black pepper to taste
2 tablespoons all-purpose flour
1 cup sour cream
Hot buttered noodles (optional)
Chopped fresh parsley for garnish

Heat oil in 5-quart Dutch oven over medium-high heat. Cook and stir onion and mushrooms in oil until onion is soft. Stir in paprika. Remove with slotted spoon; set aside.

Brown half of beef in Dutch oven over medium-high heat. Remove with slotted spoon; set aside. Brown remaining beef. Pour off drippings. Return beef, onion and mushrooms to Dutch oven. Stir in broth, caraway seeds, salt and pepper. Bring to a boil over high heat. Reduce heat to low. Cover and simmer 45 minutes or until beef is fork-tender.

Whisk flour into sour cream in small bowl. Whisk into stew. Stir until slightly thickened. Do not boil. Serve over noodles. Garnish with parsley.

Makes 6 to 8 servings

Lemon Lamb Lawry's®

2 teaspoons LAWRY'S® Lemon Pepper
1 cup water
2 pounds boneless lamb, cut into 1-inch cubes
2 tablespoons vegetable oil, divided
1 large onion, sliced
1 tablespoon olive oil
½ cup lemon juice
1 teaspoon LAWRY'S® Seasoned Salt
1½ pounds fresh green beans, cut into 1-inch pieces
1 teaspoon dried oregano

In small bowl, combine Lemon Pepper and water; let stand while browning lamb. In large skillet or Dutch oven, heat vegetable oil. Add lamb and onion and cook over medium-high heat until lamb is browned and onion is tender. Add olive oil and toss with lamb and onion to coat. Add water and lemon pepper mixture, lemon juice, Seasoned Salt, green beans and oregano. Bring to a boil over medium-high heat; reduce heat to low. Cover and simmer 1 hour, stirring occasionally. Add additional ¼ cup water during cooking if necessary.   *Makes 6 servings*

Serving Suggestion: Serve with tossed green salad and crusty bread.

Helpful Hints

The flavor of paprika can vary from mild to hot. Mild varieties are available in supermarkets, but you may have to go to an ethnic market for hotter varieties. Always store paprika in a cool dry place and replenish your supply every six months or so.

Southwestern-Style Beef Stew

Hearty Ground Beef Stew

- 1 pound ground beef
- 3 cloves garlic, minced
- 1 package (16 ounces) Italian-style frozen vegetables
- 2 cups southern-style hash brown potatoes
- 1 jar (14 ounces) marinara sauce
- 1 can (10½ ounces) condensed beef broth
- 3 tablespoons *French's*® Worcestershire Sauce

1. Brown beef with garlic in large saucepan; drain. Add remaining ingredients. Heat to boiling. Cover. Reduce heat to medium-low. Cook 10 minutes or until vegetables are crisp-tender.

2. Serve in warm bowls with garlic bread, if desired.

Makes 6 servings

Prep Time: 5 minutes
Cook Time: 15 minutes

Italian Sausage and Vegetable Stew

Slow Cooker

- 1 pound hot or mild Italian sausage, cut into 1-inch pieces
- 1 package (16 ounces) frozen mixed vegetables (onions and green, red and yellow bell peppers)
- 1 can (14½ ounces) diced Italian-style tomatoes, undrained
- 2 medium zucchini, sliced
- 1 jar (4½ ounces) sliced mushrooms, drained
- 4 cloves garlic, minced
- 2 tablespoons Italian-style tomato paste

Slow Cooker Directions

Heat large skillet over high heat until hot. Add sausage and cook about 5 minutes or until browned. Pour off any drippings.

Combine sausage, frozen vegetables, tomatoes with juice, zucchini, mushrooms and garlic in slow cooker. Cover and cook on LOW 4 to 4½ hours or until zucchini is tender. Stir in tomato paste. Cover and cook 30 minutes or until juices have thickened.

Makes 6 (1-cup) servings

Serving Suggestion: Serve with fresh hot garlic bread.

Kielbasa and Lentil Stew

- 1 pound kielbasa or smoked sausage, cut into small cubes
- ½ head (8 cups) green cabbage, shredded
- 1 large onion, chopped
- 4 carrots, shredded
- 2 cans (19 ounces *each*) lentil soup
- 1 can (16 ounces) crushed tomatoes in purée, undrained
- 3 tablespoons *Frank's*® *RedHot*® Cayenne Pepper Sauce

1. Cook and stir sausage in 5-quart saucepot over medium-high heat 3 minutes or until lightly browned. Add vegetables; cook and stir 5 minutes or until tender.

2. Stir in soup, tomatoes and *Frank's RedHot* Sauce. Heat to boiling. Reduce heat to medium-low. Cook, partially covered, 10 minutes or until heated through and flavors are blended. Ladle stew into bowls.

Makes 8 to 10 servings

Prep Time: 10 minutes
Cook Time: 20 minutes

Milwaukee Pork Stew

- 2 pounds boneless pork shoulder or sirloin, cut into ½-inch cubes
- ⅓ cup all-purpose flour
- 1½ teaspoons salt
- ¼ teaspoon black pepper
- 2 tablespoons vegetable oil
- 4 large onions, sliced ½-inch thick
- 1 clove garlic, minced
- 1 can (14½ ounces) chicken broth
- 1 can (12 ounces) beer
- ¼ cup chopped fresh parsley
- 2 tablespoons red wine vinegar
- 1 tablespoon packed brown sugar
- 1 teaspoon caraway seeds
- 1 bay leaf

Coat pork with combined flour, salt and pepper. Heat oil in Dutch oven; brown meat over medium-high heat. Add onions and garlic. Cook and stir 5 minutes. Pour off drippings. Stir in remaining ingredients. Bring to a boil. Cover; cook over medium-low heat 1 to 1¼ hours or until meat is very tender. Stir occasionally.

Makes 8 servings

Prep Time: 10 minutes
Cook Time: 90 minutes

Favorite recipe from **National Pork Board**

Helpful Hints

Traditionally, stews are economical one-dish meals that combine meat, poultry or seafood and vegetables. Long cooking allows time to tenderize tougher cuts of meat and blend flavors.

Hearty Ground Beef Stew

Stew Provençal `Slow Cooker`

2 cans (about 14 ounces each)
   beef broth, divided
⅓ cup all-purpose flour
1½ pounds pork tenderloin,
   trimmed and diced
4 red potatoes, unpeeled and
   cut into cubes
2 cups frozen cut green beans
1 onion, chopped
2 cloves garlic, minced
1 teaspoon salt
1 teaspoon dried thyme leaves
½ teaspoon black pepper

Slow Cooker Directions

Combine ¾ cup beef broth and flour in small bowl. Set aside.

Add remaining broth, pork, potatoes, beans, onion, garlic, salt, thyme and pepper to slow cooker; stir. Cover and cook on LOW 8 to 10 hours or on HIGH 4 to 5 hours. If cooking on LOW, turn to HIGH last 30 minutes. Stir in flour mixture. Cook 30 minutes to thicken. *Makes 8 servings*

Pecos "Red" Stew

2 pounds boneless pork
   shoulder or sirloin, cut into
   1½-inch cubes
2 tablespoons vegetable oil
2 cups chopped onions
1 cup chopped green bell
   pepper
¼ cup chopped fresh cilantro
3 to 4 tablespoons chili powder
2 cloves garlic, minced
2 teaspoons dried oregano
   leaves
1 teaspoon salt
½ teaspoon crushed red pepper
2 cans (14½ ounces each)
   chicken broth
3 cups cubed, peeled potatoes,
   cut in 1-inch pieces
2 cups fresh or frozen whole
   kernel corn
1 can (16 ounces) garbanzo
   beans, drained

Heat oil in Dutch oven. Brown pork over medium-high heat. Stir in onions, bell pepper, cilantro, chili powder, garlic, oregano, salt, red pepper and chicken broth. Cover; cook over medium-low heat 45 to 55 minutes or until pork is tender. Add potatoes, corn and beans. Cover; cook 15 to 20 minutes longer.

Makes 8 servings

Prep Time: 20 minutes
Cook Time: 60 minutes

Favorite recipe from **National Pork Board**

Pork and Cabbage Ragoût

1 tablespoon vegetable oil
1 pound pork tenderloin, cut
   into scant ½-inch slices
1 cup chopped onion
4 cloves garlic, minced
1½ teaspoons crushed caraway
   seeds
8 cups thinly sliced cabbage
   (1 pound) or prepared
   coleslaw mix
1 cup dry white wine
1 teaspoon chicken bouillon
   crystals
2 medium Cortland or Jonathan
   apples, peeled and cut into
   wedges
Instant potato flakes plus
   ingredients to prepare
   4 servings mashed potatoes

1. Heat oil in large saucepan over medium heat until hot. Add pork; cook and stir about 2 minutes per side or until browned and barely pink in center. Sprinkle lightly with salt and pepper. Remove from saucepan and reserve. Add onion, garlic and caraway to saucepan; cook and stir 3 to 5 minutes or until onion is tender.

2. Add cabbage, wine and chicken bouillon; bring to a boil. Reduce heat to low; simmer, covered, 5 minutes or until cabbage is wilted. Cook over medium heat, uncovered, 5 to 8 minutes or until no liquid remains.

3. Add apple wedges and reserved pork; cook, covered, 5 to 8 minutes or until apples are tender. Season to taste with salt and pepper. While ragoût is cooking, prepare potatoes according to package directions. Serve ragoût over potatoes.

Makes 4 (1-cup) servings

Tip: For a special touch, stir ⅓ cup sour cream into ragoût at end of cooking time; cook over low heat 2 to 3 minutes or until hot.

Tasty Pork Ragoût

½ pound pork loin, cubed
1 small onion, chopped
1 large clove garlic, pressed
½ teaspoon dried rosemary,
   crumbled
2 tablespoons margarine
   Salt and pepper
1 bouillon cube, any flavor
½ cup boiling water
2 cups DOLE® Cauliflower, cut
   into flowerets
1 cup sliced DOLE® Carrots
1 cup hot cooked rice

• Brown pork with onion, garlic and rosemary in margarine. Season with salt and pepper to taste.

• Dissolve bouillon in water; stir into pork mixture. Cover; simmer 20 minutes.

• Add cauliflower and carrots. Cover; simmer 5 minutes longer or until vegetables are tender-crisp. Serve with rice. *Makes 2 servings*

Prep Time: 10 minutes
Cook Time: 25 minutes

Stew Provençal

Black Bean & Pork Stew

2 (15-ounce) cans cooked black
    beans, rinsed and drained
2 cups water
1 pound boneless ham, cut into
    ¾-inch cubes
¾ pound BOB EVANS® Italian
    Dinner Link Sausage, cut
    into 1-inch pieces
¾ pound BOB EVANS® Smoked
    Sausage, cut into 1-inch
    pieces
1 pint cherry tomatoes, stems
    removed
1 medium onion, chopped
6 cloves garlic, minced
1 teaspoon red pepper flakes
⅛ teaspoon grated orange peel
    Cornbread or rolls (optional)

Preheat oven to 350°F. Combine all
ingredients except cornbread in large
ovenproof Dutch oven. Bring to a boil
over high heat, skimming foam off if
necessary. Cover; transfer to oven.
Bake 30 minutes; uncover and bake
30 minutes more, stirring occasionally.
Serve hot with cornbread, if desired,
or cool slightly, then cover and
refrigerate overnight. Remove any fat
from surface. Reheat over low heat.
Refrigerate leftovers.

Makes 8 servings

Pepper & Pineapple Pork Stew

Slow Cooker

4 top loin pork chops, cut into
    1-inch cubes
4 carrots, sliced
½ cup chicken broth
3 tablespoons teriyaki sauce
1 tablespoon cornstarch
1 (8-ounce) can pineapple
    chunks in juice, drained and
    juice reserved
1 green bell pepper, seeded and
    cut into 1-inch pieces

Slow Cooker Directions

Brown pork cubes in hot skillet, if
desired (optional). Mix pork, carrots,
broth and teriyaki in 3½-quart slow
cooker; cover and cook on LOW for
7 to 8 hours. Mix cornstarch with
reserved pineapple juice; stir into
pork mixture. Stir in pineapple and
green pepper. Cover and cook on
high 15 minutes or until thickened and
bubbly.   *Makes 4 servings*

Favorite recipe from **National Pork Board**

Savory Braised Beef

4 slices bacon
2 pounds boneless beef chuck
    or round steak, cut into
    1-inch cubes
1 large clove garlic, finely
    chopped
1 envelope LIPTON®
    RECIPE SECRETS® Beefy
    Mushroom Soup Mix*
1 can or bottle (12 ounces) beer
    or 1½ cups water
1 cup water
1 tablespoon red wine vinegar
    Hot cooked rice

*Also terrific with LIPTON® RECIPE
SECRETS® Onion, Onion-Mushroom, Beefy
Onion Soup Mix.*

1. In Dutch oven or 6-quart saucepot,
brown bacon until crisp. Remove
bacon, crumble and set aside;
reserve 1 tablespoon drippings.

2. Brown beef in two batches in
reserved drippings. Remove beef and
set aside.

3. Add garlic to drippings and cook
over medium heat, stirring frequently,
30 seconds. Return beef to Dutch
oven. Add soup mix blended with
beer and 1 cup water. Bring to a boil
over high heat.

4. Reduce heat to low and simmer
covered, stirring occasionally, 1 hour
15 minutes or until beef is tender.
Skim fat, if necessary. Stir in vinegar
and sprinkle with bacon. Serve over
rice.   *Makes 4 servings*

Skillet Sausage and Bean Stew

1 pound spicy Italian sausage,
    casing removed and sliced
    ½ inch thick
½ onion, chopped
2 cups frozen O'Brien-style
    potatoes with onions and
    peppers
1 can (15 ounces) pinto beans,
    undrained
¾ cup water
1 teaspoon beef bouillon
    granules *or* 1 beef bouillon
    cube
1 teaspoon dried oregano leaves
⅛ teaspoon ground red pepper

1. Combine sausage slices and onion
in large nonstick skillet; cook and stir
over medium-high heat 5 to 7 minutes
or until meat is no longer pink. Drain
drippings.

2. Stir in potatoes, beans, water,
bouillon, oregano and red pepper;
reduce heat to medium. Cover and
simmer 15 minutes, stirring
occasionally.   *Makes 4 servings*

Prep and Cook Time: 30 minutes

Helpful Hints

You can reduce the calories and fat
content of this dish by substituting
turkey sausage for Italian sausage.
Add hot pepper sauce to taste if you
prefer a spicier stew.

Black Bean & Pork Stew

The Best Beef Stew

Slow Cooker

½ cup plus 2 tablespoons all-purpose flour, divided
2 teaspoons salt
1 teaspoon black pepper
3 pounds beef stew meat, trimmed and cut into cubes
1 can (16 ounces) diced tomatoes in juice, undrained
3 potatoes, peeled and diced
½ pound smoked sausage, sliced
1 cup chopped leek
1 cup chopped onion
4 ribs celery, sliced
½ cup chicken broth
3 cloves garlic, minced
1 teaspoon dried thyme leaves
3 tablespoons water

Slow Cooker Directions

Combine ½ cup flour, salt and pepper in resealable plastic food storage bag. Add beef; shake bag to coat beef. Place beef in slow cooker. Add remaining ingredients except remaining 2 tablespoons flour and water; stir well. Cover and cook on LOW 8 to 12 hours or on HIGH 4 to 6 hours.

One hour before serving, turn slow cooker to HIGH. Combine remaining 2 tablespoons flour and water in small bowl; stir until mixture becomes paste. Stir mixture into slow cooker; mix well. Cover and cook until thickened. Garnish as desired.

Makes 8 servings

Pork Stew

Slow Cooker

2 tablespoons vegetable oil, divided
3 pounds fresh lean boneless pork butt, cut into 1½-inch cubes
2 medium white onions, thinly sliced
3 cloves garlic, minced
1 teaspoon salt
1 teaspoon ground cumin
¾ teaspoon dried oregano leaves
1 can (8 ounces) tomatillos, drained and chopped *or* 1 cup husked and chopped fresh tomatillos
1 can (4 ounces) chopped green chilies, drained
½ cup reduced-sodium chicken broth
1 large tomato, peeled and coarsely chopped
¼ cup fresh cilantro, chopped *or* ½ teaspoon ground coriander
2 teaspoons lime juice
4 cups hot cooked white rice
½ cup toasted slivered almonds (optional)

Slow Cooker Directions

Heat 1 tablespoon oil in large skillet over medium heat. Add pork; cook 10 minutes or until browned on all sides. Remove and set aside. Heat remaining 1 tablespoon oil in skillet. Add onions, garlic, salt, cumin and oregano; cook and stir 2 minutes or until soft.

Combine pork, onion mixture and remaining ingredients except rice and almonds in slow cooker; mix well. Cover and cook on LOW 5 hours or until pork is tender and barely pink in center. Serve over rice and sprinkle with almonds, if desired.

Makes 10 servings

Smoked Sausage Gumbo

Slow Cooker

1 can (14½ ounces) diced tomatoes, undrained
1 cup chicken broth
¼ cup all-purpose flour
2 tablespoons olive oil
¾ pound Polish sausage, cut into ½-inch pieces
1 medium onion, diced
1 green bell pepper, diced
2 ribs celery, chopped
1 carrot, peeled and chopped
2 teaspoons dried oregano
2 teaspoons dried thyme
⅛ teaspoon ground red pepper
1 cup uncooked long-grain white rice

Slow Cooker Directions

Combine tomatoes with juice and broth in slow cooker. Sprinkle flour evenly over bottom of small skillet. Cook over high heat without stirring 3 to 4 minutes or until flour begins to brown. Reduce heat to medium; stir flour about 4 minutes. Stir in oil until smooth. Carefully whisk flour mixture into slow cooker.

Add sausage, onion, bell pepper, celery, carrot, oregano, thyme and ground red pepper to slow cooker. Stir well. Cover and cook on LOW 4½ to 5 hours or until juices are thickened.

About 30 minutes before gumbo is ready to serve, prepare rice. Cook rice in 2 cups boiling water in medium saucepan. Serve gumbo over rice. *Makes 4 servings*

Note: For a special touch, sprinkle chopped parsley over each serving.

Note: If gumbo thickens upon standing, stir in additional broth.

The Best Beef Stew

Hearty Beef Barley Stew
Slow Cooker

1 tablespoon BERTOLLI® Olive Oil
1½ pounds stew meat
2 cups baby carrots
1 package (8 ounces) fresh mushrooms, sliced
2 cups (14½ ounces each) beef broth
1 can (14½ ounces) diced tomatoes, undrained
2 cups water
1 envelope LIPTON® RECIPE SECRETS® Onion Soup Mix
¾ cup barley
1 cup frozen peas

1. In 6-quart saucepot, heat oil over medium-high heat, brown beef, stirring occasionally, 4 minutes.

2. Stir in carrots, mushrooms, broth, tomatoes, water, soup mix and barley.

3. Bring to a boil over high heat. Reduce heat to medium-low and simmer, covered, 1½ hours, stirring occasionally. Stir in peas. Cook 5 minutes or until heated through.
Makes 6 servings

Slow Cooker Method: Layer carrots, mushrooms and beef in slow cooker. Combine broth, tomatoes, water, soup mix and barley. Pour over beef and vegetables. Cover. Cook on HIGH 5 to 6 hours or LOW 8 to 10 hours. Stir in peas and cook until heated through, about 5 minutes. Season, if desired, with salt and pepper.

Prep Time: 10 minutes
Cook Time: 1 hour 40 minutes

Cheeseburger Macaroni Stew

1 pound ground beef
1 can (28 ounces) crushed tomatoes in purée
1½ cups uncooked elbow macaroni
2 tablespoons *French's®* Worcestershire Sauce
1 cup shredded Cheddar cheese
1½ cups *French's®* French Fried Onions

1. Cook meat in large nonstick skillet over medium-high heat until browned and no longer pink; drain.

2. Add tomatoes, macaroni and *1½ cups water*. Bring to boiling. Boil, partially covered, 10 minutes until macaroni is tender. Stir in Worcestershire.

3. Sprinkle with cheese and French Fried Onions.   *Makes 6 servings*

Tip: For a Southwestern flavor, add 2 tablespoons chili powder to ground beef and substitute 2 tablespoons *Frank's®* RedHot Sauce for the Worcestershire.

Prep Time: 5 minutes
Cook Time: 15 minutes

Turkey Mushroom Stew
Slow Cooker

1 pound turkey cutlets, cut into 4×1-inch strips
1 small onion, thinly sliced
2 tablespoons minced green onion with top
½ pound mushrooms, sliced
1 cup half-and-half or milk
2 to 3 tablespoons all-purpose flour
1 teaspoon salt
1 teaspoon dried tarragon leaves
Black pepper to taste
½ cup frozen peas
½ cup sour cream (optional)
Puff pastry shells (optional)

Slow Cooker Directions
Layer turkey, onions and mushrooms in slow cooker. Cover and cook on LOW 4 hours. Remove turkey and vegetables to serving bowl. Turn slow cooker to HIGH.

Blend half-and-half into flour until smooth; pour into slow cooker. Add salt, tarragon and pepper to slow cooker. Return cooked vegetables and turkey to slow cooker. Stir in peas. Cover and cook 1 hour or until sauce has thickened and peas are heated through.

Stir in sour cream just before serving, if desired. Serve in puff pastry shells.
Makes 4 servings

Turkey Mushroom Stew

Chicken Stew with Dumplings

Slow Cooker

2 cups sliced carrots
1 cup chopped onion
1 large green pepper, sliced
½ cup sliced celery
2 cans (about 14 ounces each) chicken broth
⅔ cup all-purpose flour
1 pound boneless skinless chicken breasts, cut into 1-inch pieces
1 large potato, unpeeled and cut into 1-inch pieces
6 ounces mushrooms, halved
¾ cup frozen peas
1 teaspoon dried basil
¾ teaspoon dried rosemary
¼ teaspoon dried tarragon
¾ to 1 teaspoon salt
¼ teaspoon black pepper
¼ cup heavy cream

Herb Dumplings
1 cup biscuit mix
¼ teaspoon dried basil
¼ teaspoon dried rosemary
⅛ teaspoon dried tarragon
⅓ cup reduced-fat (2%) milk

Slow Cooker Directions

Combine carrots, onion, bell pepper and celery in slow cooker. Stir in chicken broth, reserving 1 cup broth. Cover and cook on LOW 2 hours.

Stir remaining 1 cup broth into flour until smooth. Stir into slow cooker. Add chicken, potato, mushrooms, peas and herbs to slow cooker. Cover and cook on LOW 4 hours or until vegetables are tender and chicken is no longer pink. Stir in salt, black pepper and heavy cream.

Combine biscuit mix and herbs in small bowl. Stir in milk to form soft dough. Spoon dumpling mixture on top of stew in 4 large spoonfuls. Cook, uncovered, 30 minutes. Cover and cook 30 to 45 minutes or until dumplings are firm and toothpick inserted in center comes out clean. Serve in shallow bowls.

Makes 4 servings

Chicken Gumbo

4 TYSON® Fresh Skinless Chicken Thighs
4 TYSON® Fresh Skinless Chicken Drumsticks
¼ cup all-purpose flour
2 teaspoons Cajun or Creole seasoning blend
2 tablespoons vegetable oil
1 large onion, chopped
1 cup thinly sliced celery
3 cloves garlic, minced
1 can (14½ ounces) stewed tomatoes, undrained
1 can (14½ ounces) chicken broth
1 large green bell pepper, cut into ½-inch pieces
½ to 1 teaspoon hot pepper sauce or to taste

PREP: CLEAN: Wash hands. Combine flour and Cajun seasoning in reclosable plastic bag. Add chicken, 2 pieces at a time; shake to coat. Reserve excess flour mixture. CLEAN: Wash hands.

COOK: In large saucepan, heat oil over medium heat. Add chicken and brown on all sides; remove and set aside. Sauté onion, celery and garlic 5 minutes. Add reserved flour mixture; cook 1 minute, stirring frequently. Add tomatoes, chicken broth, bell pepper and hot sauce. Bring to a boil. Return chicken to saucepan; cover and simmer over low heat, stirring occasionally, 30 minutes or until internal juices of chicken run clear. (Or insert instant-read meat thermometer into thickest part of chicken. Temperature should read 180°F.)

SERVE: Serve in shallow bowls, topped with hot cooked rice, if desired.

CHILL: Refrigerate leftovers immediately.

Makes 6 to 8 servings

Prep Time: 10 minutes
Cook Time: 1 hour

Country Chicken Stew

2 tablespoons butter or margarine
1 pound boneless skinless chicken breasts, cut into 1-inch cubes
½ pound small red potatoes, cut into ½-inch cubes
2 tablespoons cooking sherry
2 jars (12 ounces each) golden chicken gravy
1 bag (16 ounces) BIRDS EYE® frozen Farm Fresh Mixtures Broccoli, Green Beans, Pearl Onions and Red Peppers
½ cup water

• Melt butter in large saucepan over high heat. Add chicken and potatoes; cook about 8 minutes or until browned, stirring frequently.

• Add sherry; cook until evaporated. Add gravy, vegetables and water.

• Bring to boil; reduce heat to medium-low. Cover and cook 6 to 7 minutes.

Makes 4 to 6 servings

Prep Time: 5 minutes
Cook Time: 20 minutes

Country Chicken Stew

Chicken Gumbo

3 tablespoons vegetable oil
1 pound boneless skinless chicken breasts, cut into 1-inch pieces
½ pound smoked sausage,* cut into ¾-inch slices
1 bag (16 ounces) BIRDS EYE® frozen Farm Fresh Mixtures Broccoli, Corn and Red Peppers
1 can (14½ ounces) stewed tomatoes
1½ cups water

*For a spicy gumbo, use andouille sausage. Any type of kielbasa or turkey kielbasa can also be used.

- Heat oil in large saucepan over high heat. Add chicken and sausage; cook until browned, about 8 minutes.

- Add vegetables, tomatoes and water; bring to boil. Reduce heat to medium; cover and cook 5 to 6 minutes.   *Makes 4 to 6 servings*

Prep Time: 5 minutes
Cook Time: 20 minutes

Hearty One-Pot Chicken Stew

12 TYSON® Individually Fresh Frozen® Boneless, Skinless Chicken Tenderloins
1 box UNCLE BEN'S CHEF'S RECIPE® Traditional Red Beans & Rice
1 can (14½ ounces) diced tomatoes, undrained
3 new red potatoes, unpeeled, cut into 1-inch pieces
2 carrots, sliced ½ inch thick
1 onion, cut into 1-inch pieces

PREP: CLEAN: Wash hands. Remove protective ice glaze from frozen chicken by holding under cool running water 1 to 2 minutes. Cut into 1-inch pieces. CLEAN: Wash hands.

COOK: In large saucepan, combine chicken, beans and rice, contents of seasoning packet, 2¼ cups water, tomatoes, potatoes, carrots and onion. Bring to a boil. Cover, reduce heat; simmer 20 minutes or until internal juices of chicken run clear. (Or insert instant-read meat thermometer in thickest part of chicken. Temperature should read 170°F.)

SERVE: Serve with hot rolls, if desired.

CHILL: Refrigerate leftovers immediately.   *Makes 4 servings*

Prep Time: 10 minutes
Cook Time: 20 to 25 minutes

Easy Chicken Ragoût

2 tablespoons all-purpose flour
¼ teaspoon salt
½ teaspoon poultry seasoning
¼ teaspoon black pepper
4 boneless skinless chicken thighs (about 1½ pounds)
1 teaspoon olive oil
1 can (15 ounces) whole tomatoes, undrained
1 can (14½ ounces) chicken broth
2 cups quartered mushrooms
2 medium carrots, sliced
1 large onion, diced
½ to ¾ teaspoon dried thyme leaves
1 bay leaf
2 cups hot cooked rice

Combine flour, salt, poultry seasoning and pepper on sheet of waxed paper. Coat chicken thighs with flour mixture.

Heat oil in large saucepan over medium heat. Add chicken; cook and stir about 10 minutes or until chicken is browned on all sides. Remove chicken; drain fat from saucepan.

Return chicken to saucepan. Add tomatoes with juice, chicken broth, mushrooms, carrots, onion, thyme and bay leaf; stir to break up

tomatoes. Bring to a boil; reduce heat to low. Cover and simmer 30 minutes or until vegetables are tender and chicken is no longer pink in center, stirring occasionally. Discard bay leaf. Serve over rice.

Makes 4 servings

Gumbo in a Hurry

2 cans (14½ ounces *each*) chicken broth
1 can (14½ ounces) tomatoes, cut up, undrained
½ cup *each* minced celery and onion
¼ cup *Frank's® RedHot®* Cayenne Pepper Sauce
2 bay leaves
1 teaspoon dried thyme leaves
1 pound medium shrimp, peeled and deveined
1 can (6 ounces) crabmeat, drained
1 (4-ounce) boneless skinless chicken breast or thigh, cut into small cubes
1 package (10 ounces) frozen sliced okra, thawed
Hot cooked rice

1. Combine broth, tomatoes, *½ cup water*, celery, onion, *Frank's RedHot* Sauce and seasonings in large saucepot or Dutch oven. Heat to boiling. Stir in shrimp, crabmeat and chicken. Reduce heat to medium-low. Cook, uncovered, 10 minutes; stirring occasionally.

2. Stir in okra. Cook over medium-low heat 5 minutes or until okra is tender. *Do not boil*. Serve gumbo over rice in soup bowls. Serve with crusty French bread or garlic bread, if desired.

Makes 6 servings

Prep Time: 5 minutes
Cook Time: 15 minutes

Hearty One-Pot Chicken Stew

Shrimp Creole Stew

1½ cups raw small shrimp, shelled
1 bag (16 ounces) BIRDS EYE® frozen Farm Fresh Mixtures Broccoli, Cauliflower & Red Peppers
1 can (14½ ounces) diced tomatoes
1½ teaspoons salt
1 teaspoon hot pepper sauce
1 teaspoon vegetable oil

• In large saucepan, combine all ingredients.

• Cover; bring to boil. Reduce heat to medium-low; simmer 20 minutes or until shrimp turn opaque.

Makes 4 servings

Serving Suggestion: Serve over Spanish or white rice and with additional hot pepper sauce for added zip.

Prep Time: 5 minutes
Cook Time: 20 minutes

Mardi Gras Gumbo

1 bag SUCCESS® Rice
1 can (14½ ounces) low-sodium chicken broth
1 can (10½ ounces) chicken gumbo soup
1 can (10½ ounces) condensed tomato soup
1 can (6 ounces) crabmeat, drained and flaked

Prepare rice according to package directions.

Combine remaining ingredients in medium saucepan. Bring to a boil over medium-high heat. Reduce heat to low. Stir in rice; heat thoroughly, stirring occasionally.

Makes 4 servings

Oyster Corn Stew

40 medium oysters *or* 1 pint shucked fresh oysters including liquor*
Salt
1 cup milk
1 can (15 ounces) cream-style corn
¼ teaspoon salt
¼ teaspoon celery seeds
Dash white pepper
4 tablespoons butter or margarine
1 rib celery, chopped
1 cup cream or half-and-half
Celery leaves and grated lemon peel for garnish

Liquor is the term used to describe the natural juices of an oyster.

1. Scrub oysters thoroughly with stiff brush under cold running water. Soak oysters in mixture of ⅓ cup salt to 1 gallon water 20 minutes. Drain water; repeat 2 more times.

2. Place on tray and refrigerate 1 hour to help oysters relax.

3. Shuck oysters, reserving liquor. Refrigerate oysters. Strain oyster liquor from bowl through triple thickness of dampened cheesecloth into small bowl; set aside.

4. Place milk, corn, ¼ teaspoon salt, celery seeds and pepper in large saucepan. Bring to a simmer over medium heat; set aside.

5. Melt butter in medium skillet over medium-high heat. Add celery and cook 8 to 10 minutes or until tender. Add reserved oyster liquor; cook until heated through. Add oysters; heat about 10 minutes, just until oysters begin to curl around edges.

6. Add oyster mixture and cream to milk mixture. Cook over medium-high heat until just heated through. *Do not boil.*

7. Serve in wide-rimmed soup bowls. Garnish, if desired.

Makes 6 servings

Spicy Shrimp Gumbo

½ cup vegetable oil
½ cup all-purpose flour
1 large onion, chopped
½ cup chopped fresh parsley
½ cup chopped celery
½ cup sliced green onions
6 cloves garlic, minced
4 cups chicken broth or water*
1 package (10 ounces) frozen sliced okra, thawed (optional)
1 teaspoon salt
½ teaspoon ground red pepper
2 pounds raw medium shrimp, peeled and deveined
3 cups hot cooked rice
Fresh parsley sprigs for garnish

Traditional gumbo's thickness is like stew. If you prefer it thinner, add 1 to 2 cups additional broth.

1. For roux, blend oil and flour in large heavy stockpot. Cook over medium heat 10 to 15 minutes or until roux is dark brown but not burned, stirring often.

2. Add chopped onion, chopped parsley, celery, green onions and garlic to roux. Cook over medium heat 5 to 10 minutes or until vegetables are tender. Add broth, okra, salt and red pepper. Cover; simmer 15 minutes.

3. Add shrimp; simmer 3 to 5 minutes or until shrimp turn pink and opaque.

4. Place about ⅓ cup rice into each wide-rimmed soup bowl; top with gumbo. Garnish, if desired.

Makes 8 servings

Oyster Corn Stew

Shrimp Étouffée

- 3 tablespoons vegetable oil
- ¼ cup all-purpose flour
- 1 cup chopped onion
- 1 cup chopped green bell pepper
- ½ cup chopped carrots
- ½ cup chopped celery
- 4 cloves garlic, minced
- 1 can (14½ ounces) clear vegetable broth
- 1 bottle (8 ounces) clam juice
- ½ teaspoon salt
- 2½ pounds large shrimp, peeled and deveined
- 1 teaspoon red pepper flakes
- 1 teaspoon hot pepper sauce
- 4 cups hot cooked white or basmati rice
- ½ cup chopped flat leaf parsley

1. Heat oil in Dutch oven over medium heat. Add flour; cook and stir 10 to 15 minutes or until flour mixture is deep golden brown. Add onion, bell pepper, carrots, celery and garlic; cook and stir 5 minutes.

2. Stir in broth, clam juice and salt; bring to a boil. Simmer, uncovered, 10 minutes or until vegetables are tender. Stir in shrimp, red pepper and pepper sauce; simmer 6 to 8 minutes or until shrimp are opaque.

3. Ladle into eight shallow bowls; top each with ½ cup rice. Sprinkle with parsley. Serve with additional pepper sauce, if desired.

Makes 8 servings

Seafood Stew

- 2 tablespoons butter or margarine
- 1 cup chopped onion
- 1 cup green bell pepper strips
- 1 teaspoon dried dill weed
  Dash ground red pepper
- 1 can (14½ ounces) diced tomatoes, undrained
- ½ cup white wine
- 2 tablespoons lime juice
- 8 ounces swordfish steak, cut into 1-inch cubes
- 8 ounces bay or sea scallops, cut into quarters
- 1 bottle (8 ounces) clam juice
- 2 tablespoons cornstarch
- 2 cups frozen diced potatoes, thawed and drained
- 8 ounces frozen cooked medium shrimp, thawed and drained
- ½ cup whipping cream

1. Melt butter in Dutch oven over medium-high heat. Add onion, bell pepper, dill weed and red pepper; cook and stir 5 minutes or until vegetables are tender.

2. Reduce heat to medium. Add tomatoes with juice, wine and lime juice; bring to a boil. Add swordfish and scallops; cook and stir 2 minutes.

3. Combine clam juice and cornstarch in small bowl; stir until smooth.

4. Increase heat to high. Add potatoes, shrimp, whipping cream and clam juice mixture; bring to a boil. Season to taste with salt and black pepper. *Makes 6 servings*

Serving Suggestion: For a special touch, garnish stew with fresh lemon wedges and basil leaves.

Prep and Cook Time: 20 minutes

Shrimp Gumbo

- 1 package (16 ounces) frozen cut okra
- 1 can (16 ounces) stewed tomatoes, undrained
- 2 cups water
- ½ pound cooked ham or sausage, diced
- 1 can (8 ounces) tomato sauce
- 2 medium onions, sliced
- 2 tablespoons oil
- ½ teaspoon red pepper flakes
- 1 bay leaf
  Salt and black pepper
- 2 pounds frozen shelled deveined shrimp

Combine all ingredients except shrimp in Dutch oven. Bring to a boil over high heat. Reduce heat to low. Simmer, partially covered, 30 minutes. Add shrimp; stir well. Cook, partially covered, stirring occasionally, until shrimp are cooked through, 10 to 15 minutes longer. Remove bay leaf before serving.

Makes 6 servings

Chili Stew

- 1 box (10 ounces) BIRDS EYE® frozen Sweet Corn
- 2 cans (15 ounces each) chili
- 1 can (14 ounces) stewed tomatoes
  Chili powder

- In large saucepan, cook corn according to package directions; drain.

- Stir in chili and tomatoes; cook until heated through.

- Stir in chili powder to taste.

Makes 4 servings

Serving Suggestion: Serve with your favorite corn bread or sprinkle with shredded Cheddar cheese.

Prep Time: 2 minutes
Cook Time: 7 to 10 minutes

Shrimp Étouffée

Bean Ragoût with Cilantro-Cornmeal Dumplings

Slow Cooker

Cilantro-Cornmeal Dumplings (recipe follows)
2 cans (14½ ounces each) diced tomatoes, undrained
1½ cups chopped red bell pepper
1 large onion, chopped
1 can (15½ ounces) pinto or kidney beans, rinsed and drained
1 can (15½ ounces) black beans, rinsed and drained
2 small zucchini, sliced
½ cup chopped green bell pepper
½ cup chopped celery
1 poblano chili pepper,* seeded and chopped
2 cloves garlic, minced
3 tablespoons chili powder
2 teaspoons ground cumin
1 teaspoon dried oregano leaves
¼ teaspoon salt
⅛ teaspoon black pepper

Chili peppers can sting and irritate the skin; wear rubber gloves when handling peppers and do not touch eyes.

Slow Cooker Directions

1. Combine tomatoes with juice, red bell pepper, onion, beans, zucchini, green bell pepper, celery, poblano pepper, garlic, chili powder, cumin, oregano, salt and black pepper in slow cooker; mix well. Cover; cook on LOW 7 to 8 hours.

2. Prepare dumplings 1 hour before serving. *Turn slow cooker to HIGH.* Drop dumplings by level tablespoonfuls (larger dumplings will not cook properly) on top of ragoût. Cover; cook 1 hour or until toothpick inserted into dumpling comes out clean.   *Makes 6 servings*

Cilantro-Cornmeal Dumplings

¼ cup all-purpose flour
¼ cup yellow cornmeal
½ teaspoon baking powder
¼ teaspoon salt
1 tablespoon vegetable shortening
1 tablespoon shredded Cheddar cheese
2 teaspoons minced fresh cilantro
¼ cup milk

Slow Cooker Directions

Mix flour, cornmeal, baking powder and salt in medium bowl. Cut in shortening with pastry blender or two knives until mixture resembles coarse crumbs. Stir in cheese and cilantro. Pour milk into flour mixture. Blend just until dry ingredients are moistened.

Middle Eastern Vegetable Stew

Slow Cooker

3 cups (12 ounces) sliced zucchini
2 cups (6 ounces) cubed peeled eggplant
2 cups (8 ounces) sliced quartered sweet potatoes
1½ cups cubed peeled butternut squash
1 can (28 ounces) crushed tomatoes in purée
1 cup drained chick-peas
½ cup raisins or currants
1½ teaspoons ground cinnamon
1 teaspoon grated orange peel
¾ to 1 teaspoon ground cumin
½ teaspoon salt
½ teaspoon paprika
¼ to ½ teaspoon ground red pepper
⅛ teaspoon ground cardamom
Hot cooked rice or couscous (optional)

Slow Cooker Directions

Combine all ingredients except rice in slow cooker. Cover and cook on LOW 5 to 5½ hours or until vegetables are tender. Serve over rice.

Makes 4 to 6 servings

Tuscan Vegetable Stew

2 tablespoons olive oil
2 teaspoons minced garlic
2 packages (4 ounces each) sliced mixed exotic mushrooms *or* 1 package (8 ounces) sliced button mushrooms
¼ cup sliced shallots or chopped sweet onion
1 jar (7 ounces) roasted red peppers
1 can (14½ ounces) Italian-style stewed tomatoes, undrained
1 can (19 ounces) cannellini beans, rinsed and drained
1 bunch fresh basil leaves*
1 tablespoon balsamic vinegar
Salt
Black pepper
Grated Romano, Parmesan or Asiago cheese

If fresh basil is not available, add 2 teaspoons dried basil leaves to stew with tomatoes.

1. Heat oil and garlic in large deep skillet over medium heat. Add mushrooms and shallots; cook 5 minutes, stirring occasionally.

2. While mushroom mixture is cooking, drain and rinse peppers; cut into 1-inch pieces. Snip tomatoes in can into small pieces with scissors.

3. Add tomatoes, peppers and beans to skillet; bring to a boil. Reduce heat to medium-low. Cover and simmer 10 minutes, stirring once.

4. While stew is simmering, cut basil leaves into thin strips to measure ¼ cup packed. Stir basil and vinegar into stew; add salt and pepper to taste. Sprinkle each serving with cheese.   *Makes 4 servings*

Prep and Cook Time: 18 minutes

Bean Ragoût with Cilantro-Cornmeal Dumplings

Satisfying Chilis

Fast 'n Easy Chili

1½ pounds ground beef
1 envelope LIPTON®
    RECIPE SECRETS® Onion
    Soup Mix*
1 can (15 to 19 ounces) red
    kidney or black beans,
    drained
1½ cups water
1 can (8 ounces) tomato sauce
4 teaspoons chili powder

Also terrific with LIPTON® RECIPE SECRETS® Beefy Mushroom, Onion-Mushroom or Beefy Onion Soup Mix.

1. In 12-inch skillet, brown ground beef over medium-high heat; drain.

2. Stir in remaining ingredients. Bring to a boil over high heat. Reduce heat to low and simmer covered, stirring occasionally, 20 minutes. Top hot chili with shredded Cheddar cheese, and serve over hot cooked rice, if desired.
Makes 6 servings

First Alarm Chili: Add 5 teaspoons chili powder.

Second Alarm Chili: Add 2 tablespoons chili powder.

Third Alarm Chili: Add chili powder at your own risk.

Classic Texas Chili

¼ cup vegetable oil
3 pounds beef round or chuck,
    cut into 1-inch cubes
3 cloves garlic, minced
4 to 6 tablespoons chili powder
2 teaspoons salt
2 teaspoons dried oregano
    leaves
2 teaspoons ground cumin
2 teaspoons TABASCO® brand
    pepper sauce
1½ quarts water
⅓ cup white cornmeal
    Hot cooked rice and beans

Heat oil in large saucepan or Dutch oven. Add beef and brown on all sides. Add garlic, chili powder, salt, oregano, cumin, TABASCO® Sauce and water; stir to mix well. Bring to a boil; cover and reduce heat. Simmer 1¼ hours, stirring occasionally. Add cornmeal and mix well. Simmer, uncovered, an additional 30 minutes or until beef is tender. Garnish with chopped onion if desired. Serve with rice and beans.
Makes 6 to 8 servings

Chilly Day Chili

2 medium onions, chopped
1 green pepper, chopped
2 tablespoons vegetable oil
2 pounds lean ground beef
2 to 3 tablespoons chili powder
1 can (14½ ounces) tomatoes,
    cut into bite-size pieces
1 can (15 ounces) tomato sauce
½ cup HEINZ® Tomato Ketchup
1 teaspoon salt
¼ teaspoon black pepper
2 cans (15½ ounces each) red
    kidney beans, partially
    drained

In large saucepan or Dutch oven, cook and stir onions and green pepper in oil until tender. Add beef; cook until beef is no longer pink, stirring occasionally. Drain excess fat. Stir in chili powder, then add tomatoes, tomato sauce, ketchup, salt and pepper. Simmer, uncovered, 30 minutes, stirring occasionally. Add kidney beans; simmer additional 15 minutes.
Makes 8 servings
(about 8 cups)

Fast 'n Easy Chili

Chipotle Chili con Carne

¾ pound lean cubed beef stew meat
1 tablespoon chili powder
1 tablespoon ground cumin
  Nonstick cooking spray
1 can (about 14 ounces) beef broth
1 tablespoon minced canned chipotle chilies in adobo sauce, or to taste
1 can (14½ ounces) diced tomatoes, undrained
1 large green bell pepper *or* 2 poblano chili peppers, cut into pieces
2 cans (16 ounces each) pinto or red beans, rinsed and drained
  Chopped fresh cilantro (optional)

1. Toss beef in combined chili powder and cumin. Coat large saucepan or Dutch oven with cooking spray; heat over medium heat. Add beef; cook 5 minutes, stirring occasionally. Add beef broth and chipotle chilies with sauce; bring to a boil. Reduce heat; cover and simmer 1 hour 15 minutes or until beef is very tender.

2. With slotted spoon, transfer beef to carving board, leaving juices in saucepan. Using two forks, shred beef. Return beef to saucepan; add tomatoes and bell pepper. Bring to a boil; stir in beans. Simmer, uncovered, 20 minutes or until bell pepper is tender. Garnish with cilantro, if desired.   *Makes 6 servings*

Prep Time: 15 minutes
Cook Time: 1 hour 40 minutes

Chili Verde `Slow Cooker`

¾ pound boneless lean pork, cut into 1-inch cubes
1 large onion, halved and thinly sliced
6 cloves garlic, chopped or sliced
1 pound fresh tomatillos, coarsely chopped
1 can (about 14 ounces) chicken broth
1 can (4 ounces) diced mild green chilies
1 teaspoon ground cumin
1 can (15 ounces) Great Northern beans, rinsed and drained
½ cup lightly packed fresh cilantro, chopped
  Sour cream

Slow Cooker Directions

Spray large skillet with nonstick cooking spray and heat over medium-high heat. Add pork; cook until browned on all sides.

Combine cooked pork and all remaining ingredients except cilantro and sour cream in slow cooker. Cover and cook on HIGH 3 to 4 hours. Season to taste with salt and pepper. Gently press meat against side of slow cooker with wooden spoon to shred. Reduce heat to LOW. Stir in cilantro and cook 10 minutes. Serve with sour cream.

Makes 4 servings

Easy Slow-Cooked Chili `Slow Cooker`

2 pounds lean ground beef
2 tablespoons chili powder
1 tablespoon ground cumin
1 can (28 ounces) crushed tomatoes in purée
1 can (15 ounces) red kidney beans, drained and rinsed
1 cup water
¼ cup *Frank's® RedHot®* Cayenne Pepper Sauce
2 cups *French's®* French Fried Onions, divided
  Sour cream and shredded Cheddar cheese

Slow Cooker Directions

1. Cook ground beef, chili powder and cumin in large nonstick skillet over medium heat until browned, stirring frequently; drain. Transfer to slow cooker.

2. Stir in tomatoes, beans, water, Frank's RedHot Sauce and ½ cup French Fried Onions. Cover and cook on LOW setting for 6 hours (or on HIGH for 3 hours).

3. Serve chili topped with sour cream, cheese and remaining 1½ cups onions.   *Makes 8 servings*

Variation: For added Cheddar flavor, substitute *French's®* new Cheddar French Fried Onions for the original flavor.

Prep Time: 10 minutes
Cook Time: 6 hours

Helpful Hints

Tomatillos look like small green tomatoes with papery tan husks. They have a refreshing herbal flavor with a hint of lemon. To use them, peel away the husks, then rinse the tomatillos before chopping.

Chipotle Chili con Carne

Five-Way Cincinnati Chili

1 pound uncooked spaghetti, broken in half
1 pound ground beef chuck
2 cans (10 ounces each) tomatoes with green chilies, undrained
1 can (15 ounces) red kidney beans, drained
1 can (10½ ounces) condensed French onion soup
1¼ cups water
1 tablespoon chili powder
1 teaspoon sugar
½ teaspoon salt
¼ teaspoon ground cinnamon
½ cup chopped onion
½ cup (2 ounces) shredded Cheddar cheese

1. Cook pasta according to package directions; drain.

2. While pasta is cooking, cook beef in large saucepan or Dutch oven over medium-high heat until browned, stirring to separate; drain well. Add tomatoes with juice, beans, soup, water, chili powder, sugar, salt and cinnamon to saucepan; bring to a boil. Reduce heat to low. Simmer, uncovered, 10 minutes, stirring occasionally.

3. Serve chili over spaghetti; sprinkle with onion and cheese.

Makes 6 servings

Cook's Notes: Serve this traditional chili your way or one of the ways Cincinnatians do—two-way over spaghetti, three-way with cheese, four-way with cheese and chopped onion or five-way with beans added to the chili.

Prep/Cook Time: 20 minutes

Cowboy Chili

2 large onions, chopped
2 pounds boneless top round or sirloin steak, cut into ½-inch cubes
1 pound ground beef
1 can (28 ounces) whole tomatoes in purée, undrained
1 can (15 to 19 ounces) red kidney beans, undrained
⅓ cup *Frank's® RedHot®* Cayenne Pepper Sauce
2 packages (1¼ ounces *each*) chili seasoning mix

1. Cook and stir onions in *1 tablespoon hot oil* in large pot; transfer to bowl. Cook steak cubes and ground beef in batches in *3 tablespoons hot oil* until well-browned; drain well.

2. Add onions, *¾ cup water* and remaining ingredients to pot. Heat to boiling, stirring. Reduce heat to medium-low. Cook, partially covered, 1 hour or until meat is tender, stirring often. Garnish as desired.

Makes 10 servings

Ground Beef Variation: Substitute 3 pounds ground beef for the combination of top round and ground beef. Brown meat without oil. Proceed as in step 2. Simmer 20 minutes.

Prep Time: 15 minutes
Cook Time: 1 hour 15 minutes

Hearty Chili

2 pounds BOB EVANS® Original Recipe Roll Sausage
1½ cups chopped onions
1 (1¼-ounce) package chili seasoning
3 cups tomato sauce
3 cups tomato juice
1 (30-ounce) can chili or kidney beans
Hot pepper sauce to taste (optional)

Crumble sausage into large Dutch oven. Add onions. Cook over medium heat until sausage is browned, stirring occasionally. Drain off any drippings; stir in seasoning, then remaining ingredients. Bring to a boil over high heat. Reduce heat to low; simmer, uncovered, 30 minutes. Serve hot. Refrigerate leftovers.

Makes 8 servings

Hearty Chili with Black Beans

1 tablespoon vegetable oil
1 pound ground chuck
1 can (about 14½ ounces) beef broth
1 large onion, minced
1 green bell pepper, seeded and diced
2 teaspoons chili powder
½ teaspoon ground allspice
¼ teaspoon ground cinnamon
¼ teaspoon paprika
1 can (15 ounces) black beans, rinsed and drained
1 can (14 ounces) crushed tomatoes in purée
2 teaspoons apple cider vinegar

Heat oil in large skillet over medium high heat until hot. Add ground chuck, beef broth, onion and bell pepper. Cook and stir, breaking up meat. Cook until beef is no longer pink; drain excess fat.

Add chili powder, allspice, cinnamon and paprika. Reduce heat to medium-low; simmer 10 minutes. Add black beans, tomatoes and vinegar; bring to a boil.

Reduce heat to low; simmer 20 to 25 minutes or until chili is thickened to desired consistency. Garnish as desired.

Makes 4 servings

Five-Way Cincinnati Chili

Hearty Chili

1¼ cups dried pinto beans
1 pound ground beef or turkey
1 onion, chopped
3 tablespoons Hearty Chili Seasoning Mix (recipe follows)
1 can (28 ounces) diced tomatoes, undrained
1 can (about 14 ounces) beef broth

1. Place beans and 8 cups cold water in large saucepan. Bring to a boil over high heat. Boil 1 minute. Remove saucepan from heat. Cover; let stand 1 hour.

2. Drain beans; rinse under cold running water. Return beans to saucepan. Add 8 cups cold water. Bring to a boil over high heat. Reduce heat to medium-low. Simmer 1 hour 15 minutes or until beans are just tender, stirring occasionally. Remove saucepan from heat and drain beans; set aside.

3. Combine ground beef and onion in large saucepan. Cook over medium-high heat 6 minutes or until beef is no longer pink, stirring to crumble beef. Spoon off and discard any drippings.

4. Add seasoning mix to saucepan. Cook 1 minute, stirring frequently. Add beans, tomatoes with juice and beef broth; bring to a boil over high heat. Reduce heat to medium-low. Cover; simmer 30 minutes, stirring occasionally. Store in airtight container in refrigerator up to 3 days or freeze up to 1 month.

Makes about 8 cups

Hearty Chili Seasoning Mix

½ cup chili powder
¼ cup ground cumin
2 tablespoons garlic salt
2 tablespoons dried oregano leaves
2 teaspoons ground coriander
½ teaspoon ground red pepper

Combine all ingredients in small bowl. Store in airtight container at room temperature up to 3 months.

Makes about 1 cup

Chunky Chili

1 pound lean ground beef
1 medium onion, chopped
1 tablespoon chili powder
1½ teaspoons ground cumin
2 cans (16 ounces each) diced tomatoes, undrained
1 can (15 ounces) pinto beans, rinsed and drained
½ cup prepared salsa
½ cup (2 ounces) shredded Cheddar cheese
3 tablespoons sour cream
4 teaspoons sliced black olives

Slow Cooker Directions
Heat large skillet over medium heat. Add beef and onion; cook until beef is browned and onion is tender. Drain fat. Place beef mixture, chili powder, cumin, tomatoes, beans and salsa in slow cooker; stir. Cover and cook on LOW 5 to 6 hours or until flavors are blended and chili is bubbly. Season with salt and pepper to taste. Serve with cheese, sour cream and olives.

Makes 4 (1½-cup) servings

Serving Suggestion: Serve with tossed green salad and cornbread muffins.

Riverboat Chili

2 pounds lean ground beef
2 large onions, chopped
1 large green pepper, chopped
2 cans (14½ ounces each) FRANK'S® or SNOWFLOSS® Original Style Diced Tomatoes, undrained
1 can (14½ ounces) FRANK'S® or SNOWFLOSS® Stewed Tomatoes, undrained
⅓ cup MISSISSIPPI® Barbecue Sauce
2 bay leaves
3 whole cloves
2 teaspoons chili powder
½ teaspoon cayenne pepper
½ teaspoon paprika
4 cans (15½ ounces each) dark red kidney beans

1. Brown ground beef in large stock pot. Drain grease.

2. Add onions, green pepper, diced tomatoes, stewed tomatoes, barbecue sauce, bay leaves, cloves, chili powder, cayenne pepper and paprika. Stir well.

3. Add kidney beans and stir well.

4. Cover and simmer 2 hours, stirring occasionally. Remove and discard bay leaves.

Makes 4 to 6 servings

Microwave Directions: Crumble beef into large microwave-safe casserole dish. Cook uncovered on HIGH about 6 minutes, stirring at least twice to break up meat. Drain grease. Add onions, green pepper, diced tomatoes, stewed tomatoes, barbecue sauce, bay leaves, cloves, chili powder, cayenne pepper and paprika. Cook 1 minute. Stir well. Add kidney beans and stir well. Cover and cook 15 to 20 minutes, stirring occasionally. Remove and discard bay leaves. Cover and let stand 5 minutes.

Prep Time: 30 minutes
Cook Time: 2 hours

Hearty Chili

Winter White Chili

½ pound boneless pork loin *or*
    2 boneless pork chops, cut
    into ½-inch cubes
½ cup chopped onion
1 teaspoon vegetable oil
1 (16-ounce) can navy beans,
    drained
1 (16-ounce) can chick-peas,
    drained
1 (16-ounce) can white kernel
    corn, drained
1 (14½-ounce) can chicken broth
1 cup cooked wild rice
1 (4-ounce) can diced green
    chilies, drained
1½ teaspoons ground cumin
¼ teaspoon garlic powder
⅛ teaspoon hot pepper sauce
    Chopped parsley and
    shredded cheese

In 4-quart saucepan, sauté pork and onion in oil over medium-high heat until onion is soft and pork is lightly browned, about 5 minutes. Stir in remaining ingredients except parsley and cheese. Cover and simmer for 20 minutes. Serve each portion garnished with parsley and shredded cheese.   *Makes 6 servings*

Prep Time: 10 minutes
Cook Time: 25 minutes
Favorite recipe from **National Pork Board**

Ragú® Chili

2 pounds ground beef
1 large onion, chopped
2 cloves garlic, finely chopped
1 jar (1 pound 10 ounces)
    RAGÚ® Robusto! Pasta
    Sauce
1 can (15 ounces) red kidney
    beans, rinsed and drained
2 tablespoons chili powder

In 12-inch skillet, brown ground beef with onion and garlic over medium-high heat; drain. Stir in remaining ingredients. Simmer uncovered, stirring occasionally, 20 minutes. Serve, if desired, with shredded Cheddar cheese.

Makes 8 servings

Note: For spicier Ragú® Chili, stir in ½ teaspoon each ground cumin and dried oregano.

Soul City Chili

2 pounds ground beef
½ teaspoon LAWRY'S® Seasoned
    Salt
½ teaspoon LAWRY'S® Seasoned
    Pepper
1 pound hot Italian sausage or
    kielbasa sausage, cut into
    bite-size pieces
2 cups water
1 can (15¼ ounces) kidney
    beans, undrained
1 can (14½ ounces) stewed
    tomatoes, undrained
2 packages (1.48 ounces each)
    LAWRY'S® Spices &
    Seasonings for Chili
½ cup hickory-flavored barbecue
    sauce
¾ cup red wine

In Dutch oven, cook beef until browned and crumbly; drain fat. Add Seasoned Salt and Seasoned Pepper; mix well. Stir in sausage, water, beans, tomatoes, Spices & Seasonings for Chili and barbecue sauce. Bring to a boil over medium-high heat; reduce heat to low, simmer, uncovered, 20 minutes. Stir in wine. Heat through.

Makes about 10 servings
(9½ cups)

Serving Suggestion: Top with diced green, yellow and red bell peppers and chopped onion. Perfect with crackers, too!

Chili

2 tablespoons vegetable oil
2 pounds ground beef
2 cups finely chopped white
    onions
1 to 2 dried de arbol chiles
2 cloves garlic, minced
1 teaspoon ground cumin
½ to 1 teaspoon salt
¼ teaspoon ground cloves
1 can (28 ounces) whole peeled
    tomatoes, undrained,
    coarsely chopped
½ cup fresh orange juice
½ cup tequila or water
¼ cup tomato paste
1 tablespoon grated orange peel
    Lime wedges and cilantro
    sprigs (optional)

Heat oil in deep 12-inch skillet over medium-high heat until hot. Crumble beef into skillet. Brown 6 to 8 minutes, stirring occasionally. Pour off drippings. Reduce heat to medium. Add onions; cook and stir 5 minutes or until tender.

Crush chiles into fine flakes in mortar with pestle. Add chilies, garlic, cumin, salt and cloves to skillet. Cook and stir 30 seconds.

Stir in tomatoes with juice, orange juice, tequila, tomato paste and orange peel. Bring to a boil over high heat. Reduce heat to low. Cover and simmer 1½ hours, stirring occasionally.

Uncover skillet. Cook chili over medium-low heat 10 to 15 minutes or until thickened slightly, stirring frequently. Ladle into bowls. Garnish with lime wedges and cilantro if desired.   *Makes 6 to 8 servings*

Winter White Chili

Texas-Style Chili

1½ pounds ground beef or cubed
    round steak
1 green bell pepper, diced
1 onion, diced
1 can (2¼ ounces) diced green
    chiles, drained
1 package (1.48 ounces)
    LAWRY'S® Spices &
    Seasonings for Chili
1½ tablespoons cornmeal
1 tablespoon chili powder
1 teaspoon sugar
¼ to ½ teaspoon cayenne pepper
1 can (14½ ounces) diced
    tomatoes, undrained
¾ cup water
    Sour cream (optional)
    Shredded cheddar cheese
    (optional)

In Dutch oven or large saucepan, cook beef until browned and crumbly; drain beef, reserving fat; set beef aside. In Dutch oven, heat reserved fat. Add bell pepper and onion and cook over medium-high heat 5 minutes or until vegetables are crisp-tender. Return beef to Dutch oven. Add chiles, Spices & Seasonings for Chili, cornmeal, chili powder, sugar and cayenne pepper; mix well. Stir in tomatoes and water. Bring to a boil over medium-high heat; reduce heat to low, cover and simmer 30 minutes, stirring occasionally. *Makes 4½ cups*

Serving Suggestion: Serve topped with sour cream or cheddar cheese, if desired.

Hint: This recipe is perfect for leftover meat. Use 3½ cups shredded beef. If using shredded beef or cubed round steak, brown in 1 tablespoon vegetable oil.

Veg•All® Beef Chili

1 can (28 ounces) tomato sauce
1 pound ground beef, browned
    and drained
1 can (16 ounces) kidney beans,
    drained and rinsed
1 can (15 ounces) VEG•ALL®
    Original Mixed Vegetables,
    with liquid
1 can (14½ ounces) whole
    tomatoes, cut up
¾ cup sliced green onions
2 teaspoons chili powder
¼ teaspoon black pepper
    Corn chips
    Shredded cheese
    Diced green onions

In 3-quart saucepan, combine all ingredients except chips, cheese and diced green onions. Bring to a boil; reduce heat, cover, and simmer for 20 to 30 minutes, stirring occasionally. Serve hot with corn chips, shredded cheese, and diced green onions as toppers. *Makes 6 to 8 servings*

Prep Time: 7 minutes
Cook Time: 20 minutes

Hot Dogs with Chili

½ pound HILLSHIRE FARM® Hot
    Dogs, cut into ½-inch slices
½ cup chopped onion
2 tablespoons chopped green
    bell pepper
½ teaspoon chili powder
2 tablespoons butter
2 cans (20 ounces each) kidney
    beans, drained
1 can (10½-ounces) condensed
    tomato soup
1 teaspoon vinegar
½ teaspoon Worcestershire
    sauce

Sauté Hot Dogs, onion, green pepper and chili powder in butter until Hot Dogs are browned. Add remaining ingredients. Cover; cook over low heat 12 to 15 minutes. Stir often.
Makes 4 to 6 servings

Meaty Chili

1 pound coarsely ground beef
¼ pound ground Italian sausage
1 large onion, chopped
2 medium ribs celery, diced
2 fresh jalapeño peppers,*
    chopped
2 cloves garlic, minced
1 can (28 ounces) whole peeled
    tomatoes, undrained, cut up
1 can (15 ounces) pinto beans,
    drained
1 can (12 ounces) tomato juice
1 cup water
¼ cup ketchup
1 teaspoon sugar
1 teaspoon chili powder
½ teaspoon salt
½ teaspoon ground cumin
½ teaspoon dried thyme leaves
⅛ teaspoon black pepper

*Jalapeño peppers can sting and irritate the skin; wear rubber gloves when handling peppers and do not touch eyes. Wash hands after handling.

Cook beef, sausage, onion, celery, jalapeño peppers and garlic in 5-quart Dutch oven over medium-high heat until meat is browned and onion is tender, stirring frequently.

Stir in tomatoes with juice, beans, tomato juice, water, ketchup, sugar, chili powder, salt, cumin, thyme and black pepper. Bring to a boil over high heat. Reduce heat to medium-low; simmer, uncovered, 30 minutes, stirring occasionally.

Ladle into bowls. Garnish, if desired.
Makes 6 servings

Meaty Chili

Black and White Chili

`Slow Cooker`

Nonstick cooking spray
1 pound chicken tenders, cut into ¾-inch pieces
1 cup coarsely chopped onion
1 can (15½ ounces) Great Northern beans, drained
1 can (15 ounces) black beans, drained
1 can (14½ ounces) Mexican-style stewed tomatoes, undrained
2 tablespoons Texas-style chili powder seasoning mix

Slow Cooker Directions

Spray large saucepan with cooking spray; heat over medium heat until hot. Add chicken and onion; cook and stir 5 minutes or until chicken is browned.

Combine cooked chicken, onion, beans, tomatoes and chili seasoning in slow cooker. Cover and cook on LOW 4 to 4½ hours.

Makes 6 (1-cup) servings

Serving Suggestion: For a change of pace, this delicious chili is excellent served over cooked rice or pasta.

Bandstand Chili

2 cups chopped cooked BUTTERBALL® Boneless Young Turkey
1 tablespoon vegetable oil
1½ cups chopped onions
1½ cups chopped red bell peppers
2 tablespoons mild Mexican seasoning*
1 clove garlic, minced
1 can (28 ounces) tomato purée with tomato bits
1 can (15½ ounces) light red kidney beans, undrained

To make your own Mexican seasoning, combine 1 tablespoon chili powder, 1½ teaspoons oregano and 1½ teaspoons cumin.

Heat oil in large skillet over medium heat until hot. Add onions, bell peppers, Mexican seasoning and garlic. Cook and stir 4 to 5 minutes. Add tomato purée and beans; stir in turkey. Reduce heat to low; simmer 5 minutes. *Makes 8 servings*

Prep Time: 25 minutes

Confetti Chicken Chili

1 pound lean ground chicken or turkey
1 large onion, chopped
2 cans (about 14 ounces each) chicken broth
1 can (15 ounces) Great Northern beans, rinsed and drained
2 carrots, chopped
1 medium green bell pepper, chopped
2 plum tomatoes, chopped
1 jalapeño pepper,* finely chopped (optional)
2 teaspoons chili powder
½ teaspoon ground red pepper

Jalapeño peppers can sting and irritate the skin; wear rubber gloves when handling peppers and do not touch eyes. Wash hands after handling.

1. Heat large nonstick saucepan over medium heat until hot. Add chicken and onion; cook and stir 5 minutes or until chicken is browned. Drain fat from saucepan.

2. Add remaining ingredients to saucepan. Bring to a boil. Reduce heat to low and simmer 15 minutes.

Makes 5 servings

Prep & Cook Time: 30 minutes

Hearty Turkey Cannellini Chili

1 pound ground turkey or ground beef
1 (6.9-ounce) package RICE-A-RONI® Chicken Flavor
2 tablespoons margarine or butter
1 (14½-ounce) can diced tomatoes with garlic and onion, undrained
1 tablespoon chili powder
1 (15-ounce) can cannellini beans, drained and rinsed

1. In large skillet over medium-high heat, cook ground turkey until no longer pink. Remove from skillet; drain. Set aside.

2. In same skillet over medium heat, sauté rice-vermicelli mix with margarine until vermicelli is golden brown.

3. Slowly stir in 2¼ cups water, tomatoes, chili powder and Special Seasonings; bring to a boil. Reduce heat to low. Cover; simmer 10 minutes.

4. Stir in beans and turkey; return to a simmer. Cover; simmer 5 to 7 minutes or until rice is tender.

Makes 6 servings

Prep Time: 5 minutes
Cook Time: 30 minutes

Helpful Hints

Chili often tastes better the day after it is made, so consider preparing a double batch. Leftover chili can be served over pasta, rice or baked potatoes. Or, try it as a filling for taco shells, burritos or over hot dogs for chili dogs.

Confetti Chicken Chili

Santa Fe Skillet Chili

1 to 1¼ pounds ground turkey (93% lean)
1 cup chopped onion
1 teaspoon bottled minced garlic
1 tablespoon chili powder
1 tablespoon ground cumin
¼ to ½ teaspoon ground red pepper
1 can (15½ ounces) chili beans in spicy sauce, undrained
1 can (14½ ounces) Mexican- or chili-style stewed or diced tomatoes, undrained
1 can (4 ounces) chopped green chilies, undrained

1. Spray large deep skillet with nonstick cooking spray. Cook turkey, onion and garlic over medium-high heat, breaking meat apart with wooden spoon.

2. Sprinkle chili powder, cumin and red pepper evenly over turkey mixture; cook and stir 3 minutes or until turkey is no longer pink.

3. Stir in beans, tomatoes with juice and chilies with liquid. Reduce heat to medium; cover and simmer 10 minutes, stirring occasionally. Ladle chili into bowls.

Makes 4 servings

Serving Suggestion: Offer a variety of toppings with the skillet chili, such as chopped fresh cilantro, sour cream, shredded Cheddar or Monterey Jack cheese and diced ripe avocado. Serve with warm corn tortillas or corn bread.

Prep and Cook Time: 19 minutes

Chunky Chicken Chili

1 pound boneless skinless chicken breast, cut into bite-sized pieces
1 cup chopped onion
½ cup chopped celery
½ cup chopped carrot
2 cloves garlic, minced
1 tablespoon vegetable oil
1 can (15½ ounces) dark red kidney beans, drained
1 can (27 ounces) FRANK'S® or SNOWFLOSS® Original Style Diced Tomatoes
1 cup MISSISSIPPI® Barbecue Sauce
1 can (8 ounces) tomato sauce
1 tablespoon chili powder
½ teaspoon ground cumin
1 green bell pepper, chopped

1. In large stockpot sauté chicken, onion, celery, carrot and garlic in oil. Cook and stir until chicken is no longer pink.

2. Stir in kidney beans, tomatoes, barbecue sauce, tomato sauce, chili powder and cumin.

3. Bring to a boil then reduce heat. Simmer, uncovered, 30 minutes, stirring occasionally.

4. Add green pepper and heat through before serving.

Makes 4 to 6 servings

Prep Time: 25 minutes
Cook Time: 30 minutes

Green Flash Turkey Chili

3 tablespoons olive oil, divided
3 large stalks celery, diced
1 large green bell pepper, diced
2 green onions, sliced
2 large cloves garlic, minced
1 pound ground turkey
4 cups canned white kidney beans, drained and rinsed
1½ cups water
⅓ cup TABASCO® brand Green Pepper Sauce
1¼ teaspoons salt
¼ cup chopped fresh parsley

Heat 2 tablespoons oil in large saucepan over medium heat. Add celery and green bell pepper; cook about 5 minutes or until crisp-tender. Add green onions and garlic; cook 5 minutes, stirring occasionally. Remove vegetables to plate with slotted spoon. Add remaining 1 tablespoon oil to saucepan; cook turkey over medium-high heat until well browned, stirring frequently.

Add vegetable mixture, kidney beans, water, TABASCO® Green Pepper Sauce and salt to saucepan. Heat to boiling over high heat. Reduce heat to low; cover and simmer 20 minutes, stirring occasionally. Uncover saucepan and simmer 5 minutes. Stir in parsley just before serving.

Makes 6 servings

Santa Fe Skillet Chili

White Chicken Chili

1 to 2 tablespoons canola oil
1 onion, chopped (about 1 cup)
1 package (about 1¼ pounds) PERDUE® Fresh Ground Chicken, Turkey or Turkey Breast Meat
1 package (about 1¾ ounces) chili seasoning mix
1 can (14½ ounces) reduced-sodium chicken broth
1 can (15 ounces) cannellini or white kidney beans, drained and rinsed

In Dutch oven over medium-high heat, heat oil. Add onion; sauté 2 to 3 minutes until softened and translucent. Add ground chicken; sauté 5 to 7 minutes until no longer pink. Add chili mix and stir to combine. Add chicken broth and beans; bring to a boil. Reduce heat to medium-low; simmer 5 to 10 minutes, until all flavors are blended.

Makes 4 servings

Prep Time: 10 minutes
Cook Time: 10 to 20 minutes

Turkey Vegetable Chili Mac

Nonstick cooking spray
¾ pound ground turkey breast
½ cup chopped onion
2 cloves garlic, minced
1 can (about 15 ounces) black beans, rinsed and drained
1 can (14½ ounces) Mexican-style stewed tomatoes, undrained
1 can (14½ ounces) no-salt-added diced tomatoes, undrained
1 cup frozen corn
1 teaspoon Mexican seasoning
½ cup uncooked elbow macaroni
⅓ cup reduced-fat sour cream

1. Spray large nonstick saucepan or Dutch oven with cooking spray; heat over medium heat until hot. Add turkey, onion and garlic; cook 5 minutes or until turkey is no longer pink, stirring to crumble.

2. Stir beans, tomatoes with juice, corn and Mexican seasoning into saucepan; bring to a boil over high heat. Cover; reduce heat to low. Simmer 15 minutes, stirring occasionally.

3. Meanwhile, cook pasta according to package directions. Rinse and drain pasta; stir into saucepan. Simmer, uncovered, 2 to 3 minutes or until heated through.

4. Top each serving with dollop of sour cream. Garnish as desired.

Makes 6 servings

Chicken and Black Bean Chili

1 tablespoon vegetable oil
1 medium onion, chopped
4 boneless, skinless chicken breast halves (about 1 pound), cooked and cut into strips
2 cans (14½ ounces each) diced tomatoes, undrained
1 can (15 ounces) black beans, rinsed and drained
1 can (4 ounces) diced green chiles
½ cup water
½ teaspoon LAWRY'S® Garlic Powder with Parsley
1 package (1.48 ounces) LAWRY'S® Spices & Seasonings for Chili
½ teaspoon hot pepper sauce (optional)
1 tablespoon chopped fresh cilantro

In large, deep skillet, heat oil. Add onion and cook until tender and translucent. Add all remaining ingredients except cilantro. Bring to a boil over medium-high heat; reduce

heat to low and simmer, uncovered, 20 minutes, stirring occasionally. Stir in cilantro. *Makes 5½ cups*

Serving Suggestion: Serve with dairy sour cream and tortilla chips. Chopped avocados make a great garnish, too.

Variation: Substitute 1½ pounds ground turkey or chicken, browned in 1 tablespoon oil, for chicken.

White Bean Chili [Slow Cooker]

Nonstick cooking spray
1 pound ground chicken
3 cups coarsely chopped celery
1½ cups coarsely chopped onions
3 cloves garlic, minced
4 teaspoons chili powder
1½ teaspoons ground cumin
¾ teaspoon ground allspice
¾ teaspoon ground cinnamon
½ teaspoon black pepper
1 can (16 ounces) whole tomatoes, undrained and coarsely chopped
1 can (15½ ounces) Great Northern beans, drained and rinsed
1 cup chicken broth

Slow Cooker Directions

Spray large nonstick skillet with nonstick cooking spray; heat over high heat until hot. Add chicken; cook until browned, breaking into pieces with fork. Combine chicken, celery, onions, garlic, chili powder, cumin, allspice, cinnamon, pepper, tomatoes with juice, beans and broth in slow cooker. Cover and cook 5½ to 6 hours on LOW or until chicken is no longer pink and celery is tender.

Makes 6 servings

Turkey Vegetable Chili Mac

Chili with Beans and Corn

Slow Cooker

1 (16-ounce) can black-eyed peas or cannellini beans, rinsed and drained
1 (16-ounce) can kidney or navy beans, rinsed and drained
1 (15-ounce) can whole tomatoes, drained and chopped
1 onion, chopped
1 cup corn
1 cup water
½ cup chopped green onions
½ cup tomato paste
¼ cup diced jalapeño peppers*
1 tablespoon chili powder
1 teaspoon ground cumin
1 teaspoon prepared mustard
½ teaspoon dried oregano leaves

Jalapeño peppers can sting and irritate the skin; wear rubber gloves when handling peppers and do not touch eyes. Wash hands after handling.

Slow Cooker Directions
Combine all ingredients in slow cooker. Cover and cook on LOW 8 to 10 hours or on HIGH 4 to 5 hours.

Makes 6 to 8 servings

Southwest Chili

1 large onion, chopped
1 tablespoon olive oil
2 large tomatoes, chopped
1 (4-ounce) can chopped green chilies, undrained
1 tablespoon chili powder
1 teaspoon ground cumin
1 (15-ounce) can red kidney beans, undrained
1 (15-ounce) can Great Northern beans, undrained
¼ cup cilantro leaves, chopped (optional)

Cook and stir onion in oil in large saucepan over medium heat until onion is soft. Stir in tomatoes, chilies, chili powder and cumin. Bring to a boil. Add beans with liquid. Reduce heat to low. Cover and simmer 15 minutes, stirring occasionally. Sprinkle individual servings with cilantro.   *Makes 4 servings*

Vegetarian Rice & Black Bean Chili

2 cups UNCLE BEN'S® Hearty Soup Black Beans & Rice
2½ cups water
½ cup thinly sliced carrot
1 small zucchini, quartered lengthwise and sliced
⅓ cup diced red bell pepper
1 can (8 ounces) tomato sauce
½ cup (2 ounces) Cheddar cheese

1. Place water in medium saucepan. Stir in rice, beans and contents of seasoning packet. Bring to a boil. Add carrot. Cover; reduce heat and simmer 10 minutes.

2. Add zucchini and bell pepper. Cover; reduce heat and simmer 5 minutes. Stir in tomato sauce. Cover and simmer 8 to 10 minutes or until rice is tender. Top with cheese.

Makes 4 servings

Rice and Chick-Pea Chili

⅔ cup UNCLE BEN'S® ORIGINAL CONVERTED® Brand Rice
1 can (15 ounces) chick-peas, undrained
1 can (15 ounces) diced tomatoes, undrained
1 can (8 ounces) diced green chilies
1 cup frozen corn
¼ cup chopped fresh cilantro
1 tablespoon taco seasoning
½ cup (2 ounces) shredded reduced-fat Cheddar cheese

1. In medium saucepan, bring 1¾ cups water and rice to a boil. Cover, reduce heat and simmer 15 minutes.

2. Add remaining ingredients except cheese. Cook over low heat 10 minutes. Serve in bowls sprinkled with cheese.   *Makes 4 servings*

Serving Suggestion: To round out the meal, serve this hearty chili with corn bread and fresh fruit.

Chili with Beans and Corn

Olive-Bean Chili

3 tablespoons molasses
1½ teaspoons dry mustard
1½ teaspoons soy sauce
2 teaspoons olive oil
2 medium carrots, cut diagonally into ¼-inch slices
1 large onion, chopped
1 tablespoon chili powder
3 large tomatoes (1½ pounds), chopped
1 (15-ounce) can pinto beans, drained
1 (15-ounce) can kidney beans, drained
¾ cup California ripe olives, sliced
½ cup plain nonfat yogurt
Crushed red pepper flakes

Combine molasses, mustard and soy sauce; set aside. Heat oil in large skillet; add carrots, onion, chili powder and ¼ cup water. Cook, covered, about 4 minutes or until carrots are almost tender. Uncover and cook, stirring, until liquid has evaporated. Add molasses mixture with tomatoes, pinto beans, kidney beans and olives. Cook, stirring gently, about 5 minutes or until mixture is hot and tomatoes are soft. Ladle chili into bowls; top with yogurt. Sprinkle with pepper flakes to taste.

Makes 4 servings

Prep Time: about 15 minutes
Cook Time: about 10 minutes
Favorite recipe from **California Olive Industry**

Vegetarian Chili with Cornbread Topping

1 pound zucchini, halved and cut into ½-inch slices (about 4 cups)
1 red or green bell pepper, cut into 1-inch pieces
1 rib celery, thinly sliced
1 clove garlic, minced
2 cans (15 to 19 ounces *each*) kidney beans, rinsed and drained
1 can (28 ounces) crushed tomatoes in purée, undrained
¼ cup *Frank's® RedHot®* Cayenne Pepper Sauce
1 tablespoon chili powder
1 package (6½ ounces) cornbread mix plus ingredients to prepare mix

1. Preheat oven to 400°F. Heat *1 tablespoon oil* in 12-inch heatproof skillet* over medium-high heat. Add zucchini, bell pepper, celery and garlic. Cook and stir 5 minutes or until tender. Stir in beans, tomatoes, *Frank's RedHot* Sauce and chili powder. Heat to boiling, stirring.

2. Prepare cornbread mix according to package directions. Spoon batter on top of chili mixture, spreading to ½ inch from edges. Bake 30 minutes or until cornbread is golden brown and mixture is bubbly.

Makes 6 servings

*If handle of skillet is not heatproof, wrap in foil.

Tip: Salsa Olé! Spike up the flavor of salsa by adding *Frank's RedHot* Sauce to taste. Serve with chips or on top of fajitas and tacos.

Prep Time: 20 minutes
Cook Time: 35 minutes

Chunky Slow Cooker Vegetable Chili

1 medium onion, chopped
2 ribs celery, diced
1 carrot, diced
3 cloves garlic, minced
2 cans (about 15 ounces each) Great Northern beans, rinsed and drained
1 cup water
1 cup frozen corn
1 can (6 ounces) tomato paste
1 can (4 ounces) diced mild green chilies, undrained
1 tablespoon chili powder
2 teaspoons dried oregano leaves
1 teaspoon salt

Slow Cooker Directions
Combine all ingredients in slow cooker. Cover and cook on LOW 5½ to 6 hours or until vegetables are tender.   *Makes 6 servings*

Helpful Hints

Meatless chili gets its protein from beans—kidney beans, black beans, pinto beans, chili beans or Great Northern beans. Coupled with vegetables, meatless chili is a healthy alternative.

Vegetarian Chili with Cornbread Topping

International Fare

Lasagna Supreme

    8 ounces uncooked lasagna
      noodles
    ½ pound ground beef
    ½ pound mild Italian sausage,
      casings removed
    1 medium onion, chopped
    2 cloves garlic, minced
    1 can (14½ ounces) whole
      peeled tomatoes, undrained
      and chopped
    1 can (6 ounces) tomato paste
    2 teaspoons dried basil leaves
    1 teaspoon dried marjoram
      leaves
    1 can (4 ounces) sliced
      mushrooms, drained
    2 eggs
    2 cups (16 ounces) cream-style
      cottage cheese
    ¾ cup grated Parmesan cheese,
      divided
    2 tablespoons dried parsley
      flakes
    ½ teaspoon salt
    ½ teaspoon black pepper
    2 cups (8 ounces) shredded
      Cheddar cheese
    3 cups (12 ounces) shredded
      mozzarella cheese

1. Cook lasagna noodles according to package directions; drain.

2. Cook meats, onion and garlic in large skillet over medium-high heat until meat is brown, stirring to separate meat. Drain drippings.

3. Add tomatoes with juice, tomato paste, basil and marjoram. Reduce heat to low. Cover; simmer 15 minutes, stirring often. Stir in mushrooms; set aside.

4. Preheat oven to 375°F. Beat eggs in large bowl; add cottage cheese, ½ cup Parmesan cheese, parsley, salt and pepper. Mix well.

5. Place half the noodles in bottom of greased 13×9-inch baking pan. Spread half the cottage cheese mixture over noodles, then half the meat mixture and half the Cheddar cheese and mozzarella cheese. Repeat layers. Sprinkle with remaining ¼ cup Parmesan cheese.

6. Bake lasagna 40 to 45 minutes or until bubbly. Let stand 10 minutes.
Makes 8 to 10 servings

Note: Lasagna may be assembled, covered and refrigerated up to 2 days in advance. Bake, uncovered, in preheated 375°F oven 60 minutes or until bubbly.

Irish Stew

    1 cup fat-free reduced-sodium
      chicken broth
    1 teaspoon dried marjoram
      leaves
    1 teaspoon dried parsley leaves
    ¾ teaspoon salt
    ½ teaspoon garlic powder
    ¼ teaspoon black pepper
    1¼ pounds white potatoes, peeled
      and cut into 1-inch pieces
    1 pound lean lamb stew meat,
      cut into 1-inch cubes
    8 ounces frozen cut green
      beans
    2 small leeks, cut lengthwise
      into halves then crosswise
      into slices
    1½ cups coarsely chopped
      carrots

Slow Cooker Directions

Combine broth, marjoram, parsley, salt, garlic powder and pepper in slow cooker; mix well. Add potatoes, lamb, green beans, leeks and carrots. Cover and cook on LOW for 7 to 9 hours. *Makes 6 servings*

Lasagna Supreme

Fiesta Beef Enchiladas

    8 ounces lean ground beef
    ½ cup sliced green onions
    2 teaspoons fresh minced or
        bottled garlic
    1 cup cold cooked white or
        brown rice
    1½ cups chopped tomato, divided
    ¾ cup frozen corn, thawed
    1 cup (4 ounces) shredded
        Mexican cheese blend or
        Cheddar cheese, divided
    ½ cup salsa or picante sauce
    12 (6- to 7-inch) corn tortillas
    1 can (10 ounces) mild or hot
        enchilada sauce
    1 cup sliced romaine lettuce
        leaves

1. Preheat oven to 375°F. Spray 13×9-inch baking dish with nonstick cooking spray. Set aside. Cook ground beef in medium nonstick skillet over medium heat until no longer pink; drain. Add green onions and garlic; cook and stir 2 minutes.

2. Combine meat mixture, rice, 1 cup tomato, corn, ½ cup cheese and salsa; mix well. Spoon mixture down center of tortillas. Roll up; place seam side down in prepared dish. Spoon enchilada sauce evenly over enchiladas.

3. Cover with foil; bake for 20 minutes or until hot. Sprinkle with remaining ½ cup cheese; bake 5 minutes or until cheese melts. Top with lettuce and remaining ½ cup tomato.

Makes 4 servings

Prep Time: 15 minutes
Cook Time: 35 minutes

Pastitsio

    8 ounces uncooked elbow
        macaroni
    ½ cup cholesterol-free egg
        substitute
    ¼ teaspoon ground nutmeg
    ¾ pound lean ground lamb, beef
        or turkey
    ½ cup chopped onion
    1 clove garlic, minced
    1 can (8 ounces) tomato sauce
    ¾ teaspoon dried mint leaves
    ½ teaspoon dried oregano leaves
    ½ teaspoon black pepper
    ⅛ teaspoon ground cinnamon
    2 teaspoons margarine
    3 tablespoons all-purpose flour
    1½ cups milk
    2 tablespoons grated Parmesan
        cheese

Cook pasta according to package directions, omitting salt. Drain and transfer to medium bowl; stir in egg substitute and nutmeg.

Lightly spray bottom of 9-inch square baking dish with nonstick cooking spray. Spread pasta mixture in bottom of baking dish. Set aside.

Preheat oven to 350°F. Cook ground lamb, onion and garlic in large nonstick skillet over medium heat until lamb is no longer pink. Stir in tomato sauce, mint, oregano, black pepper and cinnamon. Reduce heat and simmer 10 minutes; spread over pasta.

Melt margarine in small nonstick saucepan. Add flour. Stir constantly for 1 minute. Whisk in milk. Cook, stirring constantly, until thickened, about 6 minutes; spread over meat mixture. Sprinkle with Parmesan cheese. Bake 30 to 40 minutes or until set. *Makes 6 servings*

Shepherd's Pie

    1 pound ground beef
    1 cup chopped onion
    1 teaspoon LAWRY'S® Seasoned
        Salt
    1 package (10 ounces) frozen
        peas and carrots, cooked
        and drained
    1 package (0.88 ounces)
        LAWRY'S® Brown Gravy Mix
    1 cup water
    1 egg, beaten
    3 cups mashed potatoes
        Paprika

In large skillet, cook ground beef and onion over medium-high heat until beef is browned; drain fat. Add Seasoned Salt and peas and carrots; mix well. Prepare Brown Gravy Mix with 1 cup water according to package directions. Add some gravy to beaten egg; gradually add egg-gravy mixture to gravy, stirring constantly. Combine gravy with meat mixture. In shallow, 2-quart casserole, place meat mixture; arrange potatoes in mounds over meat. Sprinkle top with paprika. Bake, uncovered, in 400°F. oven 15 minutes or until heated. *Makes 6 servings*

Serving Suggestion: Serve with tossed green salad.

Fiesta Beef Enchiladas

Cassoulet

Bretonne* (recipe follows)
5 slices bacon
1 pound fully-cooked smoked
    sausage, such as Polish,
    Italian or garlic, sliced
1 boneless pork loin roast
    (about ¾ pound), cubed
½ cup water
2 tablespoons packed brown
    sugar
1 tablespoon fresh lemon juice
Fresh oregano sprigs for
    garnish

*Bretonne is the classic French name for a
dish of seasoned beans.*

1. Prepare Bretonne; set aside.

2. Preheat oven to 350°F. Cook bacon
in large skillet over medium-high heat
until crisp, turning occasionally. Drain
bacon on paper towels, reserving
2 tablespoons drippings in skillet.
Crumble bacon; set aside.

3. Cut sausage into ¼-inch slices. Cut
pork into 1-inch cubes.

4. Heat bacon drippings over
medium-high heat until hot. Cook
sausage and pork in batches until
browned on all sides. Remove to
paper towels; drain well. Set aside.

5. Pour off drippings; discard. To
deglaze skillet, pour water into skillet.
Cook over medium-high heat
2 minutes, scraping up browned bits
and stirring constantly. Stir in sugar
and juice; bring to a boil. Boil
1 minute. Stir deglazed pan drippings
mixture and reserved crumbled
bacon into reserved Bretonne.

6. Spread ½ of Bretonne in lightly
greased 2½-quart ovenproof
casserole or Dutch oven. Top with
browned pork and sausage. Spoon
remaining Bretonne over browned
meats.

7. Cover and bake 2 hours. Cool
10 minutes. Serve in 8 individual
serving bowls. Garnish, if desired.
Makes 8 servings

Bretonne

1 pound dried Great Northern
    beans
2 tablespoons butter or
    margarine
2 cups chopped onion
2 cloves garlic, minced
1 can (14½ ounces) peeled,
    diced tomatoes, undrained
½ cup red wine
2 tablespoons each chopped
    fresh parsley, basil and
    thyme
¾ teaspoon salt
½ teaspoon black pepper
4 cups water
1 large carrot, peeled and cut
    into 2-inch pieces
1 large onion, peeled and halved
2 large sprigs each fresh
    parsley, basil, thyme and
    oregano

1. Rinse beans thoroughly in colander
under cold running water, picking out
debris and any blemished beans.
Place beans in large bowl; add water
to cover by 3 inches. Cover; let stand
at room temperature overnight.

2. Meanwhile, melt butter in large
saucepan over medium-high heat;
add chopped onion and garlic. Cook
8 to 10 minutes until onion is
softened, stirring frequently. Stir in
tomatoes with juice, wine, chopped
herbs, salt and pepper; bring to a
boil. Reduce heat to low; simmer,
uncovered, 20 minutes or until mixture
reduces to 2¼ cups. Transfer mixture
to small bowl; cover and refrigerate
overnight.

3. Drain beans, discarding soaking
water. Combine beans, 4 cups water,
carrot, halved onion and herb sprigs
in large saucepan or Dutch oven.
Bring to a boil over high heat. Reduce
heat to low; partially cover and
simmer 1 hour or until beans are
tender but firm.

4. Remove cooked beans to large
bowl with slotted spoon, leaving
cooking liquid in saucepan. Remove
carrot, halved onion and herb sprigs;
discard.

5. Bring bean cooking liquid to a boil
over high heat. Reduce heat to
medium; cook until bean liquid is
reduced to ½ cup. Add liquid to
cooked beans. Stir refrigerated
tomato mixture into beans until
blended.   *Makes about 6 cups*

Hungarian Lamb Goulash [Slow Cooker]

1 package (16 ounces) frozen
    cut green beans
1 cup chopped onion
1¼ pounds lean lamb stew meat,
    cut into 1-inch pieces
1 can (15 ounces) chunky
    tomato sauce
1¾ cups chicken broth
1 can (6 ounces) tomato paste
4 teaspoons paprika
3 cups hot cooked noodles

Slow Cooker Directions
Place green beans and onion in slow
cooker. Top with lamb. Combine
remaining ingredients, except
noodles in large bowl; mix well. Pour
over lamb mixture. Cover and cook on
LOW 6 to 8 hours. Stir. Serve over
noodles.   *Makes 6 servings*

Cassoulet

Greek Island Skillet

¾ pound lean ground beef
3 cups water
1 can (14 ounces) diced
    tomatoes, undrained
1 package KNORR® Recipe
    Classics™ Roasted Garlic
    Soup, Dip and Recipe Mix
2½ cups (8 ounces) uncooked
    pasta twists
1 package (10 ounces) frozen
    chopped spinach, thawed
    and drained
1 can (2¼ ounces) sliced ripe
    olives, drained (about
    ½ cup)
¼ cup crumbled feta cheese or
    grated Parmesan cheese
    (optional)

• In large skillet, sauté ground beef over medium-high heat 5 minutes or until lightly browned. Spoon off excess drippings. Add water, tomatoes and recipe mix; bring to a boil.

• Stir in pasta and return to boiling; reduce heat, cover and simmer 8 to 10 minutes or until pasta is tender, stirring frequently.

• Stir in spinach and olives. Simmer 2 minutes or until heated through. If desired, sprinkle with cheese.

Makes 4 servings

Prep Time: 25 to 30 minutes

Beef with Bean Threads and Cabbage

1 package (3¾ ounces) bean
    threads
1 boneless beef sirloin steak,
    1 inch thick (about 1 pound)
2 cloves garlic, minced
1 teaspoon minced fresh ginger
1 tablespoon peanut or
    vegetable oil
½ cup beef or chicken broth
2 tablespoons oyster sauce
2 cups coarsely chopped napa
    cabbage

1. Place bean threads in medium bowl; cover with warm water. Soak 15 minutes to soften; drain well. Cut into 2-inch lengths.

2. Cut beef across grain into ⅛-inch slices; cut each slice into 2-inch pieces. Toss beef with garlic and ginger in medium bowl.

3. Heat wok or large skillet over medium-high heat. Add oil; heat until hot. Add beef mixture; stir-fry 2 to 3 minutes until beef is barely pink in center. Add broth, oyster sauce and cabbage; stir-fry 1 minute. Add bean threads; stir-fry 1 to 2 minutes until liquid is absorbed.

Makes 4 servings

Italian Sausage Supper

1 pound mild Italian sausage,
    casing removed
1 cup chopped onion
3 medium zucchini, sliced
    (about 1½ cups)
1 can (6 ounces) CONTADINA®
    Tomato Paste
1 cup water
1 teaspoon dried basil leaves,
    crushed
½ teaspoon salt
3 cups cooked rice
1 cup (4 ounces) shredded
    mozzarella cheese
¼ cup (1 ounce) grated Romano
    cheese

1. Brown sausage with onion in large skillet, stirring to break up sausage; drain, reserving 1 tablespoon drippings.

2. Spoon sausage mixture into greased 2-quart casserole dish. Add zucchini to skillet; sauté for 5 minutes or until crisp-tender.

3. Combine tomato paste, water, basil and salt in medium bowl. Stir in rice. Spoon over sausage mixture. Arrange zucchini slices on top; sprinkle with mozzarella and Romano cheeses.

4. Cover. Bake in preheated 350°F oven for 20 minutes.

Makes 6 servings

Prep Time: 18 minutes
Cook Time: 20 minutes

Russian Borscht [Slow Cooker]

4 cups thinly sliced green
    cabbage
1½ pounds fresh beets, shredded
5 small carrots, peeled, cut
    lengthwise into halves, then
    cut into 1-inch pieces
1 parsnip, peeled, cut
    lengthwise into halves, then
    cut into 1-inch pieces
1 cup chopped onion
4 cloves garlic, minced
1 pound lean beef stew meat,
    cut into ½-inch cubes
1 can (14½ ounces) diced
    tomatoes, undrained
3 cans (14½ ounces each)
    reduced-sodium beef broth
¼ cup lemon juice
1 tablespoon sugar
1 teaspoon black pepper
    Sour cream (optional)
    Fresh parsley (optional)

Slow Cooker Directions

1. Layer ingredients in slow cooker in the following order: cabbage, beets, carrots, parsnip, onion, garlic, beef, tomatoes with juice, broth, lemon juice, sugar and pepper. Cover; cook on LOW 7 to 9 hours or until vegetables are crisp-tender.

2. Season with additional lemon juice and sugar, if desired. Dollop with sour cream and garnish with parsley, if desired.

Makes 12 servings

Mama Mia Slow Cooker Spaghetti Sauce

- 1 tablespoon olive oil
- 1 package (8 ounces) sliced mushrooms
- ½ cup finely chopped carrot
- 1 clove garlic, minced
- 1 shallot, minced
- 1 pound lean ground beef
- 2 cups canned or fresh crushed tomatoes
- ½ cup dry red wine or beef broth
- 2 tablespoons tomato paste
- 1 teaspoon salt
- 1 teaspoon dried oregano leaves
- ½ teaspoon dried basil leaves
- ¼ teaspoon black pepper
- 4 cups cooked spaghetti
  Grated Parmesan cheese (optional)

Slow Cooker Directions

1. Heat oil in large skillet over medium-high heat until hot. Add mushrooms, carrot, garlic and shallot to skillet. Cook and stir 5 minutes. Place vegetables in slow cooker.

2. Add ground beef to skillet; brown, stirring to break up meat. Drain fat. Place beef into slow cooker.

3. Add tomatoes, wine, tomato paste, salt, oregano, basil and pepper. Cover; cook on HIGH 3 to 4 hours. Serve sauce with cooked spaghetti. Sprinkle with Parmesan cheese, if desired.   *Makes 5 servings*

Italian Sausage Lasagna

- 1½ pounds BOB EVANS® Italian Roll Sausage
- 2 tablespoons olive oil
- 2 green bell peppers, thinly sliced
- 1 large yellow onion, thinly sliced
- 4 cloves garlic, minced and divided
- 1 (28-ounce) can whole tomatoes, undrained
- 1 (8-ounce) can tomato sauce
- 2 teaspoons fennel seeds
  Salt and black pepper to taste
- 1 tablespoon butter or margarine
- 1 large yellow onion, chopped
- 2 (10-ounce) packages chopped frozen spinach, thawed and squeezed dry
- 1 cup grated Parmesan cheese, divided
- 3 cups (24 ounces) low-fat ricotta cheese
- 1 pound shredded mozzarella or provolone cheese
- 9 uncooked lasagna noodles

Crumble sausage in large heavy skillet. Cook over medium heat until well browned, stirring occasionally. Remove sausage to paper towels; set aside. Drain off drippings and wipe skillet clean with paper towels. Heat oil in same skillet over medium-high heat until hot. Add green peppers, sliced onion and half the garlic. Cook, covered, over medium heat about 10 minutes or until vegetables are wilted, stirring occasionally. Stir in tomatoes with juice, tomato sauce and fennel seeds, stirring well to break up tomatoes. Bring to a boil. Reduce heat to low; simmer, uncovered, 20 to 30 minutes to blend flavors. Stir in reserved sausage. Season sauce mixture with salt and black pepper; set aside. Melt butter in small saucepan over medium-high heat; add chopped onion and remaining garlic. Cook and stir about 10 minutes or until onion is tender. Stir in spinach and ¼ cup Parmesan; set aside. Combine ricotta, mozzarella and ½ cup Parmesan in medium bowl. Season with salt and black pepper. Cook noodles according to package directions; drain.

Preheat oven to 350°F. Pour ⅓ of sauce mixture into greased 13×9-inch baking dish; spread evenly. Arrange 3 noodles over sauce mixture; spread half the spinach mixture over noodles. Spread half the cheese mixture evenly over spinach. Repeat layers once. Top with remaining 3 noodles and sauce mixture. Sprinkle with remaining ¼ cup Parmesan. Bake about 1 hour or until sauce is bubbly and cheese is browned on top. Let stand 10 to 15 minutes before slicing. Serve hot. Refrigerate leftovers.

Makes 8 servings

Helpful Hints

Fennel seeds are greenish-yellow in color and have a licorice flavor. Fennel seeds are added to many dishes but they are best known for providing the distinctive flavor of Italian sausage.

Caribbean Black Bean Casserole with Spicy Mango Salsa

2 cups chicken broth
1 cup uncooked basmati rice
2 tablespoons olive oil, divided
½ pound chorizo sausage
2 cloves garlic, minced
1 cup chopped red bell pepper
3 cups canned black beans, rinsed and drained
½ cup chopped fresh cilantro
2 small mangoes
1 cup chopped red onion
2 tablespoons white wine vinegar
2 tablespoons honey
1 teaspoon curry powder
½ teaspoon salt
½ teaspoon ground red pepper

1. Place chicken broth in medium saucepan. Bring to a boil over high heat; stir in rice. Reduce heat to low; simmer, covered, 20 minutes or until liquid is absorbed and rice is tender.

2. Heat 1 tablespoon oil in large skillet over medium heat. Add sausage; cook 8 to 10 minutes or until browned and no longer pink in center. Remove from skillet to cutting surface. Cut into ½-inch slices; set aside. Drain fat from skillet.

3. Preheat oven to 350°F. Grease 1½-quart casserole; set aside. Add remaining tablespoon oil to skillet; heat over medium-high heat. Add garlic; cook and stir 1 minute. Add bell pepper; cook and stir 5 minutes. Remove from heat. Stir in beans, sausage, rice and cilantro.

4. Spoon sausage mixture into prepared casserole; cover with foil. Bake 30 minutes or until hot.

5. Peel mangoes; remove seeds. Chop enough flesh to measure 3 cups. Combine mango and remaining ingredients in large bowl.

6. Spoon sausage mixture onto serving plates. Serve with mango salsa.   *Makes 6 servings*

Beef Bourguignon [Slow Cooker]

1 boneless beef sirloin steak, ½ inch thick, trimmed and cut into ½-inch pieces (about 3 pounds)
½ cup all-purpose flour
4 slices bacon, diced
2 medium carrots, diced
8 small new red potatoes, unpeeled, cut into quarters
8 to 10 mushrooms, sliced
20 to 24 pearl onions
3 cloves garlic, minced
1 bay leaf
1 teaspoon dried marjoram leaves
½ teaspoon dried thyme leaves
½ teaspoon salt
    Black pepper to taste
2½ cups Burgundy wine or beef broth

Slow Cooker Directions
Coat beef with flour, shaking off excess. Set aside.

Cook bacon in large skillet over medium heat until partially cooked. Add beef; cook until browned. Remove beef and bacon with slotted spoon.

Layer carrots, potatoes, mushrooms, onions, garlic, bay leaf, marjoram, thyme, salt, pepper, beef and bacon mixture and wine in slow cooker. Cover and cook on LOW 8 to 9 hours or until beef is tender. Remove and discard bay leaf.

Makes 10 to 12 servings

Moroccan Pork Tagine

1 pound well-trimmed pork tenderloin, cut into ¾-inch medallions
1 tablespoon all-purpose flour
1 teaspoon ground cumin
1 teaspoon paprika
¼ teaspoon powdered saffron *or* ½ teaspoon turmeric
¼ teaspoon ground red pepper
¼ teaspoon ground ginger
1 tablespoon olive oil
1 medium onion, chopped
3 cloves garlic, minced
2½ cups canned chicken broth, divided
⅓ cup golden or dark raisins
1 cup quick-cooking couscous
¼ cup chopped fresh cilantro
¼ cup sliced toasted almonds (optional)

1. Toss pork with flour, cumin, paprika, saffron, pepper and ginger in medium bowl; set aside.

2. Heat oil in large nonstick skillet over medium-high heat. Add onion; cook 5 minutes, stirring occasionally. Add pork and garlic; cook 4 to 5 minutes or until pork is no longer pink, stirring occasionally. Add ¾ cup chicken broth and raisins; bring to a boil over high heat. Reduce heat to medium; simmer, uncovered, 7 to 8 minutes or until pork is cooked through, stirring occasionally.

3. Meanwhile, bring remaining 1¾ cups chicken broth to a boil in medium saucepan. Stir in couscous. Cover; remove from heat. Let stand 5 minutes or until liquid is absorbed.

4. Spoon couscous onto 4 plates; top with pork mixture. Sprinkle with cilantro and almonds, if desired.

Makes 4 servings

Caribbean Black Bean Casserole with Spicy Mango Salsa

Hungarian-Style Pork Chops

1 (6.5-ounce) package RICE-A-RONI® Broccoli Au Gratin
3½ tablespoons margarine or butter, divided
1½ cups fresh or frozen cut green beans
¼ cup sour cream
1 medium onion, thinly sliced and separated into rings
4 boneless pork loin chops, about ¾ inch thick (about 1 pound)
1½ teaspoons paprika
1½ teaspoons garlic salt
¼ teaspoon cayenne pepper

1. In large skillet over medium heat, sauté rice-vermicelli mix with 2½ tablespoons margarine until vermicelli is golden brown.

2. Slowly stir in 2¼ cups water and Special Seasonings; bring to a boil. Reduce heat to low. Cover; simmer 5 minutes. Stir in green beans. Cover; simmer 10 to 15 minutes or until rice is tender. Stir in sour cream; let stand 5 minutes before serving.

3. Meanwhile, in another large skillet, melt remaining 1 tablespoon margarine over medium-high heat. Add onion; sauté 5 minutes. Push onion to edge of skillet.

4. Add pork chops; sprinkle with paprika, garlic salt and cayenne pepper. Cook uncovered, 5 minutes, over medium heat. Turn pork chops over. Cover; cook 5 to 10 more minutes or until pork is no longer pink inside. Serve pork and onion over rice. *Makes 4 servings*

Prep Time: 10 minutes
Cook Time: 25 minutes

Spicy Manicotti

3 cups ricotta cheese
1 cup grated Parmesan cheese, divided
2 eggs, beaten lightly
2½ tablespoons chopped fresh parsley
1 teaspoon dried Italian seasoning
½ teaspoon garlic powder
½ teaspoon salt
½ teaspoon black pepper
1 pound spicy Italian sausage
1 can (28 ounces) crushed tomatoes in purée, undrained
1 jar (26 ounces) marinara or spaghetti sauce
8 ounces uncooked manicotti shells

Preheat oven to 375°F. Spray 13×9-inch baking dish with nonstick cooking spray.

Combine ricotta, ¾ cup Parmesan, eggs, parsley, Italian seasoning, garlic powder, salt and pepper in medium bowl; set aside.

Crumble sausage into large skillet; brown over medium-high heat until no longer pink, stirring to separate meat. Drain sausage on paper towels; drain fat from skillet.

Add tomatoes with juice and marinara sauce to same skillet; bring to a boil over high heat. Reduce heat to low; simmer, uncovered, 10 minutes. Pour about one third of sauce into prepared dish.

Stuff each shell with about ½ cup cheese mixture. Place in dish. Top shells with sausage; pour remaining sauce over shells.

Cover tightly with foil and bake 50 minutes to 1 hour or until shells are cooked. Let stand 5 minutes before serving. Serve with remaining ¼ cup Parmesan. *Makes 8 servings*

Tijuana Tacos

1 teaspoon vegetable oil
½ cup chopped green bell pepper
½ cup chopped green onions
1 jalapeño pepper,* minced
1 pound lean ground beef
1 cup salsa
½ teaspoon ground cumin
½ teaspoon chili powder
8 taco shells
2 cups shredded lettuce
2 cups chopped tomato
1½ cups (6 ounces) shredded Cheddar cheese

Jalapeño peppers can sting and irritate the skin; wear rubber gloves when handling peppers and do not touch eyes. Wash hands after handling peppers.

Heat oil in large nonstick skillet over medium-high heat until hot. Add bell pepper, onions and jalapeño pepper; cook and stir 5 minutes or until vegetables are tender.

Add beef to vegetable mixture. Cook until no longer pink; pour off excess fat. Add salsa, cumin and chili powder to meat mixture; stir to combine.

Spoon beef mixture into taco shells. Top with lettuce, tomato and Cheddar cheese. Garnish as desired.
Makes 8 servings

Spicy Manicotti

Tijuana Torte

1 pound ground beef
1 medium onion, chopped
1 can (16 ounces) stewed
    tomatoes
1 can (8 ounces) tomato sauce
1 can (4 ounces) diced green
    chiles (optional)
1 package (1 ounce) LAWRY'S®
    Taco Spices & Seasoning
12 corn tortillas
4 cups (16 ounces) shredded
    cheddar cheese

In large skillet, brown ground beef and onion until beef is crumbly; drain fat. Add tomatoes, tomato sauce, chiles and Taco Spices & Seasoning; mix well. Bring to a boil over medium-high heat; reduce heat to low and simmer, uncovered, 10 to 15 minutes. In 13×9×2-inch baking dish, place about ¼ meat mixture, spreading to cover bottom of dish. Place 2 tortillas, side by side, on meat mixture. Top each tortilla with some meat mixture and grated cheese. Repeat until each stack contains 6 tortillas layered with meat and cheese. Bake, uncovered, in 350°F. oven 20 to 25 minutes.

Makes 4 to 6 servings

Serving Suggestion: To serve, cut each torte (stack) into quarters with a sharp knife.

Hints: Make early in the day and bake just before serving. Or, make ahead, bake and freeze. Reheat, covered, in 350°F. oven 35 to 40 minutes or until heated through. Freeze one "stack" for later use if only 2 servings are needed.

Sauerbraten [Slow Cooker]

1 boneless beef sirloin tip roast
    (1¼ pounds)
3 cups baby carrots
1½ cups fresh or frozen pearl
    onions
¼ cup raisins
½ cup water
½ cup red wine vinegar
1 tablespoon honey
½ teaspoon salt
½ teaspoon dry mustard
½ teaspoon garlic-pepper
    seasoning
¼ teaspoon ground cloves
¼ cup crushed crisp gingersnap
    cookies (5 cookies)

Slow Cooker Directions

1. Heat large nonstick skillet over medium heat until hot. Brown roast on all sides; set aside.

2. Place roast, carrots, onions and raisins in slow cooker. Combine water, vinegar, honey, salt, mustard, garlic-pepper seasoning and cloves in large bowl; mix well. Pour mixture over meat and vegetables.

3. Cover; cook on LOW 4 to 6 hours or until internal temperature of meat reaches 145°F when tested with meat thermometer inserted into thickest part of roast. Transfer roast to cutting board; cover with foil. Let stand 10 to 15 minutes before slicing. Internal temperature will continue to rise 5° to 10°F during stand time.

4. Remove vegetables with slotted spoon to bowl; cover to keep warm. Stir crushed cookies into sauce mixture in slow cooker. Cover; cook on HIGH 10 to 15 minutes or until sauce thickens. Serve meat and vegetables with sauce.

Makes 5 servings

Spanish-Style [Slow Cooker]
Couscous

1 pound lean ground beef
1 can (about 14 ounces) beef
    broth
1 small green bell pepper, cut
    into ½-inch pieces
½ cup pimiento-stuffed green
    olives, sliced
½ medium onion, chopped
2 cloves garlic, minced
1 teaspoon ground cumin
½ teaspoon dried thyme leaves
1⅓ cups water
1 cup uncooked couscous

Slow Cooker Directions

Heat skillet over high heat until hot. Add beef; cook until browned. Pour off fat. Place broth, bell pepper, olives, onion, garlic, cumin, thyme and beef in slow cooker. Cover and cook on LOW 4 hours or until bell pepper is tender.

Bring water to a boil over high heat in small saucepan. Stir in couscous. Cover; remove from heat. Let stand 5 minutes; fluff with fork. Spoon couscous onto plates; top with beef mixture.   *Makes 4 servings*

Serving Suggestion: Serve with carrot sticks.

Middle Eastern Lamb Stew

Slow Cooker

1½ pounds lamb stew meat, cubed
2 tablespoons all-purpose flour
1 tablespoon vegetable oil
1½ cups beef broth
1 cup chopped onion
½ cup chopped carrots
1 clove garlic, minced
1 tablespoon tomato paste
½ teaspoon ground cumin
½ teaspoon red pepper flakes
¼ teaspoon ground cinnamon
½ cup chopped dried apricots
1 teaspoon salt
¼ teaspoon black pepper
3 cups hot cooked noodles

Slow Cooker Directions

1. Coat lamb cubes with flour; set aside. Heat oil in large nonstick skillet over medium-high heat until hot. Brown half of lamb and transfer to slow cooker; repeat with remaining lamb. Add broth, onion, carrots, garlic, tomato paste, cumin, red pepper and cinnamon. Cover and cook on LOW 3 hours.

2. Stir in apricots, salt and black pepper. Cover and cook on LOW 2 to 3 hours, or until lamb is tender and sauce is thickened. Serve lamb over noodles.   *Makes 6 servings*

Mexican Delight Casserole

1 pound ground beef
1 medium onion, chopped
1 package (1.5 ounces) LAWRY'S® Burrito Spices & Seasonings
1 can (28 ounces) whole tomatoes, cut up
1 can (30 ounces) hominy, drained and rinsed
1 can (4 ounces) diced green chiles
4 cups tortilla chips
1½ cups (6 ounces) shredded cheddar cheese
1 can (8 ounces) tomato sauce

In large skillet, cook ground beef and onion until beef is browned; drain fat. Add Burrito Spices & Seasonings and tomatoes; mix well. Bring to a boil over medium-high heat; reduce heat to low and simmer, uncovered, 10 minutes. Combine hominy and green chiles. In 2-quart oblong casserole dish, layer half of meat mixture, tortilla chips and hominy mixture; add ½ cup cheese. Repeat layers, ending with ½ cup cheese. Top with tomato sauce and remaining ½ cup cheese. Bake, uncovered, in 350°F oven 35 minutes or until thoroughly heated.

Makes 8 servings

Serving Suggestion: Serve with a tossed green salad and fresh fruit.

Hint: Use purchased or homemade tortilla chips. To make chips, cut fresh corn tortillas into ½-inch strips. Fry in ½-inch salad oil until slightly crisp, about 30 seconds. Drain well on paper towels.

Caribbean Jerk-Style Pork

¾ cup DOLE® Pineapple Juice or Pineapple Orange Juice, divided
1 tablespoon prepared yellow mustard
1 teaspoon dried thyme leaves, crushed
¼ teaspoon crushed red pepper
12 ounces boneless pork loin chops or chicken breasts, cut into strips
½ cup DOLE® Golden or Seedless Raisins
½ cup sliced green onions
2 medium firm DOLE® Bananas, cut diagonally into ¼-inch slices
Hot cooked rice or noodles (optional)

• Stir together ½ cup juice, mustard, thyme and red pepper in small bowl; set aside.

• Place pork in large, nonstick skillet sprayed with vegetable cooking spray. Cook and stir pork over medium-high heat 3 to 5 minutes or until pork is no longer pink. Remove pork from skillet.

• Add remaining ¼ cup juice to skillet; stir in raisins and green onions. Cook and stir 1 minute.

• Stir in pork and reserved mustard mixture; cover and cook 2 minutes or until heated through. Stir in bananas. Serve over hot rice.

Makes 4 servings

Prep Time: 10 minutes
Cook Time: 10 minutes

Spinach Lasagna

1 pound ground beef
¼ pound fresh mushrooms, thinly sliced
1 medium onion, chopped
1 clove garlic, minced
1 can (28 ounces) Italian plum tomatoes, undrained
1¼ teaspoons salt, divided
¾ teaspoon dried oregano leaves
¾ teaspoon dried basil leaves
¼ teaspoon black pepper, divided
9 uncooked lasagna noodles
¼ cup plus 1 tablespoon butter or margarine, divided
¼ cup all-purpose flour
⅛ teaspoon ground nutmeg
2 cups milk
1½ cups (6 ounces) shredded mozzarella cheese, divided
½ cup freshly grated Parmesan cheese, divided
1 package (10 ounces) frozen chopped spinach, thawed and squeezed dry

1. For meat sauce, crumble ground beef into large skillet over medium-high heat. Brown 8 to 10 minutes, stirring to separate meat, until meat loses its pink color. Stir in mushrooms, onion and garlic; cook over medium heat 5 minutes or until onion is tender.

2. Press tomatoes with juice through sieve into meat mixture; discard seeds. Stir in ¾ teaspoon salt, oregano, basil and ⅛ teaspoon pepper. Bring to a boil over medium-high heat; reduce heat to low. Cover and simmer 40 minutes, stirring occasionally. Uncover and simmer 15 to 20 minutes more until sauce thickens. Set aside.

3. Add lasagna noodles to large pot of boiling salted water, 1 at a time, allowing noodles to soften and fit into pot. Cook 10 minutes or just until al dente. Drain noodles; rinse with cold water. Drain again; hang individually over pot rim to prevent sticking. Set aside.

4. For cheese sauce, melt ¼ cup butter in medium saucepan over medium heat. Stir in flour, remaining ½ teaspoon salt, remaining ⅛ teaspoon pepper and nutmeg; cook and stir until bubbly. Whisk in milk; cook and stir until sauce thickens and bubbles. Cook and stir 1 minute more. Remove from heat. Stir in 1 cup mozzarella and ¼ cup Parmesan cheeses. Stir until smooth. Set aside.

5. Preheat oven to 350°F. Spread remaining 1 tablespoon butter on bottom and sides of 12×8-inch baking dish with waxed paper. Spread noodles in single layer on clean kitchen (not paper) towel. Pat noodles dry.

6. Arrange 3 lasagna noodles in single layer, overlapping slightly, in bottom of baking dish. Top with ½ of meat sauce; spread evenly. Spread ½ of cheese sauce over meat sauce in even layer.

7. Repeat layers once, using 3 noodles, remaining meat sauce and remaining cheese sauce. Sprinkle spinach over cheese sauce in even layer; pat down lightly. Arrange remaining 3 lasagna noodles over spinach.

8. Mix remaining ½ cup mozzarella and ¼ cup Parmesan cheeses in cup. Sprinkle cheeses evenly on top of lasagna to completely cover lasagna noodles. Bake 40 minutes or until top is golden and edges are bubbly. Let lasagna stand 10 minutes before serving. Garnish as desired.

Makes 6 servings

Fettuccine with Prosciutto and Artichoke Hearts

1 package KNORR® Recipe Classics™ Leek Soup, Dip and Recipe Mix
3 cups milk
1 package (9 ounces) frozen artichoke hearts, thawed and quartered
4 ounces sliced prosciutto, smoked turkey or ham, cut into thin strips
1 cup grated Parmesan cheese
8 ounces fettuccine pasta, cooked and drained

• In 2-quart saucepan, with wire whisk, combine recipe mix and milk.

• Bring to a boil over medium-high heat, stirring constantly. Reduce heat to low and stir in artichoke hearts and prosciutto. Simmer 5 minutes. Remove from heat; stir in cheese.

• Toss with hot fettuccine. Serve, if desired, with freshly ground pepper.

Makes 4 servings

Recipe Tip: For a change of pace, substitute 2 cups fresh or frozen asparagus or peas for the artichoke hearts.

Prep Time: 20 minutes
Cook Time: 10 minutes

Helpful Hints

Prosciutto is the Italian word for ham. Typically it has been cured in salt and air dried. Unlike ham produced in the United States, prosciutto is not smoked. It is available at Italian markets, some butcher shops and large supermarkets.

Spinach Lasagna

Szechwan Beef Lo Mein

- 1 pound well-trimmed boneless beef top sirloin steak, 1 inch thick
- 4 cloves garlic, minced
- 2 teaspoons minced fresh ginger
- ¾ teaspoon red pepper flakes, divided
- 1 tablespoon vegetable oil
- 1 can (about 14 ounces) vegetable broth
- 1 cup water
- 2 tablespoons reduced-sodium soy sauce
- 1 package (8 ounces) frozen mixed vegetables for stir-fry
- 1 package (9 ounces) refrigerated angel hair pasta
- ¼ cup chopped fresh cilantro (optional)

1. Cut steak crosswise into ⅛-inch strips; cut strips into 1½-inch pieces. Toss steak with garlic, ginger and ½ teaspoon red pepper flakes.

2. Heat oil in large nonstick skillet over medium-high heat. Add half of steak to skillet; cook and stir 3 minutes or until meat is barely pink in center. Remove from skillet; set aside. Repeat with remaining steak.

3. Add vegetable broth, water, soy sauce and remaining ¼ teaspoon red pepper flakes to skillet; bring to a boil over high heat. Add vegetables; return to a boil. Reduce heat to low; simmer, covered, 3 minutes or until vegetables are crisp-tender.

4. Uncover; stir in pasta. Return to a boil over high heat. Reduce heat to medium; simmer, uncovered, 2 minutes, separating pasta with two forks. Return steak and any accumulated juices to skillet; simmer 1 minute or until pasta is tender and steak is hot. Sprinkle with cilantro, if desired.   *Makes 4 servings*

Moussaka

- 1 large eggplant
- 2½ teaspoons salt, divided
- 2 large zucchini
- 2 large russet potatoes, peeled
- ½ cup olive oil, divided
- 1½ pounds ground beef or lamb
- 1 large onion, chopped
- 2 cloves garlic, minced
- 1 cup chopped tomatoes
- ½ cup dry red or white wine
- ¼ cup chopped fresh parsley
- ¼ teaspoon ground cinnamon
- ⅛ teaspoon black pepper
- 1 cup grated Parmesan cheese, divided
- 4 tablespoons butter or margarine, divided
- ⅓ cup all-purpose flour
- ¼ teaspoon ground nutmeg
- 2 cups milk

Cut eggplant lengthwise into ½-inch-thick slices. Place in large colander; sprinkle with 1 teaspoon salt. Drain 30 minutes. Cut zucchini lengthwise into ⅜-inch-thick slices. Cut potatoes lengthwise into ¼-inch-thick slices.

Heat ¼ cup oil in large skillet over medium heat until hot. Add potatoes in single layer. Cook 5 minutes per side or until tender and lightly browned. Remove potatoes from skillet; drain on paper towels. Add more oil to skillet, if needed. Cook zucchini 2 minutes per side or until tender. Drain on paper towels. Add more oil to skillet. Cook eggplant 5 minutes per side or until tender. Drain on paper towels. Drain oil from skillet; discard.

Heat skillet over medium-high heat just until hot. Add beef, onion and garlic; cook and stir 5 minutes or until meat is no longer pink. Pour off drippings. Stir in tomatoes, wine, parsley, 1 teaspoon salt, cinnamon and pepper. Bring to a boil over high heat. Reduce heat to low. Simmer 10 minutes or until liquid is evaporated.

Preheat oven to 325°F. Grease 13×9-inch baking dish. Arrange potatoes in bottom; sprinkle with ¼ cup cheese. Top with zucchini and ¼ cup cheese, then eggplant and ¼ cup cheese. Spoon meat mixture over top.

To prepare sauce, melt butter in medium saucepan over low heat. Blend in flour, remaining ½ teaspoon salt and nutmeg with wire whisk. Cook 1 minute, whisking constantly. Gradually whisk in milk. Cook over medium heat, until mixture boils and thickens, whisking constantly. Pour sauce evenly over meat mixture in dish; sprinkle with remaining ¼ cup cheese. Bake 30 to 40 minutes or until hot and bubbly. Garnish as desired.   *Makes 6 to 8 servings*

Helpful Hints

One of the best known of all Greek dishes, Moussaka is a layered casserole that traditionally includes eggplant, beef or lamb, and a topping of a creamy white sauce.

Szechwan Beef Lo Mein

Welsh Ham and Leek Casserole

- **6 small leeks**
- **3 large tomatoes, chopped**
- **⅓ cup butter or margarine**
- **1 cup sliced celery**
- **12 thin slices deli ham**
- **2 cloves garlic, minced**
- **¼ cup all-purpose flour**
- **½ teaspoon salt**
- **¼ teaspoon white pepper**
- **⅛ teaspoon ground nutmeg**
- **2 cups milk**
- **½ cup half-and-half**
- **1 cup (4 ounces) shredded sharp white Cheddar cheese, divided**
- **¼ cup bread crumbs**

1. To prepare leeks, remove any withered outer leaves. Cut off 1 inch of leaf tops; discard. Cut off roots, then cut leeks in half crosswise. Make slit down length of each leek half, being careful not to cut through leek completely. Rinse thoroughly. Tie 2 leek halves together with kitchen string; repeat with remaining leeks. Place leeks in Dutch oven; pour in enough lightly salted water to cover. Bring to a boil over high heat. Reduce heat to low; simmer 6 to 8 minutes or until leeks are tender. Drain and pat dry. Remove strings.

2. Preheat oven to 350°F. Place tomatoes in bottom of 13×9-inch baking dish.

3. Melt butter in medium saucepan over medium heat. Add celery; cook 3 minutes or until celery is crisp-tender. Remove celery with slotted spoon, arranging evenly over tomatoes. Reserve butter in saucepan.

4. Wrap 1 ham slice around each leek half. Arrange, seam side down, in single layer in baking dish.

5. Add garlic to reserved butter in saucepan. Cook and stir over low heat 30 seconds. Stir in flour, salt, pepper and nutmeg. Cook 2 minutes, stirring constantly. Gradually whisk in milk and half-and-half until smooth. Cook until mixture boils and thickens, whisking constantly. Remove from heat. Stir in ¾ cup cheese; continue to stir until cheese melts.

6. Pour cheese sauce evenly over leeks. Sprinkle with remaining ¼ cup cheese and bread crumbs. Bake 30 minutes or until lightly browned and bubbly. *Makes 6 servings*

Traditional Spanish Chicken and Rice

- **4 TYSON® Individually Fresh Frozen® Boneless, Skinless Chicken Breasts**
- **1 box UNCLE BEN'S® COUNTRY INN® Mexican Fiesta Rice**
- **1 tablespoon olive oil**
- **2¼ cups water**
- **½ cup chopped red bell pepper**
- **½ cup frozen peas, thawed**
- **⅓ cup Spanish olives stuffed with pimientos, cut into halves**

PREP: CLEAN: Wash hands. Remove protective ice glaze from frozen chicken by holding under cool running water 1 to 2 minutes. CLEAN: Wash hands.

COOK: Heat oil in large skillet. Add chicken; cook over medium-high heat 10 to 15 minutes or until light brown. Add water, rice, contents of seasoning packet, bell pepper, peas and olives; mix well. Bring to a boil. Cover, reduce heat; simmer 10 minutes or until internal juices of chicken run clear. (Or insert instant-read meat thermometer in thickest part of chicken. Temperature should read 170°F.) Remove from heat; let stand, covered, 5 minutes or until liquid is absorbed.

SERVE: Serve with corn on the cob and wheat rolls, if desired.

CHILL: Refrigerate leftovers immediately. *Makes 4 servings*

Prep Time: 5 minutes
Cook Time: 30 minutes

Hearty Cassoulet [Slow Cooker]

- **1 tablespoon olive oil**
- **1 large onion, finely chopped**
- **4 boneless skinless chicken thighs (about 1 pound), chopped**
- **¼ pound smoked turkey sausage, finely chopped**
- **3 cloves garlic, minced**
- **1 teaspoon dried thyme leaves**
- **½ teaspoon black pepper**
- **4 tablespoons tomato paste**
- **2 tablespoons water**
- **3 cans (about 15 ounces each) Great Northern beans, rinsed and drained**
- **½ cup dry bread crumbs**
- **3 tablespoons minced fresh parsley**

Slow Cooker Directions

Heat oil in large skillet over medium heat until hot. Add onion, cook and stir 5 minutes or until onion is tender. Stir in chicken, sausage, garlic, thyme and pepper. Cook 5 minutes or until chicken and sausage are browned.

Remove skillet from heat; stir in tomato paste and water until blended. Place beans and chicken mixture in slow cooker, cover and cook on LOW 4 to 4½ hours. Just before serving, combine bread crumbs and parsley in small bowl. Sprinkle top of cassoulet. *Makes 6 servings*

Welsh Ham and Leek Casserole

Chicken Marsala

4 cups (6 ounces) uncooked broad egg noodles
½ cup Italian-style dry bread crumbs
1 teaspoon dried basil leaves
1 egg
1 teaspoon water
4 boneless skinless chicken breast halves
3 tablespoons olive oil, divided
¾ cup chopped onion
8 ounces cremini or button mushrooms, sliced
3 cloves garlic, minced
3 tablespoons all-purpose flour
1 can (14½ ounces) chicken broth
½ cup dry marsala wine
¾ teaspoon salt
¼ teaspoon black pepper
Chopped fresh parsley (optional)

Preheat oven to 375°F. Spray 11×7-inch baking dish with nonstick cooking spray.

Cook noodles according to package directions until al dente. Drain and place in prepared dish.

Meanwhile, combine bread crumbs and basil on shallow plate or pie plate. Beat egg with water on another shallow plate or pie plate. Dip chicken in egg mixture, letting excess drip off. Roll in crumb mixture, patting to coat.

Heat 2 tablespoons oil in large skillet over medium-high heat until hot. Cook chicken 3 minutes per side or until browned. Transfer to clean plate; set aside.

Heat remaining 1 tablespoon oil in same skillet over medium heat. Add onion; cook and stir 5 minutes. Add mushrooms and garlic; cook and stir 3 minutes. Sprinkle mushroom mixture with flour; cook and stir 1 minute. Add broth, wine, salt and pepper; bring to a boil over high heat. Cook and stir 5 minutes or until sauce thickens.

Reserve ½ cup sauce. Pour remaining sauce over noodles; stir until noodles are well coated. Place chicken on top of noodles. Spoon reserved sauce over chicken.

Bake, uncovered, about 20 minutes or until chicken is no longer pink in centers and sauce is hot and bubbly. Sprinkle with parsley, if desired.

Makes 4 servings

Cook's Nook: Serve with crusty Italian or French bread and tossed salad.

Greek-Style Slow Cooker Chicken Stew

2 cups cubed peeled eggplant
2 cups sliced mushrooms
¾ cup coarsely chopped onion
2 cloves garlic, minced
1 teaspoon dried oregano leaves
½ teaspoon dried basil leaves
½ teaspoon dried thyme leaves
1¼ cups low-sodium chicken broth
1½ teaspoons all-purpose flour
6 skinless chicken breasts, about 2 pounds
Additional all-purpose flour
3 tablespoons dry sherry or low-sodium chicken broth
¼ teaspoon salt
¼ teaspoon black pepper
1 can (14 ounces) artichoke hearts, drained
12 ounces uncooked wide egg noodles

Slow Cooker Directions

Combine eggplant, mushrooms, onion, garlic, oregano, basil, thyme, broth and 1½ teaspoon flour in slow cooker. Cover and cook on HIGH 1 hour.

Coat chicken very lightly with flour. Generously spray large nonstick skillet with cooking spray; heat over medium heat until hot. Cook chicken 10 to 15 minutes or until browned on all sides.

Remove vegetables to bowl with slotted spoon. Layer chicken in slow cooker; return vegetables to slow cooker. Add sherry, salt and pepper. Reduce heat to LOW and cover and cook 6 to 6½ hours or until chicken is no longer pink in center and vegetables are tender.

Stir in artichokes; cover and cook 45 minutes to 1 hour or until heated through. Cook noodles according to package directions. Serve chicken stew over noodles.

Makes 6 servings

Basque-Style Chicken & Pasta

1 pound boneless, skinless chicken thighs or pork tenderloin, cut into ¾-inch chunks
1 teaspoon dried thyme or marjoram
2 tablespoons margarine or olive oil
2 cloves garlic, minced
⅔ cup milk
1 (5.1-ounce) package PASTA RONI® Angel Hair Pasta with Parmesan Cheese
½ cup (1½ ounces) diced salami or pepperoni
⅓ cup pimiento-stuffed olives, halved

1. Toss chicken with thyme. In large skillet over medium-high heat, melt margarine. Add chicken and garlic; cook 5 minutes or until chicken is no longer pink inside.

2. Add 1⅓ cups water and milk; bring to a boil. Slowly stir in pasta, salami, olives and Special Seasonings; reduce heat to medium. Gently boil uncovered, 4 to 5 minutes or until pasta is tender, stirring occasionally. Let stand 5 minutes before serving.

Makes 4 servings

Prep Time: 15 minutes
Cook Time: 12 minutes

Chicken Marsala

Thai Turkey & Noodles

Slow Cooker

1 package (about 1½ pounds) turkey tenderloins, cut into ¾-inch pieces
1 red bell pepper, cut into short, thin strips
1¼ cups chicken broth, divided
¼ cup reduced-sodium soy sauce
3 cloves garlic, minced
¾ teaspoon red pepper flakes
¼ teaspoon salt
2 tablespoons cornstarch
3 green onions, cut into ½-inch pieces
⅓ cup creamy or chunky peanut butter (not natural-style)
12 ounces hot cooked vermicelli pasta
¾ cup peanuts or cashews, chopped
¾ cup cilantro, chopped

Slow Cooker Directions
Place turkey, bell pepper, 1 cup broth, soy sauce, garlic, red pepper flakes and salt in slow cooker. Cover and cook on LOW 3 hours.

Mix cornstarch with remaining ¼ cup broth in small bowl until smooth. Turn slow cooker to HIGH. Stir in green onions, peanut butter and cornstarch mixture. Cover and cook 30 minutes or until sauce is thickened and turkey is no longer pink in center. Stir well. Serve over vermicelli. Sprinkle with peanuts and cilantro.

Makes 6 servings

Cook's Nook: If you don't have vermicelli on hand, try substituting ramen noodles. Discard the flavor packet from ramen soup mix and drop the noodles into boiling water. Cook the noodles 2 to 3 minutes or until just tender. Drain and serve hot.

Classic Family Lasagna

1 package (1 pound) TYSON® Fresh Ground Chicken
9 lasagna noodles, cooked according to package directions
1 medium onion, chopped
½ cup chopped green bell pepper (optional)
2 cloves garlic, minced
1 jar (30 ounces) spaghetti sauce
1 container (15 ounces) ricotta cheese
¾ cup grated Parmesan cheese, divided
1 egg, beaten
¼ teaspoon black pepper
3½ cups (14 ounces) shredded mozzarella cheese

PREP: Preheat oven to 375°F. CLEAN: Wash hands. In large skillet, cook and stir chicken, onion, bell pepper and garlic over medium-high heat until chicken is no longer pink. Stir in sauce; heat through and set aside. In medium bowl, combine ricotta cheese, ½ cup Parmesan cheese, egg and black pepper; mix well. Spray 13×9-inch baking dish with nonstick cooking spray. Spread ⅓ cup sauce on bottom of dish. Top with 3 noodles, one-third of sauce, one-third of ricotta mixture and 1 cup mozzarella cheese. Repeat layers twice, except do not top with remaining 1½ cups mozzarella cheese. Cover tightly with foil sprayed lightly with nonstick cooking spray.

COOK: Bake 40 minutes. Remove foil. Top with remaining cheese. Bake 15 minutes or until bubbly and cheese is melted.

SERVE: Serve with a green salad and garlic bread, if desired.

CHILL: Refrigerate leftovers immediately. *Makes 12 servings*

Prep Time: 35 minutes
Cook Time: 1 hour

Mediterranean Chicken and Rice

4 TYSON® Fresh or Individually Fresh Frozen® Boneless, Skinless Chicken Breasts
2 cups UNCLE BEN'S® Instant Brown Rice
1 tablespoon olive oil
1 teaspoon minced garlic
1 can (15 ounces) diced tomatoes, undrained
1½ cups water
½ teaspoon dried oregano leaves
16 pitted kalamata olives
2 ounces feta cheese, crumbled

PREP: CLEAN: Wash hands. Remove protective ice glaze from frozen chicken by holding under cool running water 1 to 2 minutes. CLEAN: Wash hands.

COOK: In large nonstick skillet, heat olive oil and garlic; add chicken. Cook over medium heat 4 to 6 minutes (5 to 7 minutes if using frozen chicken) or until chicken is browned. Stir in tomatoes, water and oregano; cover. Reduce heat to low; simmer 10 minutes. Stir in rice; cover. Cook 10 minutes or until rice is cooked and internal juices of chicken run clear. (Or insert instant-read meat thermometer in thickest part of chicken. Temperature should read 170°F.) Stir in olives and sprinkle with cheese.

SERVE: For a complete Mediterranean-style meal, serve with a green salad tossed with Italian vinaigrette.

CHILL: Refrigerate leftovers immediately. *Makes 4 Servings*

Prep Time: 5 minutes
Cook Time: 30 minutes

Thai Turkey & Noodles

Coq au Vin `Slow Cooker`

- 4 slices thick-cut bacon
- 2 cups frozen pearl onions, thawed
- 1 cup sliced button mushrooms
- 1 clove garlic, minced
- 1 teaspoon dried thyme leaves
- ⅛ teaspoon black pepper
- 6 boneless skinless chicken breast halves (about 2 pounds)
- ½ cup dry red wine
- ¾ cup reduced-sodium chicken broth
- ¼ cup tomato paste
- 3 tablespoons all-purpose flour
- Hot cooked egg noodles (optional)

Slow Cooker Directions

Cook bacon in medium skillet over medium heat. Drain and crumble. Layer ingredients in slow cooker in the following order: onions, bacon, mushrooms, garlic, thyme, pepper, chicken, wine and broth. Cover and cook on LOW 6 to 8 hours.

Remove chicken and vegetables; cover and keep warm. Ladle ½ cup cooking liquid into small bowl; allow to cool slightly. Turn slow cooker to HIGH; cover. Mix cooled liquid, tomato paste and flour until smooth. Return mixture to slow cooker; cover and cook 15 minutes or until thickened. Serve over hot noodles, if desired.   *Makes 6 servings*

Cook's Nook: Coq au Vin is a classical French dish that is made with bone-in chicken, salt pork or bacon, brandy, red wine and herbs. The dish originated when farmers needed a way to cook old chickens that could no longer breed. A slow, moist cooking method was needed to tenderize the tough old birds.

Chicken Curry `Slow Cooker`

- 2 boneless skinless chicken breast halves, cut into ¾-inch pieces
- 1 small onion, sliced
- 1 cup coarsely chopped apple, divided
- 3 tablespoons raisins
- 1 clove garlic, minced
- 1 teaspoon curry powder
- ¼ teaspoon ground ginger
- ⅓ cup water
- 1½ teaspoons chicken bouillon granules
- 1½ teaspoons all-purpose flour
- ¼ cup sour cream
- ½ teaspoon cornstarch
- ½ cup uncooked white rice

Slow Cooker Directions

Combine chicken, onion, ¾ cup apple, raisins, garlic, curry powder and ginger in slow cooker. Sitr water into chicken bouillon granules and flour in small bowl until smooth. Add to slow cooker. Cover and cook on LOW 3½ to 4 hours or until onion is tender and chicken is no longer pink.

Combine sour cream and cornstarch in large bowl. Turn off slow cooker; remove insert to heatproof surface. Drain all cooking liquid from chicken mixture and stir into sour cream mixture. Add back to insert; stir well. Place insert back in slow cooker. Cover and let stand 5 to 10 minutes or until sauce is heated through.

Meanwhile, cook rice according to package directions. Serve chicken curry over rice; garnish with remaining ¼ cup apple.
Makes 2 servings

Note: For a special touch, sprinkle chicken with green onions slivers just before serving.

Turkey Stuffed Chiles Rellenos

- 1 package (1½ pounds) BUTTERBALL® 99% Fat Free Fresh Ground Turkey Breast
- 1 envelope (1¼ ounces) taco seasoning mix
- ⅓ cup water
- 6 large poblano chilies, stems on, slit lengthwise and seeded
- 1 cup (4 ounces) shredded reduced fat Cheddar cheese
- 1½ cups tomato salsa

Spray large nonstick skillet with nonstick cooking spray; heat over medium heat until hot. Brown turkey in skillet over medium-high heat 6 to 8 minutes or until no longer pink, stirring to separate meat. Add taco seasoning and water. Bring to a boil. Reduce heat to low; simmer 5 minutes, stirring occasionally. In separate pan, cook chilies in boiling water 5 minutes; remove and drain. Combine turkey mixture and Cheddar cheese. Fill chilies with mixture. Pour salsa into 11×7-inch baking dish. Place stuffed chilies slit side up in baking dish. Bake, uncovered, in preheated 400°F oven 15 minutes. Serve hot with additional salsa and sour cream, if desired.
Makes 6 servings

Prep Time: 30 minutes

Coq au Vin

Mediterranean Chicken with Dried Fruits & Olives

4 boneless, skinless chicken breast halves (about 1¼ pounds)
1½ teaspoons ground cumin
½ teaspoon salt
¼ teaspoon ground black pepper
¼ cup I CAN'T BELIEVE IT'S NOT BUTTER!® Spread
4 cloves garlic, finely chopped
1½ cups mixed dried fruits
1 cup dry white wine or chicken broth
1 cup chicken broth
½ cup pimiento-stuffed olives, sliced

Season chicken with cumin, salt and pepper. In 12-inch skillet, melt I Can't Believe It's Not Butter! Spread over medium-high heat and brown chicken. Add garlic and cook 30 seconds. Stir in dried fruits, wine, broth and olives. Bring just to a boil. Reduce heat to low and simmer uncovered, stirring occasionally, 10 minutes or until chicken is thoroughly cooked. Remove chicken to serving platter and keep warm.

Bring sauce to a boil over high heat and continue boiling, stirring occasionally, 6 minutes or until sauce is slightly thickened. To serve, spoon fruit sauce over chicken.

Makes 4 servings

Note: Recipe can be halved.

Caribbean Shrimp with Rice

Slow Cooker

1 package (12 ounces) frozen shrimp, thawed
½ cup chicken broth
1 clove garlic, minced
1 teaspoon chili powder
½ teaspoon salt
½ teaspoon dried oregano leaves
1 cup frozen peas
½ cup diced tomatoes
2 cups cooked rice

Slow Cooker Directions
Combine shrimp, broth, garlic, chili powder, salt and oregano in slow cooker. Cover and cook on LOW 2 hours. Add peas and tomatoes. Cover and cook on LOW 5 minutes. Stir in rice. Cover and cook on LOW an additional 5 minutes.

Makes 4 servings

Sicilian Fish and Rice Bake

3 tablespoons olive or vegetable oil
¾ cup chopped onion
½ cup chopped celery
1 clove garlic, minced
½ cup uncooked long-grain white rice
2 cans (14.5 ounces each) CONTADINA® Recipe Ready Diced Tomatoes, undrained
1 teaspoon salt
1 teaspoon ground black pepper
½ teaspoon granulated sugar
⅛ teaspoon cayenne pepper
1 pound firm white fish
¼ cup finely chopped fresh parsley

1. Heat oil in large skillet. Add onion, celery and garlic; sauté for 2 to 3 minutes or until vegetables are tender.

2. Stir in rice; sauté for 5 minutes or until rice browns slightly. Add undrained tomatoes, salt, black pepper, sugar and cayenne pepper; mix well.

3. Place fish in bottom of greased 12×7½-inch baking dish. Spoon rice mixture over fish; cover with foil.

4. Bake in preheated 400°F oven for 45 to 50 minutes or until rice is tender. Let stand for 5 minutes before serving. Sprinkle with parsley.

Makes 6 servings

Prep Time: 6 minutes
Cook Time: 58 minutes
Stand Time: 5 minutes

Greek-Style Shrimp & Rice

1 (7.2-ounce) package RICE-A-RONI® Rice Pilaf
2 tablespoons margarine or butter
2 cloves garlic, minced
1 teaspoon dried oregano
¼ cup dry white wine or water
1 pound uncooked large shrimp, peeled and deveined
1 medium tomato, chopped
⅓ cup pitted kalamata or ripe olives, halved
½ cup crumbled feta cheese

1. In large skillet over medium heat, sauté rice-pasta mix with margarine until pasta is golden brown. Add garlic and oregano; sauté 30 seconds.

2. Slowly stir in 1¾ cups water, wine and Special Seasonings; bring to a boil over high heat. Reduce heat to low. Cover; simmer 15 minutes.

3. Stir in shrimp, tomato and olives. Cover; simmer 5 to 10 minutes or until shrimp turn pink and rice is tender. Sprinkle with cheese. Let stand 3 minutes before serving.

Makes 4 servings

Prep Time: 10 minutes
Cook Time: 30 minutes

Caribbean Shrimp with Rice

Crab and Corn Enchilada Casserole

Spicy Tomato Sauce (recipe follows), divided
10 to 12 ounces fresh crabmeat or flaked surimi crab
1 package (10 ounces) frozen corn, thawed, drained
1½ cups (6 ounces) shredded reduced-fat Monterey Jack cheese, divided
1 can (4 ounces) diced mild green chilies
12 (6-inch) corn tortillas
1 lime, cut into 6 wedges
Sour cream (optional)

Preheat oven to 350°F. Prepare Spicy Tomato Sauce.

Combine 2 cups Spicy Tomato Sauce, crabmeat, corn, 1 cup cheese and chilies in medium bowl. Cut each tortilla into 4 wedges. Place ⅓ of tortilla wedges in bottom of shallow 3- to 4-quart casserole, overlapping to make solid layer. Spread ½ of crab mixture on top. Repeat with ⅓ layer tortilla wedges, remaining crab mixture and remaining ⅓ tortillas. Spread remaining 1 cup Spicy Tomato Sauce over top; cover.

Bake 30 to 40 minutes or until heated through. Sprinkle with remaining ½ cup cheese and bake uncovered 5 minutes or until cheese melts. Squeeze lime over individual servings. Serve with sour cream, if desired.

Spicy Tomato Sauce

2 cans (15 ounces each) no-salt-added stewed tomatoes, undrained or 6 medium tomatoes
2 teaspoons olive oil
1 medium onion, chopped
1 tablespoon minced garlic
2 tablespoons chili powder
2 teaspoons ground cumin
2 teaspoons dried oregano leaves
1 teaspoon ground cinnamon
¼ teaspoon red pepper flakes
¼ teaspoon ground cloves

Combine tomatoes with juice in food processor or blender; process until finely chopped. Set aside.

Heat oil over medium-high heat in large saucepan or Dutch oven. Add onion and garlic. Cook and stir 5 minutes or until onion is tender. Add chili powder, cumin, oregano, cinnamon, red pepper and cloves. Cook and stir 1 minute. Add tomatoes; reduce heat to medium-low. Simmer, uncovered, 20 minutes or until sauce is reduced to 3 to 3¼ cups.   *Makes 3 cups*

Italian Eggplant Parmigiana

1 large eggplant, sliced ¼ inch thick
2 eggs, beaten
½ cup dry bread crumbs
1 can (14½ ounces) DEL MONTE® Stewed Tomatoes - Italian Recipe
1 can (15 ounces) DEL MONTE Tomato Sauce
2 cloves garlic, minced
½ teaspoon dried basil
6 ounces mozzarella cheese, sliced

1. Dip eggplant slices into eggs, then bread crumbs; arrange in single layer on baking sheet. Broil 4 inches from heat until brown and tender, about 5 minutes per side.

2. *Reduce oven temperature to 350°F.* Place eggplant in 13×9-inch baking dish.

3. Combine tomatoes, tomato sauce, garlic and basil; pour over eggplant and top with cheese.

4. Cover and bake at 350°F, 30 minutes or until heated through. Sprinkle with grated Parmesan cheese, if desired.

Makes 4 servings

Prep Time: 15 minutes
Cook Time: 30 minutes

Classic French Onion Soup   `Slow Cooker`

¼ cup butter
3 large yellow onions, sliced
1 cup dry white wine
3 cans (about 14 ounces each) beef or chicken broth
1 teaspoon Worcestershire sauce
½ teaspoon salt
½ teaspoon dried thyme
1 loaf French bread, sliced and toasted
1 cup (4 ounces) shredded Swiss cheese
Fresh thyme for garnish

Slow Cooker Directions
Melt butter in large skillet over high heat. Add onions, cook and stir 15 minutes or until onions are soft and lightly browned. Stir in wine.

Combine onion mixture, beef broth, Worcestershire, salt and thyme in slow cooker. Cover and cook on LOW 4 to 4½ hours. Ladle soup into 4 individual bowls; top with bread slice and cheese. Garnish with fresh thyme, if desired.

Makes 4 servings

Classic French Onion Soup

Spicy Thai Noodles

1¼ cups water
2½ teaspoons brown sugar
2 teaspoons soy sauce
1 teaspoon LAWRY'S® Garlic
    Powder with Parsley
¾ teaspoon LAWRY'S® Seasoned
    Salt
½ teaspoon cornstarch
⅛ to ¼ teaspoon hot pepper
    flakes
¼ cup chunky peanut butter
¼ cup sliced green onion
1 tablespoon chopped fresh
    cilantro
8 ounces linguine, cooked,
    drained and kept hot
1½ cups shredded red cabbage

In large skillet, combine first seven ingredients. Bring to a boil over medium-high heat; reduce heat to low and cook, uncovered, 5 minutes. Cool 10 minutes. Stir in peanut butter, green onion and cilantro. Add hot linguine and cabbage; toss lightly to coat. Serve immediately.

Makes 4 servings

Serving Suggestion: Great served with a marinated cucumber salad.

Helpful Hints

The use of peanuts in Asian cooking probably originated in Malaysia or Indonesia. In Thailand peanut sauces are prepared with freshly ground roasted peanuts. The use of peanut butter in Thai cooking is common only to America.

Hearty Manicotti

8 to 10 dry manicotti shells
1 package (10 ounces) frozen
    chopped spinach, thawed,
    squeezed dry
1 carton (15 ounces) ricotta
    cheese
1 egg, lightly beaten
½ cup (2 ounces) grated
    Parmesan cheese
⅛ teaspoon ground black pepper
2 cans (6 ounces each)
    CONTADINA® Italian Paste
    with Italian Seasonings
1⅓ cups water
½ cup (2 ounces) shredded
    mozzarella cheese

1. Cook pasta according to package directions; drain.

2. Meanwhile, combine spinach, ricotta cheese, egg, Parmesan cheese and pepper in medium bowl; mix well.

3. Spoon into manicotti shells. Place in ungreased 12×7½-inch baking dish.

4. Combine tomato paste and water in small bowl; pour over manicotti. Sprinkle with mozzarella cheese. Bake in preheated 350°F oven for 30 to 40 minutes or until heated through.   *Makes 4 to 5 servings*

Prep Time: 15 minutes
Cook Time: 40 minutes

Four-Cheese Lasagna

½ pound ground beef
½ cup chopped onion
⅓ cup chopped celery
1 clove garlic, minced
1½ teaspoons dried basil leaves
¼ teaspoon dried oregano leaves
¼ teaspoon salt
⅛ teaspoon ground black pepper
1 package (3 ounces) cream
    cheese, cubed
⅓ cup light cream or milk
½ cup dry white wine
½ cup (2 ounces) shredded
    Wisconsin Cheddar or
    Gouda cheese
1 egg, slightly beaten
1 cup cream-style cottage
    cheese
6 ounces lasagna noodles,
    cooked and drained
6 ounces sliced Wisconsin
    Mozzarella cheese

In large skillet, brown meat with onion, celery and garlic; drain. Stir in basil, oregano, salt and pepper. Reduce heat to low. Add cream cheese and cream. Cook, stirring frequently, until cream cheese is melted. Stir in wine. Gradually add Cheddar cheese, stirring until Cheddar cheese is almost melted. Remove from heat. In small bowl, combine egg and cottage cheese.

Into greased 10×6-inch baking dish, layer ½ each of the noodles, meat sauce, cottage cheese mixture and Mozzarella cheese; repeat layers. Bake, uncovered, at 375°F, 30 to 35 minutes or until hot and bubbly. Let stand 10 minutes before cutting to serve.   *Makes 6 servings*

Prep Time: 1½ hours

Favorite recipe from **Wisconsin Milk Marketing Board**

Spicy Thai Noodles

Minestrone alla Milanese

Slow Cooker

2 cans (14½ ounces each) beef broth
1 can (14½ ounces) diced tomatoes, undrained
1 cup diced potato
1 cup coarsely chopped green cabbage
1 cup coarsely chopped carrots
1 cup sliced zucchini
¾ cup chopped onion
¾ cup sliced fresh green beans
¾ cup coarsely chopped celery
¾ cup water
2 tablespoons olive oil
1 clove garlic, minced
½ teaspoon dried basil leaves
¼ teaspoon dried rosemary
1 bay leaf
1 can (15½ ounces) cannellini beans, rinsed and drained
Grated Parmesan cheese (optional)

Slow Cooker Directions
Combine all ingredients except cannellini beans and cheese in slow cooker; mix well. Cover and cook on LOW 5 to 6 hours. Add cannellini beans. Cover and cook on LOW 1 hour or until vegetables are crisp-tender. Remove and discard bay leaf. Garnish with cheese, if desired.

Makes 8 to 10 servings

Helpful Hints

Cannellini beans are a white-skinned variety of kidney beans. If they are unavailable, you can substitute light kidney beans or Great Northern beans.

Three Cheese Baked Ziti

1 container (15 ounces) part-skim ricotta cheese
2 eggs, beaten
¼ cup grated Parmesan cheese
1 box (16 ounces) ziti pasta, cooked and drained
1 jar (1 pound 10 ounces) RAGÚ® Chunky Gardenstyle Pasta Sauce
1 cup shredded mozzarella cheese (about 4 ounces)

Preheat oven to 350°F. In large bowl, combine ricotta cheese, eggs and Parmesan cheese; set aside.

In another bowl, thoroughly combine pasta and Ragú® Chunky Gardenstyle Pasta Sauce.

In 13×9-inch baking dish, spoon ½ of the pasta mixture; evenly top with ricotta cheese mixture, then remaining pasta mixture. Sprinkle with mozzarella cheese. Bake 30 minutes or until heated through. Serve, if desired, with additional heated pasta sauce.   *Makes 8 servings*

Prep Time: 20 minutes
Cook Time: 30 minutes

Greek Spinach and Feta Pie

⅓ cup butter, melted
2 eggs
1 package (10 ounces) frozen chopped spinach, thawed and squeezed dry
1 container (15 ounces) ricotta cheese
1 package (4 ounces) crumbled feta cheese
¾ teaspoon finely grated lemon peel
¼ teaspoon black pepper
⅛ teaspoon ground nutmeg
1 package (16 ounces) frozen phyllo dough, thawed

Preheat oven to 350°F. Brush 13×9-inch baking dish lightly with butter.

Beat eggs in medium bowl. Stir in spinach, ricotta, feta, lemon peel, pepper and nutmeg. Set aside.

Unwrap phyllo dough; remove 8 sheets. Cut dough in half crosswise forming 16 rectangles about 13×8½ inches. Cover dough with damp cloth or plastic wrap to keep moist while assembling pie. Reserve remaining dough for another use.

Place 1 piece of dough in prepared dish; brush top lightly with butter. Top with another piece of dough and brush lightly with butter. Continue layering with 6 pieces of dough, brushing each lightly with butter. Spoon spinach mixture evenly over dough.

Top spinach mixture with piece of dough; brush lightly with butter. Repeat layering with remaining 7 pieces of dough, brushing each piece lightly with butter.

Bake, uncovered, 35 to 40 minutes or until golden brown.

Makes 6 servings

Minestrone alla Milanese

Light & Easy Fare

Fajita Stuffed Shells

¼ cup fresh lime juice
1 clove garlic, minced
½ teaspoon dried oregano leaves
¼ teaspoon ground cumin
1 (6-ounce) boneless lean beef round or flank steak
1 medium green bell pepper, halved and seeded
1 medium onion, cut in half
12 uncooked jumbo pasta shells (about 6 ounces)
½ cup reduced-fat sour cream
2 tablespoons shredded reduced-fat Cheddar cheese
1 tablespoon minced fresh cilantro
⅔ cup chunky salsa
2 cups shredded leaf lettuce

1. Combine lime juice, garlic, oregano and cumin in shallow nonmetallic dish. Add steak, bell pepper and onion. Cover and refrigerate 8 hours or overnight.

2. Preheat oven to 350°F. Cook pasta shells according to package directions, omitting salt. Drain and rinse well under cold water; set aside.

3. Grill steak and vegetables over medium-hot coals 3 to 4 minutes per side or until desired doneness; cool slightly. Cut steak into thin slices. Chop vegetables. Place steak slices and vegetables in medium bowl. Stir in sour cream, Cheddar cheese and cilantro. Stuff shells evenly with meat mixture, mounding slightly.

4. Arrange shells in 8-inch baking dish. Pour salsa over shells. Cover with foil; bake 15 minutes or until heated through. Arrange shells on lettuce.   *Makes 4 servings*

Creamy Ham and Garden Rotini

8 ounces uncooked rotini pasta
1 bag (16 ounces) frozen vegetable blend (broccoli, cauliflower, red peppers and corn)
4 ounces turkey ham, chopped
1½ cups fat-free (skim) milk
2 tablespoons all-purpose flour
1¼ cups (5 ounces) shredded reduced-fat Monterey Jack cheese
Black pepper

1. Preheat oven to 325°F. Spray 11×8-inch baking pan with nonstick cooking spray; set aside. Cook pasta according to package directions, omitting salt; drain. Place in bottom of prepared pan; set aside.

2. Meanwhile, add ½ cup water to large nonstick skillet. Bring to a boil over high heat. Add vegetables; return to a boil. Reduce heat to low; simmer, covered, 4 minutes. Drain. Toss vegetables and ham with pasta; set aside.

3. Combine milk and flour in small bowl; whisk until smooth. Pour milk mixture into same skillet; cook over medium-high heat, stirring constantly, until slightly thickened. Remove from heat. Pour over pasta mixture. Top with cheese; sprinkle with pepper. Cover loosely with foil. Bake 25 to 30 minutes or until heated through.

Makes 4 servings

Fajita Stuffed Shells

Baked Pasta Casserole

1½ cups (3 ounces) uncooked wagon wheel or rotelle pasta
3 ounces 95% lean ground beef sirloin
2 tablespoons chopped onion
2 tablespoons chopped green bell pepper
1 clove garlic, minced
½ cup fat-free spaghetti sauce Black pepper
2 tablespoons shredded Italian-style mozzarella and Parmesan cheese blend Peperoncini (optional)

1. Preheat oven to 350°F. Cook pasta according to package directions; drain. Return pasta to saucepan.

2. Meanwhile, heat small nonstick skillet over medium-high heat. Add beef, onion, bell pepper and garlic; cook and stir 3 to 4 minutes or until beef is browned and vegetables are crisp-tender. Drain.

3. Add beef mixture, spaghetti sauce and black pepper to pasta in saucepan; mix well. Spoon mixture into 1-quart baking dish. Sprinkle with cheese.

4. Bake 15 minutes or until heated through. Serve with peperoncini, if desired. *Makes 2 servings*

Note: To make ahead, assemble casserole as directed through step 3. Cover and refrigerate several hours or overnight. Bake, uncovered, in preheated 350°F oven for 30 minutes or until heated through.

Beef and Parsnip Stroganoff Slow Cooker

1 cube beef bouillon
¾ cup boiling water
¾ pound well-trimmed boneless top round beef steak, 1 inch thick
   Nonstick olive oil cooking spray
2 cups cubed peeled parsnips or potatoes*
1 medium onion, halved and thinly sliced
¾ pound mushrooms, sliced
2 teaspoons minced garlic
¼ teaspoon black pepper
¼ cup water
1 tablespoon plus 1½ teaspoons all-purpose flour
3 tablespoons reduced-fat sour cream
1½ teaspoons Dijon mustard
¼ teaspoon cornstarch
1 tablespoon chopped parsley
4 ounces cholesterol-free wide noodles, cooked without salt, drained and kept hot

If using potatoes, cut into 1-inch chunks and do not sauté.

Slow Cooker Directions

1. Dissolve bouillon cube in ¾ cup boiling water; cool. Meanwhile, cut steak into 2×½-inch strips. Spray large nonstick skillet with cooking spray; heat over high heat. Cook and stir beef about 4 minutes or until meat begins to brown and is barely pink. Transfer beef and juices to slow cooker.

2. Spray same skillet with cooking spray; heat over high heat. Add parsnips and onion; cook and stir until browned, about 4 minutes. Add mushrooms, garlic and pepper; cook and stir until mushrooms are tender, about 5 minutes. Transfer mushroom mixture to slow cooker; mix with beef.

3. Stir ¼ cup water into flour in small bowl until smooth. Stir flour mixture into cooled bouillon. Add to slow cooker. Cook, covered, on LOW 4½ to 5 hours or until beef and parsnips are tender.

4. Turn off slow cooker. Remove beef and vegetables with slotted spoon to large bowl; reserve cooking liquid from beef. Blend sour cream, mustard and cornstarch in medium bowl. Gradually add reserved liquid to sour cream mixture; stir well to blend. Stir sour cream mixture into beef mixture. Sprinkle with parsley; serve over noodles. Garnish, if desired. *Makes 4 servings*

Helpful Hints

Parsnips are a pale white root vegetable similar in shape to the carrot. However, the parsnip is broader at the top and has a smoother skin. Its distinctive nutty sweet flavor contributes to soups, stews and vegetable side dishes.

Beef and Parsnip Stroganoff

Beef Picante and Sour Cream Casserole

6 ounces uncooked wagon wheel pasta
8 ounces 95% lean ground beef
1½ cups reduced-sodium mild picante sauce
1 cup red kidney beans, rinsed and drained
¾ cup water
1 tablespoon chili powder
1 teaspoon ground cumin
½ cup low-fat cottage cheese
½ cup nonfat sour cream
½ cup chopped green onions, with tops
1 can (2¼ ounces) sliced black olives
¼ cup chopped fresh cilantro or fresh parsley

1. Preheat oven to 325°F. Spray 9-inch square baking pan with nonstick cooking spray; set aside. Cook pasta according to package directions, omitting salt. Drain. Place in bottom of prepared pan; set aside.

2. Brown beef in large nonstick skillet over medium-high heat 4 to 5 minutes or until no longer pink, stirring to separate beef; drain fat.

3. Add picante sauce, beans, water, chili powder and cumin; blend well. Bring to a boil over high heat. Reduce heat to low; simmer, covered, 20 minutes.

4. Combine cottage cheese, sour cream and green onions in food processor or blender; process until smooth. Spread cottage cheese mixture over pasta in prepared pan. Spoon meat mixture over cottage cheese mixture; cover with foil. Bake 20 minutes or until heated through. Remove from oven; let stand 10 minutes to allow flavors to blend. Top with olives and cilantro.

Makes 4 servings

Creamy Beef and Carrot Topped Baked Potatoes

1 tablespoon CRISCO® Oil*
1 cup shredded carrot
½ cup chopped onion
1 pound ground beef round
1 teaspoon salt
Dash of pepper
¼ cup all-purpose flour
2 cups beef broth
1 teaspoon Worcestershire sauce
6 hot baked medium potatoes

*Use your favorite Crisco Oil product.

1. Heat oil in large skillet on medium heat. Add carrot and onion. Cook and stir until tender. Add meat, salt and pepper. Cook until meat is browned, stirring occasionally. Drain. Sprinkle flour over meat mixture. Stir until blended.

2. Add broth and Worcestershire sauce to skillet. Cook and stir until thickened.

3. Place baked potatoes on serving plate. Split. Push ends toward center to open. Spoon about ½ cup meat mixture into each potato. Garnish, if desired.

Makes 6 servings

Pork, Beans and Sausage Skillet Dinner

7 ounces low-fat smoked sausage, cut into 1-inch pieces
2 cups frozen mixed vegetables
1 can (15 ounces) VAN CAMP'S® Pork and Beans
1 can (10¾ ounces) reduced-fat, reduced-sodium condensed tomato soup
2 cups cooked rice

1. In large skillet, brown sausage; drain.

2. Add vegetables, Van Camp's Beans and soup. Bring to a gentle boil; reduce heat, cover and simmer 10 minutes, stirring occasionally.

3. Stir in rice and heat through.

Makes 6 (10-ounce) servings

Stuffed Bell Peppers

1 cup chopped fresh tomatoes
1 jalapeño pepper,* seeded and
    chopped (optional)
1 teaspoon chopped fresh
    cilantro
½ clove garlic, finely minced
½ teaspoon dried oregano
    leaves, divided
¼ teaspoon ground cumin
6 ounces lean ground round
½ cup cooked brown rice
¼ cup cholesterol-free egg
    substitute *or* 1 egg white
2 tablespoons finely chopped
    onion
¼ teaspoon salt
⅛ teaspoon black pepper
2 large bell peppers, any color,
    seeded and cut in half
    lengthwise
4 sheets (12×12 inches) heavy-
    duty foil, lightly sprayed
    with nonstick cooking spray

Jalapeño peppers can sting and irritate the skin; wear rubber gloves when handling peppers and do not touch eyes. Wash hands after handling.

1. Preheat oven to 400°F.

2. Combine tomatoes, jalapeño pepper, cilantro, garlic, ¼ teaspoon oregano and cumin in small bowl. Set aside.

3. Combine beef, rice, egg substitute, onion, salt and black pepper in large bowl. Stir in ⅔ cup of tomato mixture. Spoon filling into pepper halves.

4. Place each pepper half on foil sheet. Double fold sides and ends of foil to seal packets. Place packets on baking sheet.

5. Bake 45 minutes or until vegetables are tender.

6. Remove from oven. Carefully open one end of each packet to allow steam to escape. Open packets and transfer pepper halves to serving plates. Serve with remaining tomato salsa, if desired.

Makes 6 servings

Meatball Grinders `Slow Cooker`

1 can (15 ounces) diced
    tomatoes, drained and
    juices reserved
1 can (8 ounces) reduced-
    sodium tomato sauce
¼ cup chopped onion
2 tablespoons tomato paste
1 teaspoon dried Italian
    seasoning
1 pound ground chicken
½ cup fresh whole wheat or
    white bread crumbs (1 slice
    bread)
1 egg white, lightly beaten
3 tablespoons finely chopped
    fresh parsley
2 cloves garlic, minced
¼ teaspoon salt
⅛ teaspoon black pepper
4 small hard rolls, split
2 tablespoons grated Parmesan
    cheese

Slow Cooker Directions

Combine diced tomatoes, ½ cup reserved juice, tomato sauce, onion, tomato paste and Italian seasoning in slow cooker. Cover and cook on LOW 3 to 4 hours or until onions are soft.

During the last 30 minutes of cooking time, prepare meatballs. Combine chicken, bread crumbs, egg white, parsley, garlic, salt and pepper in medium bowl. With wet hands form mixture into 12 to 16 meatballs. Spray medium nonstick skillet with cooking spray; heat over medium heat until hot. Add meatballs; cook about 8 to 10 minutes or until well-browned on all sides. Remove meatballs to slow cooker; cook 1 to 2 hours or until meatballs are no longer pink in centers and are heated through.

Place 3 to 4 meatballs in each roll. Divide sauce evenly; spoon over meatballs. Sprinkle with cheese.

Makes 4 servings

El Paso Chili Chowder

PAM® No-Stick Cooking Spray
¼ cup chopped red onions
1 can (15 ounces)
    WOLF BRAND® Turkey Chili
    with Beans
1 can (14.5 ounces) HUNT'S®
    Diced Tomatoes in Juice
1 can (14½ ounces) fat-free low-
    sodium chicken broth
2 cups frozen whole kernel corn
1 can (4 ounces) diced green
    chilies
1 tablespoons chopped fresh
    cilantro

1. Spray large saucepan with PAM Cooking Spray. Sauté onions until tender.

2. Add *remaining* ingredients. Simmer until heated through, stirring occasionally.

Makes 6 (1-cup) servings

Broccoli-Filled Chicken Roulade

- 2 cups broccoli florets
- 1 tablespoon water
- ¼ cup fresh parsley
- 1 cup diced red bell pepper
- 4 ounces fat-free cream cheese, softened
- 2 tablespoons grated Parmesan cheese
- 2 tablespoons lemon juice
- 2 tablespoons olive oil
- 1 teaspoon paprika
- ¼ teaspoon salt
- 1 egg
- ½ cup fat-free (skim) milk
- 4 cups cornflakes, crushed
- 1 tablespoon dried basil leaves
- 8 boneless skinless chicken breast halves

1. Place broccoli and water in microwavable dish; cover. Microwave at HIGH 2 minutes. Let stand, covered, 2 minutes. Drain water. Place broccoli in food processor or blender. Add parsley; process 10 seconds, scraping side of bowl if necessary. Add bell pepper, cream cheese, Parmesan cheese, lemon juice, oil, paprika and salt. Pulse 2 to 3 times or until bell pepper is minced.

2. Preheat oven to 375°F. Spray 11×7-inch baking pan with nonstick cooking spray. Lightly beat egg in small bowl. Add milk; blend well. Place cornflake crumbs in shallow bowl. Add basil; blend well.

3. Pound chicken breasts between two pieces of plastic wrap to ¼-inch thickness using flat side of meat mallet or rolling pin. Spread each chicken breast with ⅛ of the broccoli mixture, spreading to within ½ inch of edges. Roll up chicken breast from short end, tucking in sides if possible; secure with wooden picks. Dip roulades in milk mixture; roll in cornflake crumb mixture. Place in prepared baking pan. Bake 20 minutes or until chicken is no longer pink in center and juices run clear. Remove and discard wooden picks.   *Makes 8 servings*

Jalapeño Chicken & Rice in a Skillet

- 4 TYSON® Fresh or Individually Fresh Frozen® Boneless, Skinless Chicken Breasts
- 2 cups UNCLE BEN'S® Instant Rice
- 1 tablespoon olive oil
- 1 teaspoon minced garlic
- 2 cups defatted reduced-sodium chicken broth
- 1 can (15 ounces) black beans, rinsed and drained
- 1 to 2 teaspoons minced jalapeño pepper*
- ½ teaspoon ground cumin
- 2 tablespoons chopped fresh cilantro

Jalapeño peppers can sting and irritate the skin; wear rubber gloves when handling peppers and do not touch eyes. Wash hands after handling.

PREP: CLEAN: Wash hands. Remove protective ice glaze from frozen chicken by holding under cool running water 1 to 2 minutes. Pat dry. CLEAN: Wash hands.

COOK: In large nonstick skillet, heat olive oil and garlic; add chicken. Cook over medium heat 4 to 6 minutes (5 to 7 minutes if using frozen chicken) or until chicken is lightly browned. Stir in chicken broth, beans, jalapeño pepper and cumin; cover. Simmer 10 to 15 minutes or until internal juices of chicken run clear. (Or insert instant-read meat thermometer in thickest part of chicken. Temperature should read 170°F.) Stir in rice; cover. Let stand 5 minutes.

SERVE: Sprinkle with cilantro. Serve with lime wedges and salsa, if desired.

CHILL: Refrigerate leftovers immediately.   *Makes 4 servings*

Prep Time: 5 minutes
Cook Time: 30 minutes

Tuscan Pasta [Slow Cooker]

- 1 pound boneless skinless chicken breasts, cut into 1-inch pieces
- 1 can (15½ ounces) red kidney beans, rinsed and drained
- 1 can (15 ounces) tomato sauce
- 2 cans (14½ ounces each) Italian-style stewed tomatoes
- 1 jar (4½ ounces) sliced mushrooms, drained
- 1 medium green bell pepper, chopped
- ½ cup chopped onion
- ½ cup chopped celery
- 4 cloves garlic, minced
- 1 cup water
- 1 teaspoon dried Italian seasoning
- 6 ounces uncooked thin spaghetti, broken into halves

Slow Cooker Directions
Place all ingredients except spaghetti in slow cooker. Cover and cook on LOW 4 hours or until vegetables are tender.

Turn to HIGH. Stir in spaghetti; cover. Stir again after 10 minutes. Cover and cook 45 minutes or until pasta is tender. Garnish with basil and bell pepper strips, if desired.

Makes 8 servings

Broccoli-Filled Chicken Roulade

Broccoli, Chicken and Rice Casserole

1 box UNCLE BEN'S CHEF'S RECIPE® Broccoli Rice Au Gratin Supreme
2 cups boiling water
4 boneless, skinless chicken breasts (about 1 pound)
¼ teaspoon garlic powder
2 cups frozen broccoli
1 cup (4 ounces) reduced-fat shredded Cheddar cheese

1. Heat oven to 425°F. In 13×9-inch baking pan, combine rice and contents of seasoning packet. Add boiling water; mix well. Add chicken; sprinkle with garlic powder. Cover and bake 30 minutes.

2. Add broccoli and cheese; continue to bake, covered, 8 to 10 minutes or until chicken is no longer pink in center.   *Makes 4 servings*

Sweet Jalapeño Mustard Turkey Thighs

Slow Cooker

3 turkey thighs, skin removed
¾ cup honey mustard
½ cup orange juice
1 tablespoon cider vinegar
1 teaspoon Worcestershire sauce
1 to 2 fresh jalapeño peppers,* finely chopped
1 clove garlic, minced
½ teaspoon grated orange peel

*Jalapeño peppers can sting and irritate the skin; wear rubber gloves when handling peppers and do not touch eyes. Wash hands after handling.

Slow Cooker Directions

Place turkey thighs in single layer in slow cooker. Combine remaining ingredients in medium bowl. Pour mixture over turkey thighs. Cover; cook on LOW 5 to 6 hours.

Makes 6 servings

Southwest Turkey Tenderloin Stew

Slow Cooker

1 package (about 1½ pounds) turkey tenderloins, cut into ¾-inch pieces
1 tablespoon chili powder
1 teaspoon ground cumin
¼ teaspoon salt
1 red bell pepper, cut into ¾-inch pieces
1 green bell pepper, cut into ¾-inch pieces
¾ cup chopped red or yellow onion
3 cloves garlic, minced
1 can (15½ ounces) chili beans in spicy sauce, undrained
1 can (14½ ounces) chili-style stewed tomatoes, undrained
¾ cup prepared salsa or picante sauce
Fresh cilantro (optional)

Slow Cooker Directions

Place turkey in slow cooker. Sprinkle chili powder, cumin and salt over turkey; toss to coat. Add red bell pepper, green bell pepper, onion, garlic, beans with sauce, tomatoes with juice and salsa. Mix well. Cover and cook on LOW 5 hours or until turkey is no longer pink in center and vegetables are crisp-tender. Ladle into bowls. Garnish with cilantro, if desired.   *Makes 6 servings*

Southwest Tequila Chicken

1 teaspoon olive oil
1 pound skinless, boneless chicken breast
1 can (14½ ounces) Mexican stewed tomatoes
½ cup chicken broth
⅛ teaspoon green Tabasco® sauce
2 tablespoons tequila
2 tablespoons chopped cilantro
1 can (15 ounces) VEG•ALL® Original Mixed Vegetables, drained
2 teaspoons lime juice
¼ teaspoon lime zest
2 cups cooked white rice

In medium fry pan, heat oil over medium high heat; add chicken, brown on both sides.

Add tomatoes, chicken broth, Tabasco®, tequila, cilantro, VEG•ALL®, lime juice, and zest to chicken; cook 15 to 20 minutes or until liquid reduces by half.

Serve over rice.

Makes 8 servings

Chicken and Chile Pepper Stew

Slow Cooker

1 pound boneless skinless chicken thighs, cut into ½-inch pieces
1 pound small potatoes, cut lengthwise in halves and then cut crosswise into slices
1 cup chopped onion
2 poblano chili peppers,* seeded and cut into ½-inch pieces
1 jalapeño pepper,* seeded and finely chopped
3 cloves garlic, minced
3 cups fat-free reduced-sodium chicken broth
1 can (14½ ounces) no-salt-added diced tomatoes, undrained
2 tablespoons chili powder
1 teaspoon dried oregano leaves

*Chili peppers can sting and irritate the skin; wear rubber gloves when handling peppers and do not touch eyes. Wash hands after handling.

Slow Cooker Directions

1. Place chicken, potatoes, onion, poblano peppers, jalapeño pepper and garlic into slow cooker.

2. Stir together broth, tomatoes with juice, chili powder and oregano in large bowl. Pour broth mixture over chicken mixture in slow cooker; mix well. Cover; cook on LOW 8 to 9 hours.   *Makes 6 servings*

Broccoli, Chicken and Rice Casserole

Chicken Pot Pie with Cornmeal Crust

1 cup diagonally sliced carrots
½ cup diagonally sliced celery
   Nonstick cooking spray
2 cups sliced fresh mushrooms
1 can (14½ ounce) fat-free
   reduced-sodium chicken
   broth, divided
⅓ cup low-fat (1%) milk
1⅓ cup unbleached flour, divided
½ teaspoon dried thyme leaves
¼ teaspoon salt
⅛ teaspoon white pepper
⅓ cup yellow cornmeal
1 teaspoon baking powder
⅛ teaspoon salt
3 tablespoons canola and
   vegetable oil blend
4 to 5 tablespoons cold water
2 cups diced cooked chicken
   breasts
1 cup frozen peas and pearl
   onions, thawed

1. Bring 2 tablespoons water to a boil in small saucepan over medium-high heat. Add carrots and celery. Reduce heat; cover and simmer 10 minutes or until vegetables are crisp-tender.

2. Heat large nonstick skillet over high heat. Spray with cooking spray. Add mushrooms and 2 tablespoons water. Reduce heat to medium-high; cook and stir until water evaporates and mushrooms are lightly brown. Add all but ⅓ cup chicken broth to skillet. Pour milk and remaining ⅓ cup chicken broth into small jar with tight-fitting lid. Add ⅓ cup flour, thyme, salt and pepper. Shake well. Slowly stir flour mixture into chicken broth and mushrooms. Bring to a boil. Continue to cook and stir 1 minute. Cover and set aside.

3. Preheat oven to 375°F. Combine remaining 1 cup flour, cornmeal, baking powder and salt in large bowl; form a well in center. Combine oil and 4 tablespoons cold water. Pour into well; toss with fork until mixture holds together, sprinkling with additional water, if needed. Press together to form ball. Place between 2 pieces of waxed paper. Roll dough into 10-inch circle, ⅛-inch-thick. Remove top piece of waxed paper. Cut air vent into crust with knife.

4. Combine chicken broth mixture, chicken, cooked vegetables, peas and onions in large saucepan; reheat thoroughly. Coat 9-inch pie plate with nonstick cooking spray. Pour hot mixture into pie plate. Carefully place top crust over filling; remove waxed paper. Flute edge of crust; brush with additional milk, if desired. Bake for 30 to 35 minutes or until golden brown.   *Makes 6 servings*

Southern BBQ Chicken and Rice

1 cup UNCLE BEN'S® ORIGINAL
   CONVERTED® Brand Rice
4 TYSON® Individually Fresh
   Frozen® Chicken Half
   Breasts
1½ cups water
1 cup barbecue sauce, divided
1 package (6 half ears) frozen
   corn on the cob

COOK: CLEAN: Wash hands. In large skillet, combine water, rice, ¾ cup barbecue sauce and chicken. Bring to a boil. Cover, reduce heat; simmer 25 minutes. Add corn; cook 15 to 20 minutes or until internal juices of chicken run clear. (Or insert instant-read meat thermometer in thickest part of chicken. Temperature should read 170°F.) Spoon remaining ¼ cup barbecue sauce over chicken. Remove from heat; let stand 5 minutes or until liquid is absorbed.

SERVE: Serve with extra barbecue sauce and corn bread, if desired.

CHILL: Refrigerate leftovers immediately.   *Makes 4 servings*

Prep Time: none
Cook Time: 40 to 45 minutes

Easy Weeknight Chicken Cacciatore

1 tablespoon BERTOLLI® Olive
   Oil
2½ pounds chicken pieces
1 package (8 ounces) fresh
   mushrooms, sliced
1 can (28 ounces) crushed
   tomatoes
1 envelope LIPTON®
   RECIPE SECRETS® Onion
   Soup Mix
¼ cup dry red wine
½ teaspoon dried basil

1. In 6-quart saucepot, heat oil over medium-high heat and brown chicken pieces. Add mushrooms and cook 2 minutes, stirring occasionally.

2. Stir in crushed tomatoes, soup mix, wine and basil. Bring to a boil over high heat.

3. Reduce heat to low and simmer covered 30 minutes or until chicken is thoroughly cooked. Serve, if desired, over hot cooked noodles or rice.
             Makes 4 servings

Slow Cooker Method: Place mushrooms then chicken pieces in slow cooker. Stir crushed tomatoes, soup mix, wine and basil together until blended. Pour over chicken and mushrooms. Cover. Cook on HIGH 4 to 6 hours or LOW 8 hours. Serve as above.

Prep Time: 10 minutes
Cook Time: 40 minutes

Southern BBQ Chicken and Rice

Mu Shu Turkey [Slow Cooker]

1 can (16 ounces) plums,
    drained, rinsed and pitted
½ cup orange juice
¼ cup finely chopped onion
1 tablespoon minced fresh
    ginger
¼ teaspoon ground cinnamon
1 pound boneless turkey breast,
    cut into thin strips
6 (7-inch) flour tortillas
3 cups coleslaw mix

Slow Cooker Directions

1. Place plums in blender or food processor. Cover and blend until almost smooth. Combine plums, orange juice, onion, ginger and cinnamon in slow cooker; mix well. Place turkey over plum mixture. Cover; cook on LOW 3 to 4 hours.

2. Remove turkey from slow cooker and divide evenly among tortillas. Spoon about 2 tablespoons plum sauce over turkey in each tortilla; top with about ½ cup coleslaw mix. Fold bottom edge of tortilla over filling; fold in sides. Roll up to completely enclose filling. Repeat with remaining tortillas. Use remaining plum sauce for dipping.   *Makes 6 servings*

Broccoli Cheese Casserole

3 whole chicken breasts,
    skinned and halved
1½ pounds fresh broccoli
2 tablespoons margarine
½ cup chopped onion
1 clove garlic, minced
3 tablespoons all-purpose flour
1¼ cups skim milk
2 tablespoons fresh parsley
½ teaspoon salt
½ teaspoon dried oregano
    leaves, crushed
1½ cups 1% low-fat cream-style
    small curd cottage cheese
1½ cups shredded reduced-fat
    Wisconsin Cheddar cheese
¼ cup grated Wisconsin Romano
    cheese
1 jar (4½ ounces) sliced
    mushrooms, drained
6 ounces noodles, cooked and
    drained

Microwave Directions

Place chicken breasts in microwavable glass baking dish. Microwave at HIGH (100% power) 7 minutes. Cool slightly and cube. Set aside. Remove flowerets from broccoli and cut larger ones in half. Cut stems into 1-inch pieces. Place broccoli in 3-quart microwavable baking dish with ½ cup water. Cover and microwave at HIGH (100% power) 7 minutes, stirring once. Let stand, covered, 2 minutes. Drain well; set aside.

Place margarine, onion and garlic in same baking dish. Cover and microwave at HIGH (100% power) 3 minutes. Stir in flour. Gradually add milk. Add parsley, salt and oregano. Microwave at HIGH (100% power) 1 minute. Stir well; microwave 1 minute. Stir in cottage cheese. Microwave at HIGH (100% power) 2 minutes. Stir; microwave 2 minutes. Add Cheddar and Romano cheeses, stirring well. Microwave at MEDIUM-HIGH (70% power) 2 minutes. Stir in chicken, broccoli, mushrooms and noodles. Cover and microwave at MEDIUM (50% power) 5 minutes or until heated through.

Makes 6 to 8 servings

Favorite recipe from **Wisconsin Milk Marketing Board**

Helpful Hints

Fresh turkey parts are readily available at most supermarkets. Turkey breasts are sold whole or as halves with bone in or boned and rolled to form boneless halves. Breast cutlets are also available.

Mu Shu Turkey

Chicken Primavera Buffet

- 12 ounces uncooked thin spaghetti
- ¼ cup prepared pesto
- ¼ cup prepared fat-free Italian salad dressing
- ½ teaspoon red pepper flakes
- 2 cups water
- 1 cup thinly sliced carrots
- 1 cup broccoli flowerets
- 1 cup snow peas
- 1 can (4 ounces) sliced water chestnuts, drained
  Nonstick cooking spray
- 8 boneless skinless chicken breast halves

1. Preheat oven to 350°F. Cook pasta according to package directions, omitting salt. Drain and rinse well under cold water until pasta is cool; drain well. Place in large bowl; set aside.

2. Combine pesto, Italian dressing and red pepper flakes in small bowl. Reserve 1 tablespoon pesto mixture. Add remaining pesto mixture to pasta; toss to coat well.

3. In large saucepan, bring water to a boil over high heat. Add carrots, broccoli and snow peas; cook 3 minutes. Drain vegetables. Add water chestnuts and vegetables to pasta; toss to blend well. Spray 13×9-inch baking pan with nonstick cooking spray. Transfer pasta and vegetables to baking pan.

4. Spray large nonstick skillet with cooking spray; heat over medium heat until hot. Add chicken; cook until browned on both sides. Cover; cook 10 minutes or until no longer pink in center and juices run clear. Place chicken on pasta and vegetables. Pour juices from skillet over chicken. Spread reserved pesto mixture over chicken. Bake 45 minutes or until heated through.

Makes 8 servings

Sweet Slow Cooker Chicken Curry

- 1 pound boneless skinless chicken breasts, cut into 1-inch pieces
- 1 large green or red bell pepper, cut into 1-inch pieces
- 1 large onion, sliced
- 1 large tomato, seeded and chopped
- ½ cup prepared mango chutney
- ¼ cup water
- 2 tablespoons cornstarch
- 1½ teaspoons curry powder
- 1⅓ cups hot cooked rice

Slow Cooker Directions

1. Place chicken, bell pepper and onion in slow cooker. Top with tomato.

2. Mix chutney, water, cornstarch and curry powder in small bowl. Pour chutney mixture over chicken mixture into slow cooker. Cover; cook on LOW 3½ to 4½ hours. Serve over rice.

Makes 4 servings

Chicken di Napolitano

- 4 TYSON® Individually Fresh Frozen® Boneless, Skinless Chicken Breasts
- 1 box UNCLE BEN'S® COUNTRY INN® Rice Pilaf
- 1 tablespoon olive oil
- 1 can (14½ ounces) diced tomatoes, undrained
- 1¼ cups water
- ¼ cup chopped fresh basil *or* 1½ teaspoons dried basil leaves

PREP: CLEAN: Wash hands. Remove protective ice glaze from frozen chicken by holding under cool running water 1 to 2 minutes. CLEAN: Wash hands.

COOK: In large nonstick skillet, heat oil. Add chicken; cook over medium-high heat 8 to 10 minutes or until light brown. Add tomatoes, water, rice, contents of seasoning packet and basil. Bring to a boil. Cover; reduce heat. Simmer 15 to 18 minutes or until liquid is absorbed and internal juices of chicken run clear. (Or insert instant-read meat thermometer in thickest part of chicken. Temperature should read 170°F.)

SERVE: Slice chicken and serve over rice.

CHILL: Refrigerate leftovers immediately. *Makes 4 servings*

Prep Time: 5 minutes
Cook Time: 30 minutes

Helpful Hints

Boneless skinless chicken breasts are lower in fat than other chicken cuts and therefore a good choice for light cooking. However, boneless chicken breasts are expensive. Look for sales and stock up or think about deboning chicken breasts at home—it's a good way to save money.

Chicken Primavera Buffet

Turkey Vegetable Crescent Pie

    2 cans (about 14 ounces) fat-
        free reduced-sodium
        chicken broth
    1 medium onion, diced
    1¼ pounds turkey tenderloins, cut
        into ¾-inch pieces
    3 cups diced red potatoes
    1 teaspoon chopped fresh
        rosemary *or* ½ teaspoon
        dried rosemary
    ¼ teaspoon salt
    ⅛ teaspoon black pepper
    1 bag (16 ounces) frozen mixed
        vegetables
    1 bag (10 ounces) frozen mixed
        vegetables
    ⅓ cup fat-free (skim) milk plus
        additional if necessary
    3 tablespoons cornstarch
    1 package (8 ounces)
        refrigerated reduced-fat
        crescent rolls

1. Bring broth to a boil in large saucepan. Add onion; reduce heat and simmer 3 minutes. Add turkey; return to a boil. Reduce heat, cover and simmer 7 to 9 minutes or until turkey is no longer pink. Remove turkey from saucepan with slotted spoon; place in 13×9-inch baking dish.

2. Return broth to a boil. Add potatoes, rosemary, salt and pepper; simmer 2 minutes. Return to a boil and stir in mixed vegetables. Simmer, covered, 7 to 8 minutes or until potatoes are tender. Remove vegetables with slotted spoon. Drain in colander set over bowl; reserve broth. Transfer vegetables to baking dish with turkey.

3. Preheat oven to 375°F. Blend ⅓ cup milk with cornstarch in small bowl until smooth. Add enough milk to reserved broth to equal 3 cups. Heat in large saucepan over medium-high heat; whisk in cornstarch mixture, stirring constantly until mixture comes to a boil. Boil 1 minute; remove from heat. Pour over turkey-vegetable mixture in baking dish.

4. Roll out crescent roll dough and separate at perforations; arrange dough pieces decoratively over top of turkey-vegetable mixture. Bake 13 to 15 minutes or until crust is golden brown.   *Makes 8 servings*

Skillet Chicken and Rice

    1 teaspoon olive oil
    2 boneless skinless chicken
        breast halves, 2 skinless
        thighs, 2 skinless legs *or*
        any combination of 6 pieces
        (about 1½ pounds)
    1 large onion, chopped
    1 green bell pepper, seeded and
        chopped
    1 clove garlic, minced
    ½ teaspoon cumin seeds
    1 can (14 ounces) no-salt-added
        whole tomatoes, undrained
    1½ cups fat-free reduced-sodium
        chicken broth
    ¾ cup uncooked rice
    2 ounces (2 slices) turkey-ham,
        sliced into 2-inch pieces
    ¼ teaspoon salt
    ⅛ to ¼ teaspoon ground red
        pepper
    8 ounces frozen cut green
        beans, thawed

1. Heat oil in 12-inch nonstick skillet over medium-high heat. Add chicken; cook 3 minutes on each side or until browned. Remove chicken from skillet.

2. Add onion, bell pepper, garlic and cumin seeds to skillet; cook and stir 5 minutes. Stir in tomatoes, chicken broth, rice, turkey-ham, salt and red pepper; bring to a boil.

3. Return chicken to skillet, meaty side down. Cover; reduce heat. Simmer 15 minutes. Turn chicken pieces over; place green beans over chicken. Cover; simmer 20 to 30 minutes or until chicken is no longer pink in center, rice and green beans are tender and all liquid is absorbed. Garnish as desired.
          Makes 6 servings

Turkey Vegetable Crescent Pie

Spicy Turkey Casserole

- 1 tablespoon olive oil
- 1 pound turkey breast cutlets, cut into ½-inch pieces
- 2 (3-ounce) spicy chicken or turkey sausages, sliced ½-inch thick
- 1 cup diced green bell pepper
- ½ cup sliced mushrooms
- ½ cup diced onion
- 1 jalapeño pepper,* seeded and minced (optional)
- ½ cup fat-free reduced-sodium chicken broth or water
- 1 can (14 ounces) reduced-sodium diced tomatoes, undrained
- 1 teaspoon Italian seasoning
- ¼ teaspoon black pepper
- ½ teaspoon paprika
- 1 cup cooked egg yolk-free egg noodles
- 6 tablespoons grated Parmesan cheese
- 2 tablespoons coarse bread crumbs

Jalapeño peppers can sting and irritate the skin; wear rubber gloves when handling peppers and do not touch eyes. Wash hands after handling.

1. Preheat oven to 350°F. Heat oil in large nonstick skillet. Add turkey and sausages; cook and stir over medium heat 2 minutes. Add bell pepper, mushrooms, onion and jalapeño pepper, if desired. Cook and stir 5 minutes. Add chicken broth; cook 1 minute, scraping any browned bits off bottom of skillet. Add tomatoes with juice, seasonings and noodles.

2. Spoon turkey mixture into shallow 10-inch round casserole. Sprinkle with cheese and bread crumbs. Bake 15 to 20 minutes or until mixture is hot and bread crumbs are brown.

Makes 6 (1-cup) servings

Roast Turkey Breast with Apple-Cornbread Stuffing

- Nonstick cooking spray
- 1 medium onion, chopped
- 1¼ cups reduced-sodium chicken broth
- 1 package (8 ounces) corn bread stuffing mix
- 1 Granny Smith apple, diced
- ¾ teaspoon dried sage, divided
- ¾ teaspoon dried thyme leaves, divided
- 1 boneless turkey breast (1½ pounds)
- 1 teaspoon paprika
- ¼ teaspoon black pepper
- 1 cup whole-berry cranberry sauce (optional)

1. Preheat oven to 450°F. Coat 1½-quart casserole with cooking spray; set aside. Coat large saucepan with cooking spray; heat over medium heat. Add onion; cook and stir 5 minutes. Add broth; bring to a simmer. Stir in stuffing mix, apple, ¼ teaspoon sage and ¼ teaspoon thyme. Transfer mixture to prepared casserole; set aside.

2. Coat a shallow roasting pan with cooking spray. Place turkey breast in pan, skin side up; coat with cooking spray. Mix paprika, remaining ½ teaspoon sage, ½ teaspoon thyme and pepper in small bowl; sprinkle over turkey. Spray lightly with cooking spray.

3. Place turkey in preheated oven; roast 15 minutes. *Reduce oven temperature to 350°F.* Place stuffing in oven alongside turkey; continue to roast 35 minutes or until internal temperature of turkey reaches 170°F when tested with meat thermometer inserted into thickest part of breast. Transfer turkey to cutting board; cover with foil and let stand 10 to 15 minutes before carving. Internal temperature will rise 5°F to 10°F during stand time. Remove stuffing from oven; cover to keep warm. Carve turkey into thin slices; serve with stuffing and cranberry sauce, if desired.   *Makes 6 servings*

Stir-Fried Pasta with Chicken 'n' Vegetables

- 6 ounces angel hair pasta, broken in thirds (about 3 cups)
- ¼ cup *Frank's® RedHot®* Cayenne Pepper Sauce
- 3 tablespoons soy sauce
- 2 teaspoons cornstarch
- 1 tablespoon sugar
- ½ teaspoon garlic powder
- 1 pound boneless skinless chicken, cut in ¾-inch cubes
- 1 package (16 ounces) frozen stir-fry vegetables

1. Cook pasta in boiling water until just tender. Drain. Combine *Frank's RedHot* Sauce, *¼ cup water,* soy sauce, cornstarch, sugar and garlic powder in small bowl; set aside.

2. Heat 1 tablespoon oil in large nonstick skillet over high heat. Stir-fry chicken 3 minutes. Add vegetables; stir-fry 3 minutes or until crisp-tender. Add *Frank's RedHot* Sauce mixture. Heat to boiling. Reduce heat to medium-low. Cook, stirring, 1 to 2 minutes or until sauce is thickened.

3. Stir pasta into skillet; toss to coat evenly. Serve hot.

Makes 4 servings

Prep Time: 5 minutes
Cook Time: 15 minutes

Spicy Turkey Casserole

Creole Shrimp and Rice

- 2 tablespoons olive oil
- 1 cup uncooked white rice
- 1 can (15 ounces) diced tomatoes with garlic, undrained
- 1 teaspoon Creole or Cajun seasoning blend
- 1 pound peeled cooked medium shrimp
- 1 package (10 ounces) frozen okra *or* 1½ cups frozen sugar snap peas, thawed

1. Heat oil in large skillet over medium heat until hot. Add rice; cook and stir 2 to 3 minutes or until lightly browned.

2. Add tomatoes with juice, 1½ cups water and seasoning blend; bring to a boil over high heat. Reduce heat to low. Cover; simmer 15 minutes.

3. Add shrimp and okra. Cook, covered, 3 minutes or until heated through. *Makes 4 servings*

Note: Okra are oblong green pods. When cooked, they give off a viscous substance that acts as a thickener.

Prep and Cook Time: 20 minutes

Impossibly Easy Salmon Pie

- 1 can (7½ ounces) salmon packed in water, drained and deboned
- ½ cup grated Parmesan cheese
- ¼ cup sliced green onions
- 1 jar (2 ounces) chopped pimiento, drained
- ½ cup low-fat (1%) cottage cheese
- 1 tablespoon lemon juice
- 1½ cups low-fat (1%) milk
- ¾ cup reduced-fat baking and pancake mix
- 2 whole eggs
- 2 egg whites *or* ¼ cup egg substitute
- ¼ teaspoon dried dill weed
- ¼ teaspoon salt
- ¼ teaspoon paprika (optional)

1. Preheat oven to 375°F. Spray 9-inch pie plate with nonstick cooking spray. Combine salmon, Parmesan cheese, onions and pimiento in prepared pie plate; set aside.

2. Combine cottage cheese and lemon juice in blender or food processor; blend until smooth. Add milk, baking mix, whole eggs, egg whites, dill and salt. Blend 15 seconds. Pour over salmon mixture. Sprinkle with paprika, if desired.

3. Bake 35 to 40 minutes or until lightly golden and knife inserted halfway between center and edge comes out clean. Cool 5 minutes before serving. Garnish as desired.
Makes 8 servings

Shrimp Curry

- 1¼ pounds raw large shrimp
    Nonstick cooking spray
- 1 large onion, chopped
- ½ cup canned light coconut milk
- 3 cloves garlic, minced
- 2 tablespoons finely chopped fresh ginger
- 2 to 3 teaspoons hot curry powder
- ¼ teaspoon salt
- 1 can (14½ ounces) diced tomatoes
- 1 teaspoon cornstarch
- 2 tablespoons chopped fresh cilantro
- 3 cups hot cooked rice

1. Peel shrimp, leaving tails attached and reserving shells. Place shells in large saucepan; cover with water. Bring to a boil over high heat. Reduce heat to low; simmer 15 to 20 minutes. Strain shrimp stock and set aside. Discard shells.

2. Spray large skillet with cooking spray; heat over medium heat. Add onion; cover and cook 5 minutes. Add coconut milk, garlic, ginger, curry powder, salt and ½ cup shrimp stock; bring to a boil. Reduce heat to low and simmer 10 to 15 minutes or until onion is tender.

3. Add shrimp and tomatoes to skillet; return mixture to a simmer. Cook 3 minutes.

4. Stir cornstarch into 1 tablespoon cooled shrimp stock until dissolved. Add mixture to skillet with cilantro; simmer 1 to 2 minutes or just until slightly thickened, stirring occasionally. Serve over rice. Garnish with carrot and lime slices, if desired.
Makes 6 servings

Creole Shrimp and Rice

Creamy Shrimp & Vegetable Casserole

1 can (10¾ ounces) reduced-fat cream of celery soup
1 pound fresh or thawed frozen shrimp, shelled and deveined
½ cup fresh asparagus or thawed frozen asparagus, cut diagonally into 1-inch pieces
½ cup sliced mushrooms
¼ cup sliced green onions
¼ cup diced red bell pepper
1 clove garlic, minced
¾ teaspoon dried thyme leaves
¼ teaspoon black pepper
   Hot cooked rice or orzo

1. Preheat oven to 375°F. Coat 2-quart baking dish with nonstick cooking spray.

2. Combine soup, shrimp, asparagus, mushrooms, green onions, bell pepper, garlic, thyme and pepper in large bowl; mix well. Place in prepared baking dish.

3. Cover and bake 30 minutes. Serve over rice, if desired.

Makes 4 servings

Mediterranean Stew

Slow Cooker

1 medium butternut or acorn squash, peeled and cut into 1-inch cubes
2 cups unpeeled eggplant cubes (1-inch cubes)
2 cups sliced zucchini
1 can (15½ ounces) chick-peas, rinsed and drained
1 package (10 ounces) frozen cut okra
1 can (8 ounces) tomato sauce
1 cup chopped onion
1 medium tomato, chopped
1 medium carrot, thinly sliced
½ cup reduced-sodium vegetable broth
⅓ cup raisins
1 clove garlic, minced
½ teaspoon ground cumin
½ teaspoon ground turmeric
¼ to ½ teaspoon ground red pepper
¼ teaspoon ground cinnamon
¼ teaspoon paprika
6 to 8 cups hot cooked couscous or rice
   Fresh parsley (optional)

Slow Cooker Directions
Combine all ingredients except couscous and parsley in slow cooker; mix well. Cover and cook on LOW 8 to 10 hours or until vegetables are crisp-tender. Serve over couscous. Garnish with parsley, if desired.

Makes 6 servings

Vegetable Medley Quiche

Nonstick cooking spray
2 cups frozen diced potatoes with onions and peppers, thawed
1 can (10¾ ounces) reduced-fat condensed cream of mushroom soup, divided
1 (16-ounce) package frozen mixed vegetables (such as zucchini, carrots and beans), thawed and drained
1 cup cholesterol-free egg substitute *or* 4 eggs
½ cup grated Parmesan cheese, divided
¼ cup fat-free (skim) milk
¼ teaspoon dried dill weed
¼ teaspoon dried thyme leaves
¼ teaspoon dried oregano leaves
   Dash salt and pepper

1. Preheat oven to 400°F. Spray 9-inch pie plate with nonstick cooking spray; press potatoes onto bottom and side of pan to form crust. Spray potatoes lightly with nonstick cooking spray. Bake 15 minutes.

2. Combine half of soup, mixed vegetables, egg substitute and half of cheese in small bowl; mix well. Pour egg mixture into potato shell; sprinkle with remaining cheese. *Reduce oven to 375°F.* Bake 35 to 40 minutes or until set.

3. Combine remaining soup, milk and seasonings in small saucepan; mix well. Simmer over low heat 5 minutes or until heated through. Serve sauce with quiche.   *Makes 6 servings*

Mediterranean Stew

Ravioli with Homemade Tomato Sauce

3 cloves garlic, peeled
½ cup fresh basil leaves
3 cups seeded peeled tomatoes, cut into quarters
2 tablespoons tomato paste
2 tablespoons fat-free Italian salad dressing
1 tablespoon balsamic vinegar
¼ teaspoon black pepper
1 package (9 ounces) refrigerated reduced-fat cheese ravioli
2 cups shredded spinach leaves
1 cup (4 ounces) shredded part-skim mozzarella cheese

Microwave Directions

1. To prepare tomato sauce, process garlic in food processor until coarsely chopped. Add basil; process until coarsely chopped. Add tomatoes, tomato paste, salad dressing, vinegar and pepper; process using on/off pulsing action until tomatoes are chopped.

2. Spray 9-inch square microwavable dish with nonstick cooking spray. Spread 1 cup tomato sauce in dish. Layer half of ravioli and spinach over tomato sauce. Repeat layers with 1 cup tomato sauce and remaining ravioli and spinach. Top with remaining 1 cup tomato sauce.

3. Cover with plastic wrap; refrigerate 1 to 8 hours. Vent plastic wrap. Microwave at MEDIUM (50% power) 20 minutes or until pasta is tender and hot. Sprinkle with cheese. Microwave at HIGH 3 minutes or just until cheese melts. Let stand, covered, 5 minutes before serving.

Makes 6 servings

Black Bean & Rice Burritos

½ cup nonfat cottage cheese
2 tablespoons soft fresh goat cheese
1½ cups cooked brown rice or long-grain rice, kept warm
3 tablespoons minced red onion
3 tablespoons chopped fresh cilantro
¼ teaspoon ground cumin
¼ cup low sodium chicken broth, defatted
8 whole wheat tortillas (6 inches each)
¾ cup GUILTLESS GOURMET® Spicy Black Bean Dip
½ cup (2 ounces) shredded low fat Monterey Jack cheese
3 cups finely shredded lettuce
½ cup GUILTLESS GOURMET® Southwestern Grill Salsa
Fresh cilantro sprigs (optional)

Preheat oven to 350°F. Place cottage and goat cheeses in medium bowl; blend with fork until smooth. Add rice, onion, chopped cilantro and cumin. Mix well; set aside.

Place broth in shallow bowl. Working with 1 tortilla at a time, dip tortilla in broth to moisten each side. Spread 1 heaping tablespoonful bean dip on tortilla, then top with 1 heaping tablespoonful rice mixture. Roll up tortilla and place in 12×8-inch baking dish, seam side down. Repeat with remaining tortillas, bean dip and rice mixture. Cover with foil.

Bake about 25 to 30 minutes or until heated through. Remove foil; top with shredded cheese. Return to oven until cheese melts. To serve, arrange burritos on plate. Top with lettuce and salsa. Garnish with cilantro sprigs, if desired. *Makes 8 burritos*

Baked Provençal Ziti Provolone

10 ounces uncooked ziti
1 cup evaporated skimmed milk
½ cup fat-free (skim) milk
4 egg whites
1 tablespoon Dijon mustard
½ teaspoon salt
½ cup finely chopped green onions, with tops
Black pepper
4 ounces sliced provolone cheese
2 tablespoons grated Parmesan cheese

1. Preheat oven to 325°F. Spray 9-inch square baking pan with nonstick cooking spray; set aside. Cook pasta according to package directions, omitting salt; drain. Place in bottom of prepared pan.

2. Meanwhile, combine evaporated milk, fat-free milk, egg whites, mustard and salt in food processor or blender; process until smooth.

3. Sprinkle green onions over pasta. Pour egg mixture over green onions. Sprinkle with pepper and top with provolone cheese.

4. Bake 35 minutes or until heated through. Remove from oven. Sprinkle with Parmesan cheese. Let stand 5 minutes before serving.

Makes 4 servings

Ravioli with Homemade Tomato Sauce

Cannelloni with Tomato-Eggplant Sauce

1 package (10 ounces) fresh spinach
1 cup fat-free ricotta cheese
4 egg whites, beaten
¼ cup (1 ounce) grated Parmesan cheese
2 tablespoons finely chopped fresh parsley
½ teaspoon salt (optional)
8 manicotti (about 4 ounces), cooked and cooled
Tomato-Eggplant Sauce (recipe follows)
1 cup (4 ounces) shredded reduced-fat mozzarella cheese

1. Preheat oven to 350°F.

2. Wash spinach; do not pat dry. Place spinach in saucepan; cook, covered, over medium-high heat 3 to 5 minutes or until spinach is wilted. Cool slightly and drain; chop finely.

3. Combine ricotta cheese, spinach, egg whites, Parmesan cheese, parsley and salt in large bowl; mix well. Spoon mixture into manicotti shells; arrange in 13×9-inch baking pan. Spoon Tomato-Eggplant Sauce over manicotti; sprinkle with mozzarella cheese.

4. Bake manicotti, uncovered, 25 to 30 minutes or until hot and bubbly.
Makes 4 servings
(2 manicotti each)

Tomato-Eggplant Sauce

Olive oil-flavored nonstick cooking spray
1 small eggplant, coarsely chopped
½ cup chopped onion
2 cloves garlic, minced
½ teaspoon dried tarragon leaves
¼ teaspoon dried thyme leaves
1 can (16 ounces) no-salt-added whole tomatoes, undrained and coarsely chopped
Salt and black pepper

1. Spray large skillet with cooking spray; heat over medium heat until hot. Add eggplant, onion, garlic, tarragon and thyme; cook and stir about 5 minutes or until vegetables are tender.

2. Stir in tomatoes with juice; bring to a boil. Reduce heat and simmer, uncovered, 3 to 4 minutes. Season to taste with salt and pepper.
Makes about 2½ cups

Helpful Hints

Fat-free ricotta cheese is a good choice for this recipe. Although fat-free cheeses like Cheddar and mozzarella are available, they generally lack the flavor and melting properties of regular cheese. Consequently, reduced-fat Cheddar and part-skim mozzarella are better options for light cooking.

Stacked Burrito Pie

½ cup GUILTLESS GOURMET® Mild Black Bean Dip
2 teaspoons water
5 low-fat flour tortillas (6 inches each)
½ cup nonfat sour cream or plain yogurt
½ cup GUILTLESS GOURMET® Roasted Red Pepper Salsa
1¼ cups (5 ounces) shredded low-fat Monterey Jack cheese
4 cups shredded iceberg or romaine lettuce
½ cup GUILTLESS GOURMET® Salsa (Roasted Red Pepper or Southwestern Grill)
Lime slices and chili pepper (optional)

Preheat oven to 350°F. Combine bean dip and 2 teaspoons water in small bowl; mix well. Line 7½-inch springform pan with 1 tortilla. Spread 2 tablespoons bean dip mixture over tortilla, then spread with 2 tablespoons sour cream and 2 tablespoons red pepper salsa. Sprinkle with ¼ cup cheese. Repeat layers 3 more times. Place remaining tortilla on top and sprinkle with remaining ¼ cup cheese.

Bake 40 minutes or until heated through. (Place sheet of foil under springform pan to catch any juices that may seep through the bottom.) Cool slightly before unmolding. To serve, cut into 4 quarters. Place 1 cup lettuce on 4 serving plates. Top each serving with 1 quarter burrito pie and 2 tablespoons salsa. Garnish with lime slices and pepper, if desired.
Makes 4 servings

Cannelloni with Tomato-Eggplant Sauce

Fresh Vegetable Lasagna

- 8 ounces uncooked lasagna noodles
- 1 package (10 ounces) frozen chopped spinach, thawed and well drained
- 1 cup shredded carrots
- ½ cup sliced green onions
- ½ cup sliced red bell pepper
- ¼ cup chopped fresh parsley
- ½ teaspoon black pepper
- 1½ cups low-fat cottage cheese
- 1 cup buttermilk
- ½ cup plain nonfat yogurt
- 2 egg whites
- 1 cup sliced mushrooms
- 1 can (14 ounces) artichoke hearts, drained and chopped
- 2 cups (8 ounces) shredded part-skim mozzarella cheese
- ¼ cup freshly grated Parmesan cheese

1. Cook pasta according to package directions, omitting salt. Drain. Rinse under cold water; drain well. Set aside.

2. Preheat oven to 375°F. Pat spinach with paper towels to remove excess moisture. Combine spinach, carrots, green onions, bell pepper, parsley and black pepper in large bowl. Set aside.

3. Combine cottage cheese, buttermilk, yogurt and egg whites in food processor or blender; process until smooth.

4. Spray 13×9-inch baking pan with nonstick cooking spray. Arrange a third of lasagna noodles in bottom of pan. Spread with half each of cottage cheese mixture, vegetable mixture, mushrooms, artichokes and mozzarella. Repeat layers, ending with noodles. Sprinkle with Parmesan.

5. Cover and bake 30 minutes. Remove cover; continue baking 20 minutes or until bubbly and heated through. Let stand 10 minutes before serving.   *Makes 8 servings*

Three-Cheese Penne

- 2 cups uncooked penne pasta
  Nonstick cooking spray
- 2 slices whole wheat bread, cut into cubes
- 2 cups nonfat cottage cheese
- 2 cups (8 ounces) shredded reduced-fat Cheddar cheese
- 1 cup chopped Roma tomatoes, divided
- ⅓ cup sliced green onions
- ¼ cup grated Parmesan cheese
- ¼ cup low-fat (2%) milk

1. Cook pasta according to package directions, omitting salt. Drain and rinse well under cold water until pasta is cool; drain well.

2. Spray large nonstick skillet with cooking spray; heat over medium heat until hot. Place bread cubes in skillet; spray bread cubes lightly with cooking spray. Cook and stir 5 minutes or until bread cubes are browned and crisp.

3. Preheat oven to 350°F. Combine pasta, cottage cheese, Cheddar cheese, ¾ cup tomatoes, green onions, Parmesan cheese and milk in medium bowl. Spray 2-quart casserole with nonstick cooking spray. Place pasta mixture in casserole. Top with remaining ¼ cup tomatoes and cooled bread cubes.

4. Bake 20 minutes or until heated through. Garnish, if desired.
      Makes 6 servings

Double Spinach Bake

- 8 ounces uncooked spinach fettuccine noodles
- 1 cup fresh mushroom slices
- 1 green onion with top, finely chopped
- 1 clove garlic, minced
- 4 to 5 cups fresh spinach, coarsely chopped *or* 1 package (10 ounces) frozen spinach, thawed and drained
- 1 tablespoon water
- 1 container (15 ounces) fat-free ricotta cheese
- ¼ cup fat-free (skim) milk
- 1 egg
- ½ teaspoon ground nutmeg
- ½ teaspoon black pepper
- ¼ cup (1 ounce) shredded reduced-fat Swiss cheese

1. Preheat oven to 350°F. Cook noodles according to package directions, omitting salt. Drain; set aside.

2. Spray medium skillet with nonstick cooking spray. Add mushrooms, green onion and garlic. Cook and stir over medium heat until mushrooms are softened. Add spinach and water. Cover; cook until spinach is wilted, about 3 minutes.

3. Combine ricotta cheese, milk, egg, nutmeg and black pepper in large bowl. Gently stir in noodles and vegetables; toss to coat evenly.

4. Lightly coat shallow 1½-quart casserole with nonstick cooking spray. Spread noodle mixture in casserole. Sprinkle with Swiss cheese.

5. Bake 25 to 30 minutes or until knife inserted halfway into center comes out clean.
      Makes 6 (1-cup) servings

Three-Cheese Penne

Breakfast for Dinner

Breakfast Hash

1 pound **BOB EVANS®** Special
    Seasonings or Sage Roll
    Sausage
2 cups chopped potatoes
¼ cup chopped red and/or green
    bell pepper
2 tablespoons chopped onion
6 eggs
2 tablespoons milk

Crumble sausage into large skillet. Add potatoes, bell pepper and onion. Cook over low heat until sausage is browned and potatoes are fork-tender, stirring occasionally. Drain off any drippings. Whisk eggs and milk in small bowl until blended. Add to sausage mixture; scramble until eggs are set but not dry. Serve hot. Refrigerate leftovers.

Makes 6 to 8 servings

Serving Suggestion: Serve with fresh fruit.

Apple Brunch Strata

½ pound sausage, casing
    removed
4 cups cubed French bread
2 cups diced peeled Michigan
    Apples
¼ cup sliced green onions
⅓ cup sliced black olives
1½ cups (6 ounces) shredded
    sharp Cheddar cheese
2 cups reduced-fat milk
8 eggs
2 teaspoons spicy brown
    mustard
½ teaspoon salt
¼ teaspoon black pepper
    Paprika

1. Brown sausage in skillet over medium-high heat. Drain on paper towels; set aside.

2. Spray 13×9×2-inch baking dish with nonstick cooking spray. Layer half of bread cubes in bottom of dish. Crumble sausage over bread. Top with Michigan Apples, green onions, olives and cheese. Place remaining bread on top.

3. Mix milk, eggs, mustard, salt and pepper in medium bowl; pour over bread. Cover with foil and refrigerate 4 hours or overnight.

4. Preheat oven to 350°F. Bake, covered, 45 minutes. Remove foil and bake 15 minutes or until center is set. Let stand 15 minutes before serving. Sprinkle with paprika, if desired.

Makes 8 servings

Tip: Suggested Michigan Apple varieties to use include Empire, Gala, Golden Delicious, Ida Red, Jonagold, Jonathan, McIntosh or Rome.

Variation: Substitute 1 can (20 ounces) sliced Michigan Apples, drained and chopped for fresh Apples.

Favorite recipe from **Michigan Apple Committee**

Breakfast Hash

Ham and Cheese Bread Pudding

1 small loaf (8 ounces) sourdough, country French or Italian bread, cut into 1-inch-thick slices
3 tablespoons butter or margarine, softened
8 ounces ham or smoked ham, cubed
2 cups (8 ounces) shredded mild or sharp Cheddar cheese
3 eggs
2 cups milk
1 teaspoon dry mustard
½ teaspoon salt
⅛ teaspoon white pepper

1. Grease 11×7-inch baking dish. Spread 1 side of each bread slice with butter. Cut into 1-inch cubes; place on bottom of prepared dish. Top with ham; sprinkle with cheese.

2. Beat eggs in medium bowl. Whisk in milk, mustard, salt and pepper. Pour egg mixture evenly over bread mixture. Cover; refrigerate at least 6 hours or overnight.

3. Preheat oven to 350°F.

4. Bake bread pudding uncovered 45 to 50 minutes or until puffed and golden brown and knife inserted in center comes out clean. Garnish, if desired. Cut into squares. Serve immediately.   *Makes 8 servings*

Breakfast Quesadilla

6 eggs
¼ cup water
½ teaspoon garlic powder
½ teaspoon salt
1 (12-ounce) roll bulk sausage
1 cup salsa
1 (16-ounce) can ROSARITA® Traditional Refried Beans
8 burrito-sized flour tortillas
1 cup shredded Cheddar cheese
¼ cup WESSON® Oil

In medium bowl, beat together eggs, water, garlic powder and salt; set aside.

In large nonstick skillet, cook and crumble sausage until no longer pink; drain. Add egg mixture; scramble and cook until eggs are firm. Add salsa; mix well.

Spread about ½ cup beans on each of 4 tortillas. Top beans with about 1 cup egg mixture. Sprinkle each with ¼ cup cheese; top each with 1 tortilla.

Sauté each quesadilla in 1 tablespoon hot oil until golden brown, turning once. Cut into 8 slices.
Makes 8 servings

Acapulco Eggs

3 corn tortillas, cut into 2-inch strips
3 tablespoons butter or margarine
½ cup chopped onion
1 can (14½ ounces) DEL MONTE® Stewed Tomatoes - Mexican Recipe
1 cup cooked ham, cut into thin strips or shredded turkey
½ cup green pepper strips
6 eggs, beaten
¾ cup shredded Monterey Jack cheese

1. Cook tortilla strips in butter in large skillet until golden. Remove and set aside.

2. Cook onion in same skillet until tender. Drain tomatoes reserving liquid. Add reserved liquid to skillet; cook over high heat 3 minutes, stirring frequently.

3. Stir in tomatoes, meat and green pepper; heat through. Reduce heat to low; add tortillas and eggs.

4. Cover and cook 4 to 6 minutes or until eggs are set. Sprinkle with cheese; cover and cook 1 minute or until cheese is melted. Garnish with chopped cilantro or parsley, if desired.   *Makes 4 to 6 servings*

Prep Time: 10 minutes
Cook Time: 15 minutes

Sausage-Mushroom-Onion Tart

1 (9-inch) refrigerated pie crust
3 tablespoons butter
2 cups sliced fresh mushrooms
½ cup chopped onion
1 teaspoon chopped fresh parsley
1 teaspoon dried rosemary
1 cup whipping cream
1 (8-ounce) package BOB EVANS® Brown & Serve Links, sliced diagonally
2 egg yolks, lightly beaten
½ teaspoon salt
½ teaspoon black pepper
½ teaspoon hot pepper sauce

Preheat oven to 400°F. Remove pie crust from package; press into bottom and up side of greased 10-inch tart pan. Cut away excess pastry and prick crust with fork; bake 12 minutes. Meanwhile, melt butter in large skillet. Stir in mushrooms, onion, parsley and rosemary; cook and stir over medium heat until vegetables are tender. Combine cream, sausage, egg yolks, salt, black pepper and hot pepper sauce in medium bowl; add to mushroom mixture. Pour into baked shell. Bake 18 minutes or until golden brown. Refrigerate leftovers.
Makes 6 to 8 servings

Ham and Cheese Bread Pudding

Sausage Vegetable Frittata

5 eggs
¼ cup milk
2 tablespoons grated Parmesan cheese
½ teaspoon dried oregano leaves
½ teaspoon black pepper
1 (10-ounce) package BOB EVANS® Skinless Link Sausage
2 tablespoons butter or margarine
1 small zucchini, sliced (about 1 cup)
½ cup shredded carrots
⅓ cup sliced green onions with tops
¾ cup (3 ounces) shredded Swiss cheese
Carrot curls (optional)

Whisk eggs in medium bowl; stir in milk, Parmesan cheese, oregano and pepper. Set aside. Cook sausage in large skillet over medium heat until browned, turning occasionally. Drain off any drippings. Remove sausage from skillet and cut into ½-inch lengths. Melt butter in same skillet. Add zucchini, shredded carrots and onions; cook and stir over medium heat until tender. Top with sausage, then Swiss cheese. Pour egg mixture over vegetable mixture. Stir gently to combine. Cook, without stirring, over low heat 8 to 10 minutes or until center is almost set. Remove from heat. Let stand 5 minutes before cutting into wedges; serve hot. Garnish with carrot curls, if desired. Refrigerate leftovers.

Makes 4 to 6 servings

Garden Potato Casserole `Slow Cooker`

1¼ pounds baking potatoes, unpeeled and sliced
1 small green or red bell pepper, thinly sliced
¼ cup finely chopped yellow onion
2 tablespoons butter, cut into ⅛-inch pieces, divided
½ teaspoon salt
½ teaspoon dried thyme leaves
Black pepper to taste
1 small yellow squash, thinly sliced
1 cup (4 ounces) shredded sharp Cheddar cheese

Slow Cooker Directions

1. Place potatoes, bell pepper, onion, 1 tablespoon butter, salt, thyme and black pepper in slow cooker; mix well. Evenly layer squash over potato mixture; add remaining 1 tablespoon butter. Cover; cook on LOW 7 hours or on HIGH 4 hours.

2. Remove potato mixture to serving bowl. Sprinkle with cheese and let stand 2 to 3 minutes or until cheese melts. *Makes 5 servings*

Ham and Cheese Frittata

3 tablespoons CRISCO® Oil*
2 cups frozen shredded potatoes *or* 2 Idaho or Russet potatoes, peeled and shredded
¾ teaspoon salt, divided
¼ teaspoon freshly ground black pepper
½ pound baked ham, cut into ½-inch dice
6 eggs
3 tablespoons milk
¼ teaspoon Italian seasoning
1 cup (4 ounces) shredded Cheddar, Swiss or Monterey Jack cheese
¾ cup chunky spaghetti sauce, heated

Use your favorite Crisco Oil product.

1. Heat oven to 350°F.

2. Heat oil in 10- or 12-inch ovenproof skillet on medium heat. Add potatoes. Sprinkle with ½ teaspoon salt and pepper. Cook 8 minutes, or until almost brown. Add ham. Cook 2 to 3 minutes more. Turn occasionally with spatula.

3. Blend eggs with milk, Italian seasoning and remaining ¼ teaspoon salt while potatoes are cooking. Stir eggs into potatoes.

4. Bake covered at 350°F for 10 minutes. Remove from oven. Stir gently. Smooth top. Sprinkle with cheese. Return to oven. Bake 10 minutes, or until cheese is melted and eggs are set. Cut into 4 wedges. Top with spaghetti sauce.

Makes 4 servings

Prep Time: 15 minutes
Total Time: 45 minutes

Hash Brown Bake

1 packet (1 ounce) HIDDEN VALLEY® The Original Ranch® Salad Dressing & Seasoning Mix
1¼ cups milk
3 ounces cream cheese
6 cups hash browns, frozen shredded potatoes
1 tablespoon bacon bits
½ cup shredded sharp Cheddar cheese

In blender, combine salad dressing & seasoning mix, milk and cream cheese. Pour over potatoes and bacon bits in 9-inch baking dish. Top with cheese. Bake at 350°F for 35 minutes. *Makes 4 servings*

Sausage Vegetable Frittata

Egg & Sausage Casserole

½ **pound pork sausage**
3 **tablespoons margarine or butter, divided**
2 **tablespoons all-purpose flour**
¼ **teaspoon salt**
¼ **teaspoon black pepper**
1¼ **cups milk**
2 **cups frozen hash brown potatoes**
4 **eggs, hard-boiled and sliced**
½ **cup cornflake crumbs**
¼ **cup sliced green onions**

Preheat oven to 350°F. Spray 2-quart oval baking dish with nonstick cooking spray.

Crumble sausage into large skillet; brown over medium-high heat until no longer pink, stirring to separate meat. Drain sausage on paper towels. Discard fat and wipe skillet with paper towel.

Melt 2 tablespoons margarine in same skillet over medium heat. Stir in flour, salt and pepper until smooth. Gradually stir in milk; cook and stir until thickened. Add sausage, potatoes and eggs; stir to combine. Pour into prepared dish.

Melt remaining 1 tablespoon margarine. Combine cornflake crumbs and melted margarine in small bowl; sprinkle evenly over casserole.

Bake, uncovered, 30 minutes or until hot and bubbly. Sprinkle with onions.

Makes 6 servings

Make-Ahead Brunch Bake

1 **pound bulk pork sausage**
6 **eggs, beaten**
2 **cups light cream or half-and-half**
½ **teaspoon salt**
1 **teaspoon ground mustard**
1 **cup (4 ounces) shredded Cheddar cheese**
1⅓ **cups *French's*® French Fried Onions**

Crumble sausage into large skillet. Cook over medium-high heat until browned; drain well. Stir in eggs, cream, salt, mustard, ½ cup cheese and ½ can French Fried Onions; mix well. Pour into greased 12×8-inch baking dish. Refrigerate, covered, 8 hours or overnight. Bake, uncovered, at 350°F for 45 minutes or until knife inserted in center comes out clean. Top with remaining cheese and onions; bake, uncovered, 5 minutes or until onions are golden brown. Let stand 15 minutes before serving.   *Makes 6 servings*

Microwave Directions: Crumble sausage into 12×8-inch microwave-safe dish. Cook, covered, on HIGH 4 to 6 minutes or until sausage is cooked. Stir sausage halfway through cooking time. Drain well. Stir in ingredients and refrigerate as above. Cook, covered, 10 to 15 minutes or until center is firm. Stir egg mixture halfway through cooking time. Top with remaining cheese and onions; cook, uncovered, 1 minute or until cheese melts. Let stand 5 minutes.

Italian Vegetable Strata

1 **loaf Italian bread**
1⅓ **cups *French's*® French Fried Onions, divided**
1 **cup (4 ounces) shredded mozzarella cheese, divided**
1 **small zucchini, thinly sliced**
1 **red bell pepper, sliced**
5 **eggs**
2½ **cups milk**
⅓ **cup (1½ ounces) grated Parmesan cheese**
½ **teaspoon dried oregano leaves**
½ **teaspoon basil leaves**

1. Preheat oven to 350°F. Grease 3-quart shallow baking dish. Cut enough slices of bread, ½ inch thick, to arrange single layer in bottom of dish, overlapping slices if necessary. Layer ⅔ cup French Fried Onions, ⅔ cup mozzarella cheese, zucchini and bell pepper over bread.

2. Beat eggs, milk, Parmesan cheese, oregano, basil, ½ *teaspoon salt* and ¼ *teaspoon black pepper* in medium bowl. Pour over layers. Sprinkle with remaining ⅓ cup mozzarella cheese. Let stand 10 minutes.

3. Bake 45 minutes or until knife inserted in center comes out clean. Sprinkle with remaining ⅔ cup onions. Bake 5 minutes or until onions are golden. Cool on wire rack 10 minutes. Cut into squares to serve.

Makes 8 servings

Prep Time: 10 minutes
Cook Time: 50 minutes

Helpful Hints

A strata is a cross between custard and French toast. It consists of bread, cheese and often meat and/or vegetables. A mixture of eggs and milk is poured over the other ingredients and the dish is allowed to stand in the refrigerator overnight before baking.

Egg & Sausage Casserole

Spicy Sausage Skillet Breakfast

2 bags SUCCESS® Rice
Vegetable cooking spray
1 pound bulk turkey sausage
½ cup chopped onion
1 can (10 ounces) tomatoes with green chilies, undrained
1 tablespoon chili powder
1 cup (4 ounces) shredded reduced-fat Monterey Jack cheese

Prepare rice according to package directions.

Lightly spray large skillet with cooking spray. Crumble sausage into prepared skillet. Cook over medium heat until lightly browned, stirring occasionally. Add onion; cook until tender. Stir in tomatoes, chili powder and rice; simmer 2 minutes. Reduce heat to low. Simmer until no liquid remains, about 8 minutes, stirring occasionally. Sprinkle with cheese.

Makes 6 to 8 servings

Mexican Omelet Roll-Ups with Avocado Sauce

8 eggs
2 tablespoons milk
1 tablespoon margarine or butter
1½ cups (6 ounces) shredded Monterey Jack cheese
1 large tomato, seeded and chopped
¼ cup chopped fresh cilantro
8 (7-inch) corn tortillas
1½ cups salsa
2 medium avocados, chopped
¼ cup reduced-fat sour cream
2 tablespoons diced green chiles
1 tablespoon fresh lemon juice
1 teaspoon hot pepper sauce
¼ teaspoon salt

Preheat oven to 350°F. Spray 13×9-inch baking dish with nonstick cooking spray.

Whisk eggs and milk in medium bowl until blended. Melt margarine in large skillet over medium heat; add egg mixture to skillet. Cook and stir 5 minutes or until eggs are set, but still soft. Remove from heat. Stir in cheese, tomato and cilantro.

Spoon about ⅓ cup egg mixture evenly down center of each tortilla. Roll up tortillas and place seam side down in prepared dish. Pour salsa evenly over tortillas.

Cover tightly with foil and bake 20 minutes or until heated through.

Meanwhile, process avocados, sour cream, chiles, lemon juice, hot pepper sauce and salt in food processor or blender until smooth. Serve tortillas with avocado sauce.

Makes 8 servings

Cook's Nook: To reduce amount of fat in recipe, omit avocado sauce and serve with additional salsa and nonfat sour cream.

Ham 'n Egg Special Strata

¼ cup butter
2 cups sliced fresh mushrooms
1 medium onion, finely chopped
2 cups diced cooked ham
8 slices white bread, cubed
4 eggs
2½ cups milk
2 cups (8 ounces) shredded cheddar cheese
1 tablespoon prepared mustard
1 teaspoon LAWRY'S® Seasoned Salt
Dash LAWRY'S® Seasoned Pepper

In medium skillet, heat butter. Add mushrooms and onion and cook over medium-high heat until tender; stir in ham. In 13×9×2-inch baking dish, place bread cubes; arrange ham mixture over bread. In medium bowl, combine remaining ingredients; mix well. Pour over bread cubes, making sure all are moistened. Cover; refrigerate overnight. Bake, uncovered, in 325°F. oven 55 to 60 minutes. Serve immediately.

Makes 6 to 8 servings

Serving Suggestion: Serve with assorted fresh fruit in season.

Country Ham Omelets

2 tablespoons butter or margarine
3 slices HILLSHIRE FARM® Ham, chopped
½ cup finely chopped potato
¼ cup chopped green bell pepper
¼ cup chopped onion
½ cup sliced fresh mushrooms
8 to 12 eggs, beaten
½ cup (2 ounces) shredded sharp Cheddar cheese

Melt butter in medium skillet over medium heat; sauté Ham, potato, pepper and onion 3 to 4 minutes. Add mushrooms; stir and heat through.

Prepare four 2- or 3-egg omelets. Fill each with 2 tablespoons cheese and ¼ cup ham mixture. Use remaining ham mixture as omelet topping.

Makes 4 servings

Spicy Sausage Skillet Breakfast

French Toast Strata

4 ounces day-old French or
  Italian bread, cut into
  ¾-inch cubes (4 cups)
⅓ cup golden raisins
1 package (3 ounces) cream
  cheese, cut into ¼-inch
  cubes
3 eggs
1½ cups milk
½ cup maple-flavored pancake
  syrup
1 teaspoon vanilla
2 tablespoons sugar
1 teaspoon ground cinnamon
  Additional maple-flavored
  pancake syrup (optional)

1. Spray 11×7-inch baking dish with nonstick cooking spray. Place bread cubes in even layer in prepared dish; sprinkle raisins and cream cheese evenly over bread.

2. Beat eggs in medium bowl with electric mixer at medium speed until blended. Add milk, ½ cup pancake syrup and vanilla; mix well. Pour egg mixture evenly over bread mixture. Cover; refrigerate at least 4 hours or overnight.

3. Preheat oven to 350°F. Combine sugar and cinnamon in small bowl; sprinkle evenly over strata.

4. Bake, uncovered, 40 to 45 minutes or until puffed, golden brown and knife inserted in center comes out clean. Cut into squares and serve with additional pancake syrup, if desired.   *Makes 6 servings*

Cook's Nook: Serve with fresh fruit compote.

Chiles Rellenos en Casserole

3 eggs, separated
¾ cup milk
¾ cup all-purpose flour
½ teaspoon salt
1 tablespoon butter or
  margarine
½ cup chopped onion
8 peeled roasted whole chiles *or*
  2 cans (7 ounces each)
  whole green chiles, drained
8 ounces Monterey Jack cheese,
  cut into 8 slices

Condiments
  Sour cream
  Sliced green onions
  Pitted black olive slices
  Guacamole
  Salsa

Preheat oven to 350°F. Place egg yolks, milk, flour and salt in blender or food processor container fitted with metal blade; process until smooth. Pour into bowl and let stand. Melt butter in small skillet over medium heat. Add onion; cook until tender. If using canned chiles, pat dry with paper towels. Slit each chili lengthwise and carefully remove seeds. Place 1 strip cheese and 1 tablespoon onion in each chili; reshape chiles to cover cheese. Place 2 chiles in each of 4 greased 1½-cup gratin dishes or place in single layer in 13×9-inch baking dish. Beat egg whites until soft peaks form; fold into yolk mixture. Dividing mixture evenly, pour over chiles in gratin dishes (or pour entire mixture over casserole). Bake 20 to 25 minutes or until topping is puffed and knife inserted in center comes out clean. Broil 4 inches below heat 30 seconds or until topping is golden brown. Serve with condiments.
    Makes 4 servings

Corned Beef Hash

2 large russet potatoes, peeled
  and cut into ½-inch cubes
½ teaspoon salt
¼ teaspoon black pepper
¼ cup butter or margarine
1 large onion, chopped
8 ounces corned beef, finely
  chopped
1 tablespoon prepared
  horseradish, drained
¼ cup whipping cream (optional)
4 poached or fried eggs

1. Place potatoes in 10-inch skillet. Cover potatoes with water. Bring to a boil over high heat. Reduce heat to low; simmer 6 minutes. (Potatoes will be firm.) Drain potatoes in colander; sprinkle with salt and pepper.

2. Wipe out skillet with paper towel. Add butter and onion; cook and stir over medium-high heat 5 minutes. Stir in corned beef, horseradish and potatoes; mix well. Press down mixture with spatula to flatten into compact layer.

3. Reduce heat to low. Drizzle cream evenly over mixture. Cook 10 to 15 minutes. Turn mixture with spatula; pat down and continue cooking 10 to 15 minutes or until bottom is well browned. Top each serving with poached egg. Serve immediately. Garnish, if desired.
    Makes 4 servings

French Toast Strata

Crabmeat Quiche

1 (9-inch) unbaked pastry shell
4 eggs
1½ cups light cream or half-and-half
1 envelope LIPTON® RECIPE SECRETS® Savory Herb with Garlic Soup Mix*
1 cup flaked crabmeat (about 6 ounces)
1 to 2 tablespoons dry sherry (optional)
2 cups shredded Swiss cheese (about 8 ounces)

Also terrific with Lipton® Recipe Secrets® Onion-Mushroom or Golden Onion Soup Mix.

Preheat oven to 400°F.

Bake pastry shell 10 minutes. Remove from oven; *reduce oven temperature to 375°F.*

In large bowl, beat eggs. Blend in cream, soup mix, crabmeat and sherry. Sprinkle cheese in pastry shell; pour in egg mixture. Bake 40 minutes or until knife inserted in center comes out clean and pastry is golden. Garnish, if desired, with orange slices, grapes and fresh herbs. Serve hot or cold.

Makes 6 servings

Easy Brunch Frittata

Nonstick cooking spray
1 cup small broccoli florets
2½ cups (12 ounces) frozen hash brown potatoes with onions and peppers (O'Brien style), thawed
1½ cups cholesterol-free egg substitute, thawed
2 tablespoons reduced-fat (2%) milk
¾ teaspoon salt
¼ teaspoon black pepper
½ cup (2 ounces) shredded reduced-fat Cheddar cheese

1. Preheat oven to 450°F. Coat medium nonstick ovenproof skillet with nonstick cooking spray. Heat skillet over medium heat until hot. Add broccoli; cook and stir 2 minutes. Add potatoes; cook and stir 5 minutes.

2. Beat together egg substitute, milk, salt and pepper in small bowl; pour over potato mixture. Cook 5 minutes or until edges are set (center will still be wet).

3. Transfer skillet to oven; bake 6 minutes or until center is set. Sprinkle with cheese; let stand 2 to 3 minutes or until cheese is melted.

4. Cut into wedges; serve with sour cream, if desired.

Makes 6 servings

Mushroom & Onion Egg Bake

1 tablespoon vegetable oil
4 green onions, chopped
4 ounces mushrooms, sliced
1 cup low-fat cottage cheese
1 cup sour cream
6 eggs
2 tablespoons all-purpose flour
¼ teaspoon salt
⅛ teaspoon black pepper
Dash hot pepper sauce

1. Preheat oven to 350°F. Grease shallow 1-quart baking dish.

2. Heat oil in medium skillet over medium heat. Add onions and mushrooms; cook until tender. Set aside.

3. In blender or food processor, process cottage cheese until almost smooth. Add sour cream, eggs, flour, salt, pepper and hot pepper sauce; process until combined. Stir in onions and mushrooms. Pour into greased dish. Bake about 40 minutes or until knife inserted near center comes out clean.

Makes about 6 servings

Chile Rellenos Monte Cristos

1 can (4 ounces) whole roasted green chiles
8 large slices sourdough bread
4 slices SARGENTO® Deli Style Sliced Monterey Jack Cheese
4 slices SARGENTO® Deli Style Sliced Colby Cheese
2 eggs
¼ cup milk
1 teaspoon ground cumin
¼ cup butter or margarine
Powdered sugar, optional
Thick and chunky salsa, optional

1. Cut open chiles and remove any remaining seeds. Equally divide the chiles over 4 slices of bread. Top each with Monterey Jack and Colby cheeses. Place remaining bread slices on top.

2. In shallow bowl, beat eggs, milk and cumin until blended. Dip each sandwich in the egg mixture, turning carefully to coat until all liquid is absorbed by all sandwiches equally.

3. Melt butter in large skillet over medium heat. Place sandwiches in skillet. Grill (in batches if necessary) 3 to 4 minutes per side, or until browned and cheese has melted. Serve immediately. Serve with powdered sugar sprinkled on top and a spoonful of salsa, if desired.

Makes 4 servings

Prep Time: 5 minutes
Cook Time: 16 minutes

Easy Brunch Frittata

Potato and Egg Pie

1 package (20 ounces) frozen O'Brien hash brown potatoes, thawed
⅓ cup WESSON® Vegetable Oil
1½ tablespoons chopped fresh parsley
¾ cup shredded pepper-jack cheese
¾ cup shredded Swiss cheese
1 package (12 ounces) bulk breakfast sausage, cooked, crumbled and drained
1 can (4 ounces) sliced mushrooms, drained
½ cup milk
4 eggs, beaten
1 teaspoon garlic salt
¼ teaspoon pepper
4 to 6 thin tomato slices

Preheat oven to 425°F. In a medium bowl, combine potatoes and Wesson® Oil; blend to coat. Press mixture into 10-inch pie dish. Bake for 30 minutes or until golden brown; remove from oven. *Reduce oven temperature to 350°F.* Meanwhile, in large bowl, combine 1 tablespoon parsley and *remaining* ingredients *except* tomato slices; blend well. Pour into potato crust. Bake for 25 minutes or until eggs are set. Place tomato slices over pie and top with *remaining* parsley. Bake 5 to 7 minutes longer.

Makes 6 servings

Oven Breakfast Hash

2 pounds baking potatoes, unpeeled (5 or 6 medium)
1 pound BOB EVANS® Original Recipe Roll Sausage
1 (12-ounce can) evaporated milk
⅓ cup chopped green onions
1 tablespoon Worcestershire sauce
½ teaspoon salt
¼ teaspoon black pepper
¼ cup dried bread crumbs
1 tablespoon melted butter or margarine
½ teaspoon paprika

Cook potatoes in boiling water until fork-tender. Drain and coarsely chop or mash. Preheat oven to 350°F. Crumble and cook sausage in medium skillet until browned. Drain and transfer to large bowl. Stir in potatoes, milk, green onions, Worcestershire sauce, salt and pepper. Pour into greased 2½- or 3-quart casserole dish. Sprinkle with bread crumbs; drizzle with melted butter. Sprinkle with paprika. Bake, uncovered, 30 to 35 minutes or until casserole bubbles and top is browned. Refrigerate leftovers.

Makes 6 to 8 servings

Sausage & Apple Quiche

1 (9-inch) unbaked pastry shell, 1½ inches deep
½ pound bulk spicy pork sausage
½ cup chopped onion
¾ cup shredded peeled tart apple
1 tablespoon lemon juice
1 tablespoon sugar
⅛ teaspoon red pepper flakes
1 cup (4 ounces) shredded Cheddar cheese
3 eggs
1½ cups half-and-half
¼ teaspoon salt
Dash black pepper

1. Preheat oven to 450°F. Line pastry shell with foil; partially fill with uncooked beans or rice to weight shell. Bake 10 minutes. Remove foil and beans; continue baking pastry 5 minutes or until lightly browned. Let cool. *Reduce oven temperature to 375°F.*

2. Crumble sausage into large skillet; add onion. Cook and stir over medium heat until sausage is browned and onion is tender. Spoon off and discard pan drippings. Add apple, lemon juice, sugar and red pepper flakes. Cook over medium-high heat 4 minutes or until apple is barely tender and all liquid is evaporated, stirring constantly. Let cool. Spoon sausage mixture into pastry shell; top with cheese. Whisk eggs, half-and-half, salt and black pepper in medium bowl. Pour over sausage mixture. Bake 35 to 45 minutes or until filling is puffed and knife inserted in center comes out clean. Let stand 10 minutes before cutting to serve.

Makes 6 servings

Scrambled Eggs with Chicken and Sun-Dried Tomatoes

4 eggs
2 tablespoons milk
1 teaspoon dried basil leaves
Ground black pepper
5 ounces cooked chicken, chopped
¼ cup oil-packed sun-dried tomatoes, drained and cut into thin strips
2 tablespoons chopped green onion
1 tablespoon butter
1 tablespoon grated BELGIOIOSO® Romano Cheese

In medium bowl, beat together eggs, milk, basil and pepper to taste. Stir in chicken, tomatoes and onion. In large skillet, melt butter over medium heat; pour in egg mixture. Cook, without stirring, until mixture begins to set on bottom and around edges. Using large spoon or spatula, lift and fold partially cooked eggs so uncooked portion flows underneath. Continue cooking over medium heat 2 to 3 minutes. Remove from heat. Sprinkle with BelGioioso Romano Cheese and serve immediately.

Makes 3 servings

Potato and Egg Pie

Brunch Eggs Olé

    8 eggs
    ½ cup all-purpose flour
    1 teaspoon baking powder
    ¾ teaspoon salt
    2 cups (8 ounces) shredded
        Monterey Jack cheese with
        jalapeño peppers
    1½ cups (12 ounces) small curd
        cottage cheese
    1 cup (4 ounces) shredded
        sharp Cheddar cheese
    1 jalapeño pepper,* seeded and
        chopped
    ½ teaspoon hot pepper sauce
        Fresh Salsa (recipe follows)

*Jalapeño peppers can sting and irritate the
skin; wear rubber gloves when handling
peppers and do not touch eyes. Wash hands
after handling.*

1. Preheat oven to 350°F. Grease
9-inch square baking pan.

2. Beat eggs in large bowl at high
speed with electric mixer 4 to
5 minutes or until slightly thickened
and lemon colored.

3. Combine flour, baking powder and
salt in small bowl. Stir flour mixture
into eggs until blended.

4. Combine Monterey Jack cheese,
cottage cheese, Cheddar cheese,
jalapeño and hot pepper sauce in
medium bowl; mix well. Fold into egg
mixture until well blended. Pour into
prepared pan.

5. Bake 45 to 50 minutes or until
golden brown and firm in center. Let
stand 10 minutes before cutting into
squares to serve. Serve with Fresh
Salsa. Garnish as desired.

Makes 8 servings

Fresh Salsa

    3 medium plum tomatoes,
        seeded and chopped
    2 tablespoons chopped onion
    1 small jalapeño pepper,*
        stemmed, seeded and
        minced
    1 tablespoon chopped fresh
        cilantro
    1 tablespoon lime juice
    ¼ teaspoon salt
    ⅛ teaspoon black pepper

*Jalapeño peppers can sting and irritate the
skin; wear rubber gloves when handling
peppers and do not touch eyes. Wash hands
after handling.*

Stir together tomatoes, onion,
jalapeño pepper, cilantro, lime juice,
salt and black pepper in small bowl.
Refrigerate until ready to serve.

Makes 1 cup

Sausage and Cheese Potato Casserole

    1 pound BOB EVANS® Italian
        Roll Sausage
    4 cups cubed unpeeled red skin
        potatoes
    1 cup (4 ounces) shredded
        Monterey Jack cheese
    ¼ cup chopped green onions
    1 (4-ounce) can chopped green
        chiles, drained
    6 eggs
    ¾ cup milk
    ¼ teaspoon salt
    ⅛ teaspoon black pepper
    ½ cup grated Parmesan cheese

Preheat oven to 350°F. Crumble and
cook sausage in medium skillet until
browned. Drain off any drippings.
Spread potatoes in greased
13×9-inch baking pan. Top with
cooked sausage, Monterey Jack
cheese, green onions and chiles.
Whisk eggs, milk, salt and pepper in
medium bowl until frothy. Pour egg

mixture over sausage layer; bake
30 minutes. Remove from oven.
Sprinkle with Parmesan cheese; bake
15 minutes more or until eggs are set.
Refrigerate leftovers.

Makes 6 to 8 servings

Cheddar Broccoli Tart

    1½ cups milk
    3 eggs
    1 package KNORR® Recipe
        Classics™ Leek Soup, Dip
        and Recipe Mix
    1 package (10 ounces) frozen
        chopped broccoli, thawed
        and drained
    1½ cups shredded Cheddar,
        Swiss or Monterey Jack
        cheese (about 6 ounces)
    1 9-inch unbaked or frozen
        deep-dish pie crust*

*If using 9-inch deep-dish frozen prepared
pie crust, do not thaw. Preheat oven and
cookie sheet. Pour filling into pie crust; bake
on cookie sheet.*

● Preheat oven to 375°F. In large
bowl, with fork, beat milk, eggs and
recipe mix until blended. Stir in
broccoli and cheese; spoon into pie
crust.

● Bake 40 minutes or until knife
inserted 1 inch from edge comes out
clean. Let stand 10 minutes before
serving.   *Makes 6 servings*

Recipe Tip: Cheddar Broccoli Tart is
perfect for brunch or lunch. Or serve
it with a mixed green salad and soup
for a hearty dinner.

Prep Time: 10 minutes
Cook Time: 40 minutes

Brunch Eggs Olé

Bacon & Potato Frittata

2 cups frozen O'Brien-style potatoes with onions and peppers
3 tablespoons butter or margarine
5 eggs
½ cup canned real bacon pieces
¼ cup half-and-half or milk
⅛ teaspoon salt
⅛ teaspoon black pepper

1. Preheat broiler. Place potatoes in a microwavable medium bowl; microwave at HIGH 1 minute.

2. Melt butter in large ovenproof skillet over medium-high heat. Swirl butter up side of pan to prevent eggs from sticking. Add potatoes; cook 3 minutes, stirring occasionally.

3. Beat eggs in medium bowl. Add bacon, half-and-half, salt and pepper; mix well.

4. Pour egg mixture into skillet; reduce heat to medium. Stir gently to incorporate potatoes. Cover and cook 6 minutes or until eggs are set at edges (top will still be wet).

5. Transfer skillet to broiler. Broil 4 inches from heat about 1 to 2 minutes or until center is set and frittata is golden brown. Cut into wedges. *Makes 4 servings*

Serving Suggestion: Garnish frittata with red bell pepper strips, chopped chives and salsa.

Prep and Cook Time: 20 minutes

Spinach and Cheese Brunch Squares

1 box (11 ounces) pie crust mix
⅓ cup cold water
1 package (10 ounces) frozen chopped spinach, thawed and well drained
1⅓ cups *French's*® French Fried Onions
1 cup (4 ounces) shredded Swiss cheese
1 container (8 ounces) low-fat sour cream
5 eggs
1 cup milk
1 tablespoon *French's*® Zesty Deli Mustard
½ teaspoon salt
⅛ teaspoon ground black pepper

Preheat oven to 450°F. Line 13×9×2-inch baking pan with foil; spray with nonstick cooking spray. Combine pie crust mix and water in large bowl until moistened and crumbly. Using floured bottom of measuring cup, press mixture firmly into bottom of prepared pan. Prick with fork. Bake 20 minutes or until golden. *Reduce oven temperature to 350°F.*

Layer spinach, French Fried Onions and cheese over crust. Combine sour cream, eggs, milk, mustard, salt and pepper in medium bowl; mix until well blended. Pour over vegetable and cheese layers. Bake 30 minutes or until knife inserted in center comes out clean. Let stand 10 minutes. Cut into squares* to serve.

Makes 8 main-course servings

*To serve as appetizers, cut into 2-inch squares.

Tip: Next time you make omelets, create onion omelets! Sprinkle French Fried Onions across the omelet before folding over. Enjoy!

Prep Time: 20 minutes
Cook Time: 50 minutes
Stand Time: 10 minutes

Chile, Egg & Cheese Casserole

1 tablespoon WESSON® Vegetable Oil, divided
½ cup *each:* chopped green bell pepper, red bell pepper and yellow bell pepper
2 jalapeño peppers, seeded and minced
1 cup chopped onion
3 containers (8 ounces each) fat-free egg substitute (or 12 eggs)
1 teaspoon salt
10 corn tortillas, torn into bits
1 can (14.5 ounces) HUNT'S® Diced Tomatoes in Juice
1½ cups low-fat shredded Cheddar cheese, divided
PAM® No-Stick Cooking Spray
1 tablespoon chopped fresh cilantro

1. Preheat oven to 400°F.

2. In large skillet, heat *½ tablespoon* of Wesson Oil over medium-high heat. Sauté bell peppers, onion and jalapeños until tender, about 5 minutes.

3. Meanwhile, in large mixing bowl, combine egg substitute and salt; stir in tortillas. When vegetables are cooked, stir into egg mixture.

4. Pour *remaining* oil into skillet; heat over medium heat. Add egg mixture and cook about 2 minutes, or until eggs are halfway cooked; remove from heat. Stir in Hunt's Diced Tomatoes in Juice and ¾ cup cheese.

5. Transfer egg mixture to 13×9×2-inch baking dish, lightly sprayed with PAM Cooking Spray. Top with *remaining* cheese.

6. Bake, uncovered, about 25 minutes, or until lightly browned. Sprinkle with cilantro.

Makes 10 (8-ounce) servings

Bacon & Potato Frittata

Cheddar and Leek Strata

- **8 eggs, lightly beaten**
- **2 cups milk**
- **½ cup ale or beer**
- **2 cloves garlic, minced**
- **¼ teaspoon salt**
- **¼ teaspoon black pepper**
- **1 loaf (16 ounces) sourdough bread, cut into ½-inch cubes**
- **2 small leeks, coarsely chopped**
- **1 red bell pepper, chopped**
- **1½ cups (6 ounces) shredded Swiss cheese**
- **1½ cups (6 ounces) shredded sharp Cheddar cheese**

1. Combine eggs, milk, ale, garlic, salt and black pepper in large bowl. Beat until well blended.

2. Place ½ of bread cubes on bottom of greased 13×9-inch baking dish. Sprinkle ½ of leeks and ½ of bell pepper over bread cubes. Top with ¾ cup Swiss cheese and ¾ cup Cheddar cheese. Repeat layers with remaining ingredients, ending with Cheddar cheese.

3. Pour egg mixture evenly over top. Cover tightly with plastic wrap or foil. Weight top of strata down with slightly smaller baking dish. Refrigerate strata at least 2 hours or overnight.

4. Preheat oven to 350°F. Bake uncovered 40 to 45 minutes or until center is set. Garnish with fresh sage, if desired. Serve immediately.

Makes 12 servings

Helpful Hints

Leeks often collect soil between leaf layers. Trim off green tops and roots, then cut leeks in half lengthwise. Rinse under cool running water until clean.

Skillet Sausage with Potatoes and Rosemary

- **1 tablespoon vegetable oil**
- **3 cups diced red skin potatoes**
- **1 cup diced onion**
- **1 pound BOB EVANS® Original Recipe Roll Sausage**
- **½ teaspoon dried rosemary**
- **¼ teaspoon rubbed sage**
- **Salt and black pepper to taste**
- **2 tablespoons chopped fresh parsley**

Heat oil in large skillet over medium-high heat 1 minute. Add potatoes; cook 5 to 10 minutes or until slightly brown, stirring occasionally. Add onion; cook until tender. Add crumbled sausage; cook until browned. Add rosemary, sage, salt and pepper; cook and stir until well blended. Transfer to serving platter and garnish with parsley. Refrigerate leftovers.   *Makes 4 to 6 servings*

Three Cheese Asparagus and Leeks Bread Pudding

- **PAM® No-Stick Cooking Spray**
- **⅓ cup WESSON® Vegetable Oil**
- **3 small leeks, washed and cut into ½-inch slices**
- **1 pound asparagus, washed and cut into ½-inch pieces**
- **½ cup each: chopped fresh basil and parsley**
- **1 tablespoon fresh grated lemon peel**
- **2½ cups milk**
- **1 pint heavy cream**
- **5 eggs**
- **¼ pound each: grated Fontina, Parmesan and Provolone cheeses**
- **1½ teaspoons garlic salt**
- **½ teaspoon cayenne pepper**
- **½ teaspoon coarse ground pepper**
- **1 to 1½ pounds sourdough bread, cut into 1-inch cubes and lightly toasted**

Preheat oven to 375°F. Spray 4-quart oval baking dish (at least 2-inches deep) with PAM Cooking Spray; set aside. In large skillet, heat Wesson Oil until hot. Sauté leeks, asparagus, basil, parsley and lemon peel until leeks are tenders (about 10 minutes). Meanwhile, in large bowl, whisk together milk, cream and eggs. Stir in cheeses, garlic salt, peppers, sautéed vegetables and bread; toss until well coated. Spoon bread mixture into baking dish and bake 50 to 60 minutes or until top is crusty brown and knife inserted in center comes out clean. If pudding looks too brown before it's finished, cover loosely with foil. Cool 7 minutes before serving.

Makes 8 to 10 servings

Hint: For a wonderful Sunday Brunch Entrée, stir one-half pound cooked, crumbled Italian or breakfast sausage into bread mixture and bake until done.

Note: This recipe is perfect to prepare hours ahead of time or even the day before. Simply, sauté the vegetables and refrigerate. Then mix together the remaining ingredients except the bread in a large bowl and refrigerate until ready to bake. At the last minute, toss the bread with all ingredients and bake. It's a real time saver!

Prep Time: 20 minutes
Cook Time: 50 to 60 minutes

Cheddar and Leek Strata

Boston Brown Bread

Slow Cooker

3 (16-ounce) cleaned and
    emptied vegetable cans
½ cup rye flour
½ cup yellow cornmeal
½ cup whole wheat flour
3 tablespoons sugar
1 teaspoon baking soda
¾ teaspoon salt
½ cup chopped walnuts
½ cup raisins
1 cup buttermilk*
⅓ cup molasses

Soured fresh milk may be substituted. To sour, place 1 tablespoon lemon juice plus enough milk to equal 1 cup in 2-cup measure. Stir; let stand 5 minutes before using.

Slow Cooker Directions

Spray vegetable cans and 1 side of three 6-inch-square pieces of foil with nonstick cooking spray; set aside. Combine rye flour, cornmeal, whole wheat flour, sugar, baking soda and salt in large bowl. Stir in walnuts and raisins. Whisk buttermilk and molasses in medium bowl until blended. Add buttermilk mixture to dry ingredients; stir until well mixed. Spoon mixture evenly into prepared cans. Place 1 piece of foil, greased side down, on top of each can. Secure foil with rubber bands or cotton string.

Place filled cans in slow cooker. Pour boiling water into slow cooker to come halfway up sides of cans. (Make sure foil tops do not touch boiling water.) Cover and cook on LOW 4 hours or until skewer inserted in centers comes out clean. To remove bread, lay cans on side; roll and tap gently on all sides until bread releases. Cool completely on wire racks.   *Makes 3 loaves*

Spinach Pie

1 tablespoon olive oil
1 pound fresh spinach, washed,
    drained and stems removed
1 medium potato, cooked and
    mashed
2 eggs beaten
¼ cup cottage cheese
¼ cup grated BELGIOIOSO®
    Romano Cheese
Salt

Preheat oven to 350°F. Grease 8-inch round cake pan with olive oil. Tear spinach into bite-sized pieces. Combine spinach, potato, eggs, cottage cheese and BelGioioso Romano Cheese in large bowl. Spoon mixture into prepared pan. Bake 15 to 20 minutes or until set. Season to taste with salt.   *Makes 6 servings*

Fire & Ice Brunch Skillet

1 (6.8-ounce) package
    RICE-A-RONI® Spanish Rice
2 tablespoons margarine or
    butter
1 (16-ounce) jar salsa
⅓ cup sour cream
¼ cup thinly sliced green onions
4 large eggs
1 cup (4 ounces) shredded
    Cheddar cheese
Chopped cilantro (optional)

1. In large skillet over medium heat, sauté rice-vermicelli mix with margarine until vermicelli is golden brown.

2. Slowly stir in 2 cups water, salsa and Special Seasonings; bring to a boil. Reduce heat to low. Cover; simmer 15 to 20 minutes or until rice is tender.

3. Stir in sour cream and green onions. Using large spoon, make 4 indentations in rice mixture. Break 1 egg into each indentation. Reduce heat to low. Cover; cook 8 minutes or until egg yolks are set.

4. Sprinkle cheese evenly over eggs and rice. Cover; let stand 3 minutes or until cheese is melted. Sprinkle with cilantro, if desired.
        Makes 4 servings

Tip: A twist on Mexican-style huevos rancheros, serve this for brunch or as a light dinner.

Prep Time: 5 minutes
Cook Time: 30 minutes

Hash Brown Casserole

3 cartons (4 ounces *each*)
    cholesterol-free egg product
    or 6 large eggs, well beaten
1 can (12 fluid ounces)
    NESTLÉ® CARNATION®
    Evaporated Milk
1 teaspoon salt
½ teaspoon ground black pepper
1 package (30 ounces) frozen
    shredded hash brown
    potatoes
2 cups (8 ounces) shredded
    cheddar cheese
1 medium onion, chopped
1 small green bell pepper,
    chopped
1 cup diced ham (optional)

PREHEAT oven to 350°F. Grease 13×9-inch baking dish.

COMBINE egg product, evaporated milk, salt and black pepper in large bowl. Add potatoes, cheese, onion, bell pepper and ham; mix well. Pour mixture into prepared baking dish.

BAKE for 60 to 65 minutes or until set.
        Makes 12 servings

Note: For a lower fat version of this recipe, use cholesterol-free egg product, substitute NESTLÉ® CARNATION® Evaporated Fat Free Milk for Evaporated Milk and 10 slices turkey bacon, cooked and chopped, for the diced ham. Proceed as above.

Boston Brown Bread

Ham and Egg Enchiladas

2 tablespoons butter or
    margarine
1 small red bell pepper, chopped
3 green onions with tops, sliced
½ cup diced ham
8 eggs
8 (7- to 8-inch) flour tortillas
2 cups (8 ounces) shredded
    Colby-Jack cheese or
    Monterey Jack cheese with
    jalapeño peppers, divided
1 can (10 ounces) enchilada
    sauce
½ cup prepared salsa
    Sliced avocado, fresh cilantro
    and red pepper slices for
    garnish

1. Preheat oven to 350°F.

2. Melt butter in large nonstick skillet over medium heat. Add bell pepper and onions; cook and stir 2 minutes. Add ham; cook and stir 1 minute.

3. Lightly beat eggs with wire whisk in medium bowl. Add eggs to skillet; cook until eggs are set, but still soft, stirring occasionally.

4. Spoon about ⅓ cup egg mixture evenly down center of each tortilla; top with 1 tablespoon cheese. Roll tortillas up and place seam side down in shallow 11×7-inch baking dish.

5. Combine enchilada sauce and salsa in small bowl; pour evenly over enchiladas.

6. Cover enchiladas with foil; bake 20 minutes. Uncover; sprinkle with remaining cheese. Continue baking 10 minutes or until enchiladas are hot and cheese is melted. Garnish, if desired. Serve immediately.

Makes 4 servings

Sunrise Squares

1 pound BOB EVANS® Original
    Recipe Roll Sausage
2 slices bread, cut into ½-inch
    cubes (about 2 cups)
1 cup (4 ounces) shredded
    sharp Cheddar cheese
6 eggs
2 cups milk
½ teaspoon salt
½ teaspoon dry mustard

Preheat oven to 350°F. Crumble sausage into medium skillet. Cook over medium heat until browned, stirring occasionally. Drain off any drippings. Spread bread cubes in greased 11×7-inch baking dish; top with sausage and cheese. Whisk eggs, milk, salt and mustard until well blended; pour over cheese. Bake 30 to 40 minutes or until set. Let stand 5 minutes before cutting into squares; serve hot. Refrigerate leftovers. *Makes 6 servings*

Tip: You can make this tasty meal ahead and refrigerate overnight before baking.

Serving Suggestion: Serve squares between toasted English muffins.

Weekend Brunch Casserole

1 pound BOB EVANS® Original
    Recipe Roll Sausage
1 can (8 ounces) refrigerated
    crescent dinner rolls
2 cups (8 ounces) shredded
    mozzarella cheese
4 eggs, beaten
¾ cup milk
¼ teaspoon salt
⅛ teaspoon black pepper

Preheat oven to 425°F. Crumble sausage into medium skillet. Cook over medium heat until browned, stirring occasionally. Drain off any drippings. Line bottom of greased 13×9-inch baking dish with crescent roll dough, firmly pressing

perforations to seal. Sprinkle with sausage and cheese. Combine remaining ingredients in medium bowl until blended; pour over sausage. Bake 15 minutes or until set. Let stand 5 minutes before cutting into squares; serve hot. Refrigerate leftovers. *Makes 6 to 8 servings*

Serving Suggestion: Serve with fresh fruit or sliced tomatoes.

Breakfast Sausage Casserole

1 package (16 ounces) fresh
    breakfast sausage, cooked,
    drained and crumbled
4 cups cubed day-old bread
2 cups (8 ounces) shredded
    sharp cheddar cheese
2 cans (12 fluid ounces *each*)
    NESTLÉ® CARNATION®
    Evaporated Milk
10 large eggs, lightly beaten
1 teaspoon dry mustard
¼ teaspoon onion powder
    Ground black pepper to taste

GREASE 13×9-inch baking dish. Place bread in prepared baking dish. Sprinkle with cheese. Combine evaporated milk, eggs, dry mustard, onion powder and pepper in medium bowl. Pour evenly over bread and cheese. Sprinkle with sausage. Cover; refrigerate overnight.

PREHEAT oven to 325°F.

BAKE for 55 to 60 minutes or until cheese is golden brown. Cover with foil if top browns too quickly.

Makes 10 to 12 servings

Ham and Egg Enchiladas

This publisher would like to thank the companies and organizations listed below for the use of their recipes and photographs in this publication.

American Italian Pasta Company—Pasta LaBella

Barilla America, Inc.

BelGioioso® Cheese, Inc.

Birds Eye®

Bob Evans®

Butterball® Turkey Company

California Olive Industry

California Poultry Federation

Clamato® is a registered trademark of Mott's, Inc.

ConAgra Foods®

Del Monte Corporation

Dole Food Company, Inc.

Fleischmann's® Original Spread

Florida Department of Agriculture and Consumer Services, Bureau of Seafood and Aquaculture

The Fremont Company, Makers of Frank's & SnowFloss Kraut and Tomato Products

The Golden Grain Company®

Guiltless Gourmet®

Harveys® Bristol Cream®

Heinz North America

The Hidden Valley® Food Products Company

Hillshire Farm®

Holland House® is a registered trademark of Mott's, Inc.

Hormel Foods, LLC

Idaho Potato Commission

Lawry's® Foods

McIlhenny Company (TABASCO® brand Pepper Sauce)

Michigan Apple Committee

Minnesota Cultivated Wild Rice Council

Mushroom Council

National Fisheries Institute

National Honey Board

National Pork Board

National Turkey Federation

Nestlé USA

New Jersey Department of Agriculture

Norseland, Inc. / Lucini Italia Co.

Perdue Farms Incorporated

Reckitt Benckiser Inc.

Riviana Foods Inc.

Sargento® Foods Inc.

The J.M. Smucker Company

Sonoma® Dried Tomatoes

StarKist® Seafood Company

Tyson Foods, Inc.

Uncle Ben's Inc.

Unilever Bestfoods North America

USA Rice Federation

Veg-All®

Washington Apple Commission

Wisconsin Milk Marketing Board

METRIC CONVERSION CHART

VOLUME MEASUREMENTS (dry)

⅛ teaspoon = 0.5 mL
¼ teaspoon = 1 mL
½ teaspoon = 2 mL
¾ teaspoon = 4 mL
1 teaspoon = 5 mL
1 tablespoon = 15 mL
2 tablespoons = 30 mL
¼ cup = 60 mL
⅓ cup = 75 mL
½ cup = 125 mL
⅔ cup = 150 mL
¾ cup = 175 mL
1 cup = 250 mL
2 cups = 1 pint = 500 mL
3 cups = 750 mL
4 cups = 1 quart = 1 L

VOLUME MEASUREMENTS (fluid)

1 fluid ounce (2 tablespoons) = 30 mL
4 fluid ounces (½ cup) = 125 mL
8 fluid ounces (1 cup) = 250 mL
12 fluid ounces (1½ cups) = 375 mL
16 fluid ounces (2 cups) = 500 mL

WEIGHTS (mass)

½ ounce = 15 g
1 ounce = 30 g
3 ounces = 90 g
4 ounces = 120 g
8 ounces = 225 g
10 ounces = 285 g
12 ounces = 360 g
16 ounces = 1 pound = 450 g

DIMENSIONS

1/16 inch = 2 mm
⅛ inch = 3 mm
¼ inch = 6 mm
½ inch = 1.5 cm
¾ inch = 2 cm
1 inch = 2.5 cm

OVEN TEMPERATURES

250°F = 120°C
275°F = 140°C
300°F = 150°C
325°F = 160°C
350°F = 180°C
375°F = 190°C
400°F = 200°C
425°F = 220°C
450°F = 230°C

BAKING PAN SIZES

Utensil	Size in Inches/Quarts	Metric Volume	Size in Centimeters
Baking or Cake Pan (square or rectangular)	8×8×2	2 L	20×20×5
	9×9×2	2.5 L	23×23×5
	12×8×2	3 L	30×20×5
	13×9×2	3.5 L	33×23×5
Loaf Pan	8×4×3	1.5 L	20×10×7
	9×5×3	2 L	23×13×7
Round Layer Cake Pan	8×1½	1.2 L	20×4
	9×1½	1.5 L	23×4
Pie Plate	8×1¼	750 mL	20×3
	9×1¼	1 L	23×3
Baking Dish or Casserole	1 quart	1 L	—
	1½ quart	1.5 L	—
	2 quart	2 L	—